SUBSTITUTES FOR HERBS AND SPICES

IF THE RECIPE CALLS FOR:	USE INSTEAD:
Allspice	Cinnamon, cloves, and nutmeg in equal parts to equal total amount of allspice
Basil	Oregano
Caraway seeds	Anise seeds
Ground red pepper (cayenne)	Ground chili peppers
Celery seeds	Celery tops, minced
Chervil	Parsley or tarragon
Fennel seeds	Anise seeds
Marjoram	Oregano
Nutmeg	Mace
Sage	Thyme

EQUIVALENTS

DRY MEASURES

1 teaspoon	5 grams
1 ounce	28.35 grams
8 ounces	227 grams
1 pound (16 ounces)	454 grams
1 gram	0.035 ounces
50 grams	1¾ ounces
100 grams	3½ ounces
1 kilogram	2 pounds 3¼ ounces

LIQUID MEASURES

1 teaspoon	5 milliliters
1 tablespoon	15 milliliters
1 cup	237 milliliters (almost ¼ liter)
1 pint	0.473 liter (almost ½ liter)
1 quart	0.946 liter (almost 1 liter)
1 deciliter	6 tablespoons + 2 teaspoons
¼ liter	1 cup + 2¼ tablespoons
½ liter	1 pint + 4½ teaspoons
1 liter	1 quart + ¼ cup
4 liters	1 gallon + 1 cup

METRIC CONVERSION

TO CHANGE:	TO:	MULTIPLY BY:
Inches	Millimeters	25.4
Inches	Centimeters	2.54
Cubic inches	Cubic centimeters	16.4
Millimeters	Inches	0.04
Centimeters	Inches	0.4
Teaspoons	Milliliters	5
Tablespoons	Milliliters	15
Ounces (fluid)	Milliliters	30
Cups	Liters	0.2365
Pints	Liters	0.473
Quarts	Liters	0.946
Gallons	Liters	3.78
Liters	Ounces (fluid)	33.814
Milliliters	Ounces (fluid)	0.0338
Liters	Pints	2.1
Liters	Quarts	1.06
Liters	Gallons	0.26
Ounces	Grams	28.4
Pounds	Grams	454
Pounds	Kilograms	0.454
Grams	Ounces	0.035
Kilograms	Pounds	2.2

P9-DDB-718

ONE DISH MEALS

The Easy Way

The Reader's Digest Association, Inc.
Pleasantville, New York/Montreal

READER'S DIGEST

ONE DISH MEALS

The Easy Way

One-Dish Meals the Easy Way

STAFF

Project Editor
Sharon Fass Yates

Art Editor
Henrietta Stern

Editor
Paula Pines

Associate Editors
Theresa Lane
Thomas A. Ranieri

CONTRIBUTORS

Editor
Lee Fowler

Photographer
Michael Molkenthin

Editorial Assistant
Monica Smyth

Food Stylist
Polly Talbott

Art Assistant
Stefany Blyn

Assistant Food Stylist
Margaret A. Neill

Copy Editor
Virginia Croft

Prop Stylist
Debrah E. Donahue

Indexer
Sydney Wolfe Cohen

Illustrator
Dana Burns-Pizer

Recipe Developers
Jo Ann Brett
Bea Cihak (Microwave)
Georgia Downard
Sandra Rose Gluck
Paul E. Piccuito
Michele Scicolone

Special Thanks
Jeff Akellian
Susan Y. Beale
Dolores Damm
Joseph Dyas
Ben T. Etheridge
Nancy Mace

CONSULTANTS

Chief Consultant
Jean Anderson

Nutrition Consultant
Michele C. Fisher,
Ph.D. R.D.

Chart Graphics
Ronald Gross

READER'S DIGEST GENERAL BOOKS

Editor in Chief
John A. Pope, Jr.

Group Editors
Will Bradbury
Norman B. Mack
Kaari Ward

Copy Chief
Edward W. Atkinson

Managing Editor
Jane Polley

Picture Editor
Richard Pasqual

Executive Editor
Susan J. Wernert

Group Art Editors
Evelyn Bauer
Robert M. Grant
Joel Musler

Rights and Permissions
Pat Colomban

Art Director
David Trooper

Chief of Research
Laurel A. Gilbride

Head Librarian
Jo Manning

The credits and acknowledgments that appear on page 341 are hereby made a part of this copyright page.

Copyright © 1991 The Reader's Digest Association, Inc.
Copyright © 1991 The Reader's Digest Association (Canada) Ltd.
Copyright © 1991 Reader's Digest Association Far East Ltd.
Philippine Copyright 1991 Reader's Digest Association Far East Ltd.

All rights reserved. Unauthorized reproduction, in any manner, is prohibited.

READER'S DIGEST and the Pegasus logo are registered trademarks of The Reader's Digest Association, Inc.

Printed in the United States of America

Library of Congress Cataloging in Publication Data

One-dish meals the easy way.
p.   cm.
Includes index.
ISBN 0-89577-389-9
1. Casserole cookery.   I. Reader's Digest Association.
TX693.O455   1991
641.8'21—dc20   91-10972

Contents

Stuffed Veal Breast,
page 76

Seafood Newburg,
page 128

Tomatoes Stuffed with
Rice and Black-Eyed
Peas, page 184

Creamy Chicken Waldorf
Salad, page 175

Black Forest Roll,
page 312

Tex-Mex Pasta,
page 154

About This Book

ONE-DISH MEALS THE EASY WAY is a cornucopia of recipes for delicious, wholesome meals, all with one thing in common: the convenience of serving a complete meal in a single dish.

Here are recipes for the meat-and-potatoes crowd, for weight-watching calorie counters, for pasta lovers and vegetarians—even for cooks who don't have time to cook. As you turn the pages, you'll discover that some recipe ideas are brand new, others are familiar favorites with innovative twists, and many include creative variations. And every one of the 400-plus recipes has been kitchen-tested especially for this book.

Though pop-in-the-oven casseroles receive their fair share of attention, there are also mouth-watering main-course soups, stovetop stews, extra-special stir-fried dishes, microwave meals, and backyard barbecues, as well as fabulous ideas for turning tired leftovers into lively new repasts.

Many of the recipes can be prepared in advance; others can be whipped up in a jiffy; some even cook themselves by simmering slowly to delicious doneness. Whatever your choice, everything is ready at the same time, and cleanup is quick and easy.

The recipes in this book are not only flavorful but are also nutritionally well balanced. Many of them are low in fat, sodium, or calories, so select whatever dish suits your needs or satisfies your mood.

Wherever appropriate, alternate ingredients are listed. These substitutes are provided for a variety of reasons: to make the recipe more versatile, to suggest a less expensive ingredient, to save time, to reduce the amount of fat or sodium, and to enable you to make the recipe even if you don't have or can't find a particular ingredient. For many of the same reasons, some ingredients are labeled optional because they are not crucial to the success of the recipe.

Nutritional information accompanies each recipe along with preparation and cooking times. (Where an alternate ingredient is given, the nutritive analysis is based on the first ingredient listed.)

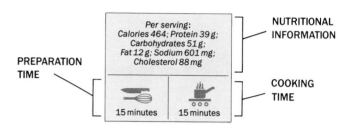

In every case we've been as precise as possible, but stoves, ovens, and personal tastes vary, and you may need to adjust cooking times to suit your own situation. Preparation times can also vary according to individual kitchen skills.

Throughout the book, bonuses abound:
- The Appetizers and Desserts chapter offers a selection of "dining companions" for before- and after-dinner treats.
- Extra Quick 'n' Easy charts at the end of Chapter 9 provide a treasury of recipes-at-a-glance.
- The Make-Ahead chapter features basics you can make when you're not busy, to have on hand when you are.
- The Cooking Basics section, the charts on the inside covers, and the introductions to recipes supply the kinds of practical information you need as you cook.

ONE-DISH MEALS THE EASY WAY is brimming with delicious, nutritious meals that are ideal for everyday fare and excellent for entertaining. So call the family to dinner . . . or invite some friends for brunch . . . or plan a festive buffet. Whatever the occasion—and whoever gathers round your table—these recipes will inspire many a satisfying meal and a multitude of warm and happy memories.

—The Editors

Eating the Healthful Way

Planning meals for a week at a time is the easiest way to assure a well-balanced diet. To help you plan, we've provided nutritional information for recipes in this book. You can see at a glance how many calories are in each serving as well as the amount of carbohydrate, protein, sodium, cholesterol, and fat. If any of the numbers seem high, remember that everything for a nutritionally sound *meal* is combined in one recipe—protein, fruit or vegetable, and carbohydrate. If you se-

lect a meal that is higher than you like in sodium or calories, choose other meals for the day that are low or moderate in those areas; if a meal is low in carbohydrate or protein, make up the difference in other meals.

Calories. A measure of energy, calories are stored by the body as fat for future use. Caloric needs vary depending on a person's age, size, metabolism, and level of physical activity. You can reduce body fat by consuming fewer calories and exercising more.

Complex carbohydrates. Found in starchy foods like grains, pastas, breads, legumes (dried beans and peas), vegetables, and some fruits, complex carbohydrates provide the body with energy. About 55 percent of your total daily calories should come from carbohydrates. Including these foods in your diet will also keep your intake of dietary fiber high. (Fiber helps food pass through the digestive system.)

Protein. Required to build and maintain muscle, bone, and nerves, protein also helps renew skin and blood. An average-size man should eat at least 56 grams each day; an average-size woman, 44 grams. Protein can come from two sources: animals and plants. Sources of animal protein—meat, poultry, fish, eggs, and milk products—are more complete; plant proteins are incomplete. However, certain plant proteins can be combined in the same meal to provide complete protein. Use any one of the following combinations:
- grains (such as wheat, cornmeal, or rice) with legumes
- grains with milk products (milk, yogurt, cheese)
- legumes with seeds (sesame, pumpkin, and sunflower seeds, and sesame paste) or nuts

Sodium. Most Americans get more of this essential nutrient each day than they need. Nutrition experts recommend that the average person limit the amount of sodium consumed each day to 3,000 to

4,000 milligrams. In 1 teaspoon of salt there are 2,132 milligrams of sodium. The easiest way to reduce your salt intake is to gradually stop adding salt to food while it's cooking or at the table. At the same time use more herbs and spices, as many of the recipes in this book do, to enhance food flavor. After a while you will find that you don't miss it. In addition, carefully check the labels of processed foods for the amount of sodium; look for salt as well as other forms of sodium, including the preservative sodium propionate, the flavor enhancer monosodium glutamate (MSG), and baking soda (sodium bicarbonate).

Cholesterol. A fatty substance produced by the liver, cholesterol is essential for the brain and nervous system; it also helps produce vitamin D and some hormones. Cholesterol is found in such foods as red meat, eggs, and whole-fat dairy products. A similar compound is also found in some seafoods. Cholesterol in foods can alter blood cholesterol levels.

There are several kinds of blood cholesterol: the "good" one is *high-density lipoprotein cholesterol,* or HDL; the less beneficial kinds are *very low-density lipoprotein cholesterol,* or VLDL, and *low-density lipoprotein cholesterol,* or LDL. When the LDL cholesterol level is too high, it can increase your risk of heart attack or stroke. Blood cholesterol levels in adults should be below 200 milligrams per deciliter. Most nutrition

The Four Food Groups

If you regularly eat foods from the basic food groups described below, your diet will include the vitamins, minerals, carbohydrates, and protein necessary for good health.

Select foods from each group every day; because it's the combined daily intake that's important, every meal doesn't have to include items from each food group.

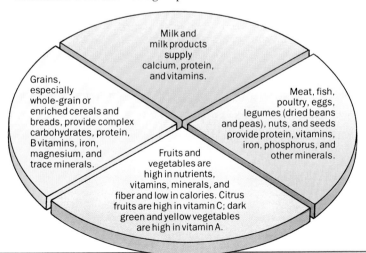

Milk and milk products supply calcium, protein, and vitamins.

Meat, fish, poultry, eggs, legumes (dried beans and peas), nuts, and seeds provide protein, vitamins, iron, phosphorus, and other minerals.

Grains, especially whole-grain or enriched cereals and breads, provide complex carbohydrates, protein, B vitamins, iron, magnesium, and trace minerals.

Fruits and vegetables are high in nutrients, vitamins, minerals, and fiber and low in calories. Citrus fruits are high in vitamin C; dark green and yellow vegetables are high in vitamin A.

Eating the Healthful Way (Continued)

experts agree that your daily intake of cholesterol should ideally be no higher than 300 milligrams. If you eat a meal that is high in cholesterol or high in fat or saturated fat (which can also increase blood cholesterol levels), other meals for that day and a few following days should be low in these substances.

Fat. Necessary for supplying energy and maintaining good health, fat also helps the body to absorb the fat-soluble vitamins A, D, E, and K. The body needs essential fatty acids each day, but the quantity needed is so small—only about 1 tablespoon—that not getting enough is rarely a problem. Any excess fat is turned into calories. A single gram of fat provides 9 calories, compared to about 4 in a gram of protein or car-

bohydrate. Nutritionists recommend limiting the consumption of fat to 30 to 35 percent or less of your daily calories.

Food labeling. Before buying a product, check its label carefully; claims on labels can be confusing. For example, *lite, natural,* and other terms have no standard definitions. But even terms that have been standardized can be misinterpreted. The term *sugar free* means the product doesn't contain sucrose—table or cane sugar—but it may contain other types of sugars such as fructose, dextrose, molasses, honey, sorbitol, or manitol. All of these add calories as well as sweetness. *Reduced sodium* means the product has at least 75 percent less sodium than the standard product, but depending on

what the standard is, this can be high or low. *Reduced calories* means that the product has one-third fewer calories than a similar food, but the actual number of calories may still be quite high.

Ingredients list. Manufacturers label product ingredients by weight, starting with the heaviest ingredient and ending with the lightest. The order doesn't tell you the actual amount of an ingredient.

On the labels below, soup A is condensed; the consumer must add water. Soup B is ready to eat. Although water is the first ingredient in soup B, the amount might be equal to or less than the total amount of water in soup A after the water is added and it's ready to eat.

The fat in soup A comes from beef stock and beef fat; this type of fat is largely saturated fat. In soup B, the fat comes from soybean and olive oils, which contain higher amounts of unsaturated fats.

Although salt is listed in the middle on both soup labels, soup A also contains sodium in the form of monosodium glutamate (MSG).

On other labels look for sugar by its chemical names: any word ending in *-ose,* as in dextrose, maltose, sucrose, and fructose. Or the sugar might be listed as molasses, corn syrup, or honey.

TYPES OF FAT	FOODS THEY ARE FOUND IN	EFFECTS ON CHOLESTEROL
Saturated fats (usually solid at room temperature)	Meat and poultry, egg yolks, whole-fat dairy products, coconut and palm oils, and most chocolate	Increase blood cholesterol levels
Monounsaturated fats	Olives, peanuts, cashews, and avocados; also found in olive and peanut oils	Raise blood cholesterol levels less than saturated fats
Polyunsaturated fats	Corn, soybeans, cottonseeds, and safflower and sunflower seeds, and in their oils; also found in almonds, walnuts, and pecans	Promote HDL cholesterol and discourage LDL and VLDL cholesterols
Omega-3 fatty acids (a type of polyunsaturated fat)	Fatty fish such as tuna, salmon, sardines, mackerel, sablefish, whitefish, bluefish, swordfish, rainbow trout, and herring	Help lower cholesterol levels

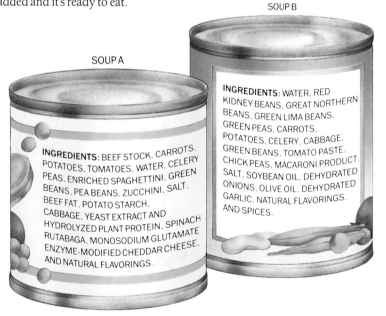

SOUP A

INGREDIENTS: BEEF STOCK, CARROTS, POTATOES, TOMATOES, WATER, CELERY PEAS, ENRICHED SPAGHETTINI, GREEN BEANS, PEA BEANS, ZUCCHINI, SALT, BEEF FAT, POTATO STARCH, CABBAGE, YEAST EXTRACT AND HYDROLYZED PLANT PROTEIN, SPINACH RUTABAGA, MONOSODIUM GLUTAMATE ENZYME-MODIFIED CHEDDAR CHEESE, AND NATURAL FLAVORINGS.

SOUP B

INGREDIENTS: WATER, RED KIDNEY BEANS, GREAT NORTHERN BEANS, GREEN LIMA BEANS, GREEN PEAS, CARROTS, POTATOES, CELERY, CABBAGE, GREEN BEANS, TOMATO PASTE, CHICK PEAS, MACARONI PRODUCT, SALT, SOYBEAN OIL, DEHYDRATED ONIONS, OLIVE OIL, DEHYDRATED GARLIC, NATURAL FLAVORINGS, AND SPICES.

Dietary Guidelines

For a healthy diet, follow these recommendations suggested by the U.S. Department of Agriculture and the Department of Health and Human Services.

- *Eat a variety of foods.* The human body needs more than 40 different nutrients for good health. These nutrients should come from a wide variety of foods, not just a selected few.

- *Maintain healthy weight.* A person who is too fat or too thin has a greater chance of developing health problems. Whether a person's weight is "healthy" depends on how much of his or her weight is fat, where in the body the fat is located, and whether the person has weight-related medical problems.

- *Choose a diet low in fat, saturated fat, and cholesterol.* A diet low in fat makes it easier to include the variety of foods you need for nutrients without exceeding your calorie needs. A diet low in saturated fat and cholesterol can help maintain a desirable level of blood cholesterol.

- *Choose a diet with plenty of vegetables, fruits, and grain products.* Eat at least three servings of vegetables, two servings of fruits, and six servings of grain products daily.

- *Use sugars only in moderation.* Sugars and many foods that contain them in large amounts supply calories but are limited in nutrients.

- *Use salt and sodium only in moderation.* Food and beverages containing salt provide most of the sodium in our diets, much of it added during processing and manufacturing.

- *If you drink alcoholic beverages, do so in moderation.* Alcoholic beverages supply calories but little or no nutrients. Each gram of alcohol contains 7 calories.

Healthful Tips

- Reduce salt, sugar, or fat gradually over a period of a month or more to prevent "cravings" from developing.

- Eat fresh fruit when you want something sweet. Buy unsweetened cereals and sweeten them with berries, bananas, raisins, or add a little sugar yourself.

- Whole milk contains 150 calories per cup (8 ounces); 2 percent low-fat milk, 120 calories; 1 percent low-fat milk, 100 calories; and skim milk, 80 calories. Reconstituted nonfat dry milk also contains 80 calories per cup.

- To get accustomed to the thinner flavor of low-fat or skim milk, mix it with whole milk; gradually increase the amount of skim or low-fat milk over a period of several weeks.

- The body uses fiber more effectively in digestion when it is coarse rather than finely ground. Check the label of cereals, breads, or crackers for the words *whole grain*, *whole wheat*, or *whole oats*.

- Choose plain breads over muffins, biscuits, corn bread, croissants, and buns that are baked with larger amounts of shortening (fat). Plain breads are lower in calories.

- Season vegetables with herbs and spices instead of butter.

- In descending order, the most polyunsaturated oils for cooking and salads are safflower, sunflower, soybean, and corn oil. Olive and peanut oils are also good, since both are monounsaturated.

- Use low-fat versions of such cheeses as cottage, ricotta, mozzarella, cream, Cheddar, and Swiss cheese. Remember, however, that even the low-fat versions of these cheeses may contain significant amounts of fat.

- Low-fat cottage cheese that has been blended until it is smooth or plain low-fat yogurt can be used as a low-fat alternative to sour cream. You can also use plain low-fat yogurt in place of mayonnaise.

- Look for ground beef labeled "very lean" or "extra lean." You'll be spared as much as half the fat of untrimmed ground beef.

- Light poultry meat has half the fat of dark poultry meat. The skin is the fattiest part of all; discard it, preferably before cooking—otherwise, after cooking.

Kitchenware

Recipes in ONE-DISH MEALS THE EASY WAY often call for cookware that can travel from stovetop to oven or broiler. Some multipurpose cookware can even go directly from freezer to stovetop or microwave oven. Many are attractive enough for serving at the table.

Use cookware that is all metal, enameled cast iron, or Pyroceram (a glass-ceramic material that is also suitable for microwaving). Because handles made of plastic and other synthetics can't withstand the heat of an oven or broiler, they are ill-suited for some recipes in this book. Avoid using glass and pottery if the dish must be transferred from oven to stovetop or broiler; sudden changes in temperature can make them shatter.

Sizes. The size of a pan or casserole may affect the outcome of a recipe. If volume or dimensions are given for a pot, pan, or casserole, try to match it as closely as possible. You may find the size on the bottom of the container. If not, measure the container to be sure. For casseroles, saucepans, and kettles, the volume is often more important than the shape. Fill the container with water, then dip the water out with a 1-cup measure, counting the number of cups. A 2-quart casserole will hold 8 cups.

For baking pans, the surface area is usually more important than the volume. If a recipe calls for a 13″ × 9″ × 2″ pan, the area is the length (13 inches) times the width (9 inches), or 117 square inches. Measure your own pans to find one with an equivalent area. The pan can be slightly deeper than the specified 2 inches but not shallower.

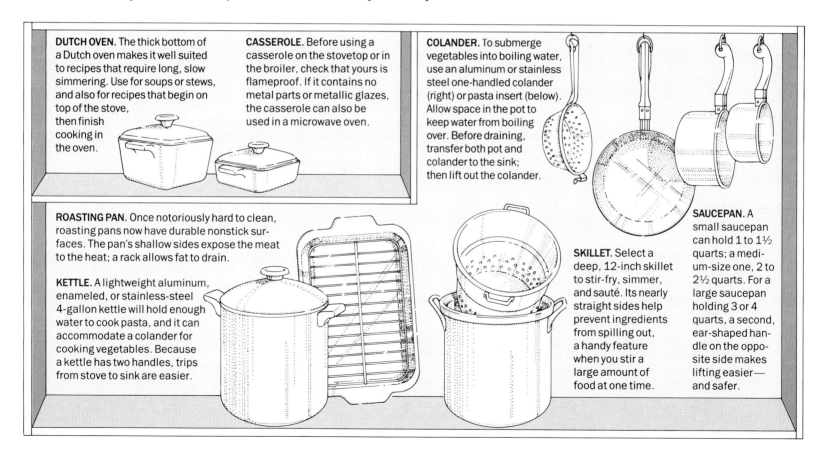

DUTCH OVEN. The thick bottom of a Dutch oven makes it well suited to recipes that require long, slow simmering. Use for soups or stews, and also for recipes that begin on top of the stove, then finish cooking in the oven.

CASSEROLE. Before using a casserole on the stovetop or in the broiler, check that yours is flameproof. If it contains no metal parts or metallic glazes, the casserole can also be used in a microwave oven.

COLANDER. To submerge vegetables into boiling water, use an aluminum or stainless steel one-handled colander (right) or pasta insert (below). Allow space in the pot to keep water from boiling over. Before draining, transfer both pot and colander to the sink; then lift out the colander.

ROASTING PAN. Once notoriously hard to clean, roasting pans now have durable nonstick surfaces. The pan's shallow sides expose the meat to the heat; a rack allows fat to drain.

KETTLE. A lightweight aluminum, enameled, or stainless-steel 4-gallon kettle will hold enough water to cook pasta, and it can accommodate a colander for cooking vegetables. Because a kettle has two handles, trips from stove to sink are easier.

SKILLET. Select a deep, 12-inch skillet to stir-fry, simmer, and sauté. Its nearly straight sides help prevent ingredients from spilling out, a handy feature when you stir a large amount of food at one time.

SAUCEPAN. A small saucepan can hold 1 to 1½ quarts; a medium-size one, 2 to 2½ quarts. For a large saucepan holding 3 or 4 quarts, a second, ear-shaped handle on the opposite side makes lifting easier— and safer.

Food Processor

A superb time-saver, the food processor is now a standard appliance in many kitchens. It can chop, grind, julienne, mince, purée, shred, and slice ingredients in less time than a cook can do manually. Mini processors are available for such tasks as mincing garlic or chopping parsley.

While the food processor is a first choice for some chores, don't use it for jobs that are better done by other appliances. Mixers are superior for mashing and beating; blenders are best for making frothy drinks. Because food processor sizes and models vary, as well as the sharpness of their blades, processing times may differ slightly from those given in a recipe.

Stir-Frying

A fast, simple cooking technique, stir-frying produces crispy vegetables and tender, succulent meat. The bright colors and fresh flavors will be welcomed by family and guests.

Stir-frying is also healthy and economical; recipes usually rely more on vegetables and less on meat, and the cooking method retains a maximum amount of nutrients. The vegetables and meats are usually served with rice, but some recipes use pasta or baby corn as alternatives.

As in Western-style cooking, there are some ingredients to keep on hand for stir-frying: fresh ginger, soy sauce, peanut oil, sesame oil, rice vinegar, and rice wine or dry sherry (see pages 14–15). You'll find that they will be in constant use.

The wok. A bowl-shaped thin metal pan, the wok allows quick stir-frying over very high heat. The old-style wok can be balanced on a ring for cooking. Newer ones have flat bottoms that can sit on a gas or electric burner; some have a nonstick surface.

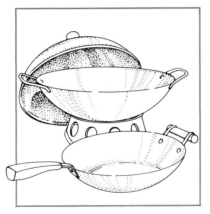

Cooking. The ingredients are first cut into small pieces of uniform size. Then, just minutes before mealtime, the food is tossed into a sizzling hot wok with just enough oil to prevent sticking.

The secret to stir-frying is in a tossing motion. It is done by lifting and turning the food with one hand while holding the wok with the other one. By keeping the food in constant motion, it is quickly cooked against the pan's hot sides and is never allowed to steam in a heap at the bottom. For stirring, use a large wooden spoon. Or you can use a wok chan—a spatula with a broad blade designed to fit the curve of the wok. It is sometimes included in a wok set.

Microwave Oven

The speed of the microwave oven has made it a popular kitchen appliance. The oven operates by using microwaves to make water molecules vibrate. The vibration creates friction, and the friction generates heat.

Because recipes cooked in a microwave oven need less oil (or butter) and water, their fat content is lower and water-soluble vitamins do not leach out. Short cooking times also guarantee that the heat-sensitive vitamins are retained.

Arranging ingredients. Thorough cooking depends on heat spreading from the outside of the food to its center. This means that food must be arranged in the oven in a specific way for even cooking. Separate large pieces of food from one another so that waves penetrate from all sides. Place ingredients that take longest to cook along the perimeter of a dish, with ingredients that take less cooking time in the center. When directed by a recipe, rearrange the ingredients in a dish or rotate the dish a half turn midway through cooking.

Cookware. Heat is distributed most evenly in a microwave in shallow round casseroles. Food in a rectangular pan cooks more quickly in the corners than elsewhere, and food at the top of a deep dish can overcook before the center or bottom is done.

Use cookware made of glass ovenware, glass ceramic, or pottery with a nonmetallic glaze. Cookware designed for use in a microwave oven is made of a heat-safe plastic and marked "Suitable for the microwave" or "Microwave safe." Utensils can be wood or microwave-safe plastic. Never assume that utensils, cookware, plastic lids, or plastic food wrap is safe for the microwave oven unless they are specifically labeled for that use.

Cookware made of or containing metal—even metallic hardware, glazes, or trim—is not suitable for microwave cooking. Because microwaves cannot penetrate metal, food will remain uncooked. In addition, arcing (electric sparks bouncing inside the oven) can occur, damaging the oven.

Plastic food wrap. Some microwave recipes call for covering the dish with plastic wrap. To prevent chemicals leaching from the plastic wrap into the food, don't allow the wrap to touch the food. To allow steam to vent during cooking, turn back one corner of the plastic wrap.

Power levels. Microwave ovens operate with different power levels, depending on the kind you own. Our recipes have been standardized for the levels given below. Check the manual for your oven to make sure they correspond.

WHEN RECIPE SAYS	SET OVEN AT
High	100%
Medium-high	70%
Medium	50%
Medium-low	30%
Low	10%

Herbs and Spices

ere is a general guide to cooking with herbs and spices, many of them used creatively in the recipes in this book. Once you've tried some of these dishes—cinnamon in a poultry dish or beef stew, for example—you'll be ready to experiment with various seasonings on your own.

Freshly snipped herbs, more flavorful than their dried counterparts, are preferred for cooking. To substitute dried herbs, use ⅓ the amount of the fresh herb called for in most cases; but for strong herbs, such as rosemary and coriander, use only ¼ of the amount. Because dried herbs lose flavor after a few months, even in tightly sealed jars, add them a little at a time, tasting for the desired flavor. Crumble dried herbs before using them to release their flavors.

If you wish to reduce sodium in your diet, decrease or omit salt from the recipe. Increase the amount of herbs and spices to add zest.

Bouquet garni. To remove herbs from the dish before serving it, make a bouquet garni. First cut a 5-inch square from a double thickness of cheesecloth, then place fresh or dried herbs (parsley and thyme sprigs plus a bay leaf) in the center. Gather the cloth's edges and tie white string around them.

Storage. To freeze freshly minced herbs for later use, place 1 tablespoon in each compartment of an ice cube tray, then add 3 to 4 tablespoons of water and freeze. Pop the frozen cubes into a plastic bag for storage in the freezer. Frozen herbs will keep for about 6 months.

NAME	CHARACTERISTICS	USE
Allspice	Spicy berries that taste like a blend of cloves, cinnamon, and nutmeg.	Add to beef dishes, yellow vegetables, breads, relishes, pickles, cakes, and pies.
Anise seeds	Small round seeds with a licorice flavor.	Enliven beef and pork dishes, fruits, breads, cakes, and cookies.
Basil	A member of the mint family, the fresh green leaves are very flavorful. Crumbled and ground dried leaves are less aromatic.	Use in chicken, fish, and tomato dishes, pasta sauce, and salads; also use for soups, stuffings, pesto sauce, and salad dressings.
Bay leaf	Belonging to the bay laurel family, leaves are dried for use. Remove bay leaves before serving a dish; they remain tough and their edges sharp, even after being cooked.	Add to poached fish or poultry dishes as well as to stocks, soups, stews, casseroles, and pasta sauces.
Caraway seeds	Small crescent-shaped seeds commonly found in rye bread.	Use to perk up pork, carrots, and coleslaw, as well as egg and cheese dishes.
Cardamom seeds	If seeds are in pods, extract them with your fingers. The seeds are also sold ground, or you can grind your own in a coffee mill or by crushing them between 2 spoons.	Use cardamom pods whole in coffee or add ground cardamom to breads, cakes, and cookies.

NAME	CHARACTERISTICS	USE
Celery seeds	Stronger tasting than fresh celery, these seeds have an intense celery flavor.	Complement beef, lamb, and vegetable stews, egg salads, and barbecue sauces.
Chervil	Similar to a combination of parsley and tarragon, chervil is available fresh or dried.	Excellent in roasted meat, poultry, fish, vegetable, and egg recipes as well as salads.
Chili powder	Named for the hot chili peppers from which it gets its red color, chili powder may also contain cumin, oregano, and garlic. The hotness varies, so use it with caution.	In addition to main-course dishes, it adds zest to barbecue sauces, dips, spreads, salad dressings, breads, and croutons.
Chives	The long, slender tubular leaves of chives have a delicate onion flavor, more fragrant than sharp.	Sprinkle freshly snipped chives on any mildly seasoned egg, cheese, fish, poultry, vegetable, or salad dish.
Cinnamon	The sweet, reddish-brown bark of the East Indian cassia tree sold either ground or as rolled sticks.	Best suited to sweetened bean dishes, yellow vegetables, cooked fruits, and baked desserts.
Cloves	These dried buds, whole or ground, give a warm, pungent flavor to foods both sweet and savory. Cloves are strong—use them sparingly.	Glazed hams can be studded with whole cloves when baked. Use ground cloves in baking, fruit desserts, and in spicy meat dishes.

NAME	CHARACTERISTICS	USE
Coriander (cilantro)	Freshly snipped coriander (sold in bunches) has a biting grassy taste and almost piercing fragrance. Coriander seeds, whole or ground, have a different, lemony flavor.	Add fresh coriander to soups and egg, cheese, fish, and poultry dishes. Add ground coriander or crushed coriander seeds to beef soups and stews and to chilies and curries.
Cumin seeds	Whole or ground, these seeds have a powerful musky aroma and flavor.	Complement meat and rice dishes, curries, chilies, and potato casseroles.
Curry powder	A mixture of many spices, the different brands vary in color, flavor, and hotness.	Use to season meats, poultry, fish, fruits, vegetables, and cream soups and sauces.
Dill	The fresh fronds of dill have a slightly lemony, salty flavor. Dried dill (dill weed) is much more intense; use it sparingly.	Add to fish, lamb, poultry, and vegetable dishes, as well as to salads, dressings, and sauces.
Fennel seeds	Either ground or whole, these seeds have a sweet anise flavor.	Use in tomato sauces for pasta and pizza and to flavor fish, salads, and carrots.
Ginger	This fresh underground plant stem has a peppery, lemony flavor; ground ginger is less aromatic, more biting.	Enhances meat, poultry, seafood, and vegetable stir-fries as well as cakes, cookies, pies, and breads.
Mace	The casing around nutmeg, mace is sold ground or as dried "blades." It tastes like nutmeg but is more delicate.	Use in poultry, fish, vegetable, and cheese dishes and in fruit desserts, custards, pound cakes, and cookies.
Marjoram	Both the fresh and dried leaves of marjoram have a strong, savory flavor.	Suitable for veal, lamb, and poultry dishes, green vegetables, and tomatoes.
Nutmeg	Available in whole seeds but usually sold ground, nutmeg has a warm, sweet flavor.	Add to beef soups and stews, yellow vegetables, breads, cakes, and fruit desserts.
Oregano	Related to marjoram, the dried leaves of oregano are available crumbled or ground.	Use in tomato dishes, pasta sauces, and salad dressings.

NAME	CHARACTERISTICS	USE
Paprika	A red powder ground from dried sweet pepper pods, paprika varies in flavor from nutty and sweet to hot.	Sprinkle over a dish as a garnish, or use as a seasoning for goulashes, fish, poultry, and potato dishes.
Parsley	A member of the carrot family, curly parsley has a mild taste; the flat-leaf, or Italian, variety is more pungent.	Use as a garnish, chopped or in sprigs. Flat-leaf parsley enhances meat, poultry, fish, and meatless main dishes.
Poppy seeds	Tiny gray seeds with a nutty flavor. Use only fresh seeds; they turn rancid quickly.	A favorite in cakes, cookies, breads, sweet pastries, and salad dressings.
Rosemary	An aromatic herb, rosemary has needle-like leaves that give off a rich, resinous scent whether fresh or dried.	Roasted meats, poultry, fish, green peas, carrots, stuffings, gravies, and casseroles benefit from its hearty flavor.
Saffron	An expensive yellow spice, sold in thread or powder form, saffron has a strong but delicate flavor.	Used sparingly, saffron enhances chicken, rice, and seafood dishes.
Sage	The fresh, ground, or dried gray-green leaves have a pungent lemony flavor; sage can be bitter if overused.	Sage is traditional in meat and poultry stuffings and is also delicious in cheese dishes.
Savory	Dried whole or ground leaves with a grassy aroma, savory has a light fragrant flavor.	Add to egg, rice, vegetable, and poultry dishes.
Sesame seeds	Pearly flat seeds with a mild nutlike flavor.	Add to stir-fries and breads and use as a garnish for chicken, fish, and vegetable dishes.
Tarragon	Fresh or dried, this herb retains its mild licorice flavor well.	Enlivens fish and poultry dishes, especially with wine or cream.
Thyme	Fresh or dried, thyme has a pungent aroma similar to sage. Discard any stems.	Equally at home with meat, poultry, seafood, eggs, cheese, vegetables, and salads.
Turmeric	The powdered yellow root lends a peppery pungency to curry powder, mustards, and relishes.	Use this potent spice in small quantities in curries, chicken, and egg dishes.

Special Ingredients

Some recipes in this book call for ingredients that may be unfamiliar to you, but they add flavorings that truly enhance a dish. If you would like to know more about a particular ingredient, look for it in the following list.

You may find that once you've tried a new ingredient in one of our recipes, you'll want to use it in other recipes on your own. For information about herbs or spices, see pages 12–13.

Ancho chilies   Dried broad, flat chili peppers that are almost black in color. They have a warm, slightly toasty flavor and vary in hotness.

Arrowroot   A starch used to thicken liquids, such as soups and sauces, without changing their flavor. Arrowroot has about the same thickening power as cornstarch but 2 to 2½ times that of flour.

Arugula (rocket)   A salad green with a sharp, peppery flavor and long bright green leaves.

Bean paste   A salty, slightly sweet paste made of fermented soybeans that is used to season Chinese food, particularly the peppery Hunan and Szechuan dishes.

Bulgur   Parched cracked wheat with some of the bran removed. Bulgur has a nutty flavor and crunchy texture. It is usually boiled or steamed and served as an alternate for potatoes or rice.

Capers   Small olive-green buds with a salty, piquant flavor. Capers are frequently used to enliven bland poultry, fish, or egg dishes. They are sold bottled and pickled in brine.

Caponata   A zesty Italian appetizer made from eggplant, zucchini, tomato paste, vinegar, and sometimes olives. Caponata is used as an ingredient in recipes or served as a spread with crackers. It is sold in cans.

Chili oil   A very hot Oriental oil used to spice up stir-fried and noodle dishes. Chili oil is made by seasoning sesame oil with chili peppers.

Chinese cabbage (bok choy)   A member of the chard family, Chinese cabbage has long gleaming-white stems topped by rich green leaves. Very crisp and crunchy, it is especially good in stir-fried dishes. Use both the leaves and stems.

Chinese celery cabbage   Long, tightly packed heads of pale lettuce-like leaves that are curled at the edges. Celery cabbage is frequently used in meat and poultry stir-fries.

Chinese egg noodles   A soft, resilient thin noodle made from wheat flour. Chinese egg noodles are good in both hot and cold Oriental dishes.

Chorizo   A pork sausage that is highly seasoned with garlic, chili, pepper, and cumin. The Mexican type is made with fresh pork; the firmer Spanish type is smoked.

Chutney   A sweet and spicy relish served with curries. Most chutneys contain mango, ginger, and raisins and range from mild to flaming hot.

Collard greens   This vegetable has smooth, flat, emerald green leaves, looks like kale, and tastes similar to turnip greens—cabbage-strong and slightly bitter.

Couscous   A tiny grain ground from semolina, the golden heart of durum wheat. Couscous has a buttery flavor that makes it an excellent companion for spicy foods. It can be steamed to make it light and fluffy or it can be soaked in hot water or stock.

Dry sherry   In wine lingo, *dry* means not sweet. Dry sherry is frequently used to flavor sauces because the alcohol vaporizes as it cooks, leaving a rich, slightly fruity taste. Use any good dry sherry from a liquor store.

Escarole   A crunchy, slightly bitter salad green with broad, wavy, fleshy leaves that are green at the outside of the head, white within. An excellent choice to fortify a mixed green salad.

Falafel   A mixture of ground dried chick peas and herbs that is moistened into a paste, then shaped into balls and deep-fried. Falafel has a nutty toasted flavor, is usually served with a sauce or salad dressing, and is sold in many supermarkets.

Feta cheese   A Greek favorite, this crumbly sheep or goat's milk cheese is preserved in brine. The sharp, salty flavor is excellent in salads.

Green chilies   A whole family of hot peppers, some round, some pear-shaped, some long and pencil-thin. As a rule, the sharper the point, the hotter the chili. The hotness of canned green chilies is usually indicated on the label.

Great Northern beans   Dried white beans used in casseroles, soups, stews, and salads.

Gruyère cheese   A smooth, nut-flavored cheese often called for in sauces because it melts smoothly.

Jalapeño peppers   Straight, smooth, 2-inch-long green chili peppers that are medium hot.

Juniper berries   Dried blue-black berries from the juniper bush. Their slightly resinous pine-needle flavor goes well with game, red meats, poultry, and sauerkraut.

Kale   A dark green cabbage with a ruffled leaf and a strong but sweet flavor. Used like collard greens, this highly nutritious vegetable can be bought fresh or frozen.

Kasha   Cracked buckwheat groats. Kasha has an earthy nutty flavor and can be served in place of rice or potatoes or incorporated into beef, poultry, and fish recipes.

ANCHO CHILI

PASILLA CHILI

JALAPEÑO PEPPER

Kielbasa A large Polish pork sausage emphatically seasoned with garlic, black pepper, and herbs. The red color comes from paprika.

Mustard greens Loose clusters of bright green leaves that are either flat or frilled. With their unmistakable mustardy bite, they complement ham, pork, and stir-fries.

Navy (pea) beans Dried small white beans used for baked beans.

Oriental oyster sauce A subtle brew made from oysters fermented in brine and soy sauce, oyster sauce intensifies food flavors without imposing its own taste.

Oriental sesame oil A clear amber oil pressed from toasted sesame seeds and used as a condiment, not a cooking oil. Its warm, smoky flavor enhances Oriental meat, vegetable, and noodle dishes.

Pasilla chilies Dried six-inch-long dark red narrow peppers. Moderately piquant, they have a rich flavor.

Peanut oil A cooking oil extracted from peanuts that is preferred for stir-frying because it withstands high heat without smoking.

Phyllo pastry Tissue-thin sheets of wheat flour pastry that are brushed with butter and layered to make crisp, flaky wrappers usually for turnovers and desserts. Sold both refrigerated and frozen in many supermarkets, phyllo is easy to use.

Pine nuts (pignolis) Blanched small seeds with a sweetly resinous taste and plump chewiness.

Pinto beans Mottled red and white beans that are exceptionally meaty and sweet and well suited to Mexican and southwestern dishes.

Porcini Wild European mushrooms prized for their meaty, rich flavor. Porcini are sold both fresh and dried and can be found in specialty stores and some supermarkets.

Prosciutto An intensely flavored dark red Italian ham that has been salted and air-dried. Usually sliced very thin, prosciutto is used in small amounts to flavor meat and poultry dishes or served with melon or fresh figs as an appetizer.

Radicchio A small, round, ruby-red chicory with white ribbed leaves. With its crunchy texture, slightly bitter taste, and bright color, radicchio is superb in green salads.

Rice wine A slightly sweet Oriental wine used in recipes to impart a delicate, almost flowery flavor. Dry sherry is a good substitute.

Rice vinegar A clear to pale gold vinegar with a light, mildly tart flavor and just a hint of sweetness. It is much less astringent than either cider vinegar or distilled white vinegar and thus much better suited to delicate Oriental dishes.

Roasted red peppers Red bell peppers that have been roasted to produce a mellow, smoky flavor. Sweeter and milder than sweet green peppers, they are exceptionally flavorful and have an incomparable silky texture. They are sold peeled and are available in jars and cans.

Rutabaga A large root vegetable often called a yellow turnip. The cooked rutabaga is sweeter than a turnip, and its golden flesh is more nutritious too.

Sesame paste (tahini) A creamy paste of ground sesame seeds that tastes and spreads something like peanut butter. Sesame paste is used in salad dressings or to mellow and blend other ingredients.

Shallots Small nut-brown onions that grow in clusters similar to garlic. Shallots taste less harsh than onions, less pungent than garlic, yet subtly combine the fragrances of both.

Shiitake (Chinese black mushrooms) Dark brown mushrooms with a rich meaty flavor and chewy consistency. Available fresh or dried, they are used frequently in Oriental stir-fries. Use only the caps.

Sorrel (sourgrass) Long-stemmed bright green leaves with an acidic tang. Sorrel adds lemony freshness to cream sauces and soups.

Straw mushrooms Small, crunchy-tender, delicately flavored caps. A fragrant addition to stir-fries, straw mushrooms are sold in the produce section of some supermarkets.

Tofu (bean curd) A bland cream-colored soybean cake that absorbs the flavors of other ingredients. Tofu is often used as a meat substitute because it is very low in fat and high in protein.

Transparent (cellophane) noodles Glassy, pleasantly slippery noodles made from bean starch. Cellophane noodles need only a brief soaking in hot water before being added to a dish. Like tofu, they are relatively tasteless and will absorb the flavor of other ingredients.

Water chestnuts Small round underwater tubers with a crystalline crunch and delicate nut flavor. They are sold in cans, whole or sliced.

Pasta

More than 600 types of pasta are available.
Since many recipes in this book offer a choice among the
different kinds, just select your favorite shape, size,
and color to enjoy a satisfying meal.

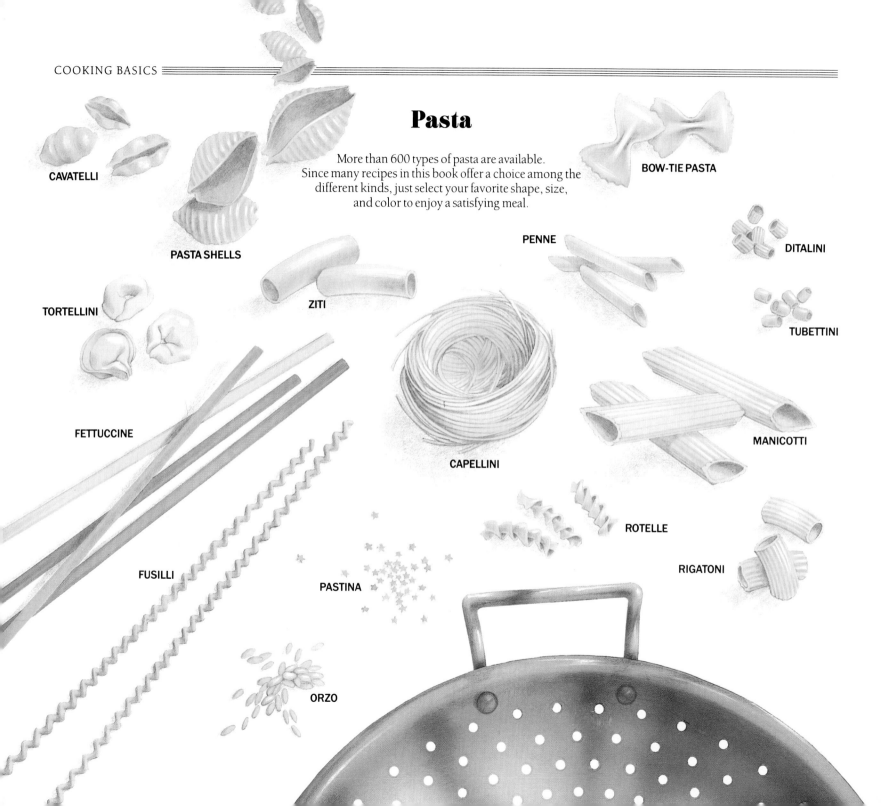

CAVATELLI

PASTA SHELLS

BOW-TIE PASTA

PENNE

DITALINI

TORTELLINI

ZITI

TUBETTINI

FETTUCCINE

CAPELLINI

MANICOTTI

FUSILLI

ROTELLE

RIGATONI

PASTINA

ORZO

Store Now, Serve Later

Sometimes it may be more convenient to make a one-dish meal ahead of time and refrigerate it for use the next day or freeze it for use weeks or months in the future. Or when planning to make a one-dish meal, you may want to double it so that you can enjoy half of it right away and the other half at a later date. Usually you can double all the ingredients, but there are exceptions, particularly when it comes to stews. If the recipe calls for large amounts of liquids, only increase the liquids by 50 percent.

Before storing. After cooking a recipe that you wish to store in the refrigerator, wait for the food to cool just enough to handle it, then refrigerate immediately. If you wish to freeze the recipe, wait until it reaches room temperature, then transfer it to the freezer. Label and date all food packages that are to be frozen.

Leftovers. When you have only a small amount of leftovers or if you're unsure how you want to use leftover food, store it in small packages or containers. This will give you a few alternatives. Wait until there are enough portions of several dishes to give each family member a choice for dinner, or use a package as a meal for one person. If you wish to incorporate leftover items, such as meat, poultry, vegetables, or grains, into a recipe, store them in half-pint containers (equivalent to 1 cup of an ingredient). Transfer any leftover canned ingredients to a glass or plastic container.

Containers. To allow room for food to expand as it freezes, leave ½ inch of space in a pint container or 1 inch of space for a quart. An overfilled glass jar may break, and too much food in a plastic container may push the lid off. If the container is too large, line it with a plastic bag and seal the bag over the food before snapping on the lid. This will prevent the food from "freezer burn," or drying out. When storing food in a plastic bag, squeeze the air from the bag before sealing it completely.

Wraps. One of two basic ways to wrap foods snugly for storage, the butcher wrap is best for poultry, bulky cuts of meat, and other irregularly shaped solid foods. Use a square piece of freezer paper, plastic freezer wrap, or aluminum foil. Place the food diagonally in the center of the square. Bring the front corner up

over it, then fold the two side corners toward the center. Keeping the wrapping taut, fold the last corner over the other three; seal with tape.

For flat foods such as steaks or fish, the drugstore wrap is best. Tear off a rectangular piece of wrapping long enough to go around the food with 12 inches to spare. With the food positioned in the center of the rectangle, pull the ends of the wrapping straight up and, holding the

two edges together, fold them over about an inch. Continue to fold until the wrapping is snug. Turn the package over. Fold the corners of the open ends inward to form triangles, then bring the ends up over the package and seal with tape.

Freezing a casserole. To free up a casserole or baking dish while a meal is stored in the freezer, line the clean dish with overlapping sheets of plastic freezer wrap. Add the food, fold over and seal the wrap, and cover the dish with foil. Freeze until solid—12 to 24 hours. Remove the food from the dish, wrap in foil, and store in the freezer. When ready to use, grease the original dish, remove the wrap and foil from the food, place the food in the dish, and reheat.

Reheating. Unless stored in small portions, most foods take too long to reheat directly from the freezer; the outside ingredients can become overcooked or dried out before the inside has defrosted and heated

through. To allow time to thaw, move the dish to the refrigerator the day before you intend to use it. Or if you have a microwave oven, you can follow the manufacturer's suggestions for defrosting in it.

For a dish that was cooked in the oven, reheat it, covered, in a preheated 350° F oven until bubbling—25 to 30 minutes. If you want the top to brown, cook, uncovered, for another 10 to 15 minutes or run briefly under the broiler. For a recipe that was cooked on top of the stove, reheat it in a covered pan over moderately low heat for 15 to 20 minutes.

What not to freeze. Any recipe that contains previously frozen food should not be frozen. Although a recipe that uses rice, pasta, or other grains or frozen vegetables should not be frozen, you can make the recipe without the grain or frozen vegetable and freeze it. Add the vegetable or cooked grain while reheating the recipe. Or use fresh vegetables instead of frozen ones.

Other food items not suitable for the freezer include:

- Buttermilk, yogurt, light cream, sour cream, cream cheese, and unwhipped heavy cream
- Omelets, frittatas, or soufflés
- Mayonnaise, including any dressing or dish containing mayonnaise
- Any vegetable that will be used uncooked, such as lettuce, cucumbers, or celery
- Raw tomatoes and potatoes

Getting Ready

Before starting a recipe, read through it carefully. Assemble all the ingredients, utensils, cookware, and any necessary equipment, such as a food processor or blender. Be sure to allow time for marinating or for frozen ingredients to thaw (or defrost them in a microwave oven according to package directions). If the recipe calls for unthawed frozen food, leave it in the freezer until you are ready to add it to the dish.

Generally, do all the rinsing, peeling, cutting, and other preparation before you start to cook. However, a number of recipes in this book save time by directing you to prepare some ingredients while others are cooking. For example, you can cut vegetables while rice or pasta is cooking.

Washing. Before opening cans, wash them with soap and water to remove any pesticides the store may have used. Fresh fruits and vegetables should be rinsed under cold running water to remove grit and chemical residues. After handling uncooked poultry, wash your hands as well as any kitchen equipment, such as a knife and cutting board, before proceeding with the recipe. This will prevent any salmonella bacteria from being transferred to foods that come into contact with those surfaces—especially important for foods that are served raw. Always wash your hands thoroughly with soap or water after handling hot peppers, and be sure to keep your hands away from your face. (You may want

to wear disposable rubber gloves.) The peppers contain a chemical irritant that can burn your skin and eyes.

Cutting. Sharp knives make cutting much easier and safer; hone your knives regularly to keep the blades keen. To prevent round vegetables like turnips and potatoes from rolling as you cut them, first remove a thin slice from one side or cut the vegetable in half lengthwise, then place it flat side down before you cut. When slicing with a chef's knife, hold the vegetable with your fingertips curled slightly under to protect them and the middle section of your fingers parallel to the broad side of the knife blade. Your fingernails can then grip the vegetable securely.

Measuring. Liquids are easiest to measure in glass measuring cups. The extra space at the top prevents spillage, and there is a lip for pouring. Measure dry ingredients in graduated measuring cups.

Cleaning up. To free space in your work area, put ingredients away as you finish using them. Replace the lids on containers and close box tops to avoid accidental spills. Keep a damp cloth or paper toweling handy for wiping the work surface. When measuring dry ingredients, grating food, or rolling dough, work on a piece of wax paper to save cleanup time; anchor the paper by moistening the counter, then laying the paper over it.

Blanching

Before freezing fresh vegetables, blanch them to destroy the enzymes that cause spoilage. Blanch small vegetables such as green beans whole; cut large ones into smaller chunks. Bring a kettle of water to a boil. Place the washed vegetables in a colander and lower into the kettle. Bring the water back to a boil, blanch for the time specified below, then transfer the vegetables to a bowl of cold water. Drain them, then store in dated and labeled plastic bags in the freezer at 0° F.

VEGETABLE	MINUTES	VEGETABLE	MINUTES
Asparagus	3	Corn kernels	3
Broccoli (florets)	3–4	Green peas	2
Brussels sprouts	3–4	Spinach and other leafy greens	2
Green beans	2		
Carrots (sliced)	3	Summer squash (sliced)	3
Cauliflower (florets)	3	Winter squash (cubed)	5–6

To measure a dry ingredient, stir it to smooth out any lumps. (If called for in a recipe, sift flour instead.) Using a spoon, gently mound the ingredient above the rim of a measuring cup, then slide the thin edge of a knife or spatula across the rim to level off the excess. For butter, margarine, vegetable shortening, or brown sugar, always pack the ingredient into the measuring cup firmly.

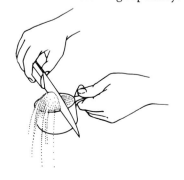

To measure a liquid ingredient, place the measuring cup on a flat surface; fill to the specified measuring line and check at eye level. For quantities less than 1/4 cup, use measuring spoons.

Cutting and Chopping

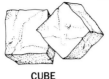

CUBE **DICE** **MINCE**

To make julienne strips, cut the vegetable in half lengthwise; lay each half on its cut side. Cut into ⅛-inch-thick slices. Stacking a few slices at a time, cut them lengthwise every ⅛ inch.

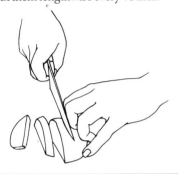

To chop or mince food, slice it with a chef's knife. Then, holding the knife's handle with one hand, the blade near its tip with the other, chop with a rocking motion, keeping the tip on the cutting board; pivot the blade as you work. Chop food into ¼-inch pieces; mince food into ⅛-inch pieces.

To cube or dice, first slice the food to the proper thickness — ½ inch for cubes or ⅛ to ¼ inch for dice. Stack a few slices at a time and cut them into strips of the same thickness. Then line up the strips and cut them crosswise into squares.

To cut an onion, peel and halve it lengthwise. With the cut side down, slice each half crosswise into ¼-inch slices. Grasp the group of slices firmly, give it a quarter turn, and slice lengthwise into ¼-inch dice.

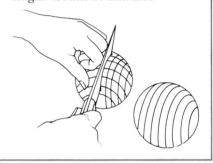

To dredge or coat food in flour or crumbs, heap the flour or crumbs on a plate; roll the food in it until evenly coated. For large amounts, place the flour or crumbs in a clean brown paper bag, add the food, and shake.

To tie a chicken for roasting, lay it on its back. (If the recipe calls for stuffing, loosely fill the neck and body cavities.) Tuck the wing tips behind the back, then tie the legs together using white string. The chicken will roast more evenly.

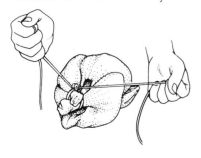

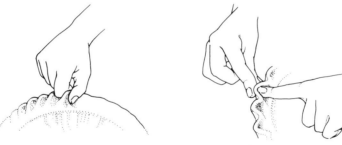

To flute a pie crust, crimp the edge by resting an index finger inside on the pastry rim; place the thumb and index finger of the other hand outside the rim. Pinch the crust between your finger and thumb to form a V shape; repeat around the pie edge. For a scalloped edge, pinch the crust between your thumb and bent index finger at a diagonal angle; repeat around the pie edge.

To snip fresh herbs, gather them into a small tight bunch. Cut crosswise every ⅛ inch with kitchen scissors. Or place the herbs, leaf ends first, into a small glass measuring cup (to prevent a mess) and cut repeatedly with scissors.

To peel tomatoes, peaches, plums, or small onions, place them in a colander and lower into a kettle of boiling water. Boil for 30 seconds for tomatoes and fruits, 1 minute for onions. Drain, run under cold water, then slip off the skins. (Or instead of a colander, remove them with a slotted spoon.)

To shell and devein shrimp, cut through the shell and a thin layer of flesh down each shrimp's back to the tail with kitchen scissors. Spread open the shell and gently lift out the shrimp. To loosen the tail meat, squeeze the tip of the tail hard; pull the shrimp free. Rinse the shelled shrimp under cold running water. Pull or scrape the dark vein out with your fingertips, then rinse the shrimp well again.

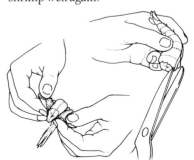

Helpful Cooking Tips

Fruits and Vegetables

To ripen fruits such as avocados, bananas, peaches, pears, and tomatoes, store them in a closed paper bag with a few ripe apples. Ripe apples release a gas that helps other fruits ripen.

For longer storage of ripened fruit, make sure they don't touch one another or any other fruit.

To prevent the flesh of apples from turning brown after cutting them, dip them in lemon juice.

Get more juice from a lemon by soaking it in hot water for 15 minutes or by microwaving it on *High* for about 30 seconds before squeezing it. Or simply roll the uncut lemon against the counter, pressing hard to release the juice.

To squeeze a few drops of lemon juice without wasting the rest, prick the peel at one end of the lemon with a fork. Squeeze out what you need and save the lemon for another use.

Grated rind from oranges and lemons freezes well. When you're ready to use the fruit, first grate the rind and store it in the freezer for later use.

Freeze fresh ginger in a plastic bag. When a recipe calls for ginger, grate or cut as much as you need from the frozen root, then return the balance to the freezer.

Peel fresh ginger by scraping the blade of a paring knife along the surface. A vegetable peeler removes too much of the juicy, richly flavored layer just beneath the skin.

Watercress and fresh herbs such as parsley, coriander, basil, and dill stay crisp in the refrigerator longer if kept with their stems in a jar containing 2 to 3 inches of water. Cover the bouquet loosely with a plastic bag. Asparagus can also be kept fresh for several days this way. Cut a slice off the bottom of each stalk. Place the bunch, stem ends down, in an inch of water in a tall, quart-size glass or plastic container.

Frozen spinach, when thawed, can be very watery. To remove excess water, place the spinach in the center of a square of paper toweling or clean white cloth. Bring up the edges to form a bag, hold the bag over the sink, and twist the top until no more water drips from it.

Salad greens stay fresh longer if your refrigerator's vegetable bin is lined with paper toweling or a clean linen towel to absorb excess moisture. Or keep several clean, dry sponges in the bin to absorb moisture.

Before using dried mushrooms, soak them in a small bowl of hot tap water until soft all the way through—about 30 minutes. Squeeze them in your fist to remove excess water, then pick out any grit from the undersides.

Take advantage of bargain prices for mushrooms that are past their prime. Slice them, sauté in butter, and freeze in recipe-size packages. They will taste as good as fresh.

To remove the canned taste from water chestnuts, soak them in the refrigerator in water for 2 to 3 days; change the water daily.

To keep bean sprouts or tofu fresh, store in the refrigerator submerged in a container of cold water; change the water daily. Bean sprouts will keep for 2 or 3 days, tofu for 1 week.

Finely chopped parsley to be used as a garnish will stay light and fluffy for hours if squeezed in a double thickness of paper toweling to remove all the moisture.

Beets, carrots, turnips, and other root vegetables are often sold whole, complete with their leafy green tops. To prevent the tops from robbing nutrients from the roots, remove all but 1 inch of them before storing the roots in the refrigerator. Use the tops in a soup or in vegetable stock.

Chill onions in the freezer for 10 to 15 minutes (or chill thoroughly in the refrigerator) before chopping them. A cold onion releases fewer eye irritants.

If you have a lot of onions to peel, put them in a large bowl of cold water in the sink and peel them under the water—tearlessly. Eye irritants are less likely to escape.

Remove the smell of onions or garlic from your hands by rinsing them, rubbing with baking powder, and rinsing again.

Freeze the liquids in which vegetables were cooked for later use in stocks and soups. They retain some of the nutrients lost from the vegetables and are a flavorful substitute for plain water.

Vegetables can often be bought more economically frozen in large bags. Tap the bag on the counter to loosen the contents, take out the quantity you need, reseal the bag, and replace immediately in the freezer.

When using dried herbs, crumble them with your fingers to release their flavors. To crush seeds, rock the bowl of a spoon over them slowly.

Meat, Poultry, and Seafood

Let meat or poultry come to room temperature before sautéing or browning it. The meat will absorb less fat, brown more quickly, and be less likely to stick.

Before sautéing or browning, pat the surface of meat, poultry, or fish dry with paper toweling. A moist surface slows browning.

To prevent sticking when sautéing or browning meat or poultry, heat the skillet for a minute before adding the oil. Then wait another minute to allow the oil to heat.

When sautéing meat, distribute it so that there is space around every piece. Crowding creates steam that prevents browning. Sauté in batches if necessary.

Before freezing leftover meat or poultry, consider how you might use it. It may be more useful if frozen already cubed, diced, or sliced for later use in recipes and in premeasured quantities such as ½ cup or 1 cup. Include this information on a label.

Marinate frozen meat as it thaws. Place the meat and marinade in a sealable plastic bag. Let thaw in the refrigerator, turning the bag over several times.

Roasts brown better in a shallow roasting pan than in a deep one because hot air can circulate more freely around them.

Ground meat and croquette mixtures will stick to your hands less as you shape the patties if you dip your hands frequently into a bowl of cold water.

Canned ham will slide out easily if, before opening the can, you run hot tap water over it to slightly melt the gelatin that surrounds the meat.

Uncooked boneless chicken breasts and other meats are much easier to slice thinly if partially frozen. Thaw frozen pieces slightly in the refrigerator or, if fresh, freeze for 45 minutes or until almost firm to the touch.

Freeze any leftover cooked fish such as salmon or halibut for later use in a salad. It will flake just as well as freshly cooked fish.

Before opening clam or oyster shells, after washing in cold water, place them in a plastic storage bag and freeze for 30 minutes. They will open more easily.

Dairy Products, Eggs, and Grains

To prevent sour cream from curdling when adding it to a hot mixture, bring it to room temperature first. When heating a dish with sour cream, stir often, and remove the pot from the stove before it reaches the boiling point.

Keep ungrated Parmesan cheese frozen; it will be much easier to grate. Cheddar, Swiss, and other hard cheeses can be shredded more easily if they are first chilled in the freezer for 15 minutes.

If you often use shredded cheese, shred more than you need, divide into recipe-size portions, and store them in labeled and dated plastic bags in the refrigerator or freezer.

Always buy large eggs. They are the standard size used in most cookbook and magazine recipes.

To halve an uncooked egg, beat together the egg white and yolk in a measuring cup, then measure out half of the beaten egg.

Store all dry foods, such as uncooked cereals, grains, dried mushrooms, and chili peppers, in tightly lidded glass jars or plastic containers. Insects can bite their way into boxes and plastic bags, and can sneak under the lids of metal canisters. If the insects persist, refrigerate the items.

If you run out of bread crumbs, substitute unsweetened dry cereal such as oatmeal or wheat or corn flakes. Crumble the cereal in an electric blender or a food processor.

To prepare rice ahead, boil it for ¾ of the normal cooking time. Drain in a colander and store, covered, in the refrigerator to prevent drying. To reheat, set the rice in a heatproof colander or a large sieve in a large saucepan with 1 inch of boiling water. Cover and steam white rice for 5 to 7 minutes, brown rice for 10 to 12 minutes.

If cooked pasta has to sit for a few minutes after draining while you finish other preparations, toss it with a tablespoon of olive or vegetable oil to keep it from clumping.

Leftover pasta that has stuck together can be separated by placing it in a colander and plunging it briefly into boiling water.

To reduce flatulence caused by eating cooked dried beans, change the water that the beans soak in several times. This removes the sugars that can cause gas; however, it also removes some nutrients.

To check baking powder for freshness, put ½ teaspoon in a cup measure and pour ¼ cup hot tap water over it. If the mixture bubbles, it is still good.

Helpful Cooking Tips (Continued)

Broths, Stocks, Soups, Stews

To remove fat from a stock, broth, or soup, cook the food the day before you'll need it. Store the food overnight in the refrigerator. The next day lift off the surface layer of hardened fat.

Freeze stock and broth in ice cube trays. When they are frozen, pop the cubes out and store in plastic bags. Each cube will equal about 3 tablespoons.

A soup or stew that turns out too thin can be thickened with instant mashed potato flakes. Add the

flakes 1 tablespoon at a time until the soup or stew reaches the desired thickness.

Oversalted soups and stews can be remedied by adding a few cubed or sliced potatoes to the pot. As the potatoes cook, they will absorb salt. Remove the potatoes and use elsewhere if desired.

Don't despair if your gravy is lumpy. To remove the lumps, whirl the gravy for a few moments in an electric blender or a food processor, beat with a wire whisk, or push through a fine sieve.

Microwave

Soften hard, dried-out brown sugar by heating it with a slice of apple in a covered heatproof container on *Low* for 1 to 2 minutes.

A stick of margarine or butter can be softened in the microwave in its own wax paper. If it is wrapped in foil, rewrap it in plastic food wrap or wax paper, or place the stick on an uncovered microwave-safe dish. Heat the stick at *Medium-low* for 30 to 40 seconds.

To toast nuts, spread ½ cup shelled nut meats in a 9-inch microwave-safe pie pan. Microwave, uncovered, on *High* until lightly browned—3 to 3½ minutes—

stirring midway. Let stand for 2 to 3 minutes. To toast 1 to 2 cups, use an 11-inch pie pan and microwave on *High* for 4 to 5½ minutes.

To peel garlic cloves easily, place 3 cloves directly on the microwave oven floor and heat on *High* until just warm—15 to 30 seconds. Squeeze the clove's end until the garlic pops from its skin.

Don't double a microwave recipe unless you intend to cook it in 2 batches. Large quantities often take longer to cook in the microwave oven than on the stove, and they tend to cook unevenly.

Barbecues

For easy cleaning, line the pan of an outdoor grill with heavy-duty aluminum foil. If the pan has vent holes, pierce the aluminum foil at those points.

Charcoal starts very slowly. Allow 20 to 40 minutes to reach grilling temperature. At that point, the coals will be coated with white ash and will glow red. Spread the coals into a layer of uniform thickness for even cooking.

To test the temperature of a barbecue fire, carefully position your hand,

palm down, above the coals at cooking height; count the number of seconds before the heat forces you to pull your hand away. Two seconds indicates a hot temperature of 400° F or more; 4 seconds corresponds to medium, or above 350° F; 5 to 6 seconds means the heat is low, 250° to 300° F.

To control cooking speed during grilling, take full advantage of any adjustments available. Raise or lower the rack; if there's a lid, adjust its height. Push more charcoal under

the food to raise the temperature; rake more to the sides to lower it. On gas-fired and electric grills, adjust the temperature knob.

Grilling sears the surface of food more quickly than it cooks the inside. Cook thick cuts of meat at lower heat than thin cuts to avoid excessive charring. Use less charcoal for fatty meats such as hamburger and steak, more for lean cuts.

Dripping fat causes flare-ups that can char the meat. Remove food from the grill during flare-ups. Let the flames burn out or dampen with a plant mister before returning the food to the grill. Try propping one side of the rack to tilt it slightly so that fat runs toward the cooler edge of the fire.

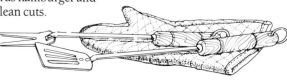

Cooking Terms

Al dente A term used to describe the tender but firm consistency of pasta cooked just to the point of doneness.

Au gratin A term used to describe a crumb- or cheese-topped shallow casserole that has been baked or broiled until the dish has a crusty brown top.

Bake To cook, uncovered, in the dry heat of an oven.

Baste To spoon or brush liquid over food while it cooks to add flavor and seal in moisture.

Batter A pourable mixture of flour, milk or other liquid, eggs, and usually leavening such as baking powder.

Beat To stir a mixture or liquid with a spoon or a hand or electric beater in a vigorous circular motion.

Blanch To submerge food briefly in boiling water and then cool immediately in cold water.

Blanched nuts Nuts with skins removed by blanching.

Blend To mix ingredients by hand or appliance to a uniform texture and color.

Boil To cook in water that is actively bubbling at 212° F.

Bone To remove bones from meat, poultry, or fish with a sharp knife.

Braise To sauté food until brown, then simmer it slowly, tightly covered, in a small amount of liquid either on top of the stove or in the oven.

Bread To coat with bread crumbs.

Broil To cook or brown food under the direct heat of a broiler.

Brown To seal in moisture and flavor by sautéing, roasting, or broiling food until its surface caramelizes.

Brush To cover food with a liquid, such as a marinade or oil, using a pastry brush.

Char To enrich the flavor of food and seal in all its juices by blackening its surface over an open flame, in a hot skillet, or in the broiler.

Chill To cool in the refrigerator or in an ice bath until uniformly cold, thickened, or gelled.

Chop To cut food into small, irregular pieces.

Clarify To make stock or melted butter clear by removing scum and other solids.

Coat To cover with a dry ingredient such as flour or with a liquid such as a batter.

Combine To stir together 2 or more ingredients until they form a uniform mixture.

Cream To beat butter or other solid shortening, sometimes with sugar, until soft and fluffy.

Crimp To seal and decorate the edges of pies and pastries by pressing with a fork or pinching with the fingers into a zigzag border.

Crisp-tender A term used to describe food soft enough to pierce with a fork yet still firm to the bite.

Cube To cut food into ½-inch or larger pieces.

Cut in To mix solid shortening into dry ingredients with a cutting motion using a pastry blender or 2 knives, usually until the texture of coarse meal.

Dice To cut food into cubes smaller than ½ inch.

Drain To remove liquid from food, usually by transferring to a sieve or colander, by using a bulb baster (especially handy for roast drippings), or by partially covering a pan and pouring off any cooking water.

Dredge To completely coat food by rolling, dipping, or shaking in flour or meal.

Drizzle To pour liquid over food in a very fine stream.

Dust To sprinkle lightly with a powder such as confectioners sugar.

Flake To break food—usually cooked fish—into small pieces with a fork.

Flameproof A term used to describe a pan or casserole that can resist intense stovetop or broiler heat.

Flute To crimp a pie crust between thumb and finger to create a scalloped edge.

Fold in To use a gentle up-and-down, over-and-under cutting and scraping motion when incorporating an airy substance, such as whipped cream or stiffly beaten egg whites, into a heavier substance to prevent loss of volume.

Garnish To decorate food before serving it, usually with sprigs of herb, slices or twists of citrus fruit, or small, compatible condiments.

Glassy A term used to describe onions that have been cooked slowly until very pale, limp, and almost transparent.

Glaze To give food a shiny surface by coating it with an ingredient such as honey, syrup, jam, or jelly.

Grate To rub food over a grater, reducing it to shreds or crumbs.

Grease To rub a baking pan with butter, margarine, or oil to prevent food from sticking.

Grill To cook food on a rack over wood, charcoal, gas, or electric heat.

Cooking Terms (Continued)

Heatproof A term used to describe a pot, pan, or casserole (including handles) made of a material that can withstand high oven temperatures but not necessarily stovetop or broiler heat.

Julienne To cut into thin strips like matchsticks.

Knead To work dough by pressing, pushing, and pulling it until satiny and elastic.

Marinate To soak food in a seasoned liquid, paste, or dry blend of herbs and spices to tenderize and flavor it.

Mince To cut food into tiny irregular pieces of 1/8 inch or less.

Mix To combine and stir ingredients together until they are evenly distributed.

Pan-broil To cook over moderately high heat in a skillet with little or no fat.

Parboil To boil vegetables until partially cooked or about half done.

Pare To remove the skin of fruits or vegetables with a knife or vegetable peeler.

Peel Same as *Pare*.

Pinch The amount of a dried herb or spice that can be held between the thumb and index finger.

Poach To cook slowly in simmering liquid.

Preheat To heat the oven or broiler to the temperature specified in the recipe before putting the food in.

Prick To puncture the surface of food, such as potatoes, eggplants, peppers, and other thin-skinned vegetables, with the tines of a sharp fork to allow steam to escape.

Purée To reduce food to a thick liquid or paste in a food mill, electric blender, or food processor.

Reduce To boil a liquid rapidly, uncovered, until it decreases in volume and thickens and its flavor intensifies.

Rind The thick fleshy covering of citrus fruits.

Roast To cook meats, poultry, fish, fruits, or vegetables, uncovered, with little or no additional liquid in the dry heat of the oven.

Sauté To brown or cook food in a small amount of fat in an uncovered skillet on top of the stove, turning as needed.

Scald To heat milk until tiny bubbles form around the edge of the pan; the milk should not boil.

Score To make shallow incisions over the surface of a food, usually meat, with a sharp knife.

Sear To cook meat quickly at high heat on the stove or in the oven to brown the surface and seal in juices.

Shell To remove the hard outer covering of such foods as nuts, shrimp, or green peas.

Shred To reduce food to narrow flakes or strings by rubbing it across a shredder.

Simmer To keep a liquid just below boiling point; bubbles form at the edges only. Also, to cook food in a simmering liquid.

Skim To remove fat, foam, or scum from the surface of soup, stock, or pan drippings with a spoon.

Skin To remove the skin of poultry or fish.

Sliver To cut into short, very thin pieces no thicker than toothpicks.

Snip To cut fresh herbs fine using kitchen scissors.

Steam To cook food on a rack or in a steamer basket over boiling water in a tightly covered pan.

Stir-fry To cook small, uniform pieces of food quickly in hot oil in a wok or deep skillet over high heat, tossing and turning them constantly.

Toss To coat food evenly with a dressing or other ingredients by gentle lifting and flipping in a container.

Truss To draw the legs of a bird tightly together with string and tuck the wings under the body so that the bird is compact, holds its shape, and roasts more evenly.

Vinaigrette A salad dressing made from oil, vinegar, and seasonings.

Whip To incorporate air into egg whites, cream, or gelatin mixtures by beating rapidly with a whisk or balloon whip in an over-and-under motion or by using an electric mixer at high speed.

Whisk An implement made of wire loops used to combine or whip ingredients; also, to whip with a whisk.

Zest The thin colored outer layer of citrus rinds without the bitter white pith; it contains aromatic oils used to flavor foods. Use a zester, grater, or paring knife to remove the zest.

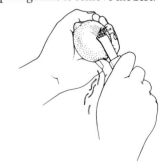

Main-Dish Soups

Nothing is more welcome than the home-sweet-home
aroma of soup simmering on the stove. Whether light and mellow, smooth
and creamy, or thick with meat or vegetables, a steaming bowl of
homemade soup is as nourishing as it is comforting. With a serving size of 2 cups,
these savory soups are not mere starters but entire meals in themselves. Many
of these recipes use stocks made from scratch (see pages 332 and 333) because they
provide the richest flavor, but canned broths are good substitutes. If you're
concerned about salt, choose low-sodium broths. If you like, accompany
with thick slices of crunchy bread and a crisp green salad.

Chicken Soup Française

A hearty soup that can also be made with 2½ cups cooked chicken or turkey. Simply reduce the cooking time in Step 3 to 2 minutes so that the poultry is heated through.

2 tablespoons olive oil

1 medium-size yellow onion, coarsely chopped

3 cloves garlic, thinly sliced

1 large sweet red pepper, cored, seeded, and diced

1 small sweet green pepper, cored, seeded, and diced

2 medium-size zucchini, halved lengthwise and sliced ¼ inch thick

½ teaspoon dried marjoram, crumbled

1 can (8 ounces) tomato sauce

4¾ cups Basic Chicken Stock (page 333) or 2¾ cups canned chicken broth plus 2 cups water

6 ounces broad egg noodles (1½ cups)

1¼ pounds skinned and boned chicken thighs or turkey drumsticks, cut into ½-inch cubes

¼ teaspoon salt

Per 16-oz. serving:
Calories 397; Protein 32 g;
Carbohydrates 28 g;
Fat 17 g; Sodium 513 mg;
Cholesterol 90 mg

30 minutes | 36 minutes

1 Heat the oil in a large saucepan over moderate heat for 1 minute. Add the onion and sauté until limp—about 5 minutes. Add the garlic and sauté 1 minute more.

2 Stir in the red and green peppers, cover, and cook over moderately low heat, stirring occasionally, until the peppers are glossy and crisp-tender—5 to 6 minutes more. Add the zucchini and marjoram, cover, and cook, stirring occasionally, until the zucchini is tender—about 7 minutes.

3 Add the tomato sauce, cover, and simmer for 5 minutes, then add the stock and bring to a boil over high heat. Add the noodles, cover, and boil for 5 minutes. Add the chicken and salt, reduce the heat to moderate, cover, and simmer until the chicken is cooked through—5 to 6 minutes more. Serves 6.

Chicken Soup Française, an all-American soup the French way—with garlic and tomatoes

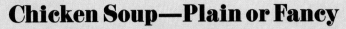
Chicken Soup—Plain or Fancy

*The simplicity of this recipe makes it extremely versatile, with each
variation as good as the classic original.*

1 tablespoon butter or margarine

1 tablespoon vegetable oil

1 pound skinned and boned chicken breasts, cut into ¾-inch cubes

1 quart Basic Chicken Stock (page 333) or 2 cups canned chicken broth plus 2 cups water

2 medium-size carrots, peeled and thinly sliced

2 medium-size stalks celery, thinly sliced

1 large yellow onion, finely chopped

½ cup long-grain white rice

2 tablespoons minced parsley

¼ teaspoon salt

⅛ teaspoon black pepper

Per 16-oz. serving:
Calories 336; Protein 34 g;
Carbohydrates 27 g;
Fat 9 g; Sodium 511 mg;
Cholesterol 74 mg

| 20 minutes | 25 minutes |

---

1 In a 5- or 6-quart Dutch oven over moderate heat, melt the butter in the oil. Add the chicken and lightly brown, stirring occasionally—about 5 minutes.

2 Add the stock, carrots, celery, onion, rice, parsley, salt, and pepper. Cover, bring to a simmer over low heat, then cook until the rice is tender—about 20 minutes. Serves 4.

Creamed Chicken Variation

Follow Steps 1 and 2 as directed. Quickly blend **2 tablespoons cornstarch** with **1 cup milk** or **half-and-half** and a **pinch of ground nutmeg**, and stir into the simmering soup. Cook, stirring, until the soup returns to a simmer and thickens—about 1 minute more. Serves 4.

Per serving: Calories 389; Protein 36 g;
Carbohydrates 34 g; Fat 11 g;
Sodium 541 mg; Cholesterol 83 mg

Mexican Variation

Follow Step 1 as directed. In Step 2, substitute **2 cups fresh corn kernels or frozen corn kernels, thawed and drained,** for the rice and add **1 cup canned crushed tomatoes** and **¼ cup chopped canned green chilies**. Simmer for 20 minutes. Sprinkle with **2 cups crumbled tortilla chips**. Serves 4.

Per serving: Calories 404; Protein 36 g;
Carbohydrates 38 g; Fat 13 g;
Sodium 703 mg; Cholesterol 74 mg

Mulligatawny Variation

In Step 1, brown **1 cup chopped peeled and cored tart apple, such as Granny Smith,** and **1½ tablespoons curry powder** along with the chicken. At the end of Step 2, quickly blend **1 cup heavy cream** with **2 tablespoons cornstarch** and **½ teaspoon grated lemon rind**. Add to the soup and cook, stirring constantly, until the soup returns to a simmer and thickens—about 1 minute more. Serves 4.

Per serving: Calories 581; Protein 35 g;
Carbohydrates 38 g; Fat 32 g;
Sodium 535 mg; Cholesterol 156 mg

Parmesan Variation

Follow Step 1 as directed. In Step 2, add **4 ounces chopped fresh spinach (3 cups)** with the other ingredients. Simmer as directed. In a small bowl, lightly beat **2 eggs**. When the rice is tender, drizzle the eggs into the soup, whisking constantly. Heat, whisking now and then, just until the soup returns to a simmer. Remove from the heat and stir in **¼ cup grated Parmesan cheese**. Serves 4.

Per serving: Calories 411; Protein 40 g;
Carbohydrates 29 g; Fat 14 g;
Sodium 685 mg; Cholesterol 216 mg

Chicken Succotash Soup

This protein-packed soup can be made ahead and refrigerated for up to 3 days in a tightly covered container. You can substitute carrots for the corn or black-eyed peas for the lima beans.

1 tablespoon olive or vegetable oil

1 large yellow onion, coarsely chopped

1 broiler-fryer (3 to 3½ pounds) with giblets, cut into 8 pieces

5 sprigs parsley, 6 black peppercorns, and 1 teaspoon each dried marjoram and thyme, crumbled and tied in cheesecloth

4 cups Basic Chicken Stock (page 333), canned chicken broth, or water

¾ teaspoon salt

¼ teaspoon black pepper

2 cups fresh or 1 package (10 ounces) frozen baby lima beans

2 cups fresh or 1 package (10 ounces) frozen corn kernels

1 cup half-and-half or light cream

⅓ cup minced parsley

Per 16-oz. serving:
Calories 400; Protein 33 g;
Carbohydrates 35 g;
Fat 15 g; Sodium 760 mg;
Cholesterol 93 mg

20 minutes | 51 minutes

1 Heat the oil in a large saucepan or 5-quart Dutch oven over moderate heat for 1 minute. Add the onion and sauté, stirring occasionally, until slightly softened—about 3 minutes. Do not brown.

2 Add the chicken, giblets, cheesecloth bag, stock, salt, and pepper to the saucepan, and bring to a boil over high heat. Reduce the heat to low, cover, and cook until the chicken is no longer pink on the inside—about 30 minutes.

3 Transfer the chicken to a plate. Remove the cheesecloth bag and giblets, then skim the fat from the stock. When the chicken is cool enough to handle, remove the skin and bones and cut the meat into bite-size pieces.

4 Meanwhile, add the lima beans to the stock and bring to a boil over high heat. Reduce the heat to moderate, cover, and cook for 10 minutes. Add the corn, return the stock to a boil, cover, and cook for 1 minute. Add the chicken and half-and-half, cover, and simmer until just heated through.

5 Stir in the parsley and adjust the salt and pepper to taste. Ladle the soup into bowls. Serves 4.

Curried Chicken Soup

The rich, satisfying flavor of this soup comes from the blend of chicken, curry, rice, and cream or yogurt. If you want to substitute turkey breast for the chicken, cut it into 6-ounce portions and cook 3 to 5 minutes longer in Step 2.

1½ pounds skinned and boned chicken breasts

¼ teaspoon salt

⅛ teaspoon black pepper

3 tablespoons unsalted butter or margarine

1 medium-size yellow onion, finely chopped

1 large stalk celery, sliced

1 medium-size carrot, peeled and sliced

2 cloves garlic, minced

1 to 2 teaspoons curry powder

5 cups Basic Chicken Stock (page 333) or canned chicken broth

1 whole bay leaf

⅓ cup long-grain white rice

1 tablespoon arrowroot blended with 1 cup heavy cream or plain low-fat yogurt

Optional garnishes:

4 teaspoons chutney

½ teaspoon paprika

Per 16-oz. serving:
Calories 603; Protein 49 g;
Carbohydrates 22 g;
Fat 35 g; Sodium 591 mg;
Cholesterol 204 mg

15 minutes | 40 minutes

1 Sprinkle the chicken with the salt and pepper. In a large saucepan over moderate heat, melt the butter. Add the chicken and sauté for 1 minute on each side, then transfer to a plate. Add the onion, celery, carrot, and garlic to the saucepan, and sauté, stirring often, for 2 minutes. Blend in the curry powder and stir 1 minute more.

2 Add the stock and bay leaf, bring to a boil, and return the chicken to the pan. Adjust the heat so that the liquid bubbles gently, partially cover, and simmer for 7 to 10 minutes or until the chicken is no longer pink inside. Transfer the chicken to a plate, let cool, then cut into bite-size pieces.

3 Bring the stock to a boil, add the rice, partially cover, and simmer for 12 to 15 minutes or until tender. Remove the bay leaf.

4 Bring the stock back to a boil, stir in the arrowroot-cream mixture, and cook, stirring constantly, for 2 minutes or until slightly thickened. Return the chicken to the pan, and adjust the salt and pepper to taste. Simmer, uncovered, for 2 to 3 minutes, until the chicken is heated through.

5 Ladle the soup into bowls and garnish each portion, if desired, with 1 teaspoon chutney and a sprinkling of paprika. Serves 4.

Spicy Chicken 'n' Chili Soup

The inspiration for this dish is pozole, a classic Mexican soup made with pork. If you wish to be more authentic, substitute 2 pounds boneless pork shoulder cut into 1½-inch cubes for the chicken breasts and cook for 1½ hours instead of 20 minutes.

1 can (4 ounces) green chilies with their liquid or 3 dried ancho chilies

4 cloves garlic, 1 sliced, 3 minced

2 pounds skinned and boned chicken breasts

6 cups Basic Chicken Stock (page 333) or canned chicken broth

1 large yellow onion, finely chopped

2 teaspoons ground cumin

1 whole bay leaf

½ teaspoon dried thyme, crumbled

¼ teaspoon salt

1 can (1 pound) hominy with its liquid or 1 can (1 pound) shoe peg corn kernels with its liquid

¼ cup minced fresh coriander (cilantro) or flat-leaf parsley

Optional garnishes:

2 cups crumbled tortilla chips

1 avocado, peeled and diced

2 scallions, including tops, thinly sliced

Per 16-oz. serving:
Calories 399; Protein 62 g;
Carbohydrates 21 g;
Fat 6 g; Sodium 1,395 mg;
Cholesterol 133 mg

30 minutes | 38 minutes

1 In a food processor or an electric blender, purée the green chilies with their liquid and the sliced garlic. If using the dried chilies, place them in a small saucepan, add 1 cup boiling water, and soak for 15 minutes. Add the sliced garlic and simmer, uncovered, for 15 minutes. Drain the liquid into a food processor. Halve the chilies, remove the seeds, stems, veins, and skins. Add the chilies and cooked garlic to the processor and purée. Wash your hands thoroughly.

2 Place the chicken breasts, stock, onion, cumin, bay leaf, thyme, minced garlic, and salt in a 4-quart Dutch oven. Set over moderately high heat; when the stock comes to a boil, adjust the heat so that it bubbles gently, cover, and simmer for 15 minutes. Remove the chicken breasts and, when cool enough to handle, cut them into bite-size pieces. Set aside.

Avocado, scallions, and tortilla chips are natural companions for Spicy Chicken 'n' Chili Soup.

3 Add the hominy and its liquid and the chili mixture to the Dutch oven and bring to a boil over moderate heat. Reduce the heat to low and simmer, uncovered, for 15 minutes. Return the chicken to the pan and adjust the salt to taste. Simmer, uncovered, for 3 to 5 minutes or until the chicken is heated through. Remove the bay leaf and stir in the coriander.

4 Ladle the soup into bowls and top each portion, if desired, with tortilla chips, avocado cubes, and sliced scallions. Serves 4.

Minestrone with Turkey Meatballs

Adding low-cholesterol meatballs to this popular vegetable soup makes it a satisfying meal.
You can substitute either kale or broccoli for the zucchini or green beans.

For the meatballs:

- 12 ounces ground turkey
- ¼ cup grated Parmesan cheese
- 1 large egg, lightly beaten
- 2 tablespoons dry bread crumbs
- 2 tablespoons minced parsley
- 1 tablespoon water

For the soup:

- 2 tablespoons olive oil
- 4 cloves garlic, thinly sliced
- 2 medium-size zucchini, halved lengthwise and sliced ¼ inch thick
- ½ teaspoon dried rosemary, crumbled
- 6 ounces mushrooms, thinly sliced
- ¾ cup canned crushed tomatoes
- 4½ cups Basic Chicken Stock (page 333) or 2½ cups canned chicken broth plus 2 cups water
- 8 ounces green beans, cut into 1½-inch lengths
- 6 ounces spaghetti, broken into 3-inch lengths
- 1 can (10½ ounces) cannellini (white kidney beans), drained and rinsed
- 2 tablespoons minced parsley

1 *For the meatballs:* In a medium-size bowl, combine the turkey, cheese, egg, bread crumbs, parsley, and water. Shape into walnut-size meatballs and set aside.

2 *For the soup:* Heat the oil for 1 minute in a large saucepan or 5-quart Dutch oven over low heat. Add the garlic and sauté for 1 minute, then add the zucchini and rosemary and sauté, stirring occasionally, until crisp-tender—about 5 minutes.

3 Add the mushrooms, cover, and cook until the mushrooms are tender—about 7 minutes. Stir in the tomatoes and stock and bring to a boil over high heat. Add the green beans and spaghetti, cover, and boil for 10 minutes.

4 Add the meatballs and cannellini, lower the heat to moderate, cover, and simmer until the meatballs are cooked through and the beans are hot—about 4 minutes. Sprinkle with the parsley and ladle into bowls. Serves 6.

Per 16-oz. serving:
Calories 341; Protein 26 g;
Carbohydrates 37 g;
Fat 10 g; Sodium 462 mg;
Cholesterol 86 mg

30 minutes

30 minutes

Minestrone with
Turkey Meatballs, an
Italian tradition with a
modern beat

Turkey, Tomato, and Barley—a shoo-in candidate for your family menu

Turkey, Tomato, and Barley Soup

A robust soup that practically cooks itself.

2 tablespoons olive or vegetable oil

2 pounds turkey or chicken drumsticks

4 medium-size stalks celery, sliced ½ inch thick

3 medium-size carrots, peeled and sliced ½ inch thick

1 large yellow onion, coarsely chopped

2 cans (1 pound each) tomatoes with their juice, broken up

3 cups water

⅓ cup medium pearl barley

1 teaspoon salt

1 teaspoon each dried marjoram and thyme, crumbled

½ teaspoon black pepper

¼ cup minced parsley

1 Heat the oil in a large saucepan or 5-quart Dutch oven over moderate heat for 1 minute. Add the drumsticks and brown on all sides—about 15 minutes.

2 Add the celery, carrots, onion, tomatoes, water, barley, salt, marjoram, thyme, and pepper, and bring to a boil over high heat. Cover, reduce the heat to low, and simmer until tender—1½ to 2 hours for turkey, 1 hour for chicken.

3 Stir in the parsley and serve. Or refrigerate the soup until cool, then skim off the fat, remove the skin and bones, and cut the meat into bite-size chunks. Reheat when ready to serve. Serves 6.

Per 16-oz. serving:
Calories 309; Protein 29 g;
Carbohydrates 22 g;
Fat 12 g; Sodium 680 mg;
Cholesterol 77 mg

 20 minutes | 2 hr. 15 min.

Meatball and Zucchini Soup

This is an excellent make-ahead. Just complete Steps 1 and 2 and refrigerate. To serve, reheat and add the zucchini as directed in Step 3.

- 1 pound lean ground beef, lamb, or turkey
- 1 large egg, lightly beaten
- 1 small yellow onion, finely chopped
- ¼ cup dry bread crumbs
- 1 teaspoon salt
- ⅛ teaspoon black pepper
- 2 tablespoons olive or vegetable oil
- ½ cup long-grain white or brown rice
- 4 scallions, including tops, finely chopped
- 2 tablespoons snipped fresh dill or 1 teaspoon dill weed
- 6 cups Basic Chicken Stock (page 333) or canned chicken broth
- 3 medium-size zucchini, diced

1 In a medium-size bowl, combine the beef, egg, onion, bread crumbs, salt, and pepper. Shape the mixture into ¾-inch balls.

2 Heat the oil in a large saucepan over moderate heat for 1 minute. Add the meatballs and brown on all sides—about 10 minutes. Add the rice, scallions, 1 tablespoon of the dill, and the stock, and bring to a simmer. Reduce the heat to low, cover, and cook until the rice is tender—about 25 minutes for white rice, 35 minutes for brown.

3 Add the zucchini and cook, uncovered, until the zucchini is tender—about 5 minutes.

4 Ladle the soup into bowls and sprinkle with the remaining dill. Serves 4 to 6.

Per 16-oz. serving:
Calories 467; Protein 47 g;
Carbohydrates 29 g;
Fat 17 g; Sodium 997 mg;
Cholesterol 172 mg

20 minutes | 43 minutes

32

Chunky Beef and Onion Soup with Biscuits

Crisp on top and dumpling-soft on the bottom, these biscuits are perfect for sopping up the onion-flavored broth. You can use a 12-ounce package of refrigerator biscuits to save time.

3 tablespoons olive or vegetable oil

1¼ pounds boneless beef chuck, cut into ½-inch cubes

5 large Spanish onions, halved and thinly sliced

1½ tablespoons sugar

2 medium-size carrots, peeled, halved lengthwise, and sliced ¼ inch thick

1¾ cups Basic Beef Stock (page 332) or canned beef broth

1 cup canned crushed tomatoes

2 cups water

¼ teaspoon salt

For the biscuits:

2 cups sifted all-purpose flour

2 teaspoons sugar

1½ teaspoons baking powder

¾ teaspoon baking soda

½ teaspoon salt

5 tablespoons butter or margarine, cut up

¼ cup minced parsley

⅔ to ¾ cup buttermilk

Per 16-oz. serving:
Calories 934; Protein 41 g;
Carbohydrates 84 g;
Fat 49 g; Sodium 1,162 mg;
Cholesterol 170 mg

 30 minutes | 1 hr. 11 min.

---

1 Heat 2 tablespoons of the oil for 1 minute in a large ovenproof saucepan or 5-quart Dutch oven over moderately high heat. Add the beef and brown on all sides—about 5 minutes—working in batches if necessary.

2 Add the remaining 1 tablespoon oil, the onions, and sugar. Lower the heat to moderate and cook, uncovered, stirring frequently, for 3 minutes. Add the carrots and cook, uncovered, stirring occasionally, until the onion is softened—about 3 minutes longer.

3 Stir in the stock, tomatoes, water, and salt. Cover and cook over moderate heat until the meat is tender—about 40 minutes.

4 *For the biscuits:* Preheat the oven to 425° F. In a medium-size bowl, combine the flour, sugar, baking powder, soda, and salt. Cut in the butter with a pastry blender or 2 knives until the mixture resembles coarse meal. Add the parsley and ⅔ cup of the buttermilk; stir until the dough just comes together. If it seems dry, lightly mix in the remaining buttermilk.

5 Turn onto a floured work surface and pat the dough into a circle about ½ inch thick. Using a floured 2-inch round cutter, cut out the biscuits. Place them, not touching, on top of the hot soup.

6 Transfer the saucepan to the oven and bake, uncovered, until the biscuits are lightly browned—12 to 14 minutes. Serves 4.

Spanish onions lend a mild flavor to Chunky Beef and Onion Soup with Biscuits.

Chinese Fire Pot

Despite its long list of ingredients, this impressive party dish is easy to prepare—and your guests do the cooking themselves. The beef, chicken, shrimp, vegetables, and dipping sauce can be prepared up to 4 hours ahead.

1 pound skinned and boned chicken breasts, put in the freezer for 45 minutes or until almost frozen

1 pound beef tenderloin, top sirloin, or flank steak, put in the freezer for 45 minutes or until almost frozen

2 tablespoons soy sauce

2 tablespoons rice wine or dry sherry

2 teaspoons Oriental sesame oil

1 pound fresh spinach, trimmed, rinsed, and dried

1 pound large shrimp, shelled and deveined

4 ounces snow peas, trimmed and rinsed

For the dipping sauce:

½ cup soy sauce

¼ cup rice wine or dry sherry

¼ cup rice vinegar or cider vinegar

2 tablespoons Oriental sesame oil

1 tablespoon chili oil or 1 tablespoon peanut oil blended with ½ teaspoon hot red pepper sauce

2 teaspoons sugar

2 cloves garlic, minced

1 tablespoon minced fresh ginger

4 scallions, including tops, thinly sliced

For the soup:

6 cups Basic Chicken Stock (page 333) or canned chicken broth

2 ounces fine transparent noodles, soaked in hot water for 30 minutes, drained, and cut into 2-inch lengths, or 2 ounces fine noodles, cooked and drained

8 ounces Chinese celery cabbage or cabbage, sliced 1½ inches thick

6 ounces firm tofu, cut into ½-inch cubes

2 tablespoons rice wine or dry sherry

¼ teaspoon salt

3 tablespoons minced fresh coriander (cilantro) or flat-leaf parsley

Per 16-oz. serving:
Calories 536; Protein 61 g;
Carbohydrates 23 g;
Fat 20 g; Sodium 2,290 mg;
Cholesterol 173 mg

1 hour   5 minutes

1 Using a sharp knife, slice the chicken and beef across the grain into very thin slices. Arrange the slices on a platter. In a small bowl, combine the soy sauce, rice wine, and sesame oil; brush the mixture over the beef and chicken. Cover the platter with plastic wrap and chill until ready to serve.

2 Put the spinach in a small bowl, cover with moist paper toweling, then plastic wrap, and chill until ready to serve. Arrange the shrimp and snow peas on separate platters, cover with plastic wrap, and chill until ready to serve.

3 *For the dipping sauce:* In an electric blender or food processor, blend all the ingredients except the scallions for 10 to 15 seconds. Transfer to a bowl, cover with plastic wrap, and chill until ready to serve. Chill the sliced scallions separately.

4 *For the soup:* Just before serving, place all the ingredients except the coriander in a large saucepan over moderately high heat. Bring to a boil, remove from the heat, cover, and let stand for 5 to 10 minutes.

5 In the center of the dinner table, set a Chinese fire pot (available at Oriental specialty stores) or a large fondue pot, chafing dish, or electric skillet or wok. Arrange the platters of beef, chicken, shrimp, and vegetables around the pot. Divide the dipping sauce equally among 6 small bowls and top each with the sliced scallions. Set a bowl of the sauce at each place, along with a plate, fondue fork or long-handled kitchen fork, dinner knife, and fork.

6 Bring the soup back to a boil, stir in the coriander, and ladle two-thirds of it into the fire pot. Adjust the flame so that the soup simmers gently. Let the guests use their fondue forks to dip each food—chicken, beef, shrimp, and vegetables—into the soup for 30 to 60 seconds, then into their own dipping sauce bowls before placing the food on their plates.

7 When all of the food has been eaten, add the remaining soup to the fire pot, then divide equally among the 6 bowls. Serves 6.

Pork and Noodle Soup, Oriental Style

If you put the pork in the freezer until it is partially frozen (about 45 minutes), it will be much easier to cut into matchsticks.

2 tablespoons vegetable oil

1 pound boneless pork shoulder, trimmed and cut into matchstick strips

1 clove garlic, minced

1 tablespoon minced fresh ginger

8 cups Basic Chicken Stock (page 333) or canned chicken broth

1 pound kale, mustard greens, or spinach, trimmed, rinsed, and cut into bite-size pieces

8 scallions, including tops, thinly sliced

2 cups fine egg noodles

½ teaspoon salt

⅛ teaspoon black pepper

1 tablespoon Oriental sesame oil (optional)

1 Heat the oil in a large saucepan over moderate heat for 1 minute. Add the pork, garlic, and ginger, and stir-fry until the pork is no longer pink—about 2 minutes.

2 Add the stock and bring to a simmer, then reduce the heat to low, cover, and cook for 15 minutes.

3 Stir in the kale and scallions, cover, and simmer for 10 minutes. Add the noodles and cook, covered, until the kale and noodles are tender—about 5 minutes more. Stir in the salt and pepper and, if desired, the sesame oil. Serves 4.

Per 16-oz. serving:
Calories 542; Protein 42 g;
Carbohydrates 44 g;
Fat 21 g; Sodium 933 mg;
Cholesterol 128 mg

| 20 minutes | 35 minutes |

For special occasions, a Chinese fire pot (available at Oriental specialty stores) makes an unusual centerpiece, but a fondue pot or electric skillet works just as well. Serve with extra noodles or rice, if you like, and pass a basket of fortune cookies for dessert.

Lentil Soup with Knockwurst — a down-home favorite plus a fancy variation

Lentil Soup with Knockwurst

The combination of spicy sausage and mild-flavored lentils takes the chill out of cold days.

2 tablespoons vegetable oil

1 pound knockwurst or kielbasa, sliced ¼ inch thick

2 medium-size carrots, peeled and finely chopped

1 large yellow onion, finely chopped

1 medium-size stalk celery, finely chopped

1 clove garlic, minced

¼ cup minced parsley

8 ounces dried lentils (1¼ cups), sorted and rinsed

1 cup canned tomatoes with their juice, chopped

1 whole bay leaf

3 cups Basic Beef Stock (page 332) or canned beef broth

1½ cups water

½ teaspoon salt

⅛ teaspoon black pepper

Per 16-oz. serving: Calories 629; Protein 31 g; Carbohydrates 46 g; Fat 36 g; Sodium 1,719 mg; Cholesterol 65 mg

30 minutes	53 minutes

1 Heat the oil in a 4-quart saucepan over moderate heat for 1 minute. Add the knockwurst and brown lightly, stirring occasionally, for 5 minutes. Drain on paper toweling. Remove all but 1 tablespoon of fat from the pan.

2 In the same pan, sauté the carrots, onion, celery, garlic, and parsley over moderately low heat until the onion is tender—about 5 minutes.

3 Add the lentils, tomatoes, bay leaf, stock, water, and knockwurst, and bring to a simmer. Reduce the heat to low, partially cover, and cook for 40 minutes or until the lentils are tender. Season with the salt and pepper and discard the bay leaf. Serves 4.

Red Wine Variation

In Step 2, use **3 cloves garlic** instead of 1. In Step 3, add **1 cup dry red wine** and **1 teaspoon ground cumin** along with the lentils. Cook as directed. Just before serving, stir in **2 teaspoons lemon juice.** Garnish each serving with a lemon slice. Serves 4.

Per serving: Calories 679; Protein 31 g; Carbohydrates 48 g; Fat 36 g; Sodium 1,725 mg; Cholesterol 65 mg

Quick Potato and Ham Soup

Instead of sauerkraut, you can use 2 cups thinly sliced cabbage. Add it after the potatoes have cooked for 10 minutes, then return the soup to a boil and continue cooking. To enhance the flavor, substitute 1¾ cups beer for half of the stock and add more caraway seeds.

1 tablespoon olive or vegetable oil

1 tablespoon butter or margarine

1 large yellow onion, coarsely chopped

8 ounces baked or boiled ham, cut into ½-inch cubes

1 can or package (1 pound) sauerkraut, drained and rinsed

1 pound all-purpose potatoes (about 3), peeled and cut into ½-inch cubes

3½ cups Basic Beef Stock (page 332) or canned beef broth

1 teaspoon caraway seeds

¼ teaspoon black pepper

1 In a 5-quart Dutch oven or saucepan, heat the oil and butter over moderate heat until bubbly. Add the onion and sauté, stirring occasionally, for 3 to 5 minutes or until pale golden.

2 Add the ham and brown lightly, stirring occasionally, for 5 minutes. Add the sauerkraut, potatoes, stock, caraway seeds, and pepper, then bring to a boil over high heat.

3 Reduce the heat to moderate, cover, and cook for 15 to 20 minutes or until the potatoes are tender. Serves 4.

Per 16-oz. serving: Calories 305; Protein 19 g; Carbohydrates 31 g; Fat 12 g; Sodium 1,485 mg; Cholesterol 41 mg

| 15 minutes | 33 minutes |

Lemon Soup with Lamb

Light yet filling, this soup is just as good when beef is substituted for the lamb. To make ahead, refrigerate the soup after Step 2, then, just before serving, add the greens and cream and reheat (but do not boil).

2 pounds boneless lamb shoulder or lamb or beef stew meat, cut into 1½-inch cubes

1 large yellow onion, coarsely chopped

1 medium-size stalk celery, coarsely chopped

1 small carrot, peeled and coarsely chopped

6 cups Basic Chicken Stock (page 333) or canned chicken broth

2 cups water

1 teaspoon each fresh minced rosemary and thyme or ½ teaspoon each dried rosemary and thyme, crumbled

¼ teaspoon salt

⅛ teaspoon black pepper

½ cup orzo or other small pasta such as tubettini

3 large eggs

⅓ cup fresh lemon juice

2 cups fresh spinach, collard greens, or escarole, trimmed, rinsed, and cut crosswise into thin strips

½ cup heavy cream (optional)

3 tablespoons snipped fresh dill

Dill sprigs (optional garnish)

1 In a large saucepan over high heat, bring the lamb, onion, celery, carrot, stock, water, herbs, salt, and pepper to a boil. Reduce the heat to low, partially cover, and simmer for 30 minutes, occasionally skimming off any scum.

2 Strain the stock into a large heatproof bowl and discard the vegetables. Return the lamb and stock to the saucepan and bring to a boil over moderately high heat. Add the orzo and cook, uncovered, at a slow boil, stirring occasionally, until the pasta is just tender—about 10 minutes. Set aside.

3 In a medium-size bowl, beat the eggs until frothy, then beat in the lemon juice. Gradually whisk 1 cup of the hot stock into the egg mixture, then slowly stir the mixture back into the saucepan. Cook over low heat, stirring constantly, until slightly thickened—1 to 2 minutes.

4 Stir the spinach into the soup, then blend in the cream, if desired, and the dill. Ladle into soup bowls and garnish with dill sprigs. Serves 4 to 6.

Per 16-oz. serving: Calories 558; Protein 60 g; Carbohydrates 23 g; Fat 22 g; Sodium 695 mg; Cholesterol 385 mg

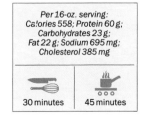

| 30 minutes | 45 minutes |

Sweet Corn Chowder with Shrimp and Red Peppers

An exquisite flavor combination makes this dish ideal for company.

2 tablespoons olive or vegetable oil

1 large yellow onion, finely chopped

1 large all-purpose potato, peeled and diced

1 whole bay leaf

½ teaspoon dried marjoram, crumbled

⅛ teaspoon ground nutmeg

1¾ cups Basic Chicken Stock (page 333) or canned chicken broth

1 can (17 ounces) cream-style corn

1 package (10 ounces) frozen corn kernels, thawed

1¾ cups milk

¼ teaspoon black pepper

1 jar (7 ounces) roasted red peppers, drained and thinly sliced

1 pound large shrimp, shelled and deveined

1 Heat the oil for 1 minute in a large saucepan over moderate heat. Add the onion and sauté, stirring, until limp—about 5 minutes.

2 Add the potato, bay leaf, marjoram, nutmeg, and stock, and bring to a boil. Lower the heat to moderate, cover, and cook at a gentle boil until the potato is just tender—about 10 minutes.

3 Add the cream-style corn, corn kernels, milk, and black pepper, and bring to a rapid boil. Lower the heat to moderate, add the red peppers and shrimp, and boil gently, uncovered, until the shrimp are just cooked through—about 3 minutes. Remove the bay leaf. Serves 6.

Per 16-oz. serving:
Calories 280; Protein 17 g;
Carbohydrates 37 g;
Fat 9 g; Sodium 417 mg;
Cholesterol 80 mg

25 minutes | 23 minutes

To keep the shrimp tender, serve this Sweet Corn Chowder right away. If you must reheat, do it gently over very low heat.

Crab and Black Mushroom Soup

Black mushrooms can be found in the Oriental section of most supermarkets and in specialty food stores.

½ cup long-grain white or brown rice

1 package (1 ounce) dried Chinese black mushrooms

1 cup boiling water

2 tablespoons vegetable oil

3 scallions, including tops, finely chopped

1 tablespoon minced fresh ginger

8 ounces fresh crabmeat or frozen crabmeat (thawed and drained), picked over

¼ teaspoon salt

⅛ teaspoon black pepper

4 cups Basic Chicken Stock (page 333) or 2 cans (13¾ ounces each) chicken broth mixed with ½ cup water

2 tablespoons soy sauce

1 tablespoon dry sherry

1 cup frozen green peas, thawed

2 tablespoons cornstarch blended with ¼ cup cold water

2 large eggs beaten with a pinch of salt

1 teaspoon Oriental sesame oil or to taste

4 scallion tops, thinly sliced (optional garnish)

1 Cook the rice according to package directions. Meanwhile, in a small heatproof bowl, soak the mushrooms in the boiling water for 15 minutes. Drain and save the water, then slice the mushrooms, discarding the stems.

2 In a wok or large saucepan over moderately high heat, heat the oil for 1 minute. Add the scallions and ginger and stir-fry for 30 seconds. Add the crabmeat, mushrooms, salt, and pepper, and stir-fry for 1 minute.

3 Add the stock, soy sauce, sherry, and mushroom water, and bring to a boil. Add the peas, reduce the heat to low, and simmer, uncovered, until the peas are tender—about 3 minutes.

4 Bring the stock to a boil over high heat and blend in the cornstarch mixture. Reduce the heat to low and simmer the soup, stirring constantly, until it is slightly thickened—about 1 minute.

5 Remove from the heat and slowly add the beaten eggs in a thin stream. Stir in the sesame oil and adjust the salt and pepper to taste. Divide the rice among 4 bowls, ladle in the soup, and sprinkle with the scallion tops if desired. Serves 4.

Bring a taste of the Far East to your table with Crab and Black Mushroom Soup.

Per 16-oz. serving:
Calories 344; Protein 24 g;
Carbohydrates 36 g;
Fat 11 g; Sodium 1,437 mg;
Cholesterol 160 mg

15 minutes	20 minutes

Black Bean Soup with Ham and Sweet Potatoes

The perfect end to a long day. If you have any soup left over, thin it with a little water or tomato juice before reheating.

- 2 tablespoons olive oil
- 3 medium-size red or yellow onions, coarsely chopped
- 4 cloves garlic, thinly sliced
- 1 large sweet green pepper, cored, seeded, and diced
- 2 medium-size sweet potatoes, peeled and cut into 1-inch cubes
- 1½ cups canned crushed tomatoes
- ¾ teaspoon each ground cumin and coriander
- ½ teaspoon each ground ginger and salt
- ¼ teaspoon ground red pepper (cayenne)
- 3½ cups water
- 1 cup cooked white or brown rice
- 4 cups cooked black beans or 2 cans (1 pound each) black beans, drained and rinsed
- 6 ounces boiled or baked ham, cut into matchstick strips
- 3 tablespoons lime juice
- 2 limes, cut into wedges (optional garnish)

1 Heat the oil in a 5-quart Dutch oven over moderate heat for 1 minute. Add the onions and garlic and sauté, stirring frequently, until limp—about 5 minutes. Add the green pepper and sauté, stirring occasionally, until it is tender—about 5 minutes more. Stir in the sweet potatoes and tomatoes and cook, uncovered, until slightly thickened—4 minutes.

2 Mix in the cumin, coriander, ginger, salt, and red pepper. Add the water and bring to a boil over high heat, then cover, reduce the heat to low, and simmer until the sweet potatoes are tender—about 20 minutes.

3 Stir in the rice, beans, and ham, and cook, uncovered, until heated through—about 5 minutes. Stir in the lime juice.

4 Ladle the soup into bowls and garnish with the lime wedges if desired. Serves 4.

> Per 16-oz. serving:
> Calories 527; Protein 26 g;
> Carbohydrates 79 g;
> Fat 13 g; Sodium 821 mg;
> Cholesterol 24 mg

25 minutes	42 minutes

White Bean and Cabbage Soup

If you don't have time to soak the beans overnight, try this quick method: Place the beans in a saucepan and add enough water to cover by 3 inches. Boil for 2 minutes, then remove from the heat, cover, and let the beans stand for 1 hour. Drain, then follow Step 1 as directed.

- 1 cup dried navy or pea beans, sorted and soaked overnight in water to cover, then drained
- 2 smoked ham hocks (about 1 pound)
- 7 cups water
- 12 sprigs parsley, 1 teaspoon dried thyme, crumbled, 4 whole cloves, and 1 bay leaf, crumbled, tied in cheesecloth
- 3 tablespoons olive or vegetable oil
- 1 large yellow onion, finely chopped
- 2 medium-size carrots or 2 small parsnips, peeled and sliced ¼ inch thick
- 1 medium-size stalk celery, sliced ¼ inch thick
- 4 cloves garlic, minced
- 1 large all-purpose potato or white turnip, peeled and cut into 1-inch cubes
- ½ small head cabbage, shredded
- ¼ teaspoon salt
- ⅛ teaspoon black pepper
- ¼ cup minced parsley
- ¼ cup grated Parmesan cheese (optional)

1 In a large saucepan over moderately high heat, bring the beans, ham hocks, water, and cheesecloth bag to a boil. Cover, reduce the heat to low, and simmer for 20 minutes.

2 Meanwhile, heat the oil for 1 minute in a 10-inch skillet over moderate heat. Add the onion, carrots, celery, and garlic, and sauté, stirring occasionally, until the onion is limp—about 5 minutes.

3 Stir the sautéed vegetables, potato, cabbage, salt, and pepper into the saucepan, cover, and simmer until the beans and potato are tender—about 20 minutes. Discard the cheesecloth bag and adjust the salt and pepper to taste.

4 Ladle the soup into bowls and sprinkle with parsley. Pass the Parmesan cheese if desired. Serves 4.

> Per 16-oz. serving:
> Calories 611; Protein 30 g;
> Carbohydrates 51 g;
> Fat 33 g; Sodium 969 mg;
> Cholesterol 66 mg

35 minutes	45 minutes

Double Pea Soup

A hint of mint and ginger gives this creamy soup a new, fresh taste. To add crunch, sprinkle each serving with toasted sesame seeds.

2 tablespoons olive or vegetable oil

1 can (7 ounces) Vienna sausages, sliced ¼ inch thick

3 medium-size yellow onions, finely chopped

3 cloves garlic, minced

4 scallions, including tops, thinly sliced

2 cups chopped lettuce (Boston, iceberg, or red leaf)

¼ cup minced fresh mint or 2 teaspoons mint flakes, crumbled

1 teaspoon ground ginger

6 cups water

1½ cups dried split green peas, sorted and rinsed

1 teaspoon salt

1 package (10 ounces) frozen green peas, thawed

2 cups milk

¾ cup grated Parmesan cheese (3 ounces)

Per 16-oz. serving:
Calories 354; Protein 20 g;
Carbohydrates 35 g;
Fat 15 g; Sodium 734 mg;
Cholesterol 28 mg

 25 minutes | 54 minutes

1 Heat the oil in a large saucepan or 5-quart Dutch oven over moderate heat for 1 minute. Add the sausages and sauté, stirring occasionally, until lightly browned—about 2 minutes. Remove from the pan and set aside. Add the onions and garlic and sauté, stirring occasionally, until limp—about 5 minutes.

2 Add the scallions and toss to coat with the oil, then stir in the lettuce, mint, and ginger. Cover and cook for 5 minutes. Add the water, split peas, and salt, and bring the mixture to a boil. Reduce the heat to low, cover, and simmer 30 minutes longer. Add the green peas and simmer, covered, until both the split peas and green peas are tender—about 5 minutes.

3 In a food processor or an electric blender, purée the soup, working in batches if necessary, for 20 seconds. Return the soup to the saucepan, stir in the milk, then add the sausages. Cover, set over moderate heat, and bring to serving temperature—3 to 5 minutes. Adjust the salt to taste and sprinkle with the cheese. Serves 8.

Double Pea Soup—twice as good as the standard version

41

Pasta and Bean Soup

This popular soup—known as pasta e fagioli in Italian—is closely related to minestrone, but its taste and texture are entirely different. To make ahead, omit the pasta. Before serving, reheat, using water or broth to thin if necessary, then add the pasta as directed.

- 2 tablespoons olive oil
- 1 large yellow onion, finely chopped
- 1 medium-size stalk celery, finely chopped
- 1 can (8 ounces) tomato sauce
- 1 clove garlic, minced
- 2 tablespoons minced parsley
- ½ teaspoon dried rosemary, crumbled
- 4 cups cooked Great Northern beans or 2 cans (1 pound each) cannellini (white kidney beans), drained and rinsed
- 4 cups Basic Beef Stock (page 332) or canned beef broth
- 1 cup small elbow pasta
- ½ cup grated Parmesan cheese (2 ounces)
- ½ teaspoon salt
- ⅛ teaspoon black pepper

1 Heat the oil in a 4-quart saucepan over moderate heat for 1 minute. Add the onion and celery, and sauté, stirring occasionally, until very soft—about 10 minutes.

2 Stir in the tomato sauce, garlic, parsley, and rosemary. Cover and cook 5 minutes more.

3 Add the beans and stock, then bring to a simmer over moderate heat. Stir in the pasta and cook, uncovered, stirring frequently, until tender—about 10 minutes more. Stir in the cheese, salt, and pepper, then taste and adjust as desired. Serves 4.

Per 16-oz. serving:
Calories 473; Protein 27 g;
Carbohydrates 66 g;
Fat 13 g; Sodium 1,341 mg;
Cholesterol 10 mg

10 minutes | 28 minutes

Garden Vegetable Soup

If you wish, add 1½ cups of sliced cooked turkey cut into matchstick strips.

- 3 quarts water
- 3 medium-size all-purpose potatoes, peeled and diced
- 3 medium-size carrots, peeled and sliced
- 1 large yellow onion, coarsely chopped
- 1 teaspoon salt
- 2 cups cooked Great Northern beans or 1 can (1 pound) cannellini (white kidney beans), drained and rinsed
- 8 ounces green beans, cut into ½-inch lengths
- 2 medium-size zucchini, diced
- 2 large tomatoes, peeled, seeded, and diced, or 2 cans (1 pound each) tomatoes with their juice, chopped
- 1 cup 1-inch pieces thin spaghetti
- 3 cloves garlic, minced
- ½ cup minced fresh basil or parsley
- ¼ teaspoon black pepper
- 1¼ cups grated Parmesan cheese (5 ounces)
- ¼ cup olive oil, preferably extra virgin

1 In a 5-quart Dutch oven over moderately high heat, bring the water, potatoes, carrots, onion, and salt to a boil. Reduce the heat to low, partially cover, and cook until the potatoes are tender—20 minutes.

2 Add the Great Northern beans, green beans, zucchini, tomatoes, and spaghetti. Cover and simmer, stirring occasionally, 10 minutes more. Remove from the heat.

3 Stir in the garlic, basil, and pepper. Sprinkle with ½ cup of the cheese and drizzle with the olive oil. Adjust the salt and pepper to taste and pass the remaining cheese. Serves 8.

Per 16-oz. serving:
Calories 323; Protein 15 g;
Carbohydrates 41 g;
Fat 12 g; Sodium 803 mg;
Cholesterol 12 mg

25 minutes | 45 minutes

Green Fettuccine Soup

Because the pasta has to be reheated, be sure not to overcook it in Step 1.

- 1 package (12 ounces) spinach fettuccine
- 3 tablespoons olive or vegetable oil
- 1 large yellow onion, coarsely chopped
- 4 cloves garlic, minced
- 6 cups Basic Chicken Stock (page 333) or canned chicken broth
- 2 packages (10 ounces each) frozen chopped spinach, thawed and drained
- 1½ cups cubed cooked ham or chicken
- ½ teaspoon each ground nutmeg and salt
- ¼ teaspoon black pepper
- ½ cup (2 ounces) grated Parmesan cheese (optional)

1 Cook the fettuccine according to package directions until barely done. Drain, then toss with 1 tablespoon of the oil and set aside.

2 In a large saucepan, heat the remaining oil for 1 minute over moderate heat. Add the onion and sauté, stirring occasionally, for 3 minutes. Add the garlic and continue sautéing until the onion is limp—about 2 minutes more.

3 Add the stock, cover, and bring to a boil over high heat. Add the spinach, ham, nutmeg, salt, and pepper, and bring to a boil, then reduce the heat to moderate and cook, uncovered, for 3 to 4 minutes. Stir in the fettuccine and heat until warmed through—about 1 minute.

4 Ladle the soup into bowls and serve with the Parmesan cheese if desired. Serves 6.

Per 16-oz. serving: Calories 437; Protein 23 g; Carbohydrates 50 g; Fat 16 g; Sodium 831 mg; Cholesterol 23 mg

20 minutes | 23 minutes

Chick Pea, Pasta, and Spinach Soup

You can also use 1 pound of fresh escarole or Swiss chard for this quick-cooking Italian soup.

- 2 tablespoons olive oil
- 1 large yellow onion, finely chopped
- 2 cloves garlic, minced
- ½ teaspoon dried marjoram, crumbled
- ¼ teaspoon dried rosemary, crumbled
- 1 pound fresh spinach, trimmed and rinsed, or 1 package (10 ounces) frozen chopped spinach, unthawed
- 1 can (1 pound) chick peas, drained
- 6 cups Basic Beef Stock (page 332) or 2 cups canned beef broth plus 4 cups of water
- 1 cup small tube-shaped pasta such as tubettini or ditalini (8 ounces)
- ¼ teaspoon salt
- ⅛ teaspoon black pepper
- ½ cup (2 ounces) grated Parmesan cheese (optional)

1 Heat the oil in a 3-quart saucepan over moderate heat for 1 minute. Add the onion and sauté until brown—about 10 minutes. Stir in the garlic, marjoram, and rosemary, and sauté 2 minutes longer. Add the spinach, cover, and cook over moderate heat until tender—about 5 minutes more.

2 Add the chick peas and stock and bring to a simmer over moderate heat. Add the pasta and cook, uncovered, stirring occasionally, 10 minutes more, until the pasta is just tender. Stir in the salt and pepper, then taste and adjust as needed. Serve with the Parmesan cheese if desired. Serves 4.

Per 16-oz. serving: Calories 331; Protein 17 g; Carbohydrates 46 g; Fat 11 g; Sodium 1,047 mg; Cholesterol 0 mg

20 minutes | 35 minutes

Chick Pea, Pasta, and Spinach Soup— serve with Parmesan cheese and thick slices of crusty bread.

Peppery Corn Soup

Hot Mexican jalapeños add bite to this thick, creamy soup.

6 slices bacon

2 tablespoons vegetable oil

1 large yellow onion, finely chopped

2 medium-size stalks celery, thinly sliced

2 medium-size carrots, peeled and diced

1 pound all-purpose potatoes (about 3), peeled and diced

¾ teaspoon salt

¼ teaspoon black pepper

2 cups Basic Chicken Stock (page 333) or canned chicken broth

2 cups milk

2 cups fresh or 1 package (10 ounces) frozen corn kernels, thawed

1 to 2 tablespoons minced, seeded, canned jalapeño peppers (wash your hands after handling hot peppers)

½ cup shredded low-fat Cheddar or Monterey Jack cheese

1 tablespoon minced fresh coriander (cilantro), flat-leaf parsley, or chives

1 In a deep 12-inch skillet or large saucepan over moderate heat, cook the bacon until crisp. Drain the bacon on paper toweling, then crumble. Discard the pan drippings.

2 In the same skillet, heat the oil for 1 minute over moderate heat. Add the onion, celery, and carrots, and sauté, stirring frequently, until soft—about 10 minutes. Add the potatoes, salt, black pepper, and stock. Adjust the heat so that the mixture bubbles gently, then cover and simmer for 15 minutes or until the potatoes are tender.

3 Add the milk and corn, cover, and simmer 5 minutes more; stir in the jalapeño peppers and the Monterey Jack cheese.

4 Taste for salt and pepper and adjust as needed. Ladle into soup bowls, then sprinkle the crumbled bacon and minced coriander on each portion. Serves 4.

Per 16-oz. serving:
Calories 439; Protein 20 g;
Carbohydrates 57 g;
Fat 16 g; Sodium 1,025 mg;
Cholesterol 25 mg

30 minutes | 40 minutes

Potato-Cheese Soup, Mexican Style

If you want more zip in this rich, creamy soup, add a sprinkling of chili powder or increase the amount of chili peppers. You can cool it down with a dollop or two of sour cream.

3 tablespoons chopped canned green chilies (from a 4-ounce can) or 1 dried ancho or pasilla chili (about 6 inches long)

3 tablespoons unsalted butter or margarine

1 large yellow onion, coarsely chopped

4 medium-size all-purpose potatoes, peeled and cut into ½-inch cubes

2 small sweet peppers (red, green, or 1 of each), cored, seeded, and diced

2 cloves garlic, minced

4 cups Basic Chicken Stock (page 333) or canned chicken broth

1 whole bay leaf

¼ teaspoon salt

1½ teaspoons ground cumin

1 cup whole or low-fat milk

½ cup sour cream or plain low-fat yogurt

2 cups shredded low-fat Monterey Jack or Cheddar cheese

¼ cup minced fresh coriander (cilantro) or flat-leaf parsley (optional garnish)

Per 16-oz. serving:
Calories 551; Protein 25 g;
Carbohydrates 34 g;
Fat 36 g; Sodium 740 mg;
Cholesterol 45 mg

 25 minutes | 40 minutes

1 Set the chopped green chilies aside. If using the dried chili, preheat the oven to 350° F. Place the chili in a pie pan and roast, uncovered, for 10 minutes. Transfer the chili to a small bowl, break it in half, cover with ½ cup boiling water, and soak for 15 minutes; drain. Discard the stem, seeds, and veins and set the chili aside. (Wash your hands after handling the chilies.)

2 In a large saucepan over moderate heat, melt the butter. Add the onion and sauté, stirring occasionally, until limp—about 5 minutes. Add the potatoes, sweet peppers, and garlic, and stir-fry for 2 minutes. Add the stock, bay leaf, and salt, and bring to a boil over high heat. Reduce the heat to low, cover, and simmer until the potatoes are tender—about 20 minutes. Discard the bay leaf.

3 Place the soup, chili, and cumin in a food processor or an electric blender and purée until smooth—about 1 minute—working in batches if necessary. Strain the soup back into the saucepan.

4 Set the saucepan over moderately low heat and stir in the milk and sour cream. Bring to a simmer and cook, stirring constantly, for 5 minutes. (Do not let the soup boil; it may curdle.) Add 1 cup of the cheese, a little at a time, stirring until it has melted. Turn off the heat and adjust the salt to taste.

5 Ladle the soup into bowls and top each portion with 1 tablespoon each of the cheese and coriander. Pass the remaining cheese. Serves 4.

Top this smooth and spicy Potato-Cheese Soup, Mexican Style, with a generous amount of croutons, scallions, and chopped tomatoes.

45

Sweet Red Pepper Soup with Ricotta Dumplings

It's definitely worth the time to make fresh orange juice for this splendid soup.

2	tablespoons olive or vegetable oil
1	large yellow onion, thinly sliced
4	cloves garlic, crushed
1	medium-size carrot, peeled and thinly sliced
1	large all-purpose potato, peeled and thinly sliced
3	large sweet red peppers, cored, seeded, and thinly sliced
¾	cup canned crushed tomatoes
3	strips orange zest (colored part of the rind), each about 3 inches long and ½ inch wide
½	teaspoon each ground ginger and salt
2	cups water
1¼	cups freshly squeezed orange juice (about 3 oranges)

For the ricotta dumplings:

1	cup low-fat ricotta cheese
2	tablespoons softened butter or margarine
1	large egg plus 1 large egg white
½	cup sifted all-purpose flour
¼	teaspoon salt
⅛	teaspoon black pepper
3	tablespoons minced parsley

Per 16-oz. serving:
Calories 390; Protein 14 g;
Carbohydrates 41 g;
Fat 20 g; Sodium 618 mg;
Cholesterol 103 mg

40 minutes

43 minutes

1 Heat 1 tablespoon of the oil for 1 minute in a large saucepan over moderate heat. Add the onion and garlic and sauté, stirring frequently, until limp—about 5 minutes. Add the carrot, potato, red peppers, and remaining oil. Cover, reduce the heat to low, and cook until the sweet peppers are tender—about 8 minutes more.

2 Stir in the tomatoes, orange zest, ginger, salt, water, and ¾ cup of the orange juice, and bring to a boil over high heat. Reduce the heat to low, partially cover, and simmer until the potatoes are tender—about 25 minutes.

3 *For the dumplings:* In a medium-size bowl, combine the cheese, butter, egg, egg white, flour, salt, pepper, and parsley. Bring a large saucepan of water to a gentle simmer over low heat and drop the dumpling mixture by the tablespoon into the water. Cook the dumplings, covered, until set and no longer doughy—8 to 10 minutes. Remove with a slotted spoon and set aside.

4 Purée the red pepper mixture in a food processor or an electric blender for 1 minute, then push through a sieve. Return the mixture to the saucepan, stir in the remaining orange juice, and set over low heat until heated through—do not boil. Adjust the salt to taste and place the dumplings on top. Serves 4.

Creamy Tortellini Soup

Unexpected company? Keep frozen tortellini on hand and you can have this elegant dish on the table in minutes.

1 package (1 pound) frozen cheese or meat tortellini

3 tablespoons olive or vegetable oil

1 medium-size yellow onion, coarsely chopped

5 cloves garlic, minced

4 cups Basic Chicken Stock (page 333) or canned chicken broth

1 package (10 ounces) frozen green peas, thawed and drained

2 cups plain low-fat yogurt, well stirred, or sour cream

¼ teaspoon black pepper

⅓ cup minced parsley

½ cup grated Parmesan cheese (2 ounces) (optional)

1 Cook the tortellini according to package directions. Drain, then add 1 tablespoon of the oil and toss; set aside.

2 Heat the remaining 2 tablespoons of oil in a large saucepan over moderate heat for 1 minute. Add the onion and garlic and sauté, stirring occasionally, until slightly softened—about 3 minutes.

3 Add the stock and the peas, cover, and bring to a boil over high heat. Reduce the heat to low and whisk in the yogurt. Add the tortellini and pepper and heat through but do not boil.

4 Stir in the parsley and adjust the pepper to taste. Pass the grated Parmesan cheese. Serves 4.

Per 16-oz. serving: Calories 607; Protein 34 g; Carbohydrates 75 g; Fat 19 g; Sodium 904 mg; Cholesterol 70 mg

10 minutes | 20 minutes

White Gazpacho

A refreshing change from the traditional tomato-based cold soup. Be sure to allow extra time for chilling the gazpacho—or prepare it the night before.

2 medium-size all-purpose potatoes, peeled and cut into 1-inch cubes

2 large cucumbers, peeled, halved lengthwise, seeded, and coarsely chopped

9 scallions, including tops, sliced ¼ inch thick

½ cup walnuts

2 cups buttermilk

1 cup plain low-fat yogurt

2 tablespoons olive or vegetable oil

1 teaspoon prepared horseradish

¼ teaspoon hot red pepper sauce

¼ teaspoon salt

1 sweet red pepper, cored, seeded, and finely chopped

4 plum tomatoes, cored and finely chopped

4 hard-cooked large eggs, 3 chopped (white part only), 1 thinly sliced

1 In a large saucepan of boiling water, cook the potatoes, uncovered, until tender; drain and let cool.

2 Meanwhile, in a food processor or an electric blender, purée the cucumbers, ½ cup of the scallions, the walnuts, buttermilk, yogurt, oil, horseradish, hot red pepper sauce, and salt until smooth—15 to 20 seconds.

3 Transfer to a large bowl and stir in the sweet red pepper, tomatoes, and cooked potatoes. Cover with plastic wrap and refrigerate for several hours or until well chilled.

4 To serve, adjust the salt and hot red pepper sauce to taste, then stir in the chopped eggs. Garnish with the egg slices and remaining scallions. Serves 4.

Per 16-oz. serving: Calories 367; Protein 17 g; Carbohydrates 41 g; Fat 17 g; Sodium 379 mg; Cholesterol 77 mg

25 minutes | 20 minutes

Sweet Red Pepper Soup with Ricotta Dumplings— as spectacular as it looks

47

Gingered Tofu and Noodle Soup

Ginger and scallions add pizzazz to this delicate soup.

- **1 package (8 ounces) fine egg noodles**
- **2 tablespoons olive oil**
- **5 scallions, including tops, sliced diagonally 1 inch thick**
- **3 tablespoons minced fresh ginger**
- **5 cups Basic Chicken Stock (page 333) or canned chicken broth**
- **1 small head cabbage, finely sliced**
- **12 ounces firm tofu, cut into ½-inch cubes**
- **¼ teaspoon salt**
- **⅛ teaspoon black pepper**

Per 16-oz. serving:
Calories 479; Protein 28 g;
Carbohydrates 51 g;
Fat 19 g; Sodium 471 mg;
Cholesterol 2 mg

25 minutes | 10 minutes

1 Cook the noodles according to package directions, drain, then toss with 1 tablespoon of the oil and set aside.

2 In a large saucepan, heat the remaining oil over moderate heat for 1 minute. Add the scallions and ginger and stir-fry for 1 to 2 minutes or until crisp-tender.

3 Add the stock and bring to a boil over high heat. Add the cabbage, reduce the heat to moderate, and cook, uncovered, for 1 to 2 minutes or until crisp-tender. Stir in the cooked noodles and the tofu, salt, and pepper. Serves 4.

When you're in the mood for a light meal, try Gingered Tofu and Noodle Soup.

48

meat

Whether you're in the mood for hearty beef,
rich pork, tender lamb, or lean veal, you'll find a cornucopia of choices
in the pages that follow: everything from fancy roasts to down-home casseroles, from
simmering stews to quick skillet suppers, from hungry-man meat pies to
lighter stir-fries. And while meat is certainly the star, the supporting cast has been
carefully chosen to guarantee a well-balanced meal. If you're watching fat or
cholesterol, choose lean cuts and trim off any visible fat.

Pot Roast—Plain or Fancy

*Here are three recipes in one: a basic pot roast with an Italian accent,
a Tex-Mex version featuring chunks of corn on the cob, and a version starring
a variety of fruits. Delicious—any way you slice it.*

2 tablespoons olive oil

4 pounds boned and rolled beef roast (bottom round, rump, or chuck)

1 large yellow onion, coarsely chopped

1 cup Chianti or other dry red wine

1 can (1 pound) tomatoes with their juice, chopped

2 teaspoons dried basil, crumbled

1 teaspoon salt

⅛ teaspoon black pepper

4 small all-purpose potatoes, peeled and cut into 1-inch cubes

4 medium-size carrots, peeled and cut into 2-inch lengths

4 medium-size stalks celery, cut into 2-inch lengths

4 medium-size zucchini, sliced ½ inch thick

---

*Per serving:
Calories 591; Protein 72 g;
Carbohydrates 24 g;
Fat 20 g; Sodium 534 mg;
Cholesterol 206 mg*

| 20 minutes | 3 hr. 16 min. |

---

1 Preheat the oven to 375° F. Heat the oil in a 6-quart flame-proof casserole or Dutch oven over moderate heat for 1 minute. Using paper toweling, blot the roast dry, add it to the casserole, and brown on all sides—about 10 minutes. Remove the roast and set aside.

2 Skim all but 2 tablespoons of the drippings from the casserole, then add the onion and sauté until soft—about 5 minutes. Stir in the wine, scraping up any browned bits from the bottom of the casserole.

3 Return the roast to the casserole and add the tomatoes, basil, salt, and pepper. Bring to a simmer, cover, and transfer the casserole to the oven. Bake for 2½ hours, turning the roast every 30 minutes.

4 Add the potatoes, carrots, and celery, cover, and bake for 15 minutes. Add the zucchini, cover, and bake until the meat and vegetables are tender—15 minutes more.

5 Transfer the meat and vegetables to a serving platter. Skim any excess fat from the casserole drippings, then spoon the drippings over the roast and vegetables. Serves 8.

Mexican Pot Roast Variation

Follow Step 1 as directed. In Step 2, add **2 minced garlic cloves** and **1 cored, seeded, and chopped sweet green pepper** along with the onion. Then substitute **1 cup Basic Beef Stock (page 332) or canned beef broth** for the wine. In Step 3, omit the basil and add **3 tablespoons chili powder** and **½ teaspoon each ground red pepper (cayenne)** and **cinnamon** along with the tomatoes, salt, and pepper. In Step 4, eliminate the potatoes, carrots, celery, and zucchini. Add **2 cans (1 pound each) red kidney beans, drained,** then cover and bake for 15 minutes or until the beef is tender. Add **4 ears fresh or partially thawed frozen corn, cut into 2-inch pieces,** and **1 large sweet red pepper, cored, seeded, and cut into matchstick strips.** Cover and bake 15 minutes more. For a thicker sauce, mash some of the beans with the back of a spoon. Serve as directed in Step 5, wreathing the roast with the beans, corn, and sweet red pepper and sprinkling with **¼ cup minced fresh coriander (cilantro) or flat-leaf parsley.** Serves 8.

*Per serving: Calories 664; Protein 79 g;
Carbohydrates 40 g; Fat 21 g;
Sodium 916 mg; Cholesterol 206 mg*

Fruited Pot Roast Variation

Follow Step 1 as directed. In Step 2, substitute **2 cups Basic Beef Stock (page 332) or canned beef broth** for the wine. In Step 3, omit the tomatoes and basil and add **½ teaspoon ground cinnamon, 1 whole bay leaf,** and a **2- by ½-inch strip of orange zest (colored part of the rind),** then proceed as directed. In Step 4, omit the potatoes, carrots, celery, and zucchini, and add **2 pounds sweet potatoes, peeled and cut into 1-inch cubes,** and **½ cup each pitted prunes, dried apricots, and raisins.** Cover and bake until the potatoes are tender—about 30 minutes. Remove the bay leaf and serve as directed in Step 5, wreathing the roast with the sweet potatoes and fruits and topping all with some of the casserole drippings. Serves 8.

*Per serving: Calories 666; Protein 73 g;
Carbohydrates 48 g; Fat 20 g;
Sodium 466 mg; Cholesterol 206 mg*

Roast Beef Royale

An American classic embellished by carrots, potatoes,
parsnips, and a creamy horseradish sauce

A wreath of sweet potatoes, dried apricots, raisins,
and prunes—spiced with orange and cinnamon—dresses up
this fruited variation of Pot Roast—Plain or Fancy.

- 2 large baking potatoes, peeled and cut into 2-inch cubes
- 4 medium-size carrots, peeled and cut into 1-inch lengths
- 4 medium-size parsnips, peeled and quartered
- 2 medium-size yellow onions, quartered lengthwise
- 3 tablespoons olive or vegetable oil
- ½ teaspoon dried marjoram, crumbled
- ½ teaspoon salt
- ¼ teaspoon black pepper
- 2½ pounds beef eye round roast

For the sauce:

- 1 cup sour cream or ½ cup each sour cream and plain low-fat yogurt
- ¼ cup finely grated fresh horseradish or drained bottled horseradish
- 2 tablespoons white vinegar
- ¼ teaspoon sugar
- ¼ teaspoon salt

Per serving:
Calories 864; Protein 58 g;
Carbohydrates 60 g;
Fat 44 g; Sodium 1,038 mg;
Cholesterol 180 mg

20 minutes	1–1¼ hr.

1 Preheat the oven to 450° F. Cook the potatoes in a large saucepan of boiling water, covered, over moderately high heat for 3 minutes. Add the carrots and parsnips, cover, and cook 2 minutes more. Drain.

2 Put the potatoes, carrots, and parsnips in a 13" x 9" x 2" roasting pan. Mix in the onions, oil, marjoram, and half the salt and pepper.

3 Pat the roast dry with paper toweling, sprinkle it with the remaining salt and pepper, and place it in the center of the pan, surrounded by the vegetables.

4 Roast the beef and vegetables, uncovered, for 20 to 25 minutes or until the beef is brown on the outside. Reduce the oven temperature to 350° F. Continue roasting, turning the roast and vegetables occasionally, for 32 to 36 minutes for rare, 40 to 44 for medium, or 44 to 48 for well-done. Cover the roast loosely with foil and let it rest for 15 minutes before carving.

5 *For the sauce:* While the roast rests, combine the sour cream, horseradish, vinegar, sugar, and salt in a medium-size bowl. Serves 4 to 6.

Beef Stroganoff Supreme

*Choose between the classic stroganoff, made with beef tenderloin, and a hamburger version
that gives you the same rich flavor in less time and at half the cost.*

- 3 tablespoons vegetable oil
- 1½ pounds beef tenderloin or boneless sirloin, cut into thin 2-inch-long strips
- ½ teaspoon salt
- ¼ teaspoon black pepper
- 1 medium-size yellow onion, finely chopped
- 8 ounces mushrooms, thinly sliced
- 2 tablespoons all-purpose flour
- 1½ cups Basic Beef Stock (page 332) or canned beef broth
- 1 package (10 ounces) frozen green peas, thawed and drained
- ½ cup sour cream or plain low-fat yogurt
- 2 teaspoons Dijon mustard
- 8 ounces medium-wide egg noodles, cooked according to package directions
- 2 tablespoons unsalted butter or margarine
- 1 tablespoon poppy seeds

1 Heat 2 tablespoons of the oil in a 10-inch nonstick skillet over moderately high heat for 1 minute. Add the beef, salt, and pepper, and brown, stirring, for 2 to 3 minutes. Using a slotted spoon, transfer the beef to a plate and set aside.

2 Heat the remaining 1 tablespoon oil for 1 minute. Reduce the heat to moderate, add the onion, and sauté, stirring, for 5 minutes or until soft. Add the mushrooms and sauté, stirring, 5 minutes more.

3 Reduce the heat to moderately low, blend in the flour, and cook, stirring, for 3 minutes. Raise the heat to moderately high, add the stock, and cook, stirring constantly, until thick and smooth—3 to 5 minutes.

4 Return the beef to the skillet, add the peas, and cook, uncovered, stirring occasionally, for 5 minutes. Whisk in the sour cream and mustard, then simmer, stirring, just until heated through—1 to 2 minutes. Toss the noodles with the butter and poppy seeds, then top each portion with the beef mixture. Serves 4.

Hamburger Stroganoff Variation

Shape 1½ *pounds ground beef sirloin or round* into 4 patties. In Step 1, brown the patties for 2 to 3 minutes on each side. Follow Steps 2 and 3 as directed. In Step 4, cook for 5 to 7 minutes or until heated through. Serves 4.

Per serving: Calories 907; Protein 69 g; Carbohydrates 60 g; Fat 42 g; Sodium 611 mg; Cholesterol 198 mg

---

Per serving:
Calories 863; Protein 53 g;
Carbohydrates 60 g;
Fat 45 g; Sodium 573 mg;
Cholesterol 157 mg

15 minutes	30 minutes

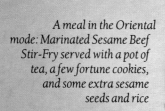

A meal in the Oriental mode: Marinated Sesame Beef Stir-Fry served with a pot of tea, a few fortune cookies, and some extra sesame seeds and rice

Marinated Sesame Beef Stir-Fry

Stir-frying—tossing food quickly in a deep skillet over high heat—is a wonderful way to cook. It's not only fast and easy but healthy too. And the results are tender meat and crisp, colorful vegetables.

For the marinade:
- 2 tablespoons reduced-sodium soy sauce
- 2 tablespoons cornstarch blended with ¼ cup water
- 2 tablespoons peanut or vegetable oil
- 1 tablespoon dry sherry
- ½ teaspoon sugar
- 1½ pounds boneless sirloin or flank steak, cut diagonally into thin 2-inch-long strips
- 1 cup long-grain white rice

For the sauce:
- ⅓ cup reduced-sodium soy sauce
- 2 tablespoons dry sherry
- 1½ teaspoons chili oil or 1½ teaspoons peanut oil blended with ¼ teaspoon hot red pepper sauce
- 1 tablespoon cornstarch blended with ¼ cup Basic Beef Stock (page 332) or canned beef broth
- 2 tablespoons Oriental oyster sauce (optional)

For the stir-fry:
- 4 tablespoons peanut or vegetable oil
- 1 tablespoon minced fresh ginger
- 1 tablespoon minced garlic
- 1½ pounds asparagus, cut into 1½-inch lengths, or 1 package (10 ounces) frozen cut asparagus, thawed
- ⅛ teaspoon salt
- ½ cup Basic Beef Stock (page 332) or canned beef broth
- 1 tablespoon Oriental sesame oil
- 2 tablespoons sesame seeds

1 *For the marinade:* In a medium-size bowl, combine the soy sauce, cornstarch, oil, sherry, and sugar. Add the beef and marinate for 20 to 30 minutes at room temperature. Meanwhile, cook the rice according to package directions.

2 *For the sauce:* In a medium-size bowl, combine the soy sauce, sherry, chili oil, cornstarch mixture, and, if desired, the oyster sauce, and set aside.

3 *For the stir-fry:* Heat 2 tablespoons of the peanut oil in a 12-inch nonstick skillet or wok over moderately high heat for 1 minute. Add the beef and brown for 2 to 3 minutes; transfer to a plate.

4 Heat the remaining 2 tablespoons peanut oil in the skillet for 1 minute. Add the ginger and garlic and stir-fry for 30 seconds. Add the asparagus and salt and stir-fry for 1 minute. Add the stock, bring to a boil, cover, and steam for 1 minute. Uncover, return the beef to the skillet, and stir-fry for 30 seconds. Add the sauce and cook, stirring constantly, for 1 to 2 minutes or until thickened. Add the sesame oil and sprinkle the sesame seeds on top. Serve over the rice. Serves 4.

Per serving:
Calories 771; Protein 63 g;
Carbohydrates 51 g;
Fat 35 g; Sodium 1,102 mg;
Cholesterol 155 mg

| 30 minutes | 20 minutes |

Savory Swiss Steak

Try this when you're in the mood for a real meat-and-potatoes meal.

- 1 **pound top round steak**
- ¾ **teaspoon salt**
- ¼ **teaspoon black pepper**
- 4 **medium-size stalks celery, sliced ¾ inch thick**
- 1 **large yellow onion, thickly sliced**
- ¾ **cup Basic Beef Stock (page 332) or canned beef broth**
- ¼ **cup bottled chili sauce**
- 1 **teaspoon dry mustard**
- ¾ **teaspoon dried thyme, crumbled**
- 1 **pound all-purpose potatoes (about 3), peeled and cut into eighths**
- 8 **ounces rutabaga (yellow turnip), peeled and cut into ½-inch cubes**
- 3 **tablespoons olive or vegetable oil**
- 3 **tablespoons all-purpose flour**

Per serving:
Calories 428; Protein 25 g;
Carbohydrates 39 g;
Fat 19 g; Sodium 750 mg;
Cholesterol 62 mg

| 20 minutes | 1 hr. 51 min. |

1 Preheat the oven to 350° F. Center the steak on a 26- by 18-inch sheet of heavy-duty foil, then place it in a 13″ x 9″ x 2″ baking pan. Sprinkle each side of the steak with ¼ teaspoon of the salt and ⅛ teaspoon of the pepper. Cover with the celery and onion and set aside.

2 In a small bowl, combine the stock, chili sauce, mustard, and ½ teaspoon of the thyme. Pour over the meat and vegetables. Fold the foil over the meat and vegetables and seal tightly. Bake for 1 hour.

3 Unwrap the foil and add the potatoes and rutabaga, submerging them in the liquid as much as possible. Sprinkle with the remaining salt, pepper, and thyme. Reseal, and bake 40 to 45 minutes more or until the meat and vegetables are tender.

4 Unwrap the foil and drain the liquid into a medium-size heat-proof bowl; measure out 2 cups (or add water to total 2 cups) and set aside. Reseal the foil to keep the meat and vegetables warm.

5 Heat the oil in a medium-size saucepan over moderate heat for 1 minute. Blend in the flour. Gradually add the 2 cups of liquid and cook, stirring constantly, for 3 to 5 minutes or until thickened and smooth. Transfer the meat and vegetables to a serving platter and pour half the gravy over all. Serve the remaining gravy in a sauceboat. Serves 4.

Steak Creole with Cheese Grits, a mouth-watering southern dish that is a coast-to-coast favorite

Steak Creole with Cheese Grits

Grits is made from hominy (puffed and dried corn kernels) that is ground into meal.

3 pounds boneless chuck steak (2 inches thick), patted dry
¼ cup all-purpose flour
½ teaspoon salt
¼ teaspoon black pepper
3 tablespoons vegetable oil
1 medium-size yellow onion, thickly sliced
1 medium-size stalk celery, thickly sliced
2 medium-size sweet green peppers, cored, seeded, and sliced
2 cloves garlic, minced
1½ cups Basic Beef Stock (page 332) or canned beef broth
1 can (8 ounces) tomato sauce
1 teaspoon brown sugar
½ teaspoon each dried basil, thyme, and oregano, crumbled
1 whole bay leaf
⅛ teaspoon ground red pepper (cayenne)

For the grits:

3 cups water
¼ teaspoon salt
1 cup hominy grits
1 tablespoon unsalted butter or margarine
1 cup shredded Cheddar, Gruyère, or mozzarella cheese
1 large egg, lightly beaten
¼ teaspoon paprika (optional garnish)

1 Dredge the steak in the flour, shaking off any excess, and sprinkle with half the salt and black pepper. Heat the oil for 1 minute in a 3-quart flameproof casserole over moderately high heat. Add the steak and brown for 6 to 7 minutes on each side. Remove the steak and set aside.

2 Preheat the oven to 350° F. Add the onion, celery, green peppers, and remaining salt and black pepper to the casserole, and cook over moderate heat, stirring occasionally, for 5 minutes. Stir in the garlic, stock, tomato sauce, sugar, basil, thyme, oregano, bay leaf, and red pepper, and bring to a boil. Return the steak to the casserole and spoon some of the vegetable mixture over it. Cover, transfer to the oven, and bake until the steak is tender—1½ to 2 hours.

3 For the grits: Bring the water to a boil in a medium-size saucepan over moderately high heat. Add the salt and grits, reduce the heat to low, and simmer, stirring constantly, until thickened—about 15 minutes. Remove from the heat, beat in the butter, cheese, and egg, and let cool for 15 minutes.

4 Raise the oven temperature to 400° F. Remove the casserole from the oven, skim any fat from the drippings, and remove the bay leaf. Spoon some of the sauce from the bottom of the casserole over the steak, arrange the grits in mounds on top, then sprinkle them with the paprika if desired.

5 Return the casserole to the oven and bake, uncovered, for 25 to 30 minutes or until bubbling. Serves 6.

Per serving:
Calories 742; Protein 79 g;
Carbohydrates 197 g;
Fat 32 g; Sodium 815 mg;
Cholesterol 267 mg

20 minutes   2 hr. 30 min.

55

Short Ribs with Lentils and Rice

The lentils add extra protein to this filling dish. A salad of sliced avocados and oranges with vinaigrette dressing makes a nice accompaniment.

2 tablespoons olive oil

4 pounds meaty beef short ribs or pork spareribs, cut into 3-inch pieces (ask the butcher to cut them)

2 large yellow onions, coarsely chopped

2 cloves garlic, minced

3 large sweet peppers (green, red, yellow, or a combination), cored, seeded, and diced

1 whole bay leaf

1 teaspoon salt

1 teaspoon dried thyme, crumbled

½ teaspoon dried rosemary, crumbled

¼ teaspoon black pepper

4 cups water

8 ounces (1¼ cups) dried lentils, sorted and rinsed

½ cup long-grain white rice

1 cup canned tomatoes with their juice, chopped

2 tablespoons minced parsley

1 Heat the oil in a 5-quart Dutch oven or flameproof casserole over moderate heat for 1 minute. Working in 3 batches, add the ribs and brown on all sides—about 10 minutes per batch. Remove the ribs and set aside.

2 Add the onions, garlic, and peppers to the Dutch oven and sauté, stirring occasionally, for 10 minutes or until softened. Return the ribs to the Dutch oven, add the bay leaf, salt, thyme, rosemary, black pepper, and water, and bring to a simmer. Cover, reduce the heat to low, and simmer for 1 hour.

3 Stir in the lentils, cover, and simmer 30 minutes more. Stir in the rice and tomatoes, cover, and simmer until the rice and meat are tender—about 25 minutes. Remove the bay leaf, sprinkle with the parsley, and adjust the salt and pepper to taste. Serves 6.

Per serving:
Calories 741; Protein 47 g;
Carbohydrates 44 g;
Fat 41 g; Sodium 546 mg;
Cholesterol 144 mg

15 minutes	2 hr. 38 min.

A hearty meal for a hungry crew—
Short Ribs with Lentils and Rice

Old-Fashioned Beef Stew

You can easily turn this American favorite into a hearty lamb stew by using cubes of boneless lamb shoulder.

2 tablespoons all-purpose flour
½ teaspoon salt
¼ teaspoon black pepper
1 pound boneless beef chuck or bottom round, cut into 1-inch cubes
2 tablespoons vegetable oil
2 large yellow onions, coarsely chopped
6 ounces small whole mushrooms
1 pound all-purpose potatoes (about 3), peeled and cut into ¾-inch cubes
8 medium-size carrots, peeled and sliced ½ inch thick
2¼ cups Basic Beef Stock (page 332) or canned beef broth
1 cup dry red wine
1 whole bay leaf
½ teaspoon dried thyme, crumbled
3 medium-size parsnips, peeled and quartered
1 pint fresh or 1 package (10 ounces) frozen Brussels sprouts, unthawed
¼ cup minced parsley

1 Mix the flour, salt, and pepper in a small paper bag. Add the beef, half at a time, and shake until the beef is well coated.

2 Heat the oil in a 5-quart Dutch oven over moderately high heat for 1 minute. Add half the beef and brown on all sides, turning frequently, for 5 to 8 minutes. Transfer to a plate and repeat for the remaining beef.

3 Add the onions to the Dutch oven and sauté, stirring occasionally, for 3 minutes or until slightly softened. Add the mushrooms and sauté, stirring occasionally, for 2 minutes or until lightly golden.

4 Return the beef to the Dutch oven and add the potatoes, carrots, stock, wine, bay leaf, and thyme. Bring the mixture to a boil, reduce the heat to low, cover, and simmer for 1 hour.

5 Add the parsnips, cover, and cook for 15 minutes. Add the Brussels sprouts, cover, and cook 15 minutes more or until the vegetables are tender. Remove the bay leaf and stir in the parsley. Serves 4.

Per serving:
Calories 664; Protein 46 g;
Carbohydrates 78 g;
Fat 16 g; Sodium 506 mg;
Cholesterol 103 mg

20 minutes | 1 hr. 54 min.

Dad's Favorite Beef Stew

Beer gives this stew its distinctive nutty flavor.

3 pounds boneless beef chuck, cut into 2-inch cubes
½ teaspoon salt
¼ teaspoon black pepper
2 tablespoons vegetable oil
3 large yellow onions, thickly sliced
1 teaspoon sugar
1 can (12 ounces) lager beer
1½ cups Basic Beef Stock (page 332) or canned beef broth
1½ teaspoons dried thyme, crumbled
1 whole bay leaf
8 medium-size carrots, peeled and cut into 1½-inch lengths
1 pound small new potatoes (about 8), unpeeled
2 tablespoons arrowroot or cornstarch blended with ¼ cup cold water
1½ tablespoons white wine vinegar

1 Season the beef with half the salt and pepper. Heat the oil in a Dutch oven or 5-quart flameproof casserole over moderately high heat for 1 minute. Working in batches, add the beef and brown on all sides—about 7 minutes per batch. Transfer to a plate.

2 Add the onions, season with the remaining salt and pepper, and sauté over moderate heat, stirring occasionally, for 8 to 10 minutes or until lightly browned. Add the sugar and cook, stirring, 1 minute more.

3 Return the beef to the Dutch oven and add the beer, stock, thyme, and bay leaf. Bring the stew to a boil, reduce the heat to moderately low, cover, and simmer for 1½ hours or until the beef is tender. Add the carrots and potatoes, cover, and simmer 20 to 30 minutes more.

4 Remove the cover and bring the liquid to a boil over moderately high heat. Blend in the arrowroot mixture and cook, stirring constantly, for 2 to 3 minutes or until the sauce thickens. Stir in the vinegar and remove the bay leaf. Serves 8.

Per serving:
Calories 489; Protein 54 g;
Carbohydrates 27 g;
Fat 16 g; Sodium 304 mg;
Cholesterol 155 mg

15 minutes | 2 hr. 30 min.

Classic Beef Goulash

Here's a traditional Hungarian goulash that you can make with beef, pork, or veal,
plus a quick ground beef version that can be on the table in less than an hour. For a festive presentation, garnish with
dollops of sour cream and thin slices of store-bought roasted sweet red pepper.

2 tablespoons vegetable oil

1½ pounds boneless beef chuck, pork, or veal shoulder, cut into 1-inch cubes

½ teaspoon salt

3 medium-size yellow onions, coarsely chopped

4 cloves garlic, thinly sliced

2 tablespoons paprika

1½ teaspoons caraway seeds

1 cup dry red wine

3 medium-size carrots, peeled and sliced ¼ inch thick

¼ cup tomato paste

1 cup Basic Chicken Stock (page 333) or canned chicken broth

3 medium-size all-purpose potatoes, peeled and coarsely shredded

1 cup frozen peas, thawed and drained

1 cup sour cream or plain low-fat yogurt

> Per serving:
> Calories 508; Protein 41 g;
> Carbohydrates 32 g;
> Fat 21 g; Sodium 455 mg;
> Cholesterol 120 mg

20 minutes   2 hr. 9 min.

1 Preheat the oven to 350° F. Heat the oil in a 5-quart Dutch oven or flameproof casserole over moderately high heat for 1 minute. Working in batches, add the beef, sprinkle it with salt, and brown on all sides for about 5 minutes. With a slotted spoon, transfer the beef to a large plate and set aside.

2 Add the onions and garlic to the Dutch oven, reduce the heat to moderately low, and sauté, stirring occasionally, until golden—about 7 minutes. Stir in the paprika and caraway seeds and sauté for 1 minute. Add the wine, raise the heat to high, and boil, uncovered, for 3 minutes. Stir in the carrots, tomato paste, stock, and browned beef, and bring to a boil. Cover, transfer to the oven, and bake until the beef is almost tender—about 1 hour 10 minutes.

3 Stir in the potatoes, cover, and continue baking until the potatoes and beef are tender—about 30 minutes more. Transfer the Dutch oven to the stovetop and stir in the peas. Cook, uncovered, over moderate heat until the peas are tender—about 4 minutes. Stir in the sour cream and heat just to serving temperature—do not boil. Serves 6.

Ground Beef Variation

In Step 1, decrease the vegetable oil to 1 tablespoon and substitute *1½ pounds lean ground beef* for the chuck, then proceed as directed. In Step 2, proceed as directed but add the potatoes along with the carrots. Do not transfer the casserole to the oven, but let it simmer, covered, for 30 minutes or until the carrots are tender. Add the peas and sour cream as directed in Step 3. Serves 4.

Per serving: Calories 483; Protein 42 g; Carbohydrates 32 g; Fat 18 g; Sodium 482 mg; Cholesterol 120 mg

Beef Casserole, Persian Style

To peel fresh small white onions easily, put them in a sieve and immerse for 1 minute in a large pan of boiling water; when they are cool, slip off the skins.

- 1 tablespoon vegetable or olive oil
- 1 pound boneless beef chuck, cut into ¾-inch cubes
- ½ teaspoon salt
- ⅛ teaspoon black pepper
- 2¼ cups Basic Beef Stock (page 332) or canned beef broth
- 1½ teaspoons ground cinnamon
- 12 ounces small white onions, peeled, or 8 ounces frozen small white onions
- 8 ounces butternut squash or sweet potatoes, peeled, and cut into ½-inch cubes
- 3 tablespoons balsamic or white vinegar
- 1 tablespoon honey
- 1 cup pitted prunes
- 1 can (10 ounces) chick peas, drained and rinsed
- ¾ cup (5 ounces) couscous or quick-cooking brown rice

1 Heat the oil in a 4-quart Dutch oven or flameproof casserole over moderately high heat for 1 minute. Sprinkle the beef with the salt and pepper, then brown in the oil, stirring frequently, for 5 to 8 minutes.

2 Add the stock and cinnamon. Bring to a boil, reduce the heat to low, cover, and simmer for 1 hour.

3 Stir in the onions, squash, vinegar, and honey, and bring the mixture back to a boil. Lower the heat, cover, and simmer for 30 minutes or until the meat and vegetables are tender.

4 Add the prunes and chick peas, cover, and heat just until the mixture returns to a boil—about 2 minutes. Meanwhile, start cooking the couscous according to package directions. Serve the beef mixture on a bed of couscous. Serves 4.

> Per serving:
> Calories 677; Protein 50 g;
> Carbohydrates 91 g;
> Fat 14 g; Sodium 486 mg;
> Cholesterol 103 mg

25 minutes	1 hr. 49 min.

When you're in the mood for something exotic, try this tantalizing Beef Casserole, Persian Style.

59

Chunky Chili

Since everybody loves chili, why not make extra and keep some in the freezer for unexpected guests? Use sour cream, shredded Cheddar cheese, chopped canned green chilies, and chopped onions for garnishes.

- **2** tablespoons vegetable or olive oil
- **1½** pounds boneless beef chuck, cut into ¾-inch cubes
- **1** large sweet green pepper, cored, seeded, and coarsely chopped
- **1** large sweet red pepper, cored, seeded, and coarsely chopped
- **1** large yellow onion, coarsely chopped
- **1** clove garlic, minced
- **1** can (1 pound 12 ounces) tomatoes with their juice, broken up
- **1** can (6 ounces) tomato paste
- **1** cup Basic Beef Stock (page 332) or canned beef broth
- **1** can (1 pound 3 ounces) red kidney beans, drained and rinsed
- **1** package (10 ounces) frozen corn kernels, thawed and drained
- **2** tablespoons chili powder
- **½** teaspoon ground cumin
- **¼** teaspoon salt
- **⅛** teaspoon ground red pepper (cayenne)

1 Heat 1 tablespoon of the oil in a 5-quart Dutch oven over moderately high heat for 1 minute. Add the beef and brown on all sides—about 10 minutes. Transfer to a large plate lined with paper toweling.

2 Reduce the heat to moderate, add the remaining 1 tablespoon oil, the peppers, and onion to the Dutch oven, and sauté, stirring frequently, for 5 minutes or until soft. Add the garlic and sauté, stirring frequently, 2 minutes more.

3 Add the tomatoes, tomato paste, stock, beans, corn, chili powder, cumin, salt, and red pepper, and bring to a boil. Return the beef to the Dutch oven, reduce the heat to low, cover, and cook until tender—about 1 hour. If a thinner sauce is desired, add a little water. Serves 6.

Create your own design when you decorate this Chili Pie with the extra pastry dough.

Per serving:
Calories 454; Protein 45 g;
Carbohydrates 40 g;
Fat 14 g; Sodium 756 mg;
Cholesterol 103 mg

20 minutes

1 hr. 20 min.

Chili Pie

If you're in a hurry, you can serve this spicy Tex-Mex chili in a prepared pie crust, without the crust, or in taco shells. For an extra flourish, top it with sliced avocado and a generous spoonful of sour cream.

For the crust:

- 1 cup pie crust mix
- ½ cup yellow cornmeal
- 2 teaspoons sugar
- ⅛ teaspoon ground red pepper (cayenne)
- 1 tablespoon butter or margarine
- ¼ cup ice water

For the filling:

- 1 tablespoon vegetable oil
- 1 medium-size sweet green pepper, cored, seeded, and coarsely chopped
- 4 scallions, white part thinly sliced; green tops thinly sliced (optional garnish)
- 3 cloves garlic, minced
- 2 teaspoons unsweetened cocoa
- 1 teaspoon chili powder
- ¾ teaspoon each ground cinnamon, coriander, and cumin
- ¼ teaspoon salt
- 1 pound lean ground beef or turkey
- 1 cup canned crushed tomatoes
- 1 can (10½ ounces) red kidney or black beans, drained and rinsed
- ¾ cup frozen corn kernels, thawed and drained
- 1 cup sour cream or plain low-fat yogurt (optional topping)

1 *For the crust:* In a medium-size bowl, combine the pie crust mix, cornmeal, sugar, and red pepper. Using 2 knives, cut in the butter until the mixture resembles coarse meal. Add the water and stir just until the mixture comes together.

2 Preheat the oven to 350° F. Place the dough between 2 sheets of floured wax paper and roll into a 12-inch circle. Remove the top piece of wax paper, invert the dough onto a 9-inch pie pan, then peel off the remaining paper. (If it sticks, chill the pan and dough for 20 minutes, then remove the paper.) Press the dough into the pie pan and flute the edge. Line the pastry shell with wax paper, weight it with dried beans or rice, and bake, uncovered, until lightly crisped around the edges—about 20 minutes. Remove from the oven and set aside.

3 *For the filling:* Heat the oil in a 12-inch skillet over moderate heat for 1 minute. Add the green pepper and sauté, stirring occasionally, until soft—about 5 minutes. Stir in the white part of the scallions and garlic and sauté 2 minutes longer. Stir in the cocoa, chili powder, cinnamon, coriander, cumin, and salt, and sauté 1 minute longer. Add the beef and sauté until browned—about 5 minutes. Stir in the tomatoes, beans, and corn.

4 Spoon the filling into the baked pie shell and bake, uncovered, until bubbling—12 to 15 minutes. Spoon dollops of sour cream on top of the pie and sprinkle with the sliced scallion tops if desired. Serves 4.

Per serving:
Calories 654; Protein 46 g;
Carbohydrates 60 g;
Fat 26 g; Sodium 854 mg;
Cholesterol 111 mg

30 minutes | 35 minutes

Ground Beef Moussaka

A multilayered meal that can also be made in the traditional Greek fashion—with ground lamb.

- 1 medium-size eggplant, sliced ½ inch thick
- 1 teaspoon salt
- 1 tablespoon olive or vegetable oil
- 1 large yellow onion, finely chopped
- 2 cloves garlic, minced
- 1 pound lean ground beef
- 2 tablespoons tomato paste
- ¼ teaspoon each dried basil and oregano, crumbled
- ½ teaspoon black pepper
- ⅛ teaspoon ground cinnamon
- ½ cup grated Parmesan cheese (2 ounces)
- 2 tablespoons dry bread crumbs
- 2 tablespoons minced parsley
- 1 large egg, lightly beaten
- 2 cups part-skim ricotta cheese
- 1 large egg or 2 large egg whites, lightly beaten
- ¼ cup parsley leaves
- ⅛ teaspoon ground nutmeg
- 1¼ pounds frozen hash brown potatoes, thawed

Per serving:
Calories 884; Protein 65 g;
Carbohydrates 62 g;
Fat 43 g; Sodium 1,180 mg;
Cholesterol 258 mg

 20 minutes   1 hr. 26 min.

1 Preheat the oven to 350° F. Sprinkle the eggplant slices with ¼ teaspoon of the salt, place on a lightly greased baking sheet, and bake, uncovered, for 15 minutes or until tender. Transfer the eggplant to the bottom of a lightly greased 13" x 9" x 2" baking pan, overlapping the slices slightly, and set aside. Reduce the oven temperature to 325° F.

2 Heat the oil in a 12-inch skillet over moderate heat for 1 minute. Add the onion and sauté, stirring frequently, for 3 minutes. Add the garlic and sauté, stirring frequently, for 2 minutes. Add the beef and brown, stirring to break up any clumps, for 5 minutes. Reduce the heat to low.

3 Mix in the tomato paste, basil, oregano, ½ teaspoon of the remaining salt, and ⅛ teaspoon of the pepper. Simmer, uncovered, stirring occasionally, for 15 minutes. Remove from the heat and stir in the cinnamon, 2 tablespoons of the Parmesan cheese, the bread crumbs, and minced parsley; set aside. When cool, stir in the egg.

4 Place the ricotta cheese, the other egg, parsley leaves, nutmeg, and remaining Parmesan cheese, salt, and pepper in a food processor or an electric blender and purée for 1 minute or until smooth; set aside.

5 Spread half the meat mixture evenly over the eggplant slices, then arrange all the potatoes in a layer, followed by the remaining meat mixture. "Frost" with the ricotta mixture.

6 Bake, uncovered, for 45 minutes or until lightly browned and bubbling. Let stand for 10 minutes before serving. Serves 4 to 6.

A fresh Greek-style salad adds a splash of color to Ground Beef Moussaka.

Beef and Spinach with Noodle Topping

*A recipe so versatile you can use ground turkey
or veal for the beef; shredded Cheddar, Monterey Jack, or fontina for the
Parmesan cheese; and frozen green peas for the spinach.*

3 tablespoons vegetable oil
1 large yellow onion, finely chopped
2 tablespoons all-purpose flour
2½ cups low-fat or whole milk
¾ teaspoon dried marjoram, crumbled
½ teaspoon salt
¼ teaspoon black pepper
6 ounces medium-wide egg noodles, cooked according to package directions
⅔ cup grated Parmesan cheese (3 ounces)
1 package (10 ounces) frozen leaf spinach, thawed, drained, and squeezed dry
2 medium-size carrots, peeled and coarsely shredded
1¼ pounds lean ground beef
1 large egg, lightly beaten

Per serving:
Calories 765; Protein 69 g;
Carbohydrates 52 g;
Fat 31 g; Sodium 941 mg;
Cholesterol 205 mg

15 minutes | 1 hour

1 Preheat the oven to 400° F. Heat 1 tablespoon of the oil in a large saucepan over moderate heat for 1 minute. Add the onion and sauté, stirring occasionally, until soft—5 minutes. Transfer the onion to an ungreased 3-quart casserole.

2 Add the remaining oil to the saucepan and heat for 1 minute. Reduce the heat to low, whisk in the flour, and cook, stirring constantly, until bubbling—about 3 minutes. Stir in the milk, marjoram, salt, and pepper, and cook, stirring constantly, until slightly thickened—3 to 5 minutes. Transfer ½ cup of the cream sauce to a medium-size bowl, add the cooked noodles, mix gently, and set aside.

3 Add the cheese, spinach, and carrots to the remaining sauce and cook over low heat, stirring constantly, for 2 minutes. Transfer to the casserole with the onion. Add the beef and egg to the casserole and mix well. Pack down lightly.

4 Layer the noodle mixture on top of the beef. Cover the casserole with foil and bake for 25 minutes. Uncover and bake until the noodles are golden and the mixture is set—15 to 20 minutes. Serves 4.

Beef 'n' Barley Casserole

*This casserole refrigerates well, so you can make it up to 2 days ahead
or double the recipe and enjoy the leftovers.*

1¼ pounds lean ground beef
1 large yellow onion, finely chopped
1 clove garlic, minced
12 ounces mushrooms, thinly sliced
4 cups Basic Beef Stock (page 332) or 2 cups canned beef broth mixed with 2 cups water
8 ounces medium pearl barley, rinsed
4 medium-size carrots, peeled and thinly sliced
4 medium-size stalks celery, thinly sliced
½ teaspoon dried thyme, crumbled
1 whole bay leaf
Pinch each ground cinnamon and nutmeg
1 teaspoon salt
⅛ teaspoon black pepper
¼ cup minced parsley

Per serving:
Calories 556; Protein 55 g;
Carbohydrates 61 g;
Fat 10 g; Sodium 963 mg;
Cholesterol 129 mg

20 minutes | 1 hour

1 Brown the beef lightly in a 5-quart flameproof casserole or Dutch oven over moderate heat—about 5 minutes. Add the onion and garlic and sauté, stirring occasionally, until soft—about 5 minutes. Add the mushrooms and sauté, stirring occasionally, until lightly browned—about 5 minutes.

2 Add the stock, barley, carrots, celery, thyme, bay leaf, cinnamon, nutmeg, salt, and pepper, and bring to a simmer. Cover, reduce the heat to low, and simmer for 30 minutes, stirring occasionally.

3 Uncover and cook until the barley is tender and most of the liquid is absorbed—10 to 15 minutes. Remove the bay leaf, adjust the salt and pepper to taste, and sprinkle with the parsley. Serves 4 to 6.

Sweet-and-Sour Meatball Stew

Instead of rice, you can use ½ cup couscous, a quick-cooking grain that's a good companion for sweet-and-sour foods.

- 8 ounces lean ground beef
- 8 ounces ground pork
- 1 cup soft whole wheat bread crumbs (2 slices)
- ½ cup low-fat milk
- 1 small yellow onion, finely chopped
- 1 teaspoon grated lemon rind
- ¼ teaspoon black pepper
- 3 tablespoons vegetable oil
- 1 can (20 ounces) pineapple chunks, drained (reserve juice)
- 2 tablespoons red wine vinegar
- 2 tablespoons reduced-sodium soy sauce
- 2 tablespoons packed light brown sugar
- 1 tablespoon dry sherry
- ½ teaspoon minced fresh ginger or ¼ teaspoon each ground ginger and grated lemon rind
- 1 cup Basic Beef Stock (page 332) or canned beef broth
- 1 large sweet green pepper, cored, seeded, and chopped
- 1 large sweet red pepper, cored, seeded, and chopped
- 2 cloves garlic, minced
- ½ cup long-grain white rice
- 12 ounces fresh snow peas, trimmed, or 2 packages (9 ounces each) frozen snow peas, unthawed

1 Place the beef, pork, bread crumbs, milk, onion, lemon rind, and black pepper in a large bowl. Mix well and shape into 1-inch balls.

2 Heat 1 tablespoon of the oil in a 12-inch skillet over moderate heat for 1 minute. Add half of the meatballs and sauté, turning often, for 5 to 8 minutes or until well browned. Using a slotted spoon, transfer to a large plate. Add another tablespoon of the oil to the skillet and brown the remaining meatballs. Transfer to the plate. Discard the pan drippings.

3 Meanwhile, combine the pineapple juice, vinegar, soy sauce, sugar, sherry, and ginger. Add enough stock to make 2 cups; set aside.

4 Heat the remaining 1 tablespoon oil in the skillet for 1 minute. Add the green and red peppers and sauté, stirring, for 2 to 3 minutes. Add the garlic and sauté, stirring frequently, 2 minutes more or until the peppers are lightly golden.

5 Return the meatballs to the skillet, add the stock mixture, and bring to a boil. Stir in the rice, reduce the heat to low, cover, and simmer for 10 minutes. Add the snow peas, cover, and continue simmering until the rice and snow peas are tender —about 10 minutes more. Stir in the pineapple and heat to serving temperature. Serves 4.

Per serving:
Calories 706; Protein 39 g;
Carbohydrates 73 g;
Fat 29 g; Sodium 592 mg;
Cholesterol 92 mg

25 minutes   47 minutes

Sloppy Joes Updated

The addition of butternut squash, scallions, and green pepper turns this old favorite into a well-balanced meal. For a spicier sauce, add ¼ to ½ teaspoon hot red pepper sauce or a 4-ounce can of green chilies, drained and chopped. For a sweeter flavor, add ¼ cup chopped dried apricots.

1½	tablespoons vegetable oil
1	large sweet green pepper, cored, seeded, and coarsely chopped
5	scallions, including tops, thinly sliced
1	cup peeled and coarsely shredded butternut squash or carrots
1¼	pounds lean ground beef, pork, or turkey
2	cups canned crushed tomatoes
1	tablespoon steak sauce
¼	cup golden raisins
2	tablespoons orange juice
¼	teaspoon salt
4	hamburger buns or kaiser rolls

1 Heat the oil in a 12-inch skillet over moderate heat for 1 minute. Add the pepper and sauté, stirring occasionally, until softened—about 5 minutes. Add the scallions and squash and sauté, stirring occasionally, until the squash is softened—about 5 minutes longer.

2 Add the beef and sauté, stirring frequently, until browned—about 5 minutes. Stir in the tomatoes, steak sauce, raisins, orange juice, and salt, and simmer, uncovered, until the beef is cooked through and the sauce is thick and glossy—about 5 minutes longer. Spoon into buns. Serves 4.

> Per serving:
> Calories 503; Protein 50 g;
> Carbohydrates 38 g;
> Fat 16 g; Sodium 756 mg;
> Cholesterol 129 mg

12 minutes	21 minutes

What better way to cap an afternoon of play than with Sloppy Joes Updated?

Quick Beef and Ziti with Three Cheeses

This dish has the same great taste as lasagne, but it can be made in less than half the time.

8	ounces ziti, macaroni, or other small pasta
1	pound lean ground beef
1	medium-size yellow onion, finely chopped
1	jar (2 pounds) Italian tomato or spaghetti sauce
1	package (10 ounces) Italian green beans, partially thawed but not drained
1	cup part-skim ricotta cheese
1	cup shredded low-fat mozzarella cheese (4 ounces)
¼	cup grated Parmesan cheese

> Per serving:
> Calories 887; Protein 64 g;
> Carbohydrates 89 g;
> Fat 30 g; Sodium 1,499 mg;
> Cholesterol 143 mg

5 minutes	27 minutes

1 Bring a large saucepan of water to a boil over high heat. Add the ziti and cook, uncovered, until tender but still firm to the bite—about 10 minutes. Drain well and set aside.

2 Meanwhile, sauté the beef and onion in a deep 12-inch skillet over moderate heat, stirring frequently to break up any clumps, until the beef is browned—about 5 minutes. Drain off the excess fat. Stir in the tomato sauce and bring to a simmer. Add the green beans, reduce the heat to low, and simmer, uncovered, for 10 minutes.

3 Stir in the cooked ziti, then place large spoonfuls of the ricotta on top but not touching. Sprinkle the mozzarella in between. Cover and cook just until the mozzarella melts and the ziti and beans are heated through—about 10 minutes. Sprinkle with the Parmesan cheese. Serves 4.

All-in-One Meat Loaf Dinner

This dish is similar in flavor to stuffed cabbage, but it's much easier to make.

3 tablespoons vegetable oil

2 pounds cabbage, coarsely shredded

1 medium-size yellow onion, thinly sliced

1 can (1 pound) tomatoes with their juice, chopped

1 teaspoon sugar

½ teaspoon salt

¼ teaspoon black pepper

1⅔ cups Basic Beef Stock (page 332) or canned beef broth

¾ cup long-grain white or brown rice

2 large eggs

1 pound lean ground beef

3 tablespoons soft bread crumbs

4 scallions, including tops, thinly sliced

½ cup shredded Swiss cheese (2 ounces)

¼ teaspoon dried thyme, crumbled

2 tablespoons minced parsley

Per serving:
Calories 624; Protein 51 g;
Carbohydrates 50 g;
Fat 25 g; Sodium 766 mg;
Cholesterol 223 mg

30 minutes	1 hr. 25 min.

1 Preheat the oven to 350° F. Spread the oil in a 14" x 11" x 3" baking pan. Add the cabbage, onion, tomatoes, sugar, and half the salt and pepper, and mix well. Cover with foil and bake for 45 minutes, stirring occasionally.

2 Meanwhile, bring the stock to a simmer in a medium-size sauce-pan over moderate heat. Stir in the rice, reduce the heat to low, cover, and simmer until all the water is absorbed—20 minutes for white rice, 35 to 40 minutes for brown.

3 In a large bowl, beat the eggs lightly, then add the beef, 2 tablespoons of the bread crumbs, ¼ cup of the scallions, and the remaining salt and pepper, and mix well.

4 Cover a 12- by 10-inch sheet of wax paper with the remaining tablespoon of bread crumbs. Pat the beef mixture firmly on top of the crumbs so that the paper is entirely covered; set aside.

5 Mix the cheese, thyme, and remaining scallions into the rice, and spread on top of the beef, leaving a 1-inch border all around.

6 Beginning with a long edge, roll the beef up jelly-roll fashion, pulling off the wax paper as you go. When you reach the end of the paper, pinch the meat together at both ends, enclosing the rice, then pinch the seam to seal.

7 Remove the baking pan from the oven and push the cabbage mixture to the sides with a wooden spoon. Using the wax paper to help lift the beef roll, place it, seam side down, in the center of the pan. Bake, uncovered, for 40 minutes. Sprinkle with the parsley just before serving. Serves 4.

Mozzarella Meat Loaf Pie

This easy-as-pie recipe features a ground beef crust filled with layers of chopped tomato, spinach, and cheese — all topped with mashed potatoes. If you're watching cholesterol, substitute ground turkey for the ground beef. To save time, use 3 cups of prepared instant mashed potatoes instead of homemade.

- 4 medium-size all-purpose potatoes, peeled and quartered
- 1 teaspoon salt
- ½ cup skim milk
- 1 pound lean ground beef
- 3 tablespoons fine dry bread crumbs
- 1 large egg, lightly beaten
- 1 clove garlic, crushed
- ½ teaspoon dried oregano, crumbled
- 1 large tomato, cored, seeded, and chopped, or 1 cup drained and chopped canned tomatoes
- 1 cup shredded low-fat mozzarella cheese (4 ounces)
- 1 package (10 ounces) frozen chopped spinach, cooked and drained well

Per serving:
Calories 479; Protein 51 g;
Carbohydrates 39 g;
Fat 13 g; Sodium 891 mg;
Cholesterol 173 mg

20 minutes   50 minutes

1 Preheat the oven to 350° F. In a covered large saucepan, cook the potatoes with half the salt in boiling water until tender — about 20 minutes. Drain, then mash the potatoes with the milk until smooth. Adjust the salt to taste and set aside.

2 In a large bowl, combine the beef, remaining salt, bread crumbs, egg, garlic, and oregano. Make a crust by pressing the mixture across the bottom and up the sides of a greased 9-inch pie pan.

3 Fill the "meat crust" with the following layers: the tomato, the cheese, then the spinach. Top with the mashed potatoes and smooth with a rubber spatula. Bake, uncovered, until the "crust" shrinks from the sides of the pan — about 30 minutes. Serves 4.

A cheese and rice filling turns familiar fare into an irresistible All-in-One Meat Loaf Dinner.

Roast Pork with Red Cabbage, Apples, and Potatoes

A wonderful dish for Sunday dinner that takes just 15 minutes to prepare. If the potatoes are thin-skinned, you don't even need to peel them.

- 2 tablespoons vegetable oil
- 3 pounds boneless pork loin
- 1 medium-size yellow onion, finely chopped
- 4 cups thinly sliced red cabbage (about 2 pounds)
- 2 pounds small new potatoes, peeled and quartered
- 3 medium-size tart green apples, peeled, cored, and thinly sliced
- 2 tablespoons dark brown sugar
- 1 teaspoon salt
- ¼ teaspoon black pepper
- 1 cup dry white wine
- 1 tablespoon red wine vinegar

1 Preheat the oven to 375° F. Heat the oil in an 8-quart flameproof casserole over moderate heat for 1 minute. Add the pork and brown on all sides—about 10 minutes. Remove the pork and set aside.

2 Add the onion to the casserole and sauté, stirring occasionally, until soft—about 5 minutes. Stir in the cabbage, potatoes, apples, sugar, salt, pepper, wine, and vinegar, and bring to a simmer, then return the pork to the casserole.

3 Transfer the casserole to the oven. Bake, uncovered, stirring the cabbage mixture and turning the pork occasionally, about 1½ hours or until a meat thermometer inserted in the center of the thickest part of the pork reads 155° F. Serves 6.

> *Per serving:*
> *Calories 666; Protein 51 g;*
> *Carbohydrates 49 g;*
> *Fat 27 g; Sodium 508 mg;*
> *Cholesterol 150 mg*

| 15 minutes | 1 hr. 48 min. |

Pork Chop and Lima Bean Skillet

A hint of orange and brown sugar makes the difference in this tempting recipe. If you want to reheat any leftovers, add 2 tablespoons water, cover the skillet, and set over low heat for 10 minutes.

- 2 tablespoons vegetable oil
- 4 thick center-cut pork rib chops (8 ounces each)
- 1 large yellow onion, finely chopped
- 4 medium-size carrots, peeled and thinly sliced
- 2 cloves garlic, minced
- 1 can (1 pound) tomatoes with their juice, chopped
- 2 tablespoons dark brown sugar
- ½ teaspoon grated orange zest (colored part of rind)
- 1 teaspoon salt
- ⅛ teaspoon black pepper
- 1 package (10 ounces) frozen baby lima beans, partially thawed but not drained

1 Heat the oil in a 12-inch skillet over moderate heat for 1 minute. Add the pork chops and brown for 5 minutes per side. Transfer to a plate.

2 Skim all but 2 tablespoons of the drippings from the skillet. Add the onion and sauté over moderate heat, stirring occasionally, until soft—5 minutes. Stir in the carrots and garlic and sauté 5 minutes more. Add the tomatoes, sugar, orange zest, salt, and pepper, and bring to a simmer. Cover, reduce the heat to low, and simmer for 10 minutes.

3 Stir in the lima beans, then return the pork chops to the skillet, pushing them down into the liquid. Simmer, uncovered, until the pork is tender and no longer pink on the inside—about 20 minutes. Serves 4.

> *Per serving:*
> *Calories 516; Protein 38 g;*
> *Carbohydrates 36 g;*
> *Fat 25 g; Sodium 868 mg;*
> *Cholesterol 108 mg*

| 15 minutes | 53 minutes |

Stuffed Pork Chop Supper

Arrange these savory chops on a bed of fresh arugula or steamed collard greens, mustard greens, or kale, and serve the extra stuffing in a bowl.

- 8 loin pork chops (6 ounces each)
- 1 tablespoon lime or lemon juice
- ¾ teaspoon ground coriander
- ½ teaspoon salt
- 4 tablespoons olive oil
- 1 large sweet red pepper, cored, seeded, and finely chopped
- 3 small zucchini, finely chopped (3 cups)
- 12 ounces mushrooms, finely chopped
- 3 scallions, including tops, finely chopped
- 2¼ cups soft bread crumbs
- 3 tablespoons prepared mustard

Per serving:
Calories 567; Protein 42 g;
Carbohydrates 21 g;
Fat 35 g; Sodium 650 mg;
Cholesterol 122 mg

| 25 minutes | 37 minutes |

1 Preheat the oven to 350° F. Holding a sharp knife horizontal to the work surface and starting at the rib bone, cut a pocket in each chop (or have your butcher do it). Sprinkle the chops with the lime juice, coriander, and salt.

2 Heat 1 tablespoon of the oil in a 12-inch skillet over moderate heat for 1 minute. Add the chops and brown for 5 minutes on each side. Transfer the chops to a plate and discard the pan drippings.

3 Add the remaining 3 tablespoons oil to the skillet and heat over moderate heat for 1 minute. Add the pepper, zucchini, mushrooms, and scallions, and sauté until soft and all the liquid has evaporated—5 minutes. Remove from the heat and stir in the bread crumbs and mustard.

4 Spoon a little of the stuffing into each chop pocket (you do not need to sew or skewer them shut). Cover the chops with a ½-inch layer of stuffing and spoon the remainder into a lightly greased 13" x 9" x 2" baking dish. Place the chops on top, cover with foil, and bake until the pork is no longer pink on the inside—about 20 minutes. Serves 4.

Add a more piquant touch to this Stuffed Pork Chop Supper by sprinkling the chops with fresh lime juice.

Curried Pork Chop Bake

A touch of curry turns pork chops, cabbage, and potatoes into a mouth-watering dinner. Garnish each plate with sprigs of watercress.

- 2 tablespoons vegetable or olive oil
- 4 pork loin or rib chops, about ¾ inch thick
- 1 teaspoon salt
- ¼ teaspoon black pepper
- 2 large yellow onions, thinly sliced
- 2 teaspoons curry powder
- 1 cup apple juice
- 1 pound all-purpose potatoes (about 3), peeled and sliced ¼ inch thick
- 3 medium-size carrots, peeled and coarsely shredded
- 2 cups thinly sliced cabbage

> Per serving:
> Calories 540; Protein 36 g;
> Carbohydrates 44 g;
> Fat 25 g; Sodium 657 mg;
> Cholesterol 108 mg

20 minutes	1 hr. 46 min.

1 Preheat the oven to 350° F. Heat the oil in a 12-inch ovenproof skillet or shallow 3-quart flameproof casserole over moderately high heat for 1 minute. Sprinkle the chops with ¼ teaspoon of the salt and ⅛ teaspoon of the pepper, add to the skillet, and brown for 5 minutes on each side. Transfer the chops to a plate and discard all but 1 tablespoon of the skillet drippings.

2 Add the onions and curry powder to the skillet and sauté, stirring frequently, for 5 minutes or until soft. Pour in ¼ cup of the apple juice, scraping up any browned bits on the bottom of the skillet.

3 Place the potatoes on top of the onions. Toss the carrots and cabbage together on a sheet of wax paper and scatter them on top of the potatoes. Sprinkle with the remaining salt and pepper.

4 Arrange the pork chops in the skillet and spoon half the vegetable mixture on top. Pour in the remaining apple juice. Cover the skillet, transfer to the oven, and bake for 1½ hours or until the pork chops and vegetables are tender. Serves 4.

Pork Medley with Sauerkraut

Juniper berries are too bitter to eat raw, but when cooked, they provide a distinctively sweet flavor.

- 2 tablespoons vegetable oil
- 1 medium-size yellow onion, thinly sliced
- 2 medium-size carrots, peeled and thinly sliced
- 2 cans or packages (1 pound each) sauerkraut, drained and rinsed
- 2 cups Basic Chicken Stock (page 333) or canned chicken broth
- ½ cup dry white wine
- 6 juniper berries (optional)
- 1 teaspoon caraway seeds
- 1 whole bay leaf
- ¼ teaspoon salt
- ¼ teaspoon black pepper
- 1¼ pounds all-purpose potatoes (about 4), peeled and cut into 1½-inch cubes
- 4 smoked pork chops (1 pound)
- 2 knockwurst (8 ounces), pricked with a fork
- 8 ounces kielbasa or other garlic sausage, pricked with a fork

> Per serving:
> Calories 778; Protein 38 g;
> Carbohydrates 47 g;
> Fat 47 g; Sodium 2,525 mg;
> Cholesterol 124 mg

20 minutes	51 minutes

1 Heat the oil in a 3-quart flameproof casserole over moderate heat for 1 minute. Add the onion and carrots and sauté, stirring occasionally, for 7 minutes or until the onion is golden.

2 Add the sauerkraut and cook, stirring, for 1 minute. Add the stock, wine, juniper berries (if desired), caraway seeds, bay leaf, salt, pepper, and potatoes. Bring the mixture to a boil, cover, reduce the heat to low, and simmer for 20 minutes.

3 Meanwhile, preheat the broiler. Arrange the pork chops, knockwurst, and kielbasa on the rack of a broiling pan and broil 4 inches from the heat for 3 to 4 minutes on each side or until lightly golden. Cut the kielbasa and knockwurst into thick slices.

4 Add the meats to the casserole, spooning the sauerkraut and potatoes over and around them. Cover and simmer 20 minutes longer. Remove the bay leaf. Serves 4.

Barbecued Ribs, South American Style

Raisins and banana add a south-of-the-Equator flavor to a standard American dish. You can substitute 3 pounds of chicken legs for the ribs —just shorten the baking time in Step 2 to 45 minutes.

- 3 medium-size yellow onions, coarsely chopped
- 4 cloves garlic, crushed
- 1 tablespoon sugar
- 1¼ cups water
- 3 pounds pork spareribs or beef short ribs, cut into 2-rib widths
- 2¼ cups canned crushed tomatoes
- 3 tablespoons red wine vinegar
- 2 tablespoons molasses
- 1 large banana, peeled and sliced ½ inch thick
- ¼ cup raisins
- 2 teaspoons ground ginger
- ¾ teaspoon dried oregano, crumbled
- ¼ teaspoon hot red pepper sauce
- 8 ounces green beans, trimmed and cut into 1-inch lengths
- 1 cup long-grain white or brown rice

Flat-leaf parsley sprigs (optional garnish)

Per serving:
Calories 870; Protein 46 g;
Carbohydrates 79 g;
Fat 42 g; Sodium 354 mg;
Cholesterol 162 mg

 20 minutes   1 hr. 52 min.

1 Preheat the oven to 350° F. Place the onions and garlic in a 5-quart Dutch oven and sprinkle with the sugar. Add 1 cup of the water and simmer, uncovered, over moderate heat until the water has evaporated and the onions are very soft— about 10 minutes.

2 Add the ribs, the remaining water, and the tomatoes, vinegar, molasses, banana, raisins, ginger, oregano, and red pepper sauce, and mix well. Bring to a boil, cover, and transfer to the oven. Bake until the ribs are well-done—about 1 hour 20 minutes.

3 Stir in the green beans, cover, and bake until the beans are tender— 15 to 20 minutes more. Meanwhile, cook the rice according to package directions. Serve with the rice and garnish with the parsley sprigs if desired. Serves 4.

Blanketed by a sweet, tangy sauce—Barbecued Ribs, South American Style

Pork and Broccoli Stir-Fry

This stir-fry also works well with beef, lamb, or chicken, but the chicken takes about 2 minutes less to cook. You'll find oyster sauce, bean paste, and baby corn in the Oriental section of your supermarket or at a specialty food store.

For the marinade:
- 2 tablespoons reduced-sodium soy sauce
- 1 tablespoon dry sherry
- 1 teaspoon Oriental sesame oil
- 1½ pounds boneless pork loin or lean shoulder, thinly sliced

For the sauce:
- ⅓ cup Basic Chicken Stock (page 333) or canned chicken broth
- ¼ cup reduced-sodium soy sauce
- 2 tablespoons dry sherry
- 2 teaspoons Oriental sesame oil
- 2 teaspoons cornstarch
- 1 teaspoon hot bean paste (optional)
- 2 tablespoons Oriental oyster sauce (optional)

For the stir-fry:
- 2 tablespoons peanut or vegetable oil
- 3 shallots or scallions, including tops, finely chopped
- 1 tablespoon minced fresh ginger
- 1 tablespoon minced garlic
- 2 cups fresh or 1 package (10 ounces) frozen broccoli florets, thawed
- 1 can (14 ounces) whole baby corn, drained and rinsed

1 *For the marinade:* In a medium-size bowl, combine the soy sauce, sherry, and oil. Add the pork, toss well, and marinate for 20 minutes.

2 *For the sauce:* In another medium-size bowl, combine the stock, soy sauce, sherry, oil, cornstarch, and, if desired, the bean paste and oyster sauce; set aside.

3 *For the stir-fry:* Heat the oil in a 12-inch skillet or wok over moderately high heat for 1 minute. Add the shallots, ginger, and garlic, and stir-fry for l minute. Add the pork and stir-fry for 2 to 3 minutes or until no longer pink. Add the broccoli and corn and toss. Stir the sauce, mix into the skillet, bring to a simmer, cover, and cook over moderately low heat for 4 to 5 minutes or until the broccoli is just crisp-tender. Serves 4 to 6.

Per serving:
Calories 472; Protein 39 g;
Carbohydrates 25 g;
Fat 24 g; Sodium 1,267 mg;
Cholesterol 114 mg

30 minutes | 11 minutes

Pork and Apple Pie

If you prefer to make the crust from scratch (or with 1½ cups of pie crust mix), add 1 teaspoon sugar and 1 teaspoon paprika to the dry ingredients for extra flavor.

- 1 frozen 9-inch deep-dish pie crust
- 3 slices bacon, diced
- 12 ounces boneless pork shoulder, cut into ¾-inch cubes
- ½ teaspoon salt
- 1 large yellow onion, coarsely chopped
- 2 medium-size carrots, peeled, halved lengthwise, and sliced ¼ inch thick
- 2 medium-size white turnips, peeled and cut into ½-inch cubes
- 1 large McIntosh apple, peeled, cored, and cut into ½-inch cubes
- 1 tablespoon all-purpose flour
- ½ teaspoon each dried sage and rosemary, crumbled
- ⅛ teaspoon black pepper
- 1 cup apple cider

1 Thaw the pie crust at room temperature for about 30 minutes. Meanwhile, cook the bacon in a 12-inch skillet over moderate heat until slightly crisp—4 minutes. Using a slotted spoon, transfer to paper toweling to drain. Remove all but 2 tablespoons of the drippings from the skillet, then add the pork, sprinkle with half of the salt, and brown on all sides—10 minutes. Remove with a slotted spoon and set aside.

2 Preheat the oven to 350° F. Add the onion, carrots, turnips, and apple to the skillet, and toss to coat with the drippings. Stir in the flour, sage, rosemary, pepper, and the remaining salt. Pour in the cider and bring to a boil over high heat, stirring constantly. Return the pork and bacon to the skillet and remove from the heat.

3 Spoon the mixture into a 9-inch pie pan. Remove the pie crust from its pan and ease it on top; flute the edge. Make decorative slashes in the crust to let steam escape.

4 Bake the pie, uncovered, for 1 hour 20 minutes. Insert a small skewer through a steam vent in the crust and pierce a piece of the pork to see if it's tender. If not, bake the pie 20 minutes longer, covering the crust with foil if it is overbrowning. Serves 4.

Per serving:
Calories 482; Protein 23 g;
Carbohydrates 39 g;
Fat 24 g; Sodium 754 mg;
Cholesterol 131 mg

30 minutes | 1 hr. 36 min.

Pork and Apple Pie, a perfect pairing of fruit and meat.
Why not make two so that you can freeze one for another time?

Sausage and Potato Pie

A thin potato crust filled with sausage, mozzarella cheese, and zucchini.

- 2 tablespoons olive oil
- 1 large sweet red pepper, cored, seeded, and cut into strips ¼ inch wide
- 1 medium-size zucchini, thinly sliced
- 2 teaspoons minced garlic
- ½ teaspoon black pepper
- ¼ cup minced fresh basil or ¼ cup minced flat-leaf parsley mixed with 2 teaspoons crumbled dried basil
- 1 pound sweet Italian sausage, casings removed, or diced kielbasa or ham
- 3 medium-size all-purpose potatoes, peeled and very thinly sliced
- 1 cup grated Parmesan cheese (4 ounces)
- 2 cups shredded mozzarella, Monterey Jack, fontina, or Cheddar cheese (8 ounces)

Per serving:
Calories 500; Protein 27 g;
Carbohydrates 17 g;
Fat 36 g; Sodium 1,192 mg;
Cholesterol 91 mg

 20 minutes 1 hour

1 Preheat the oven to 425° F. Heat 1 tablespoon of the oil in a 12-inch skillet over moderately high heat for 1 minute. Add the red pepper and zucchini and sauté, stirring occasionally, until soft—about 5 minutes. Stir in the garlic, black pepper, and basil, and sauté 2 minutes longer. Add the sausage, breaking up any clumps, and sauté until no longer pink but not quite cooked through—about 5 minutes. Remove from the heat.

2 Toss the potatoes with the remaining 1 tablespoon oil. Spread ¼ of the potatoes, overlapping slightly, over the bottom of a lightly greased 10-inch pie pan or a 13" x 9" x 2" baking dish. Spread ⅓ of the skillet mixture on top, followed by ⅓ each of the Parmesan and mozzarella cheeses. Press each layer down with your hands. Repeat the layers twice, finishing with a top layer of potatoes.

3 Cover the pie with foil, set in the lower third of the oven, and bake for 40 minutes. Remove the foil and bake until the potatoes are crisp and cooked through—5 to 10 minutes more.

4 Remove the pie from the oven and let stand for 10 minutes at room temperature. Carefully pour off any fat, then cut the pie into wedges. Serves 6.

73

Baked Ham and Spinach au Gratin

With a few handy ingredients, you can turn a pound of ham into a nutritious meal that will please the whole family.

- 3 tablespoons butter or margarine
- 1 cup frozen chopped onions, thawed and drained
- 3 cloves garlic, minced
- 3 tablespoons all-purpose flour
- 1½ teaspoons dry mustard
- 2 cups low-fat milk
- 1 cup shredded Cheddar, Swiss, or Monterey Jack cheese (4 ounces)
- 1 package (10 ounces) frozen chopped spinach, thawed and drained
- ¼ teaspoon black pepper
- 1 package (1 pound 4 ounces) refrigerated shredded potatoes or frozen hash browns, thawed
- 1 pound boiled or baked ham, cut into ½-inch cubes

1 Preheat the oven to 375° F. Melt the butter in a medium-size saucepan over moderate heat. Add the onions and sauté, stirring occasionally, for 2 to 3 minutes or until pale golden. Add the garlic and sauté, stirring occasionally, 2 to 3 minutes more.

2 Blend in the flour and mustard, then gradually whisk in the milk. Cook, stirring constantly, until thickened and smooth—3 to 5 minutes. Add the cheese, stir until melted, remove from the heat, and mix in the spinach and pepper.

3 Arrange half the potatoes in a lightly greased 12″ x 7″ x 2″ baking dish, pour on half the spinach mixture, and scatter with the ham. Top with the remaining potatoes and spinach mixture.

4 Cover with foil, set on a baking sheet, and bake for 30 minutes. Remove the foil and bake 15 minutes longer or until the potatoes are tender. Serves 4 to 6.

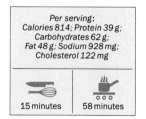

Per serving:
Calories 814; Protein 39 g;
Carbohydrates 62 g;
Fat 48 g; Sodium 928 mg;
Cholesterol 122 mg

15 minutes	58 minutes

Ham and Corn Custard with Sweet Red Peppers

This creamy dish is real comfort food. For a meatless meal, omit the ham and double the amount of cheese.

- 1 can (12 ounces) evaporated skim milk or 1½ cups low-fat milk
- 1 package (10 ounces) frozen corn kernels, thawed and drained
- ¼ cup yellow cornmeal
- 4 large eggs
- 1 tablespoon sugar
- ¼ teaspoon salt
- ⅛ teaspoon each black pepper and ground red pepper (cayenne)
- 1 cup shredded Cheddar, Swiss, or Monterey Jack cheese (4 ounces)
- 4 ounces baked or boiled ham, finely diced (1 cup)
- 1 jar (7 ounces) roasted sweet red peppers or pimientos, drained and finely chopped
- 2 scallions, including tops, thinly sliced

1 Preheat the oven to 400° F. In a small saucepan, heat the milk over low heat until almost simmering. Meanwhile, place 1 cup of the corn and the cornmeal in a food processor or an electric blender and whirl for 10 to 15 seconds or until smooth. Add the warm milk, eggs, sugar, salt, black pepper and ground red pepper, and whirl 5 to 10 seconds more. Transfer the mixture to a large bowl.

2 Stir in the cheese, ham, roasted peppers, scallions, and remaining corn. Pour the mixture into a lightly greased 1½-quart soufflé dish.

3 Bake, uncovered, for 15 minutes, then lower the oven temperature to 350° F and bake, uncovered, 35 minutes longer or until set. If the custard threatens to over-brown, cover with foil during the last 10 minutes of baking. Serve warm or at room temperature. Serves 4.

Per serving:
Calories 422; Protein 28 g;
Carbohydrates 39 g;
Fat 18 g; Sodium 845 mg;
Cholesterol 262 mg

15 minutes	52 minutes

Ham and Sweet Potatoes in Orange Sauce

Ham never tasted so good, thanks to the perfect blend of orange juice and sweet potatoes.

3 tablespoons vegetable oil

1 tablespoon butter or margarine

8 ounces frozen small white onions, unthawed

1 pound sweet potatoes, peeled and cut into ¾-inch cubes

1 pound boiled or baked ham, cut into ¾-inch cubes (3 cups)

3 tablespoons all-purpose flour

3 cups Basic Chicken Stock (page 333) or canned chicken broth

¾ cup orange juice

1 teaspoon grated orange zest (colored part of the rind)

¼ teaspoon black pepper

2 cups fresh or 1 package (10 ounces) frozen broccoli florets, thawed

Per serving:
Calories 528; Protein 28 g;
Carbohydrates 47 g;
Fat 26 g; Sodium 1,740 mg;
Cholesterol 72 mg

20 minutes | 55 minutes

1 Heat the oil and butter in a 5-quart Dutch oven over moderately high heat for 2 minutes. Add the onions and sauté, stirring occasionally, for 8 to 10 minutes or until golden brown. Transfer to a large plate. Add the potatoes and sauté, stirring occasionally, for 5 minutes or until lightly browned. Transfer to the plate. Add the ham to the Dutch oven and sauté, stirring occasionally, for 5 to 8 minutes or until lightly browned. Transfer to a separate plate.

2 Reduce the heat to moderate. Whisk the flour into the ham drippings and cook, stirring constantly, for 2 minutes. Gradually whisk in the stock and orange juice and cook, stirring constantly, for 3 to 5 minutes or until slightly thickened. Stir in the orange zest and pepper.

3 Return the potatoes to the Dutch oven, bring to a boil over moderate heat, cover, and cook for 10 minutes or until almost tender. Add the sautéed ham and onions and the broccoli, return to a boil, cover, and cook for 10 minutes or until all the vegetables are tender and the ham is heated through. Serves 4 to 6.

Hawaiian Variation

Follow Step 1 as directed. In Step 2, omit the orange juice and substitute *1 can (1 pound 4 ounces) pineapple chunks*. Drain the juice, reserving ¾ cup. Add the pineapple chunks to the Dutch oven along with the chicken stock. In Step 3, add the reserved juice with the broccoli. Serves 4 to 6.

Per serving: Calories 580; Protein 28 g;
Carbohydrates 61 g; Fat 26 g;
Sodium 1,742 mg; Cholesterol 72 mg

The Hawaiian variation of Ham and Sweet Potatoes in Orange Sauce — garnished with fresh orange and pineapple

Stuffed Veal Breast

This herb stuffing turns a thrifty cut of meat into company fare. You can substitute 3 cups cooked spinach or Swiss chard for the green peas.

- 3 tablespoons unsalted butter or margarine
- 3 tablespoons vegetable oil
- 3 medium-size yellow onions, coarsely chopped
- 1½ pounds mushrooms, coarsely chopped (about 4 cups)
- 1½ teaspoons dried thyme, crumbled
- 3 cups fresh or 1½ packages (10 ounces each) frozen green peas, thawed and drained
- 3 cups cooked long-grain white or brown rice
- 3 large eggs, lightly beaten
- 1½ cups grated Parmesan cheese (6 ounces)
- 1 teaspoon salt
- ¼ teaspoon black pepper
- 1 bone-in breast of veal with pocket (about 4 pounds)
- 1 clove garlic, minced
- ½ teaspoon dried sage, crumbled
- 6 medium-size carrots, peeled and cut into 2-inch lengths
- 4 medium-size white turnips, peeled and quartered
- 8 shallots or 4 ounces frozen small white onions, thawed

1 Heat the butter and oil in a 12-inch skillet over moderate heat for 1 minute. Add the onions and sauté, stirring occasionally, until soft—about 5 minutes. Add the mushrooms and thyme and sauté, stirring often, until lightly browned—about 10 minutes.

2 Preheat the oven to 350° F. Transfer the onion mixture to a large bowl. Add the peas, rice, eggs, cheese, salt, and pepper, and mix thoroughly. Stuff about ⅓ of the mixture into the veal pocket; do not overstuff or the filling will ooze out. Close the opening with skewers or sew it shut. Place the extra stuffing in a lightly greased 1-quart casserole, cover with foil, and refrigerate.

3 Place the veal, bone side down, in a greased 13" x 9" x 2" roasting pan. Rub with the garlic and sprinkle with the sage. Cover the pan with foil and bake for 1 hour, then add the carrots, turnips, and shallots. Cover with the foil again and bake 1 hour more.

4 Remove the foil from the veal, place the casserole of extra stuffing, covered, in the oven, and bake until the veal is browned—30 minutes more. To serve, remove the skewers or string and slice the veal between the bones. Serve the extra stuffing on the side. Serves 6.

> *Per serving:*
> *Calories 997; Protein 64 g;*
> *Carbohydrates 67 g;*
> *Fat 57 g; Sodium 1,015 mg;*
> *Cholesterol 308 mg*

| 30 minutes | 2 hr. 46 min. |

Veal Chop Skillet Dinner

If you prefer pork chops, substitute okra or limas for the green beans.

- 2 tablespoons vegetable oil
- 4 veal shoulder chops (8 ounces each)
- 8 small new potatoes, unpeeled
- 4 medium-size carrots, peeled and cut into 1½-inch lengths
- 2 cloves garlic, minced
- 1 medium-size yellow onion, finely chopped
- 1 cup Basic Beef or Basic Chicken Stock (page 332 or 333) or canned beef or chicken broth
- ½ teaspoon each salt and dried thyme, crumbled
- ⅛ teaspoon black pepper
- 8 ounces green beans, trimmed and cut into 1-inch lengths, or 1 package (10 ounces) frozen cut green beans, thawed and drained

1 Heat the oil in a 12-inch skillet over moderate heat for 1 minute. Add the veal chops and brown on both sides—about 15 minutes in all. Discard any excess fat.

2 Add the potatoes, carrots, garlic, onion, stock, salt, thyme, and pepper. Cover, reduce the heat to low, and simmer for 30 minutes.

3 Add the green beans, cover, and cook until the veal and vegetables are tender—about 15 minutes more. Serves 4.

> *Per serving:*
> *Calories 409; Protein 26 g;*
> *Carbohydrates 36 g;*
> *Fat 18 g; Sodium 432 mg;*
> *Cholesterol 144 mg*

| 15 minutes | 1 hour |

Creamy Veal and Mushroom Stew

The dried mushrooms, available in some supermarkets and most health food and Oriental grocery stores, add a special earthy taste to this elegant dish. If you don't use them, add 2 ounces more fresh mushrooms and substitute chicken stock for the soaking liquid.

1½	cups water
½	ounce dried porcini, shiitake, or Polish mushrooms
1½	pounds stewing veal, sliced ¼ inch thick
¾	teaspoon salt
¼	cup all-purpose flour
⅓	cup olive oil
8	shallots, halved if large (optional)

12	ounces mushrooms, quartered
⅓	cup dry sherry
2½	teaspoons minced fresh tarragon or ¾ teaspoon dried tarragon, crumbled
8	ounces broad egg noodles
1	package (10 ounces) frozen green peas, thawed and drained
½	cup light cream or half-and-half
2	tablespoons lemon juice

Per serving:
Calories 832; Protein 48 g;
Carbohydrates 70 g;
Fat 40 g; Sodium 563 mg;
Cholesterol 200 mg

 30 minutes   55 minutes

1 Bring the water to a boil in a small saucepan. Remove from the heat, add the dried mushrooms, and let soak for 30 minutes at room temperature.

2 Meanwhile, sprinkle the veal with ¼ teaspoon of the salt, then dredge in the flour, shaking off any excess. Heat 3 tablespoons of the oil in a 5-quart Dutch oven over moderately high heat for 1 minute. Working in batches, brown the veal—about 5 minutes per batch. Using a slotted spoon, transfer to a bowl and set aside; add more oil to the Dutch oven if needed.

3 Preheat the oven to 350° F. Add the shallots if desired and fresh mushrooms to the Dutch oven. Reduce the heat to low and sauté, shaking the pan occasionally, until the shallots and mushrooms are slightly softened, about 5 minutes. Add the sherry and cook for 2 minutes, scraping up any browned bits from the bottom of the pan.

4 With your fingers, carefully lift the dried mushrooms from the soaking water. Rinse off any dirt, then add them to the Dutch oven. Strain the soaking water through dampened cheesecloth or paper toweling into the Dutch oven, then add the tarragon and veal. Bring to a boil over high heat, cover, transfer to the oven, and bake until the veal is tender—about 30 minutes. After the veal has been in the oven for 20 minutes, start cooking the noodles according to package directions.

5 When the veal is tender, transfer the Dutch oven to the stovetop and stir in the peas, cream, lemon juice, and remaining salt. Cook, uncovered, over moderate heat until the peas are heated through and the sauce is slightly thickened—about 5 minutes. Serve over the noodles. Serves 4 to 6.

When preparing this Stuffed Veal Breast, don't overstuff the pocket or the filling may spill out during cooking.

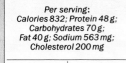

Lamb Shanks, Italian Style

Wine, tomatoes, and rosemary flavor this economical cut of lamb, which is slow-cooked until the meat practically falls off the bone. It's a good company dish that's easy on the budget.

4 lamb shanks (14 ounces each)
2 tablespoons vegetable oil
8 large shallots or 2 medium-size yellow onions, finely chopped
2 cloves garlic, minced
2 medium-size sweet green peppers, cored, seeded, and cut lengthwise into strips ½ inch wide
1 cup dry white wine
1 can (1 pound) tomatoes with their juice, chopped

2 teaspoons minced fresh rosemary or ½ teaspoon dried rosemary, crumbled
½ teaspoon salt
¼ teaspoon black pepper
1 cup Basic Beef Stock (page 332) or canned beef broth
1 cup orzo (rice-shaped pasta), pastina, or long-grain white rice
⅓ cup minced parsley

> Per serving:
> Calories 657; Protein 52 g;
> Carbohydrates 56 g;
> Fat 25 g; Sodium 670 mg;
> Cholesterol 113 mg

20 minutes | 2 hours

1 Using paper toweling, blot the lamb shanks dry. Heat the oil in a 6-quart Dutch oven or flameproof casserole over moderate heat for 1 minute. Add the shanks and brown well on all sides—10 minutes. Remove the shanks and set aside.

2 Add the shallots and garlic to the Dutch oven and sauté, stirring frequently, until softened—about 5 minutes. Add the green peppers and sauté, stirring occasionally, until soft—about 5 minutes more. Stir in the wine, scraping up any browned bits on the bottom of the pan.

3 Return the shanks to the pan. Add the tomatoes, rosemary, salt, pepper, and stock. Cover, reduce heat to low, and simmer, turning and basting the shanks occasionally with pan juices, until tender—1½ hours. Skim excess fat.

4 Add the orzo, cover, and simmer until tender—10 minutes. Stir in all but 2 tablespoons of the parsley and sprinkle the remainder on top. Serves 4.

Lamb is more common in Greek than Italian cooking, but these Lamb Shanks, Italian Style are an international success.

French Lamb Chop Casserole

Serve this succulent casserole with pasta, couscous, or polenta.

- 6 tablespoons olive oil
- 1 medium-size eggplant, cut into 1-inch cubes
- 1 medium-size zucchini, sliced ¼ inch thick
- 1 large sweet green pepper, cored, seeded, and cut into 1-inch squares
- 1 medium-size yellow onion, thinly sliced
- 1 can (1 pound) tomatoes, drained and chopped
- 1 tablespoon minced garlic
- ½ teaspoon each dried rosemary, thyme, and basil, crumbled
- ½ teaspoon salt
- ¼ teaspoon black pepper
- 2 tablespoons tomato paste
- 4 shoulder lamb chops (8 ounces each)
- ¼ cup all-purpose flour
- 2 tablespoons minced fresh basil or parsley
- 2 tablespoons grated Parmesan cheese

Per serving:
Calories 592; Protein 45 g;
Carbohydrates 20 g;
Fat 36 g; Sodium 682 mg;
Cholesterol 160 mg

30 minutes   59 minutes

1 Heat 2 tablespoons of oil in a 12-inch skillet over moderately high heat for 1 minute. Add the eggplant and sauté, stirring occasionally, until golden brown on all sides—5 to 6 minutes. Transfer the eggplant to an ungreased shallow 2-quart casserole.

2 Heat 2 more tablespoons of oil in the skillet for 1 minute; add the zucchini and sauté until lightly browned on both sides—about 3 minutes. With a slotted spoon, transfer the zucchini to the casserole.

3 Preheat the oven to 375° F. Add the green pepper and onion to the skillet and sauté, stirring, until softened—5 minutes. Stir in the tomatoes, garlic, rosemary, thyme, basil, and half the salt and black pepper. Cook, uncovered, stirring occasionally, until thickened—2 minutes. Mix in the tomato paste, transfer to the casserole, and toss lightly.

4 Dredge the lamb chops in the flour, shake off any excess, and sprinkle with the remaining salt and pepper. Add the remaining 2 tablespoons oil to the skillet and heat over moderate heat for 1 minute. Brown the chops for 5 minutes on each side. Transfer to the casserole and spoon some of the vegetable mixture on top.

5 Cover the casserole with foil and bake until the chops are tender—about 30 minutes. Sprinkle with the fresh basil and cheese. Serves 4.

Piquant Lamb Stew

Green chilies and garlic add spice to this lamb and zucchini stew. You can make it with either yogurt or sour cream. Yogurt has a slightly tart flavor and is lower in fat; sour cream is a bit more mellow.

- 2 tablespoons butter or margarine
- 1 tablespoon vegetable oil
- 1 large yellow onion, coarsely chopped
- 1 can (4 ounces) green chilies, drained and coarsely chopped (wash your hands after handling the chilies)
- 1 clove garlic, minced
- ½ teaspoon salt
- ½ teaspoon ground cinnamon
  Pinch ground cloves
- ¼ teaspoon black pepper
- 3 pounds boneless lamb shoulder, cut into 1-inch cubes
- 1 cup water
- 1½ cups long-grain white rice
- 2 medium-size zucchini, sliced ¼ inch thick
- 1 tablespoon cornstarch
- 1 cup plain low-fat yogurt or sour cream
- 2 tablespoons minced fresh coriander (cilantro) or flat-leaf parsley

Per serving:
Calories 597; Protein 49 g;
Carbohydrates 46 g;
Fat 22 g; Sodium 356 mg;
Cholesterol 179 mg

25 minutes   1 hr. 58 min.

1 Heat the butter and oil in a 5-quart Dutch oven over moderate heat for 1 minute. Add the onion and sauté, stirring occasionally, until soft—about 5 minutes.

2 Add the chilies, garlic, salt, cinnamon, cloves, and pepper, and sauté for 5 minutes. Add the lamb and sauté, stirring occasionally, until lightly browned—about 10 minutes.

3 Stir in the water, cover, reduce the heat to low, and simmer until the lamb is tender—about 1½ hours. About 20 minutes before the lamb is done, cook the rice according to package directions.

4 Skim any fat from the surface of the stew, then stir in the zucchini, cover, and cook for 5 minutes. In a small bowl, blend the cornstarch with 2 tablespoons of the yogurt. Whisk in the remaining yogurt, then stir the mixture into the Dutch oven. Bring the stew just to serving temperature, stirring constantly, but do not boil. Sprinkle with the coriander and serve over the rice. Serves 6.

Lamb Pilaf with Apricots and Raisins

We prefer brown rice in this recipe, but you can easily substitute white and reduce the cooking time in Step 1 by 10 minutes. If you want to use leftover cooked lamb, omit Step 2 and add the meat in Step 3.

2 tablespoons butter or margarine

1 cup long-grain brown rice

1 large yellow onion, coarsely chopped

2 tablespoons minced fresh ginger

2 cloves garlic, minced

2 cups Basic Beef Stock (page 332) or canned beef broth

3 tablespoons olive or vegetable oil

1 pound boneless lean leg of lamb or pork loin, cut into ¾-inch cubes

¼ teaspoon salt

⅛ teaspoon black pepper

2 small zucchini, diced

4 ounces small mushrooms, halved

½ cup chopped dried apricots

½ cup dark or golden raisins

½ cup minced parsley

Per serving:
Calories 477; Protein 28 g;
Carbohydrates 44 g;
Fat 22 g; Sodium 385 mg;
Cholesterol 90 mg

20 minutes | 50 minutes

1 Melt the butter in a medium-size saucepan over moderate heat. Add the rice, onion, 1 tablespoon of the ginger, and the garlic, and sauté until the rice is pale gold—3 to 4 minutes. Add the stock and bring to a boil. Reduce the heat to low, cover, and simmer about 30 minutes or until most of the liquid is absorbed.

2 Meanwhile, heat 1 tablespoon of the oil in a 12-inch skillet over moderately high heat for 1 minute. Sprinkle the lamb with the salt and pepper, add to the skillet, and brown on all sides—about 10 minutes. Using a slotted spoon, transfer the lamb to a plate lined with paper toweling and set aside.

3 Add the remaining oil to the skillet, reduce the heat to moderate, and heat for 1 minute. Add the zucchini and the remaining ginger and sauté until the zucchini is softened—about 3 minutes. Add the mushrooms and sauté until tender—3 to 4 minutes more. Set aside.

4 Add the apricots and raisins to the rice, cover, and continue cooking until all the liquid is absorbed—about 10 minutes more.

5 Return the lamb to the skillet, add the rice mixture, toss well to mix, and bring just to serving temperature, uncovered, over moderate heat. Stir in the parsley. Serves 4.

Lamb Pilaf with Apricots and Raisins —an easy dish with the special dash of ginger and garlic

Poultry

Of all the foods you can plan a menu with,
poultry is by far the most versatile —suitable for both everyday
meals and elegant dinners. Chicken, turkey, duck, and Cornish hens
all have a simple, subtle flavor that's compatible with just about anything:
zesty tomato sauce, fruity stuffing, even pungent garlic purée.
Whenever possible, these recipes use skinned poultry to minimize fat
and cholesterol. However you prepare poultry, make sure it's thoroughly
cooked by following the directions carefully.

Roast Chicken with Garden Vegetables

In Step 3, add 1 more tablespoon of oil if you don't have enough pan drippings.

- **2** tablespoons butter or margarine, softened
- **4** cloves garlic, crushed
- **1** teaspoon each dried marjoram and thyme, crumbled
- **1** whole roasting chicken (4 to 4½ pounds)
- **1** teaspoon salt
- **½** teaspoon black pepper
- **1** pound (about 8) small new potatoes, unpeeled
- **4** small carrots, peeled and cut into 3-inch lengths
- **1** package (1 pound) frozen small white onions, thawed and drained
- **2** packages (9 ounces each) frozen whole green beans, thawed
- **1** tablespoon olive or vegetable oil

Per serving:
Calories 929; Protein 78 g;
Carbohydrates 46 g;
Fat 50 g; Sodium 858 mg;
Cholesterol 243 mg

20 minutes | 2 hr. 15 min.

1 Preheat the oven to 425° F. In a small bowl, combine the butter, garlic, marjoram, and thyme. Rub the chicken inside and out first with the salt and pepper, then with the butter mixture. Tuck the wing tips behind the back and tie the legs together.

2 Place the chicken, breast side up, on a rack in a large roasting pan, and roast, uncovered, for 15 minutes. Reduce the oven temperature to 325° F. Add the potatoes and carrots to the pan, coat with the drippings, then continue roasting the chicken, uncovered, for 1 hour 30 minutes.

3 In a medium-size bowl, toss the onions and beans with the oil, then place on top of the other vegetables in the roasting pan. Roast 30 minutes more, basting frequently with the pan drippings, until the vegetables are tender and a chicken leg moves easily in the hip socket. If the chicken browns too quickly, cover with foil.

4 Transfer the chicken to a serving platter and let stand for 10 minutes. Meanwhile, cover the vegetables loosely with foil and set in the oven turned down to the keep-warm setting. Serves 4.

Braised Chicken, Moroccan Style

Braising the chicken—cooking it slowly in a small amount of
liquid over low heat—is a great way to make it more tender and flavorful.
If you don't have couscous, use quick-cooking rice. If you like your
food spicier, add ½ to 1 teaspoon hot red pepper sauce.

- 1 whole roasting chicken (3½ to 4 pounds)
- 1 teaspoon salt
- 2 tablespoons olive oil
- 1 large yellow onion, cut into large pieces
- 1½ teaspoons ground turmeric
- ¾ teaspoon each ground ginger and coriander
- 1 cinnamon stick, split lengthwise, or ½ teaspoon ground cinnamon
- ¼ teaspoon black pepper
- 3 cups water
- 1 medium-size sweet red pepper, cored, seeded, and cut into 1-inch squares
- 3 small zucchini, sliced ½ inch thick
- 4 medium-size carrots, peeled and cut into 2-inch lengths
- 1 can (1 pound 3 ounces) chick peas, drained and rinsed
- ¾ cup (5 ounces) couscous

1 Sprinkle the chicken inside and out with half of the salt. Tuck the wing tips behind the back, tie the legs together, and set aside.

2 Heat the oil in a 4-quart Dutch oven or flameproof casserole over moderate heat for 1 minute. Add the onion and sauté until soft—5 minutes. Stir in the turmeric, ginger, coriander, cinnamon stick, and black pepper, and sauté 2 minutes longer.

3 Add the chicken and turn until lightly coated with the spices. Add the water and remaining ½ teaspoon salt and bring to a boil. Reduce the heat to low, cover, and simmer for 45 minutes. Stir in the red pepper, zucchini, and carrots. Cover and simmer until the vegetables are tender and a chicken leg moves easily in the hip socket—15 to 20 minutes more.

4 Add the chick peas and simmer, uncovered, for 3 to 4 minutes or until heated through. Remove from the heat and discard the cinnamon stick. Transfer the chicken and vegetables to a plate.

5 Add the couscous to the Dutch oven, remove from the heat, cover, and let stand for 5 minutes or until the couscous is tender. (Some of the liquid will not be absorbed.) Spoon the couscous onto a serving platter and place the chicken and vegetables on top. Serves 4.

Per serving:
Calories 1,064; Protein 83 g;
Carbohydrates 83 g;
Fat 46 g; Sodium 772 mg;
Cholesterol 199 mg

20 minutes | 1 hr. 24 min.

Braised Chicken, Moroccan Style—
flavored with a delicious blend of hot
and sweet spices

Roast Chicken Stuffed with Mashed Potatoes

Although this recipe calls for carrots and Brussels sprouts, onions, potatoes, turnips, beets, and sweet peppers are all good cooked in the pan with the chicken.

For the stuffing:

- 2 pounds all-purpose potatoes, peeled, cooked, and mashed, or 3 cups prepared instant mashed potatoes
- 2 tablespoons minced parsley
- 2 tablespoons butter or margarine
- 1 clove garlic, minced
- ¼ cup low-fat milk
- ¼ teaspoon salt

For the chicken:

- 1 whole roasting chicken (5 to 5½ pounds)
- ½ teaspoon salt
- ¼ teaspoon black pepper
- 1 teaspoon dried sage, crumbled
- 8 medium-size carrots, peeled and cut into 1-inch lengths
- 1 medium-size yellow onion, thinly sliced
- 1 pint fresh or 1 package (10 ounces) frozen Brussels sprouts, thawed and drained
- 1 cup Basic Chicken Stock (page 333) or canned chicken broth

Per serving:
Calories 1,168; Protein 99 g;
Carbohydrates 70 g;
Fat 57 g; Sodium 882 mg;
Cholesterol 301 mg

 30 minutes   2 hrs.

1 *For the stuffing:* In a large bowl, combine the potatoes, parsley, butter, garlic, milk, and salt.

2 *For the chicken:* Preheat the oven to 350° F. Stuff the chicken loosely with the potato mixture and tie the legs together. Place the remaining stuffing in a greased 1-quart baking dish, cover with foil, and refrigerate.

3 Sprinkle the chicken with the salt, pepper, and sage, then place breast side up in a medium-size roasting pan. Roast, uncovered, basting occasionally, for 1 hour. Skim the excess fat from the drippings, then scatter the carrots and onion around the chicken.

4 Roast, uncovered, 15 minutes more. Add the Brussels sprouts to the pan. Set the covered dish of extra stuffing in the oven with the chicken until heated through. Roast the chicken, uncovered, 40 minutes more or until a leg moves easily in the hip socket and the vegetables are tender.

5 Transfer the chicken and vegetables to a serving platter and let stand for 10 minutes.

6 Meanwhile, add the stock to the roasting pan, set over moderate heat, and cook, scraping up any browned bits from the bottom of the the pan, for 5 minutes. Strain the juices into a gravy boat and serve at the table along with the extra stuffing. Serves 6.

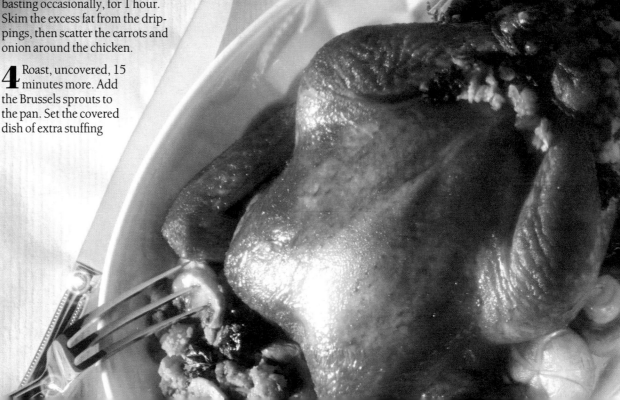

Roast Chicken with Prune and Corn Bread Stuffing

We used packaged corn bread stuffing to save time, but homemade corn bread would be even more delicious. You can make the stuffing several hours ahead and store it, covered with foil, in the refrigerator, but do not stuff the bird until you are ready to roast it.

For the stuffing:
- 1 cup pitted prunes
- ½ cup port, dry red wine, or apple juice
- 2 tablespoons olive or corn oil
- 1 large yellow onion, coarsely chopped
- 1 medium-size carrot, peeled and coarsely shredded
- 3 cloves garlic, minced
- 12 ounces mushrooms, thinly sliced
- 1 cup almonds, coarsely chopped
- 10 ounces kale or spinach, trimmed, rinsed, and coarsely shredded, or 1 package (10 ounces) frozen chopped spinach, thawed and drained
- ¼ cup (½ stick) unsalted butter or margarine
- 1½ cups Basic Chicken Stock (page 333) or canned reduced-sodium chicken broth
- 2 packages (8 ounces each) corn bread stuffing mix

For the chicken:
- 1 whole roasting chicken (about 5 pounds)
- ¼ teaspoon salt (optional)

Per serving:
Calories 1,801; Protein 118 g; Carbohydrates 131 g; Fat 90 g; Sodium 1,914 mg; Cholesterol 315 mg

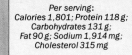

25 minutes | 1 hr. 52 min.

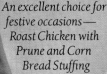

An excellent choice for festive occasions— Roast Chicken with Prune and Corn Bread Stuffing

1 *For the stuffing:* Place the prunes and port in a small bowl and set aside.

2 Heat 1 tablespoon of the oil in a 12-inch skillet over low heat for 1 minute. Add the onion, carrot, and garlic, and sauté, stirring occasionally, until softened—about 5 minutes. Add the mushrooms and sauté, stirring frequently, until tender—8 to 10 minutes.

3 Add the almonds and kale, stir to coat with the skillet drippings, then add the prunes and port, butter, and stock. Sauté until the butter has melted. Transfer to a large bowl, add the stuffing mix, and mix thoroughly.

4 *For the chicken:* Preheat the oven to 450° F. Fill the chicken cavity with ⅓ of the stuffing. Place the remaining stuffing in a lightly greased 1½-quart casserole, cover with foil, and refrigerate. Tie the chicken legs together, tuck the wing tips behind the back, sprinkle with the salt, if desired, and brush with the remaining oil. Place the chicken, breast side up, in a medium-size roasting pan.

5 Roast the chicken, uncovered, for 35 minutes, then reduce the oven temperature to 350° F and continue roasting until a leg moves easily in its socket—about 1 hour more. For the last 40 minutes, set the casserole of extra stuffing in the oven and bake along with the bird. If the chicken starts to overbrown, cover with foil. Let stand for 10 minutes before serving. Serves 4 to 6.

Rice-Stuffed Chicken with Gravy

Spinach, basil, and Parmesan cheese add great taste to roast chicken. To toast the nuts, scatter them in a pie pan or on a baking sheet and place, uncovered, in a 350° F oven for 10 minutes.

For the stuffing:

- 4 cups cooked long-grain white rice
- 2 packages (10 ounces each) frozen chopped spinach, cooked and drained well
- 2 large eggs, lightly beaten
- ½ cup minced fresh basil or flat-leaf parsley
- ½ cup pine nuts or coarsely chopped almonds or walnuts, toasted
- ½ cup grated Parmesan cheese (2 ounces)
- 2 tablespoons olive oil
- 1 teaspoon minced garlic

For the chicken:

- 1 whole roasting chicken (5 to 5½ pounds)
- 2 tablespoons olive oil
- ½ teaspoon salt
- ⅛ teaspoon black pepper
- 12 shallots or 24 fresh or frozen small white onions, partially thawed
- 6 large carrots, peeled and quartered
- 2½ cups Basic Chicken Stock (page 333) or canned chicken broth

1 *For the stuffing:* In a large bowl, mix the rice, spinach, eggs, basil, pine nuts, cheese, oil, and garlic. Set aside.

2 *For the chicken:* Preheat the oven to 350° F. Rub the chicken with the oil and sprinkle with the salt and pepper. Tuck the wing tips behind the back, then loosely stuff the chicken and tie the legs together. Spoon the remaining stuffing into a greased 1½-quart casserole, cover with foil, and refrigerate.

3 Place the chicken, breast side up, in a medium-size roasting pan and roast, uncovered, basting occasionally, for 1 hour. Skim the excess fat from the drippings, then scatter the shallots and carrots around the chicken.

4 Bake, uncovered, until the vegetables are tender and a chicken leg moves easily in the hip socket—about 45 minutes more. Meanwhile, mix 1 cup of the stock into the stuffing in the casserole, cover with foil, and bake alongside the chicken for the last 20 minutes or until heated through.

5 Transfer the chicken and vegetables to a serving platter and let stand for 10 minutes.

6 Add the remaining stock to the roasting pan. Set over moderate heat and cook, scraping up any browned bits from the bottom of the pan, for 5 minutes. Strain the juices into a gravy boat and pass at the table. Serves 6.

Portuguese Chicken—a wonderful new way to serve chicken

Per serving:
Calories 996; Protein 77 g;
Carbohydrates 56 g;
Fat 53 g; Sodium 767 mg;
Cholesterol 267 mg

30 minutes

1 hr. 50 min.

Portuguese Chicken

*This traditional recipe calls for port wine because
its sweetness contrasts nicely with the ham and olives. However, it's also
good made with all red wine, or, if you prefer, you can omit the
wine entirely and use 1½ cups chicken stock.*

2 tablespoons olive oil
1 broiler-fryer (3½ pounds), skinned and cut into 8 serving pieces
¾ cup port or Madeira
¾ cup dry red wine
⅔ cup canned crushed tomatoes
⅓ cup orange juice
1 pound small new potatoes (about 8), unpeeled and quartered
4 ounces baked or boiled ham, cut into ½-inch cubes
¼ cup thickly sliced pitted or pimiento-stuffed green olives
1 pound kale or spinach, trimmed, rinsed, then stacked and cut into strips ½ inch wide

*Per serving:
Calories 788; Protein 76 g;
Carbohydrates 40 g;
Fat 29 g; Sodium 821 mg;
Cholesterol 213 mg*

23 minutes   1 hr. 4 min.

1 Heat the oil in a deep 12-inch skillet over moderate heat for 1 minute. Add the chicken and sauté on all sides until no longer pink on the outside—about 10 minutes. Transfer the chicken to a bowl and set aside. Discard the skillet drippings.

2 Add the port and red wine to the skillet, raise the heat to high, and cook, scraping up any browned bits from the bottom, until the mixture comes to a boil. Stir in the tomatoes, orange juice, potatoes, ham, and olives, and bring to a boil again.

3 Return the chicken to the skillet, cover, reduce the heat to low, and simmer, stirring occasionally, until the chicken and potatoes are tender—about 40 minutes. Stir in the kale, cover, and cook until tender—about 10 minutes more. Serves 4.

Chicken Jambalaya

We made this classic Creole dish just spicy enough for average tastes. If you like your food very spicy, add more hot red pepper sauce and use hot sausage instead of ham.

2 tablespoons vegetable oil

1 broiler-fryer (3½ pounds), skinned and cut into 8 serving pieces

¼ teaspoon salt

¼ teaspoon black pepper

1 large yellow onion, finely chopped

2 medium-size stalks celery, thinly sliced

2 medium-size sweet green peppers, cored, seeded, and coarsely chopped

1 can (1 pound) crushed tomatoes

4 ounces baked or boiled ham, cubed (1 cup)

2 cloves garlic, minced

1 whole bay leaf

1 teaspoon paprika

½ teaspoon dried thyme, crumbled

¼ teaspoon salt

5 drops hot red pepper sauce

1 cup long-grain white rice

1 cup water

¼ cup minced parsley

Per serving:
Calories 752; Protein 76 g;
Carbohydrates 50 g;
Fat 28 g; Sodium 1,144 mg;
Cholesterol 213 mg

25 minutes | 1 hr. 5 min.

1 Heat the oil in a 6-quart flame-proof casserole or Dutch oven over moderately high heat for 1 minute. Add the chicken and brown for 6 to 7 minutes on each side. Transfer the chicken to a plate and sprinkle with the salt and black pepper. Skim off all but 2 tablespoons of the casserole drippings.

2 Add the onion to the casserole and sauté, stirring frequently, until soft—5 minutes. Add the celery and green peppers and sauté 5 minutes more.

3 Stir in the tomatoes, ham, garlic, bay leaf, paprika, thyme, salt, and red pepper sauce. Add the chicken, pushing it underneath the liquid. Cover, reduce the heat to low, and simmer for 15 minutes.

4 Stir in the rice and water, cover, and cook until the rice is tender and the chicken is no longer pink on the inside—20 to 25 minutes. If the casserole liquid reduces too much, add a little water to prevent scorching. Remove the bay leaf and sprinkle with the parsley. Serves 4.

Inspired by the renowned cuisine of New Orleans— Chicken Jambalaya

Sausage and Okra Variation

In Step 1, first brown *8 ounces sweet or hot Italian-style pork sausage, cut into ½-inch slices*, in the oil— about 10 minutes. Transfer the sausage to a plate and set aside. Brown the chicken as directed and follow Steps 2 and 3. In Step 4, cook the rice for 15 minutes, then stir in the browned sausage and *1 package (10 ounces) partially thawed frozen okra.* Cover and simmer 10 minutes more or until the rice and okra are tender. Serves 4 to 6.

Per serving: Calories 931; Protein 85 g;
Carbohydrates 55 g; Fat 42 g;
Sodium 1,863 mg; Cholesterol 249 mg

Honey and Lemon Chicken

If you use whole chicken legs, separate them first into thighs and drumsticks. For breasts, cook for only 35 to 40 minutes in Step 3.

- 1 large zucchini, halved lengthwise and sliced ½ inch thick
- 8 ounces fresh small white onions, peeled (see page 59 for an easy way to peel skins) or ½ package (8 ounces) frozen small white onions, unthawed
- 3 medium-size carrots, peeled and sliced ½ inch thick
- 3 pounds chicken parts
- ¼ cup orange juice, freshly squeezed preferred
- ¼ cup lemon juice, freshly squeezed preferred
- ¼ cup honey
- ¼ cup (½ stick) unsalted butter or margarine, melted
- 3 tablespoons Dijon mustard
- 1 large clove garlic, minced
- 1 tablespoon grated lemon rind
- 1 tablespoon minced fresh ginger (optional)
- ½ teaspoon salt
- ¼ teaspoon black pepper
- 1 cup long-grain brown, white, or wild rice

1 Preheat the oven to 400° F. Place the zucchini in a sieve, immerse in a large saucepan of boiling water for 1 minute, lift out, and set aside. Add the onions and carrots to the boiling water and cook, uncovered, for 6 minutes; drain well.

2 Place the chicken, onions, and carrots in a lightly greased medium-size baking pan and set aside. In a small bowl, combine the orange juice, lemon juice, honey, butter, mustard, garlic, lemon rind, ginger, salt, and pepper. Pour over the chicken and vegetables.

3 Cover and bake for 50 minutes, basting frequently with the juices. After 20 minutes, begin cooking the rice according to package directions. After 50 minutes, add the zucchini to the vegetables in the baking pan, cover, and bake 10 minutes longer or until the chicken is no longer pink on the inside.

4 Make a bed of rice on a large platter, arrange the chicken on top, and wreathe the vegetables around the edge. Serves 4.

> **Per serving:**
> Calories 778; Protein 58 g;
> Carbohydrates 44 g;
> Fat 43 g; Sodium 609 mg;
> Cholesterol 202 mg

20 minutes | 1 hr. 7 min.

Chicken in Red Wine Casserole

Rich and robust, this dish is based on a French favorite, coq au vin. *To reduce the fat, you can omit the bacon and remove the skin from the chicken.*

- 4 strips bacon, cut into 1-inch pieces
- 1 broiler-fryer (3 to 3½ pounds), quartered and patted dry
- ½ teaspoon salt
- ¼ teaspoon black pepper
- 2 tablespoons olive or vegetable oil
- 1 pound fresh small white onions, peeled (see page 59 for an easy way to peel skins) or 1 package (1 pound) frozen small white onions, thawed
- 8 ounces small new potatoes, unpeeled
- 8 ounces mushrooms, sliced
- 2 medium-size carrots, peeled and thickly sliced
- 1 cup dry red wine
- 1 can (1 pound 12 ounces) crushed tomatoes
- 2 cloves garlic, minced
- ½ teaspoon each dried rosemary and thyme, crumbled
- 1 whole bay leaf
- 1 package (10 ounces) frozen green peas, thawed and drained
- 2 tablespoons minced parsley

1 Cook the bacon in a 5-quart flameproof casserole over moderate heat, stirring, until crisp—about 5 minutes. Drain on paper toweling. Discard the drippings.

2 Sprinkle the chicken with the salt and pepper. Heat the oil in the casserole over moderately high heat for 1 minute. Add the chicken and brown for 6 to 7 minutes on each side. Transfer to a plate.

3 Add the onions, potatoes, mushrooms, and carrots to the casserole, and cook, uncovered, stirring occasionally, for 5 minutes. Add the wine, bring to a boil, and boil, uncovered, for 1 minute. Return the chicken to the casserole and add the tomatoes, garlic, rosemary, thyme, and bay leaf. Bring to a boil again, reduce the heat to moderately low, cover, and simmer for 45 minutes or until the potatoes are tender and the chicken is no longer pink on the inside.

4 Add the peas and the bacon, cover, and simmer 5 minutes more. Remove the bay leaf. Sprinkle the chicken with the parsley just before serving. Serves 4 to 6.

> **Per serving:**
> Calories 838; Protein 66 g;
> Carbohydrates 46 g;
> Fat 41 g; Sodium 975 mg;
> Cholesterol 176 mg

20 minutes | 1 hr. 19 min.

Basil Chicken with Tomatoes, Squash, and Barley

The ancient Greeks considered basil the royal herb, and you'll know why after just one taste of this dish.

3 pounds chicken parts, skinned
½ teaspoon salt
¼ teaspoon black pepper
3 tablespoons olive or vegetable oil
1 large yellow onion, chopped
2 cloves garlic, minced
1 small sweet green pepper, cored, seeded, and diced
½ cup dry white wine (optional)
1 can (14 ounces) stewed tomatoes with their juice
½ cup Basic Chicken Stock (page 333) or canned chicken broth
¼ teaspoon each dried basil and thyme, crumbled
1 cup medium pearl barley
1 medium-size zucchini, cut into 1-inch cubes
1 medium-size yellow squash, cut into 1-inch cubes
¼ cup minced fresh basil or parsley

Per serving:
Calories 696; Protein 64 g;
Carbohydrates 55 g;
Fat 26 g; Sodium 726 mg;
Cholesterol 169 mg

30 minutes | 52 minutes

1 Pat the chicken dry with paper toweling and sprinkle with the salt and black pepper. Heat the oil for 1 minute in a 4-quart flameproof casserole or Dutch oven over moderately high heat. Add the chicken and sauté for 5 minutes on each side. Transfer to a plate and set aside.

2 Reduce the heat to moderate. Add the onion, garlic, and green pepper to the casserole, and sauté, stirring, for 5 minutes or until slightly softened. Add the wine if desired, and boil, uncovered, for 1 minute. Return the chicken to the casserole.

3 Add the tomatoes, stock, basil, and thyme. Bring to a boil, adjust the heat so that the liquid bubbles gently, cover, and simmer for 25 minutes or until the chicken is no longer pink on the inside. Meanwhile, cook the barley according to package directions.

4 Add the zucchini and yellow squash to the casserole, cover, and cook for 5 minutes. Stir in the barley, cover, and simmer 5 minutes more. Sprinkle with the basil before serving. Serves 4 to 6.

Chicken Paprikash

German-style noodles (spaetzle) are a natural for this traditional Hungarian dish, but you can use regular noodles just as well. For the cauliflower, you can substitute frozen peas, diced carrots, or cut green beans.

2¼ pounds chicken thighs, drumsticks, or breasts
½ teaspoon salt
¼ teaspoon black pepper
2 tablespoons vegetable oil
1 large yellow onion, sliced
1 large sweet red pepper, cored, seeded, and cut into ¾-inch squares
1 tablespoon paprika
1¾ cups Basic Chicken Stock (page 333) or canned chicken broth
1 package (10½ ounces) spaetzle
1 package (10 ounces) frozen cauliflower florets, thawed and drained
1 cup sour cream or plain low-fat yogurt

Per serving:
Calories 936; Protein 67 g;
Carbohydrates 64 g;
Fat 44 g; Sodium 603 mg;
Cholesterol 213 mg

10 minutes | 51 minutes

1 Sprinkle the chicken with the salt and black pepper. Heat the oil in a 12-inch skillet over moderately high heat for 1 minute. Add the chicken and brown on each side for 6 to 7 minutes. Drain on paper toweling. Discard all but 1 tablespoon of the drippings.

2 Reduce the heat to moderate. Add the onion and red pepper to the skillet and sauté, stirring occasionally, for 6 to 8 minutes or until softened. Add the paprika and sauté, stirring occasionally, 2 minutes more or until the onion is golden.

3 Add the stock, stirring to loosen any browned bits on the bottom of the skillet. Return the chicken to the skillet and bring the mixture to a boil. Cover, reduce the heat to low, and simmer for 5 minutes.

4 Gradually stir in the spaetzle, submerging them in the liquid. Return to a boil, cover, and cook for 10 minutes. Add the cauliflower and return to a boil. Cover and cook for 5 minutes or until the cauliflower is tender. Add the sour cream, and stir for 1 to 2 minutes over low heat without boiling. Serves 4 to 6.

Chicken Fricassee Supreme

Noodles and lima beans lend distinction to this dish.

2½ pounds chicken thighs and
    drumsticks
½ teaspoon salt
¼ teaspoon black pepper
3 tablespoons vegetable oil
1 medium-size leek, chopped
1 medium-size stalk celery,
    chopped
4 ounces mushrooms, sliced
½ cup dry white wine (optional)
1½ cups Basic Chicken Stock
    (page 333) or canned chicken
    broth
1 teaspoon fresh or ½ teaspoon
    dried tarragon, crumbled
1 whole bay leaf
4 ounces wide egg noodles
2 tablespoons unsalted butter or
    margarine
1 package (10 ounces) frozen
    baby lima beans or green peas,
    thawed and drained
1½ tablespoons cornstarch
1 cup heavy cream or half-and-
    half
1 teaspoon lemon juice
2 tablespoons minced fresh
    tarragon or parsley
3 tablespoons dry bread crumbs

Per serving:
Calories 938; Protein 58 g;
Carbohydrates 49 g;
Fat 56 g; Sodium 611 mg;
Cholesterol 257 mg

 20 minutes   1 hr. 19 min.

1 Sprinkle the chicken with the salt and pepper. Heat the oil in a deep 12-inch skillet over moderately high heat for 1 minute. Add the chicken and brown over moderate heat for 5 minutes on each side; transfer the chicken to a plate.

2 Preheat the oven to 400° F. Add the leek, celery, and mushrooms to the skillet, reduce the heat to moderate, and sauté, stirring occasionally, for 5 minutes or until limp. Add the wine if you like, raise the heat to high, and boil, uncovered, for 1 minute. Add the stock, dried tarragon, and bay leaf, return the chicken to the skillet, and bring to a boil. Reduce the heat to low, cover, and simmer for 25 minutes.

Chicken Fricassee Supreme— a scrumptious version of an old favorite

3 Meanwhile, cook the noodles according to package directions and drain well. Place in a medium-size baking pan, add 1 tablespoon of the butter, and toss well; set aside.

4 Add the lima beans to the skillet, cover, and simmer for 5 minutes. Mix the cornstarch with the cream and slowly stir into the skillet. Raise the heat to moderately high and cook, stirring constantly, until thickened—3 minutes. Remove the bay leaf, stir in the lemon juice and

fresh tarragon, and spoon the chicken and vegetable mixture evenly over the noodles.

5 Sprinkle the bread crumbs on top and dot with the remaining 1 tablespoon butter. Bake, uncovered, for 25 minutes or until bubbling. Transfer to the broiler and broil 4 inches from the heat for 1 to 2 minutes or until tipped with brown. Serves 4.

Salami and ground red pepper add zip to Chicken and Mushrooms in Zesty Tomato Sauce.

Chicken and Mushrooms in Zesty Tomato Sauce

If you don't have orzo (rice-shaped pasta), use long-grain white rice and cook it for 20 minutes in Step 3.

2 tablespoons olive oil

4 chicken legs and thighs (about 4 pounds), skinned

1 medium-size yellow onion, coarsely chopped

1 clove garlic, minced

2 medium-size sweet green peppers, cored, seeded, and thinly sliced

10 ounces mushrooms, halved (quartered if large)

1 can (1 pound) tomato sauce

½ teaspoon salt

¼ teaspoon ground red pepper (cayenne)

6 thin slices hard salami, cut into matchstick strips

1 cup orzo or pastina

2½ cups water

¼ cup minced parsley

Per serving:
Calories 955; Protein 88 g;
Carbohydrates 54 g;
Fat 41 g; Sodium 1,564 mg;
Cholesterol 289 mg

 25 minutes

 1 hour

1 Heat the oil in a 6-quart flame-proof casserole or Dutch oven over moderately high heat for 1 minute. Add the chicken and brown for 6 to 7 minutes on each side. Transfer the chicken to a plate.

2 Add the onion, garlic, green peppers, and mushrooms to the casserole, and sauté, stirring frequently, for 10 minutes. Stir in the tomato sauce, salt, and red pepper, then add the browned chicken. Spoon the sauce over the chicken and sprinkle with the salami. Cover, reduce the heat to low, and simmer for 20 minutes.

3 Stir in the orzo and water. Cover and simmer, stirring occasionally, until the orzo is tender and the chicken is no longer pink on the inside—15 minutes more. Sprinkle with the parsley. Serves 4.

Chicken Cacciatore

Watercress makes this popular Italian dish taste better than ever.

- 2 tablespoons olive oil
- 2 pounds whole chicken legs (thighs and drumsticks)
- ½ teaspoon salt
- ¼ teaspoon black pepper
- 1 large yellow onion, finely chopped
- 4 ounces small mushrooms, halved
- 2 cloves garlic, minced
- 1 can (1 pound) tomatoes with their juice, quartered
- ½ cup tomato sauce
- ¾ cup dry white wine, Basic Chicken Stock (page 333), or canned chicken broth
- ¾ teaspoon dried tarragon, crumbled
- 2 cups peeled and cubed butternut squash or yellow squash
- 3 ounces medium-wide egg noodles
- 1 medium-size bunch watercress, rinsed

Per serving:
Calories 536; Protein 46 g;
Carbohydrates 38 g;
Fat 23 g; Sodium 783 mg;
Cholesterol 139 mg

15 minutes | 55 minutes

1 Heat the oil in a deep 12-inch skillet over moderately high heat for 1 minute. Add the chicken, sprinkle with half the salt and pepper, and sauté for 6 to 7 minutes on each side or until golden brown. Drain on paper toweling. Discard all but 1 tablespoon of the drippings.

2 Reduce the heat to moderate. Add the onion and sauté, stirring occasionally, for 5 minutes or until limp. Add the mushrooms and garlic and sauté, stirring occasionally, 3 minutes more.

3 Add the tomatoes, tomato sauce, wine, tarragon, and remaining salt and pepper. Return the chicken to the skillet, bring the mixture to a boil, and reduce the heat to low. Cover and simmer for 15 minutes.

4 Add the squash, cover, and simmer for 5 minutes. Stir in the noodles, submerging them in the liquid, and return to a boil. Adjust the heat so that the liquid bubbles gently, cover, and simmer for 5 minutes or until the chicken, vegetables, and noodles are tender.

5 Meanwhile, remove about 2 inches of stems from the watercress. Lay the watercress on top of the skillet mixture, cover, and heat until the watercress is slightly wilted—about 5 minutes. Serves 4.

Grandma's Best Chicken and Onion Casserole

A hearty home-style dish. If you prefer to use fresh onions, see page 59 for an easy way to remove their skins.

- 2 whole skinned and boned chicken breasts (about 1¼ pounds), halved
- ¼ cup all-purpose flour
- ½ teaspoon salt
- ¼ teaspoon black pepper
- ¼ cup vegetable oil
- 8 ounces frozen small white onions (2 cups), thawed and drained
- 4 ounces mushrooms, quartered
- 1¼ cups Basic Chicken Stock (page 333) or canned chicken broth
- 1 clove garlic, minced
- 2 teaspoons tomato paste
- ¼ teaspoon each dried rosemary, crumbled, and fennel seeds, crushed
- 4 ounces thick-sliced bacon, cut into 1½-inch pieces
- 1 pound baking potatoes, peeled, cut into 1-inch cubes, and patted dry
- 1 package (10 ounces) frozen cut asparagus or broccoli florets, thawed and drained
- 2 tablespoons minced parsley

Per serving:
Calories 612; Protein 49 g;
Carbohydrates 41 g;
Fat 29 g; Sodium 870 mg;
Cholesterol 103 mg

20 minutes | 46 minutes

1 Dredge the chicken in the flour, shaking off any excess, and sprinkle with the salt and pepper. Heat 2 tablespoons of the oil in a 4-quart Dutch oven over moderately high heat for 1 minute. Add the chicken and brown for 4 minutes on each side. Transfer to a plate.

2 Add the onions and mushrooms to the Dutch oven and cook, stirring occasionally, over moderate heat for 5 to 7 minutes or until the onions are golden. Add the stock, garlic, tomato paste, rosemary, and fennel seeds, then return the chicken to the Dutch oven. Cover and simmer for 15 minutes.

3 Meanwhile, cook the bacon in a 10-inch skillet over moderate heat until crisp—about 5 minutes. Drain on paper toweling and discard the pan drippings. Add the remaining oil to the skillet and heat over moderate heat for 1 minute. Add the potatoes and brown, turning occasionally, for 10 to 12 minutes. Transfer to a plate.

4 Add the asparagus to the Dutch oven, cover, and simmer for 3 minutes or until barely tender. Add the potatoes and bacon, cover, and cook for 5 minutes or until the chicken and vegetables are tender. Before serving, sprinkle with the parsley. Serves 4.

Chicken Breasts Catalan

This recipe was inspired by the cooking of Catalonia—a region noted for its blend of French and Spanish cuisine.

- 3 whole skinned and boned chicken breasts (about 2 pounds), halved
- 1 teaspoon salt
- ¼ teaspoon black pepper
- 2 tablespoons olive oil
- 1 large yellow onion, sliced ¼ inch thick
- 1 medium-size sweet red pepper, cored, seeded, and cut into strips ½ inch wide
- 3 cloves garlic, minced
- 1 can (1 pound) tomatoes with their juice, quartered
- 1 cup Basic Chicken Stock (page 333) or canned chicken broth
- 1 whole bay leaf
- 1 teaspoon dried basil, crumbled
- ¾ cup long-grain white rice
- 1 package (10 ounces) frozen green peas, unthawed
- ¾ cup pitted small black olives

1 Sprinkle the chicken with half of the salt and black pepper. Heat the oil in a deep 12-inch skillet over moderately high heat for 1 minute. Add the chicken and brown for 3 minutes on each side. Drain on paper toweling.

2 Reduce the heat to moderate. Add the onion and red pepper to the skillet and sauté, stirring occasionally, for 3 minutes. Add the garlic and sauté, stirring occasionally, for 2 minutes or until the onion is limp.

3 Add the tomatoes, stock, bay leaf, basil, and remaining salt and black pepper to the skillet. Bring the mixture to a boil, stir in the rice, then reduce the heat to low. Cover and simmer for 10 minutes.

4 Add the chicken, cover, and cook 10 minutes more. Add the peas and return to a boil. Reduce the heat to low, cover and simmer for 5 to 10 minutes or until the chicken is no longer pink on the inside and the vegetables are tender. Stir in the olives and heat until bubbling—1 to 2 minutes more. Remove the bay leaf. Serves 4.

> **Per serving:**
> *Calories 550; Protein 62 g;*
> *Carbohydrates 48 g;*
> *Fat 12 g; Sodium 1,032 mg;*
> *Cholesterol 131 mg*

| 15 minutes | 49 minutes |

Chicken and Cabbage in Mustard Sauce

The sharp flavor of Dijon mustard and the tart taste of a Granny Smith apple make a surprisingly good combination.

- 1 tablespoon unsalted butter or margarine
- 1 tablespoon olive oil
- 2 whole skinned and boned chicken breasts (about 1¼ pounds), halved
- ½ teaspoon salt
- ¼ teaspoon black pepper
- 1 medium-size yellow onion, thinly sliced
- 1 small head cabbage, coarsely shredded
- 1 teaspoon caraway seeds
- 3 cups Basic Chicken Stock (page 333) or canned chicken broth
- 1 medium-size Granny Smith apple, peeled, cored, and sliced ¼ inch thick
- ⅔ cup orzo (rice-shaped pasta) or other small pasta
- ½ cup sour cream or plain low-fat yogurt
- ½ cup milk blended with 2 teaspoons cornstarch
- 2 to 3 tablespoons Dijon mustard
- 2 tablespoons snipped fresh dill or ½ teaspoon dill weed

1 Heat the butter and oil in a 4-quart Dutch oven over moderate heat for 1 minute. Sprinkle the chicken breasts on both sides with the salt and pepper, add to the Dutch oven, and sauté for 2 minutes on each side. Transfer to a plate.

2 Add the onion to the Dutch oven and sauté, stirring, for 5 minutes or until soft. Add the cabbage and caraway seeds, cover, and cook, stirring occasionally, for 5 minutes. Add the stock, cover, and cook 5 minutes more. Stir in the apple and orzo, cover, and cook another 5 minutes.

3 Mix in the sour cream, milk mixture, and mustard to taste, and cook, stirring constantly, until slightly thickened—about 2 minutes. Return the chicken to the Dutch oven, cover, reduce the heat to low, and cook without boiling for 8 to 10 minutes or until no longer pink on the inside. Sprinkle with the dill before serving. Serves 4.

> **Per serving:**
> *Calories 484; Protein 44 g;*
> *Carbohydrates 37 g;*
> *Fat 17 g; Sodium 767 mg;*
> *Cholesterol 107 mg*

| 15 minutes | 37 minutes |

Stuffed Chicken Rolls in Tomato Sauce

Try this recipe when you want something special. If need be, you can make it a day ahead; before serving, bring to a simmer over moderately low heat for 10 minutes or until heated through.

⅓ cup olive oil

1 medium-size yellow onion, finely chopped

6 ounces mushrooms, finely chopped

4 ounces smoked ham or prosciutto, finely chopped

2 packages (10 ounces each) frozen chopped spinach, thawed and drained

2 cloves garlic, minced

1 cup cooked long-grain white rice or soft bread crumbs

⅓ cup grated Parmesan cheese

½ teaspoon salt

¼ teaspoon black pepper

4 whole skinned and boned chicken breasts (about 2½ pounds), halved and pounded ¼ inch thick

½ cup all-purpose flour

2 jars (1 pound 10 ounces each) marinara sauce

1 package (1 pound) frozen small white onions, thawed and drained

1½ cups Basic Chicken Stock (page 333) or canned chicken broth

1 Heat 3 tablespoons of the oil in a 12-inch nonstick skillet over moderate heat for 1 minute. Add the yellow onion and mushrooms and sauté, stirring, for 3 minutes. Add the ham and half of the spinach and cook, stirring, 3 minutes more. Transfer to a bowl and add the garlic, rice, cheese, salt, and pepper.

2 Spoon ⅛ of the stuffing onto the center of each piece of chicken, leaving a ½-inch border all around, and roll up. Tie the ends of each roll with string.

3 Dredge the chicken rolls in the flour, shaking off any excess. Heat the remaining oil in a 3-quart flameproof casserole over moderate heat for 1 minute. Add the chicken rolls and brown on all sides — about 5 minutes.

4 Add the marinara sauce, white onions, remaining spinach, and stock. Bring the liquid to a boil, adjust the heat so that the mixture bubbles gently, cover, and simmer for 30 minutes. Transfer the chicken rolls to a platter, remove the strings, and spoon the sauce on top. Serves 6 to 8.

Per serving: Calories 675; Protein 62 g; Carbohydrates 52 g; Fat 27 g; Sodium 2,382 mg; Cholesterol 125 mg
35 minutes	44 minutes

Chicken Breasts Catalan — a meal that echoes its rich European heritage

Chicken and Corn Bread Skillet

This recipe calls for dark meat because it's more flavorful and stays moist.
If you prefer white meat, cook it for only 3 minutes in Step 3 before checking for doneness.

1 pound skinned and boned chicken thighs, cut into 1-inch cubes
½ teaspoon salt
⅛ teaspoon black pepper
¼ cup unsifted all-purpose flour
¼ cup olive oil
1 medium-size yellow onion, finely chopped
3 cloves garlic, minced
1 small carrot, peeled, halved lengthwise, and thinly sliced
2 cups chopped canned tomatoes with their juice
2 medium-size stalks celery, coarsely chopped
1¼ teaspoons grated orange rind
1 whole bay leaf
⅔ cup frozen green peas, thawed and drained

For the corn bread:
¾ cup yellow cornmeal
¼ cup unsifted all-purpose flour
2 teaspoons sugar
1½ teaspoons baking powder
½ teaspoon salt
¼ teaspoon baking soda
½ cup buttermilk
1 large egg, lightly beaten
2 tablespoons melted butter or vegetable oil

1 Preheat the oven to 400° F. Sprinkle the chicken with the salt and pepper, then dredge in the flour, shaking off any excess. Heat 2½ tablespoons of the oil in a 10-inch ovenproof skillet over moderately high heat for 1 minute. Add the chicken and sauté, stirring occasionally, until no longer pink on the outside—about 5 minutes. Transfer to a large plate.

2 Add the remaining oil, the onion, and garlic to the skillet. Sauté over moderate heat, stirring occasionally, until soft—about 5 minutes. Add the carrot and sauté until soft—about 5 minutes. Stir in the tomatoes, celery, orange rind, and bay leaf. Cook, uncovered, until slightly thickened—about 7 minutes more.

3 If desired, remove ¼ cup of the sauce from the skillet and set aside for garnishing. Return the chicken to the skillet and cook, uncovered, for 4 to 5 minutes or until no longer pink on the inside. Remove the skillet from the heat and discard the bay leaf. Stir in the peas.

4 *For the corn bread:* In a medium-size bowl, combine the cornmeal, flour, sugar, baking powder, salt, and soda. In another bowl, whisk together the buttermilk, egg, and butter. Form a well in the center of the dry ingredients and stir in the liquid mixture until just combined—the batter should be lumpy.

5 Spoon the batter on top of the chicken, leaving a slight border. Transfer the skillet to the oven and bake, uncovered, for 15 minutes or until the corn bread is lightly browned. If using the sauce as garnish, drizzle it over the corn bread during the last minute of cooking. Serves 4.

Tex-Mex Variation

Follow Step 1 as directed. In Step 2, after sautéing the carrot, add *3 tablespoons minced fresh coriander (cilantro)* or *½ teaspoon each ground coriander* and *ground cumin*, plus ⅛ *teaspoon ground red pepper (cayenne)*. Proceed as directed, omitting the orange rind. (If you prefer a hot sauce, add *1 finely chopped, cored, and seeded jalapeño pepper*; wash your hands thoroughly after handling.) In Step 4, add *½ cup shredded Monterey Jack cheese* to the dry ingredients. After stirring in the liquid ingredients, add *½ cup chopped, cored, and seeded sweet red pepper* and *1 can (4 ounces) chopped mild green chilies*, drained. Follow Step 5 as directed. Serves 4.

Per serving: Calories 712; Protein 39 g; Carbohydrates 51 g; Fat 40 g; Sodium 1,331 mg; Cholesterol 150 mg

Per serving:
Calories 595; Protein 31 g;
Carbohydrates 48 g;
Fat 31 g; Sodium 1,131 mg;
Cholesterol 150 mg

25 minutes | 43 minutes

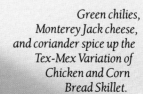

Green chilies, Monterey Jack cheese, and coriander spice up the Tex-Mex Variation of Chicken and Corn Bread Skillet.

Easiest Ever Chicken 'n' Dumplings

If these dumplings are to be fluffy, cook them covered—no peeking!

2 tablespoons unsalted butter or margarine
1 large yellow onion, coarsely chopped
3 cloves garlic, minced
1 pound skinned and boned chicken thighs, cut into pieces 1½ inches wide
½ teaspoon each dried marjoram and sage, crumbled
¼ teaspoon salt
⅛ teaspoon black pepper
1 cup Basic Chicken Stock (page 333) or canned reduced-sodium chicken broth
1 package (10 ounces) frozen mixed vegetables, thawed and drained

For the dumplings:

3 tablespoons minced parsley
1½ cups unsifted self-rising flour
3 tablespoons vegetable shortening
⅔ cup buttermilk

Per serving:
Calories 561; Protein 32 g;
Carbohydrates 50 g;
Fat 26 g; Sodium 849 mg;
Cholesterol 97 mg

25 minutes

23 minutes

1 Melt the butter in a 4-quart Dutch oven or flameproof casserole over moderate heat. Add the onion and garlic and sauté, stirring occasionally, until soft—about 5 minutes. Stir in the chicken and sauté until no longer pink on the outside—5 minutes more. Stir in the marjoram, sage, salt, pepper, stock, and vegetables, and keep over moderate heat while you make the dumplings.

2 *For the dumplings:* In a medium-size bowl, mix the parsley with the flour. Cut in the shortening with a pastry blender or 2 knives until the mixture resembles coarse meal. Stir in the buttermilk until the dough just holds together and is soft but firm; if too stiff, mix in 1 to 2 tablespoons more buttermilk.

3 Bring the mixture in the Dutch oven to a boil, uncovered, over moderate heat. Drop rounded tablespoons of the dumpling dough on top without letting them touch. Reduce the heat to low, cover, and simmer for 12 minutes without removing the lid. Serves 4.

Fiesta Chicken

The secret ingredient in this Mexican dish is the chocolate in the sauce. For parties, serve with bowls of sour cream, sliced avocado, and canned black beans (drain and rinse them first to remove excess sodium).

- 2 tablespoons olive oil
- 4 cloves garlic, thinly sliced
- 1¼ pounds skinned and boned chicken thighs or breasts, cut into pieces 1½ inches wide
- ¼ teaspoon salt
- 1 teaspoon chili powder
- 1 can (14½ ounces) stewed tomatoes with their juice
- 1 package (10 ounces) frozen green beans, thawed and drained
- 1 can (4 ounces) green chilies, drained and chopped (wash your hands after handling the chilies)
- 2 squares (1 ounce each) semisweet chocolate, coarsely chopped
- ½ teaspoon ground cinnamon
- 3 tablespoons minced fresh coriander (cilantro) or 3 tablespoons minced parsley plus 1½ teaspoons ground coriander
- 1 tablespoon lime juice
- ⅓ cup pumpkin seeds (optional)
- 8 flour tortillas, 7½ to 8 inches in diameter
  Fresh coriander (cilantro) or flat-leaf parsley sprigs (optional garnish)

1 Heat the oil in a 5-quart Dutch oven or flameproof casserole over moderate heat for 1 minute. Add the garlic and sauté, stirring frequently, for 2 minutes. Add the chicken and salt and sauté until the chicken is no longer pink on the outside— about 5 minutes.

2 Stir in the chili powder and cook for 1 minute. Add the tomatoes, breaking them up with a spoon, and the beans, chilies, chocolate, cinnamon, and coriander. Bring to a boil, reduce the heat to low, cover, and simmer until the sauce has thickened and the chicken is no longer pink on the inside— 15 minutes for dark meat, 10 minutes for light.

3 Stir in the lime juice and sprinkle the pumpkin seeds on top if desired. Serve with the tortillas and garnish, if you like, with the coriander sprigs. Serves 4.

Per serving:
Calories 595; Protein 35 g;
Carbohydrates 57 g;
Fat 27 g; Sodium 496 mg;
Cholesterol 96 mg

| 20 minutes | 26 minutes |

Chicken Risotto with Spring Vegetables

Our easy version of this Italian rice dish does not have to be stirred constantly, as the traditional recipe does. For a succulent shellfish variation, substitute 1 pound of shelled and deveined shrimp for the chicken and sauté it just 2 minutes in Step 1, then proceed as directed.

- 2 tablespoons butter or margarine
- 2 tablespoons olive oil
- 1 pound skinned and boned chicken breasts, cut into 1-inch cubes
- ½ teaspoon salt
- ¼ teaspoon black pepper
- 1 medium-size yellow onion, finely chopped
- 1½ cups long-grain white rice
- 3 cups Basic Chicken Stock (page 333) or 2 cups canned chicken broth mixed with 1 cup water
- 1 cup fresh or ½ package (5 ounces) frozen cauliflower florets, thawed
- 2 medium-size carrots, peeled and diced
- 1 large stalk celery, diced
- 1 cup drained canned tomatoes, diced
- 4 ounces asparagus or green beans, cut into ½-inch lengths, or ½ package (5 ounces) frozen cut asparagus or green beans, thawed and drained
- ½ cup grated Parmesan cheese (2 ounces)
- 2 tablespoons minced fresh basil or flat-leaf parsley

1 Heat the butter and oil in a deep 12-inch skillet (not iron) over moderate heat. Add the chicken and sauté, stirring frequently, until no longer pink on the outside— 5 minutes. Sprinkle with half of the salt and pepper. With a slotted spoon, transfer the chicken to a plate and set aside.

2 Add the onion to the skillet and sauté, stirring frequently, until limp— 5 minutes. Stir in the rice, then add the stock and remaining salt and pepper. Cover and bring to a boil, reduce the heat to low, and simmer for 10 minutes.

3 Stir in the cauliflower, carrots, and celery, cover, and simmer for 5 minutes. Return the chicken to the skillet and stir in the tomatoes and asparagus. Cover and simmer until the rice and vegetables are tender— 5 minutes more. Remove from the heat, then stir in the cheese and basil. Serves 4.

Per serving:
Calories 614; Protein 42 g;
Carbohydrates 69 g;
Fat 18 g; Sodium 950 mg;
Cholesterol 91 mg

| 25 minutes | 33 minutes |

Gingered Chicken and Broccoli Stir-Fry

This versatile recipe also works well with an equal amount of beef, pork, or lamb.

- ¼ cup reduced-sodium soy sauce
- 1 tablespoon dry sherry
- 2 teaspoons cornstarch
- 1 pound skinned and boned chicken breasts, cut crosswise into strips ¼ inch wide
- 3 tablespoons vegetable oil
- 2 pieces fresh ginger, each 1-inch long, peeled and cut into matchstick strips
- 2 cloves garlic, crushed
- 2 cups fresh or 1 package (10 ounces) frozen broccoli florets, thawed and drained
- 1 large sweet red pepper, cored, seeded, and cut into strips ¼ inch wide
- 2 cups water
- 1 cup small pasta, such as bow ties or orzo, or quick-cooking white rice
- ¼ cup pine nuts or slivered almonds

1 In a medium-size bowl, blend the soy sauce, sherry, and cornstarch. Stir in the chicken, turning to coat evenly, and set aside.

2 Heat 1 tablespoon of the oil for 1 minute in a deep 12-inch skillet or wok over moderately high heat. Add the ginger and stir-fry for 1 to 2 minutes or until lightly golden; drain on paper toweling. Add the garlic to the skillet and stir-fry for 1 to 2 minutes or until lightly golden. Using a slotted spoon, remove and discard.

3 Add another tablespoon of the oil to the skillet and heat for 1 minute. Add the broccoli and stir-fry for 3 to 4 minutes or until bright green. Add the red pepper and stir-fry for 2 to 3 minutes or until crisp-tender. Using a slotted spoon, transfer the vegetables to a medium-size bowl and set aside.

4 Heat the remaining oil in the skillet for 1 minute, add the chicken mixture, and stir-fry for 3 minutes or until the chicken is no longer pink. Transfer to the bowl with the vegetables.

5 Slowly add the water to the skillet, bring to a boil, and add the pasta. Reduce the heat to moderate and cook, uncovered, for 10 minutes or until the liquid is absorbed, stirring occasionally. Return the chicken and vegetables to the skillet, add the pine nuts, and heat through for 3 to 5 minutes. Sprinkle with the reserved ginger. Serves 4.

Per serving:
Calories 468; Protein 34 g;
Carbohydrates 46 g;
Fat 16 g; Sodium 773 mg;
Cholesterol 66 mg

30 minutes   34 minutes

It's easy to make an authentic Chinese dinner in your home with Gingered Chicken and Broccoli Stir-Fry.

Chicken and Walnut Stir-Fry

Crunchy and colorful. Although this recipe uses asparagus, you may want to try either 1 pound of sliced zucchini or 2 cups of broccoli florets.

1 large egg white
1 tablespoon dry sherry or port
1 teaspoon cornstarch
½ teaspoon salt
⅛ teaspoon black pepper
1 pound skinned and boned chicken breasts, cut crosswise into strips ¼ inch wide
2 tablespoons vegetable oil
1 tablespoon minced fresh ginger
1 clove garlic, minced
4 scallions, including tops, cut into ½-inch lengths
4 medium-size carrots, peeled and cut into matchstick strips
1½ cups long-grain white rice
3 cups Basic Chicken Stock (page 333) or canned chicken broth
2 tablespoons reduced-sodium soy sauce
1 pound asparagus, cut into 1-inch lengths, or 1 package (10 ounces) frozen cut asparagus, thawed and drained
½ cup walnuts, toasted (page 86)

1 In a medium-size bowl, beat the egg white, sherry, cornstarch, salt, and black pepper until smooth. Add the chicken and stir to coat.

2 Heat the oil in a deep 12-inch skillet over moderate heat for 1 minute. Add the ginger and garlic and stir-fry for 30 seconds. Add the chicken and stir-fry until no longer pink on the outside—about 5 minutes. Using a slotted spoon, transfer the chicken to a plate and set aside.

3 Add the scallions, carrots, rice, stock, and soy sauce to the skillet. Cover, reduce the heat to low, and simmer for 10 minutes.

4 Return the chicken to the skillet, add the asparagus, cover, and simmer until the rice is tender and the chicken is no longer pink on the inside—10 minutes more. Sprinkle the walnuts on top. Serves 4.

Per serving:
Calories 629; Protein 42 g;
Carbohydrates 74 g;
Fat 18 g; Sodium 784 mg;
Cholesterol 66 mg

| 25 minutes | 27 minutes |

Serve Curried Chicken and Rice with your favorite sweet or spicy chutney.

Curried Chicken and Rice

If you like more fire in your curry, add another 2 teaspoons of curry powder. You can substitute turkey breast for the chicken or you can make Curried Shrimp and Rice by cooking 1¼ pounds of shelled and deveined shrimp for 2 minutes in Step 1 and 5 minutes in Step 3.

2 tablespoons butter or margarine

1¼ pounds skinned and boned chicken breasts, cut into strips ½ inch wide

½ teaspoon salt

⅛ teaspoon black pepper

1 large yellow onion, coarsely chopped

2 cloves garlic, minced

2 teaspoons curry powder

¾ teaspoon ground cinnamon

⅛ teaspoon ground cloves

1 cup long-grain white rice

2 cups Basic Chicken Stock (page 333) or canned chicken broth

1 cup drained canned tomatoes, coarsely chopped

2 cups fresh or 1 package (10 ounces) frozen cauliflower florets, unthawed

½ cup raisins

1 cup frozen green peas, unthawed

½ cup plain low-fat yogurt or sour cream

1 Melt the butter in a 12-inch skillet over moderate heat. Add the chicken and sauté until no longer pink on the outside — 5 minutes. With a slotted spoon, transfer the chicken to a plate and sprinkle with the salt and pepper.

2 Add the onion and garlic to the skillet and sauté until soft — about 5 minutes. Add the curry powder, cinnamon, and cloves, and sauté, stirring, 2 minutes more. Stir in the rice, stock, tomatoes, cauliflower, and raisins. Cover, reduce the heat to low, and simmer for 15 minutes.

3 Return the chicken to the skillet, add the peas, cover, and simmer for 10 minutes. Remove from the heat and stir in the yogurt. Serves 4.

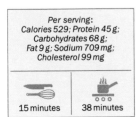

Per serving:
Calories 529; Protein 45 g;
Carbohydrates 68 g;
Fat 9 g; Sodium 709 mg;
Cholesterol 99 mg

15 minutes   38 minutes

Chicken and Eggplant Parmigiana

Instead of cutlets, this recipe calls for ground chicken, which saves both time and money. Serve it with a crunchy Italian bread.

1 medium-size eggplant, peeled and sliced ¼ inch thick

3 tablespoons olive oil

1 large yellow onion, finely chopped

1 clove garlic, minced

1 pound ground chicken

1 can (14 ounces) Italian-style plum tomatoes with their juice, halved

3 tablespoons tomato paste

¾ teaspoon dried basil, crumbled

½ teaspoon dried oregano, crumbled

½ teaspoon salt

⅛ teaspoon black pepper

3 tablespoons pastina

½ cup grated Parmesan cheese (2 ounces)

1 cup shredded part-skim mozzarella cheese (4 ounces)

Per serving:
Calories 429; Protein 35 g;
Carbohydrates 20 g;
Fat 24 g; Sodium 955 mg;
Cholesterol 82 mg

17 minutes   1 hr. 9 min.

1 Preheat the oven to 350° F. Grease a large baking sheet. Lightly brush both sides of the eggplant slices with the oil, using half the total amount. Place them on the baking sheet, overlapping slightly if necessary, and bake, uncovered, for 5 minutes. Transfer to a plate.

2 Meanwhile, heat the remaining 1½ tablespoons oil in a 10-inch skillet over moderate heat for 1 minute. Add the onion and garlic and sauté, stirring occasionally, for 3 minutes or until slightly softened.

3 Add the chicken and sauté, stirring, for 10 minutes or until no longer pink. Stir in the tomatoes, tomato paste, basil, oregano, salt, and pepper. Bring to a boil and cook, uncovered, for 5 minutes.

4 Spoon a thin layer of the chicken mixture into an ungreased 11″ x 7″ x 2″ baking dish. Sprinkle with 1 tablespoon of the pastina, top with ⅓ of the eggplant, and sprinkle with ⅓ each of the Parmesan and mozzarella cheeses. Repeat the layering twice, ending with the mozzarella. Bake, uncovered, for 45 minutes or until bubbling. Serves 4.

101

Turkey Breast with Roast Garlic Purée

Whether you use a conventional oven or a microwave (we give instructions for both), the garlic purée is easy to make. You can also use it to spice up roast chicken or double the amount and dress up a roast turkey.

For the garlic purée:

- 1 **large whole head garlic, unpeeled**
- ⅓ **cup firmly packed fresh basil or flat-leaf parsley leaves**
- 1 **tablespoon olive oil**
- 1 **teaspoon lemon juice**

For the turkey breast:

- 1¾ **pounds boneless whole turkey breast**
- 12 **ounces sweet Italian sausage, casings removed and crumbled**
- 10 **ounces spinach, rinsed, dried, and torn into bite-size pieces, or 1 package (10 ounces) frozen chopped spinach, thawed and drained well**
- 3 **tablespoons unsalted butter or margarine**
- 1 **cup Basic Chicken Stock (page 333) or canned chicken broth**
- 1¼ **teaspoons poultry seasoning**
- 12 **slices white bread, toasted and cut into 1-inch cubes, or 6 cups cubed corn bread**
- 2 **teaspoons olive oil**
- ¼ **teaspoon salt**
- 2 **large yellow onions, quartered**
- 1 **pint cherry tomatoes**

Per serving:
Calories 906; Protein 55 g;
Carbohydrates 55 g;
Fat 53 g; Sodium 1,824 mg;
Cholesterol 172 mg

25 minutes	1 hr. 28 min.

1 *For the garlic purée:* To microwave, place the garlic head in a 1-quart microwave-safe dish, cover with ¼ cup water, then cover the dish with microwave-safe plastic wrap. Microwave at full power until the garlic is soft—4½ to 5 minutes. To bake, preheat the oven to 400° F. Wrap the garlic head in foil and bake for 40 minutes or until the packet feels soft when squeezed.

2 Preheat the oven (or reduce the oven temperature) to 375°F. When cool enough to handle, remove the plastic wrap or foil from the garlic and cut ½ inch off the tip (not the root end). With your fingers, squeeze the garlic pulp out of the skin into a food processor or an electric blender; discard the skin. Add the basil, oil, and lemon juice, and whirl to make a paste—about 30 seconds.

3 *For the turkey breast:* Carefully loosen the turkey skin with your fingers and stuff the garlic purée between the skin and the breast meat; set aside.

4 In a 12-inch skillet over moderate heat, cook the sausage, stirring occasionally, until no longer pink—about 4 minutes. Add the spinach, butter, stock, and poultry seasoning, mix well, and cook, uncovered, 4 minutes more or until the butter has melted. Transfer to a large bowl, add the bread cubes, and toss to mix.

5 Place ⅔ of the stuffing in a lightly greased 1½-quart casserole and cover with foil. Place the remaining stuffing in the bottom of a lightly greased medium-size roasting pan. Place the turkey on top, skin side up, brush with the oil, and sprinkle with the salt. Scatter the onions around the turkey, cover the pan with foil, and roast 40 minutes.

6 Reduce the oven temperature to 350° F. Uncover the turkey, place the casserole of extra stuffing in the oven, and continue roasting the turkey 35 to 40 minutes longer or until the juices run yellow, not pink. Add the tomatoes to the pan for the last 10 minutes of cooking. Serves 4 to 6.

Turkey Cassoulet

The classic French cassoulet is an all-day affair made with goose, lamb, sausage, and smoked pork. Our streamlined version, which uses turkey and canned beans, has the same hearty flavor as the original but can be prepared in much less time.

1 pound kielbasa, sliced ½ inch thick

2 tablespoons olive oil

6 turkey drumsticks (about 4¼ pounds), skinned

1 large yellow onion, finely chopped

1 garlic clove, minced

1 can (1 pound) crushed tomatoes

6 large carrots, peeled and coarsely chopped

3 medium-size stalks celery, coarsely chopped

½ teaspoon salt

¼ teaspoon black pepper

2 cans (1 pound each) cannellini (white kidney beans) with their liquid

1 cup Basic Chicken Stock (page 333) or canned chicken broth

½ cup fine dry bread crumbs

1 Preheat the oven to 350° F. Lightly brown the kielbasa on all sides in a 6-quart flameproof casserole or Dutch oven over moderate heat—about 5 minutes. Transfer to a platter and discard the drippings.

2 Add the olive oil to the casserole and heat over moderately high heat for 1 minute . Working in 2 batches, add the turkey and sauté for 12 to 15 minutes per batch, turning the drumsticks so that they brown on all sides. Transfer the turkey to the platter with the kielbasa.

3 Add the onion and garlic to the casserole and sauté, stirring frequently, until soft—5 minutes. Add the tomatoes, carrots, celery, salt, and pepper, and simmer, uncovered, for 10 minutes. Stir in the beans and stock, return the turkey and sausage to the casserole, and bring to a simmer.

4 Transfer the casserole to the oven, cover, and bake for 45 minutes. Sprinkle with the bread crumbs and bake, uncovered, 15 minutes more or until the top is crusty and the turkey is no longer pink on the inside. Serves 6.

Per serving:
Calories 925; Protein 87 g;
Carbohydrates 44 g;
Fat 43 g; Sodium 1,571 mg;
Cholesterol 242 mg

25 minutes	1 hr. 53 min.

Turkey Cassoulet guarantees a drumstick for everyone.

Turkey Cutlet Skillet Dinner

This dish is also delicious made with pork, veal, or chicken cutlets.

- 1 cup long-grain white or brown rice
- ⅓ cup all-purpose flour
- ½ teaspoon each salt and dried marjoram, crumbled
- ⅛ teaspoon black pepper
- 1¼ pounds turkey cutlets
- 3 tablespoons olive oil
- 1 large sweet red pepper, cored, seeded, and cut into 1-inch squares
- 1 medium-size zucchini, halved lengthwise and sliced ¼ inch thick
- 8 ounces mushrooms, thinly sliced
- ¾ cup dry red wine
- 1 cup Basic Chicken Stock (page 333) or canned chicken broth

Per serving:
Calories 488; Protein 26 g;
Carbohydrates 50 g;
Fat 17 g; Sodium 413 mg;
Cholesterol 55 mg

10 minutes	26 minutes

1 Cook the rice according to package directions. Meanwhile, on a sheet of wax paper, combine the flour, salt, marjoram, and black pepper. Dredge the cutlets in the flour mixture, shaking off any excess.

2 Heat the oil in a 12-inch skillet over moderately high heat for 1 minute. Add the cutlets and sauté until golden brown and cooked through—2 to 3 minutes on each side. Transfer to a plate and set aside.

3 Add the red pepper and zucchini to the skillet, reduce the heat to moderate, and sauté, stirring occasionally, until softened—about 5 minutes. Add the mushrooms and sauté until tender—3 to 4 minutes more.

4 Pour in the wine, raise the heat to high, and boil, uncovered, for 2 minutes. Add the stock and cook 2 to 3 minutes longer or until slightly reduced; remove from the heat.

5 About 5 minutes before the rice is done, return the turkey to the skillet and heat, uncovered, over moderate heat, until warmed through—about 5 minutes. Serve over the hot rice. Serves 4.

Turkey Cutlet Skillet Dinner—a quick, easy, and delectable meal

Curried Turkey Tetrazzini

This updated classic is an ideal make-ahead that can be reheated in just 15 to 20 minutes. If you're not fond of curry, you can omit it and stir in 1 tablespoon Dijon mustard or 1 to 2 teaspoons lemon juice at the end of Step 3.

¼ cup (½ stick) unsalted butter or margarine

1 large yellow onion, finely chopped

1 large stalk celery, thinly sliced

8 ounces mushrooms, thinly sliced

1 tablespoon curry powder

4 cups Basic Chicken Stock (page 333) or canned chicken broth

¼ teaspoon each dried thyme and marjoram, crumbled

⅔ cup orzo (rice-shaped pasta) or other small pasta

1 cup half-and-half

1 tablespoon all-purpose flour

2 cups fresh or 1 package (10 ounces) frozen broccoli florets, thawed and drained

1 pound turkey tenderloins or cutlets, cut into pieces 1½ inch wide

½ teaspoon salt

¼ teaspoon black pepper

¼ cup fine dry bread crumbs

Per serving:
Calories 500; Protein 28 g;
Carbohydrates 44 g;
Fat 24 g; Sodium 660 mg;
Cholesterol 97 mg

25 minutes | 54 minutes

1 Preheat the oven to 400° F. Melt the butter in a large saucepan over moderate heat. Add the onion, celery, and mushrooms, cover, and steam for 5 minutes. Blend in the curry powder and cook, stirring constantly, for 1 minute. Reduce the heat to moderately low, add the stock, thyme, and marjoram, and simmer, uncovered, for 3 minutes. Add the orzo and simmer, uncovered, stirring occasionally, for 5 minutes.

2 In a small bowl, blend the half-and-half and flour until smooth, Mix into the saucepan and bring to a boil, whisking constantly. Add the broccoli, turkey, salt, and pepper. Simmer, uncovered, stirring occasionally, for 4 to 6 minutes or until the broccoli is tender.

3 Spoon all into a greased 13" x 9" x 2" flameproof baking dish and sprinkle the crumbs on top. Bake, uncovered, for 25 to 30 minutes or until bubbling. Transfer to the broiler and broil 4 inches from the heat for 1 to 2 minutes or until lightly browned. Serves 4.

Orange-Flavored Turkey Stir-Fry

Asparagus, broccoli, and green beans are all good alternatives to snow peas.

1 cup long-grain white or brown rice

¼ cup reduced-sodium soy sauce

1 tablespoon dry sherry

2 teaspoons cornstarch

1 pound turkey cutlets, cut crosswise into strips ½ inch wide

3 tablespoons vegetable oil

3 tablespoons finely slivered orange zest (colored part of the rind)

1 clove garlic, finely slivered

8 scallions, including tops, cut diagonally into 1-inch lengths

8 ounces snow peas, trimmed

1 can (15 ounces) baby corn, drained and halved

¼ teaspoon crushed red pepper flakes

⅓ cup orange juice, freshly squeezed preferred

Per serving:
Calories 531; Protein 26 g;
Carbohydrates 72 g;
Fat 17 g; Sodium 1,030 mg;
Cholesterol 44 mg

28 minutes | 18 minutes

1 Cook the rice according to package directions. Meanwhile, in a medium-size bowl, combine the soy sauce, sherry, and cornstarch. Add the turkey, toss well to coat, and set aside.

2 Heat 1 tablespoon of the oil in a deep 12-inch skillet or wok over moderately high heat for 1 minute. Add the orange zest and stir-fry for 1 to 2 minutes. Using a slotted spoon, transfer the zest to paper toweling. Add the garlic and stir-fry for 1 to 2 minutes; remove and discard. Add the scallions and snow peas and stir-fry for 2 to 3 minutes. Transfer to a medium-size bowl and set aside.

3 Add another tablespoon of the oil to the skillet and heat over moderately high heat for 1 minute. Add the corn and stir-fry for 2 to 3 minutes. Transfer to the bowl with the vegetables.

4 Add the remaining 1 tablespoon oil to the skillet and heat over moderately high heat for 1 minute. Add the turkey–soy sauce mixture and stir-fry for 3 minutes or until the meat is no longer pink. If necessary, add more oil. Add the red pepper flakes and orange juice and stir constantly to loosen any browned bits on the bottom of the skillet. Return the vegetables and orange zest to the skillet and heat for 1 to 2 minutes. Serve over the rice. Serves 4.

Turkey Roll Surprise

Ground turkey frames a colorful mosaic of mashed potatoes, leeks, and carrots on a bed of spinach. You can use leftover or instant mashed potatoes, or make them from scratch using 3 large all-purpose potatoes.

4	large eggs
3	cups mashed potatoes
1	cup grated Parmesan cheese (4 ounces)
3	leeks or 9 scallions, including tops, finely chopped
3	medium-size carrots, peeled and finely chopped
1¼	teaspoons salt
1¼	pounds ground turkey
2	tablespoons whole or low-fat milk
2	tablespoons soft bread crumbs
2	tablespoons minced parsley
½	teaspoon dried rosemary, crumbled
1	package (10 ounces) frozen chopped spinach, unthawed
1	jar (15 ounces) Italian tomato or marinara sauce

Per serving:
Calories 661; Protein 57 g;
Carbohydrates 64 g;
Fat 22 g; Sodium 2,550 mg;
Cholesterol 329 mg

20 minutes | 35 minutes

1 Preheat the oven to 375° F. In a small bowl, lightly beat 3 of the eggs. Add the mashed potatoes, cheese, leeks, carrots, and ¾ teaspoon of the salt; mix well and set aside.

2 In a large bowl, beat the remaining egg lightly. Add the turkey, milk, bread crumbs, parsley, rosemary, and remaining ½ teaspoon salt; mix well with your hands. On a large sheet of plastic wrap, pat the turkey mixture into a 14″ x 7″ x ½″ rectangle. Spread ⅓ of the potato mixture on top, leaving a 1-inch border all around. Beginning with a long side and using the plastic wrap to lift, roll up the turkey jelly roll style. Place the remaining mashed potatoes in a lightly greased 1½-quart baking dish, cover with foil, and set aside.

3 Transfer the turkey roll, using the plastic wrap to lift, to an ungreased jelly roll pan or large roasting pan. Bake, uncovered, for 35 minutes or until the turkey is firm and no longer pink. Place the extra mashed potatoes in the oven 15 minutes after the turkey roll goes in.

4 About 5 minutes before serving, cook the spinach according to package directions. Meanwhile, in an uncovered medium-size saucepan over moderate heat, bring the tomato sauce to a simmer. Drain the spinach, mix with 1 tablespoon of the turkey drippings, and transfer to a platter. Cut the turkey roll into 1-inch slices and arrange on top of the spinach. Pass the tomato sauce and extra potatoes separately. Serves 4.

Confetti Hash

Beets bring a rosy color to this turkey hash. For an extra fillip, you can top it off with a poached egg.

- ¼ cup (½ stick) unsalted butter or margarine
- 1 large yellow onion, finely chopped
- 12 ounces ground turkey
- 10 ounces frozen hash brown potatoes, thawed
- 2 cans (8 ounces each) no-salt-added sliced beets, drained and diced
- 1 small zucchini, shredded and squeezed dry
- 1 teaspoon salt
- ½ teaspoon each dried sage and rosemary, crumbled
- ¼ teaspoon black pepper
- ¼ cup water

1 Melt 2 tablespoons of the butter in a 12-inch skillet over moderate heat. Add the onion, cover, and cook, stirring occasionally, until soft —about 5 minutes. Transfer to a large bowl.

2 Add the turkey, potatoes, beets, zucchini, salt, sage, rosemary, and pepper to the same bowl and mix well.

3 Add another tablespoon of the butter to the skillet and melt over moderately low heat. Add the turkey mixture, pat it down, and cook, uncovered, until a light crust forms on the bottom—about 10 minutes.

4 Turn the hash over, add the remaining 1 tablespoon butter to the bottom of the skillet, and cook, uncovered, for 10 minutes or until a crust forms on the second side. Turn again, cover, and cook 10 minutes longer. Turn a third time, then lift up an edge of the hash and pour the water into the skillet. Cook, uncovered, another 10 minutes or until the turkey and potatoes are cooked through and crusty. Serves 4.

Per serving:
Calories 408; Protein 23 g;
Carbohydrates 32 g;
Fat 22 g; Sodium 673 mg;
Cholesterol 86 mg

15 minutes | 47 minutes

Turkey Loaf Deluxe

Tomato sauce dresses up a tasty low-fat loaf. You can substitute a combination of ground pork, beef, or veal for the turkey.

- 2 tablespoons vegetable oil
- 4 medium-size all-purpose potatoes, peeled and sliced ¼ inch thick
- 2 medium-size sweet green peppers, cored, seeded, and thinly sliced
- 1½ medium-size yellow onions, 1 thinly sliced, ½ finely chopped
- ¾ teaspoon salt
- ¼ teaspoon black pepper
- 1 large egg
- 1 pound ground turkey
- ½ cup fine dry bread crumbs
- ¼ cup minced parsley
- 1 tablespoon Worcestershire sauce
- 2 medium-size zucchini, thinly sliced
- 1 can (8 ounces) tomato sauce

1 Preheat the oven to 400° F. In a greased medium-size roasting pan, mix the oil, potatoes, green peppers, and sliced onion. Sprinkle with ¼ teaspoon of the salt and ⅛ teaspoon of the black pepper and bake, uncovered, for 20 minutes.

2 In a large bowl, beat the egg lightly. Add the turkey, bread crumbs, chopped onion, parsley, Worcestershire sauce, and remaining salt and pepper, and combine. Shape the mixture into an 8" x 5" x 3" loaf.

3 Reduce the oven temperature to 350° F. Remove the roasting pan from the oven, add the zucchini, and mix well, then push the vegetables to the sides of the pan. Place the turkey loaf in the center and pour the tomato sauce over all.

4 Return the pan to the oven and bake, uncovered, stirring the vegetables occasionally, until the turkey loaf is no longer pink on the inside and the vegetables are tender—about 35 minutes more. Serves 4.

Per serving:
Calories 439; Protein 33 g;
Carbohydrates 50 g;
Fat 13 g; Sodium 914 mg;
Cholesterol 127 mg

20 minutes | 55 minutes

Turkey Roll Surprise includes a terrific bonus for mashed potato lovers— a casserole of the savory stuffing is served on the side.

107

Turkey Enchiladas

The cool, fresh taste of watercress and arugula makes a delicious difference in this Mexican dish. You can also use fresh kale, spinach, or collard greens as long as you have 5 cups of chopped greens.

- 2 tablespoons vegetable oil
- 1 large yellow onion, chopped
- 1 clove garlic, minced
- 8 flour tortillas, 7½ to 8 inches in diameter
- 1 pound ground turkey
- 1 bunch arugula, thicker stems removed, rinsed, drained, and chopped (about 2½ cups)
- 1 bunch watercress, thicker stems removed, rinsed, drained, and chopped (about 2½ cups)
- 1 can (4 ounces) green chilies, drained and chopped (wash your hands after handling the chilies)
- 1 can (10 ounces) enchilada sauce
- 1½ tablespoons chili powder
- 1 teaspoon ground cumin
- ¼ teaspoon salt
- ½ teaspoon ground red pepper (cayenne) (optional)
- 1 cup shredded Monterey Jack cheese (4 ounces)
- 1 cup sour cream or plain low-fat yogurt (optional)

1 Preheat the oven to 325° F. Heat the oil in a 12-inch skillet over moderate heat for 1 minute. Add the onion and garlic and sauté, stirring occasionally, until soft—5 minutes.

2 Wrap the tortillas in foil and heat in the oven for 15 minutes. Meanwhile, add the turkey to the skillet and sauté, breaking up the clumps, until no longer pink—10 minutes. Stir in the arugula, watercress, chilies, ½ cup of the enchilada sauce, chili powder, cumin, salt, and red pepper if desired. Bring to a boil and cook, uncovered, for 5 minutes.

3 Remove the tortillas from the oven. When cool enough to handle, place a tortilla on a sheet of wax paper and spoon ½ cup of the turkey mixture on top, leaving a 1-inch border all around. Roll the tortilla up tightly, being careful not to let the filling leak out at the edges. Place seam side down in a greased medium-size baking dish. Repeat with the remaining tortillas and filling.

4 Pour the remaining enchilada sauce over the tortillas and sprinkle with the cheese. Bake, uncovered, for 30 minutes or until the sauce is bubbling and the cheese has melted. Serve the sour cream on the side if desired. Serves 4.

> **Per serving:**
> *Calories 572; Protein 41 g;*
> *Carbohydrates 52 g;*
> *Fat 24 g; Sodium 969 mg;*
> *Cholesterol 74 mg*

25 minutes | 51 minutes

Barbecued Cornish Hens with Chili Rice

Corn, chilies, and cheese bring a Tex-Mex flavor to Cornish hens.

- ¾ cup long-grain white rice
- 2 Rock Cornish hens (1 to 1½ pounds each), split
- 2 tablespoons olive oil
- ¼ teaspoon salt
- ¼ teaspoon black pepper
- 1 can (12 ounces) corn kernels, drained
- 1 jar (6 ounces) pimientos, drained and diced
- 1 can (4 ounces) green chilies, drained and chopped (wash your hands after handling the chilies)
- 1 cup shredded Monterey Jack or Cheddar cheese (4 ounces)
- ½ cup sour cream
- ⅔ cup bottled barbecue sauce

1 Preheat the broiler. Cook the rice according to package directions. Meanwhile, brush the hens with the oil, then sprinkle with the salt and pepper. Arrange them, skin side down, in a lightly greased medium-size baking pan and broil 6 inches from the heat for 10 minutes; turn and broil 10 minutes more or until nicely browned. Reduce the oven temperature to 400° F.

2 Mix the rice, corn, pimientos, chilies, cheese, and sour cream in a large bowl. Spoon the barbecue sauce over the hens, then wreathe the rice mixture around them.

3 Bake, uncovered, for 20 to 30 minutes or until the legs move easily in the hip sockets. Serves 4.

> **Per serving:**
> *Calories 705; Protein 54 g;*
> *Carbohydrates 55 g;*
> *Fat 30 g; Sodium 999 mg;*
> *Cholesterol 213 mg*

16 minutes | 50 minutes

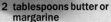

Country-Style Cornish Hens

Thanks to its nutlike flavor, bulgur makes a wonderful stuffing.

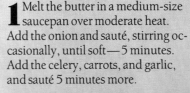

2 tablespoons butter or
   margarine
1 medium-size yellow onion,
   finely chopped
2 medium-size stalks celery,
   finely chopped
2 medium-size carrots, peeled
   and finely chopped
1 clove garlic, minced
4 cups Basic Chicken Stock
   (page 333) or canned chicken
   broth
2 cups bulgur (12 ounces)
¾ teaspoon salt
½ teaspoon black pepper

4 Rock Cornish hens (1 to 1½
   pounds each)
1 teaspoon dried sage, crumbled
½ cup chopped shallots or yellow
   onion
1 package (10 ounces) frozen
   artichoke hearts, partially
   thawed and drained
10 ounces small mushrooms

Per serving:
Calories 937; Protein 98 g; Carbohydrates 90 g; Fat 21 g; Sodium 1,018 mg; Cholesterol 215 mg

20 minutes	1 hr. 31 min.

1 Melt the butter in a medium-size saucepan over moderate heat. Add the onion and sauté, stirring occasionally, until soft—5 minutes. Add the celery, carrots, and garlic, and sauté 5 minutes more.

2 Add 3½ cups of the stock, the bulgur, ¼ teaspoon of the salt, and ⅛ teaspoon of the pepper. Cover, reduce the heat to low, and simmer, stirring occasionally, until the liquid is absorbed and the bulgur is tender—20 minutes.

3 Preheat the oven to 375° F. Fill the hens loosely with the stuffing and tie the legs together. Sprinkle with the sage and the remaining salt and pepper. Arrange breast side up, not touching, in 1 large or 2 smaller roasting pans, leaving enough room for the vegetables. Spoon the remaining stuffing into a greased 1½-quart casserole and set aside.

4 Roast the hens, uncovered, basting occasionally with the pan drippings, for 30 minutes. Scatter the shallots, artichoke hearts, and mushrooms around the hens, and baste with the drippings.

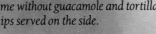

Turkey Enchiladas wouldn't be the same without guacamole and tortilla chips served on the side.

5 Pour the remaining stock over the stuffing in the casserole, cover with foil, and set in the oven with the hens. Roast the hens, uncovered, another 30 minutes, stirring the pan vegetables twice, until the legs move easily in the hip sockets and the vegetables are tender. Serves 4.

Asparagus and Brown Rice Variation

Eliminate Step 1. In Step 2, increase the stock to 4¼ cups and bring to a simmer over moderate heat in a medium-size saucepan. Add **2 cups long-grain brown rice, 2 cored, seeded, and coarsely chopped sweet red peppers, ½ teaspoon crumbled dried thyme,** and ¼ teaspoon of the salt and ⅛ teaspoon of the pepper. Cover and simmer over low heat until the rice is tender—35 to 40 minutes. Stir in **7 coarsely chopped scallions (including half of the tops).** Stuff the hens as directed in Step 3. In Step 4, roast the hens for 40 minutes and omit the artichoke hearts and mushrooms. Add **1 package (10 ounces) partially thawed frozen cut asparagus** to the pan and baste with the pan juices. In Step 5 pour an additional ¼ cup stock over the stuffing in the casserole, then proceed as directed. Serves 4.

Per serving: Calories 953; Protein 100 g; Carbohydrates 101 g; Fat 16 g; Sodium 934 mg; Cholesterol 201 mg

Marinated Cornish Hens with Apricot Stuffing

An impressive dish that's not as complicated as it looks. If you're short on time, marinate the hens for just 10 or 15 minutes while you make the stuffing.

For the marinade:
- ¼ cup reduced-sodium soy sauce
- ¼ cup rice wine or dry sherry
- ¼ cup vegetable oil
- 2 tablespoons cider vinegar
- 2 tablespoons Dijon mustard
- 2 tablespoons honey
- 2 cloves garlic, minced
- 1 tablespoon minced fresh ginger or ½ teaspoon each ground ginger and finely grated lemon or orange rind
- 2 Rock Cornish hens (about 1½ pounds each)

For the stuffing:
- 3 tablespoons unsalted butter or margarine
- 1 large yellow onion, finely chopped
- 1 medium-size stalk celery, finely chopped
- 1 package (10 ounces) frozen green peas, thawed and drained
- 4 cups cooked quick-cooking or long-grain white rice
- ½ cup Basic Chicken Stock (page 333) or canned chicken broth
- 4 ounces dried apricots, chopped (1 cup)
- ½ cup toasted slivered almonds (page 86)
- ¼ teaspoon each dried thyme and sage, crumbled
- ½ teaspoon salt
- ¼ teaspoon black pepper

For the glaze:
- ½ cup apricot preserves

Per serving:
Calories 1,144; Protein 76 g;
Carbohydrates 117 g;
Fat 40 g; Sodium 1,350 mg;
Cholesterol 223 mg

35 minutes | 1 hr. 12 min.

1 *For the marinade*: In a large bowl, combine the soy sauce, wine, oil, vinegar, mustard, honey, garlic, and ginger. Place a large plastic bag inside another (to double the thickness), add the hens and the marinade, and seal. Refrigerate for 3 hours or overnight. Drain the hens, reserving the marinade, and pat dry with paper toweling. Preheat the oven to 400° F.

2 *For the stuffing:* Melt the butter in a 12-inch skillet over moderate heat. Add the onion and celery and sauté, stirring occasionally, until soft—5 minutes. Remove from the heat and stir in the peas, rice, stock, apricots, almonds, thyme, sage, salt, and pepper; mix well. Fill each hen loosely with stuffing and tie the legs together. Place the remaining stuffing in a greased 1½-quart casserole and cover with foil; set aside.

3 *For the glaze:* In a small saucepan over moderate heat, combine the reserved marinade and the apricot preserves. Bring to a boil, stirring constantly, then reduce the heat to low and simmer, uncovered, stirring occasionally, until thickened— about 5 minutes.

4 Arrange the hens, breast side up, in a medium-size baking pan and spoon the glaze over them. Roast, uncovered, basting occasionally, for 1 hour or until the legs move easily in the hip sockets. Bake the covered casserole of stuffing in the oven along with the hens for the last 40 minutes.

5 Remove the strings and split each hen in half. Serve with the extra stuffing. Serves 4.

When your friends expect a four-star meal, serve them Marinated Cornish Hens with Apricot Stuffing.

Duck Normandy

This dish is surprisingly ungreasy because most of the fat is rendered out when the duck is browned. Serve it over spaetzle—tiny tear-shaped German noodles —or regular noodles. You can use a roasting chicken instead of the duck.

- 1 duck (4 pounds), skinned and cut into 8 serving pieces
- 2 large yellow onions, halved and thinly sliced
- 3 cloves garlic, thinly sliced
- 3 medium-size McIntosh apples (about 1 pound), peeled, cored, and thinly sliced
- ½ cup water
- 1¼ pounds cabbage, coarsely shredded
- 1 teaspoon caraway seeds
- 1 teaspoon salt

- ⅔ cup dry white wine
- ¼ cup white wine vinegar or white vinegar
- ⅔ cup half-and-half or heavy cream
- 1 package (10½ ounces) spaetzle

Per serving:
Calories 1,149; Protein 90 g;
Carbohydrates 88 g;
Fat 45 g; Sodium 815 mg;
Cholesterol 305 mg

25 minutes | 1 hr. 40 min.

1 Brown the duck in a 5-quart Dutch oven over moderately high heat, turning the pieces, until quite a bit of fat has rendered out—about 10 minutes. Transfer the duck to a plate and pour off all but 2 tablespoons of the drippings.

2 Reduce the heat to moderate, add the onions to the Dutch oven, and sauté, stirring frequently, until limp—7 to 10 minutes. Add the garlic and sauté 2 minutes longer. Add the apples and water, cover, and simmer for 15 minutes. Stir in the cabbage, caraway seeds, and salt, and cook, stirring constantly, 3 minutes. Stir in the wine and vinegar.

3 Return the duck to the Dutch oven, cover, and simmer for 40 minutes or until almost tender. Stir in the half-and-half, cover, and simmer 20 minutes longer. Meanwhile, cook the spaetzle according to package directions.

4 Spoon the spaetzle onto a deep platter, arrange the duck, apples, and cabbage on top, then ladle the sauce over all. Serves 4.

Stir-Fried Duck with Chinese Noodles

If you prefer, substitute turkey or chicken breast for the duck, and asparagus for the broccoli.

1 large egg white, lightly beaten

3 tablespoons dry sherry

6 tablespoons peanut or vegetable oil

4 teaspoons cornstarch

½ teaspoon salt

1 pound skinned and boned duck breast, frozen until almost firm (about 45 minutes), then cut into 2½- by ½-inch strips

½ cup Basic Chicken Stock (page 333) or canned chicken broth

3 tablespoons reduced-sodium soy sauce

6 scallions, including tops, thinly sliced

1 tablespoon minced fresh ginger

1 tablespoon minced garlic

4 ounces mushrooms, thinly sliced

3 medium-size carrots, peeled and cut into matchstick strips

2 cups fresh or 1 package (10 ounces) frozen broccoli florets, thawed and drained

⅛ teaspoon red pepper flakes

2 tablespoons Oriental sesame oil

8 ounces Chinese noodles or thin spaghetti, cooked according to package directions

Optional garnishes:

2 tablespoons thinly sliced scallion tops

2 tablespoons minced fresh coriander (cilantro) or flat-leaf parsley

Per serving:
Calories 707; Protein 33 g;
Carbohydrates 57 g;
Fat 38 g; Sodium 1,454 mg;
Cholesterol 81 mg

40 minutes | 10 minutes

1 In a medium-size bowl, combine the egg white, 1 tablespoon each of the sherry and oil, 1 teaspoon of the cornstarch, and ¼ teaspoon of the salt. Add the duck, stir to coat, and let stand for 20 minutes, stirring occasionally.

2 Meanwhile, in a small bowl, combine the stock, soy sauce, and remaining sherry and cornstarch. Set aside.

3 Heat 3 tablespoons of the remaining oil in a wok or 12-inch skillet over moderately high heat for 1 minute. Add the duck and stir-fry for 3 minutes. Transfer to a plate.

4 Add the remaining 2 tablespoons oil to the wok and heat for 1 minute. Add the scallions, ginger, and garlic, and stir-fry for 30 seconds. Add the mushrooms, carrots, broccoli, red pepper flakes, and remaining salt, and stir-fry for 1 minute.

5 Stir the stock mixture and pour into the wok. Reduce the heat to moderate, cover, and simmer for 2 minutes. Return the duck to the wok and cook and stir for 1 minute or until heated through. Stir in 1 tablespoon of the sesame oil.

6 Toss the cooked noodles with the remaining sesame oil. Place the noodles on a serving platter and spoon the duck mixture on top. Garnish with the scallion tops and coriander if desired. Serves 4.

Duck with a difference — Stir-Fried Duck with Chinese Noodles

Fish and Shellfish

The catch of the day, enticingly displayed in many
markets across America, is an inspiration to try any number of these
dishes. Most recipes offer a choice of fish, enabling you to select the best of
what's in season. If the recipe calls for a firm-fleshed lean white fish, try
haddock, pollock, cod, scrod, or flounder. If the fish you want isn't on display,
head for the frozen food section of your supermarket. And there's always
canned salmon; never out of season, it's perfect for
light-as-a-cloud Salmon Pastry Puff.

Fish in Foil

*There's hardly any cleanup with this recipe because the fish
and vegetables are cooked in aluminum foil.*

- 2 tablespoons unsalted butter or margarine, melted
- 8 ounces fine egg noodles
- 4 large carrots, peeled and thinly sliced
- ½ cup heavy cream or half-and-half
- 4 scallions, including tops, thinly sliced
- 2 tablespoons snipped fresh dill or minced parsley or ½ teaspoon dill weed
- ½ teaspoon salt
- ⅛ teaspoon black pepper
- 2 cups loosely packed watercress or spinach leaves
- 4 flounder fillets or other lean white fish such as scrod or haddock (1½ pounds), thawed if frozen

Per serving:
Calories 532; Protein 35 g;
Carbohydrates 51 g;
Fat 20 g; Sodium 416 mg;
Cholesterol 141 mg

15 minutes   22 minutes

1 Preheat the oven to 325° F. Fold four 20- by 12-inch sheets of heavy-duty foil in half crosswise, then open each sheet like a book and brush one "page" with 1 teaspoon of the melted butter, leaving a 2-inch margin all around.

2 Bring a large saucepan of water to a boil over high heat. Add the noodles and carrots and cook, uncovered, stirring occasionally, for 5 minutes or until almost tender. Drain well and toss with the cream and half of the scallions, dill, salt, and pepper.

3 Divide the noodle mixture evenly among the 4 buttered foil "pages" and top each with ½ cup of the watercress, then a fish fillet. Spoon on the remaining butter and sprinkle with the remaining scallions, dill, salt, and pepper.

4 Fold the foil over, enclosing the food, and seal the edges by folding over twice. Place the foil packets on a baking sheet and bake for 15 minutes. To serve, slit the foil and slide the fish, noodles, and vegetables onto serving plates. Serves 4.

Flounder Divan

*Assembling this meal is exceptionally fast if you use instant
mashed potatoes. If you prefer fresh, cook 3 medium-size potatoes, drain,
and mash. You can make the sauce several hours ahead of time, but
reheat it gently before proceeding with the recipe.*

- 2 tablespoons unsalted butter or margarine
- 2 tablespoons all-purpose flour
- 1½ cups whole milk
- 1 cup shredded low-fat Cheddar cheese (4 ounces)
- 6 dashes hot red pepper sauce
- 1 tablespoon lemon juice (freshly squeezed preferred)
- 1 package (10 ounces) frozen chopped broccoli, thawed and drained
- 1⅓ cups mashed potatoes
- 4 flounder fillets (6 ounces each)

Per serving:
Calories 416; Protein 39 g;
Carbohydrates 34 g;
Fat 14 g; Sodium 573 mg;
Cholesterol 125 mg

20 minutes   32 minutes

1 Preheat the oven to 400° F. Melt the butter in an ovenproof 10-inch skillet over moderate heat. Blend in the flour and cook, stirring, until golden—about 3 minutes. Gradually whisk in the milk, then cook, whisking constantly, until thickened—about 4 minutes longer.

2 Stir in ¾ cup of the cheese, the red pepper sauce, and lemon juice, and heat, uncovered, just until the cheese melts—about 2 minutes. Mix in the broccoli.

3 Spoon ⅓ cup of the mashed potatoes onto each flounder fillet and fold over. Lay the fillets in the skillet and spoon some of the sauce on top.

4 Cover and bake for 20 minutes. Top with the remaining cheese, transfer to the broiler, and broil 4 inches from the heat for 2 minutes or until tipped with brown. Serves 4.

Fillets with Lemon-Parsley Sauce

A great dish to make in summer when fresh tomatoes and zucchini are at their best. Any firm-fleshed fish fillets, even frozen, can be used in this recipe.

- 1 tablespoon olive oil
- 1 medium-size yellow onion, finely chopped
- 2 cloves garlic, thinly sliced
- 1 cup long-grain white rice
- 2 teaspoons finely grated lemon rind
- ½ teaspoon salt
- 2½ cups water
- 2 medium-size zucchini, thinly sliced
- 3 plum tomatoes, cored and coarsely chopped
- 1 tablespoon fresh lemon juice
- 4 thick flounder or haddock fillets (1½ pounds)

For the sauce:
- ⅓ cup olive oil
- ⅓ cup fresh lemon juice
- ¼ cup firmly packed flat-leaf parsley leaves

Per serving:
Calories 523; Protein 31 g;
Carbohydrates 49 g;
Fat 23 g; Sodium 376 mg;
Cholesterol 85 mg

20 minutes | 34 minutes

1 Heat the oil in a deep 12-inch skillet or 4-quart Dutch oven over low heat for 1 minute. Add the onion and garlic and sauté, stirring occasionally, until limp—about 5 minutes.

2 Add the rice, lemon rind, and salt, and stir to mix. Add the water, raise the heat to moderate, and bring to a boil. Reduce the heat to moderately low, cover, and cook for 12 minutes. Stir in the zucchini, tomatoes, and lemon juice, cover, and cook 4 minutes more.

3 Lay the fish on top of the rice mixture, reduce the heat to low, cover, and cook for 10 minutes or until the fish flakes at the touch of a fork. Transfer the fish and rice mixture to a large platter.

4 *For the sauce:* Blend the oil, lemon juice, and parsley in a food processor or an electric blender at high speed for 15 to 20 seconds. Spoon over the fish and serve. Serves 4.

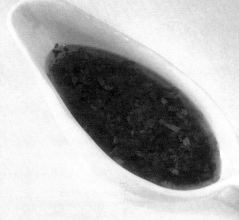

Fillets with Lemon-Parsley Sauce—a light meal with a refreshing citrus flavor

Flounder Florentine

You can prepare this recipe through Step 4 several hours ahead of time; cover and refrigerate until ready to proceed.

- 4 flounder fillets (4 to 6 ounces each)
- ½ teaspoon salt
- ¼ teaspoon black pepper
- 1½ cups milk or evaporated skim milk
- 8 ounces spinach fettuccine
- ¼ cup (½ stick) unsalted butter or margarine
- ¼ cup all-purpose flour
- 1½ cups Basic Chicken Stock (page 333) or canned chicken broth or fish stock (page 254)
- 1 teaspoon Dijon mustard
- ¼ teaspoon ground nutmeg
- ⅓ cup plus 2 tablespoons grated Parmesan cheese
- ⅓ cup plus 2 tablespoons shredded Gruyère or Swiss cheese
- 1 package (10 ounces) frozen chopped spinach, thawed and drained

Per serving:
Calories 612; Protein 41 g;
Carbohydrates 56 g;
Fat 24 g; Sodium 812 mg;
Cholesterol 125 mg

5 minutes | 31 minutes

1 Preheat the oven to 400° F. Fold the flounder fillets in half crosswise, place in a deep 10-inch skillet, and sprinkle with the salt and pepper. Add the milk, cover, and bring to a simmer over moderate heat. Cook until the fish is firm but still slightly resilient—about 1 minute. Transfer the fish to a plate and the milk to a large measuring cup.

2 Cook the fettuccine according to package directions and drain well. Transfer to an ungreased shallow 2-quart flameproof casserole and toss with 1 tablespoon of the butter.

3 Meanwhile, melt the remaining 3 tablespoons butter in the skillet over moderate heat. Blend in the flour and cook, stirring, for 1 minute. Mix in the reserved milk and the stock and cook, stirring constantly, for 3 minutes or until slightly thickened. Reduce the heat to low and simmer, uncovered, stirring occasionally, for 5 minutes. Remove from the heat and whisk in the mustard, nutmeg, and ⅓ cup each of the Parmesan and Gruyère cheeses.

4 Spread the spinach over the fettuccine and top with the fish, then the sauce. Sprinkle with the remaining 2 tablespoons of each cheese.

5 Bring to a simmer over moderate heat, transfer to the oven, and bake, uncovered, for 15 minutes or until bubbling. Transfer to the broiler and broil 4 inches from the heat for 1 to 2 minutes or until tipped with brown. Serves 4.

Catch-of-the-Day Dinner

A succulent dish that can also be made on the barbecue or over a campfire. Wrap the potatoes in a foil packet and cook for 15 minutes, turning the packet over halfway through. Add the zucchini and tomatoes, reseal, and cook 7 minutes more. Finally, add the trout, reseal, and cook for 10 minutes.

- 1 pound small new potatoes (about 8), halved
- 3 tablespoons olive oil
- ¾ teaspoon salt
- ½ teaspoon dried rosemary, crumbled
- 3 small zucchini, quartered lengthwise
- 12 ounces plum tomatoes, cut into cubes but not peeled or cored
- 2 whole rainbow or brook trout, bluefish, mackerel, or whiting (12 ounces each), cleaned and boned
- 1 lemon, thinly sliced

1 Preheat the oven to 450° F. Place the potatoes in an ungreased 11" x 7" x 2" baking pan and sprinkle with 1½ tablespoons of the oil, ¼ teaspoon of the salt, and the rosemary. Bake, uncovered, for 15 minutes, shaking the pan after 7 minutes.

2 Add the zucchini, tomatoes, another ½ tablespoon of the oil, and ¼ teaspoon of the salt, and bake, uncovered, 7 minutes longer.

3 Sprinkle the fish with the remaining salt and lay the lemon slices inside each one. Arrange the fish on top of the vegetables, drizzle with the remaining oil, and bake, uncovered, for 15 minutes. Serves 4.

> Per serving:
> Calories 379; Protein 37 g;
> Carbohydrates 32 g;
> Fat 11 g; Sodium 650 mg;
> Cholesterol 152 mg

30 minutes	37 minutes

South Carolina Fish Stew

This dish, often called pine bark stew, can be traced to the Revolutionary War, when southern troops, using whatever food they could find in the wild, cooked a similar concoction on slabs of pine bark.

- 1 cup quick-cooking or long-grain white rice
- 3 slices bacon, diced
- 3 medium-size stalks celery, chopped
- 1 large sweet green pepper, cored, seeded, and diced
- 1 large yellow onion, coarsely chopped
- 1 can (1 pound) crushed tomatoes
- 2 bottles (8 ounces each) clam juice or 2 cups fish stock (page 254)
- 2 cups water
- 2 tablespoons white vinegar
- 2 tablespoons balsamic or cider vinegar
- ½ teaspoon each ground cinnamon and cloves
- ¼ teaspoon salt
- ½ teaspoon hot red pepper sauce
- 8 ounces catfish or trout fillets, cut into ¾-inch squares
- 8 ounces perch fillets, cut into ¾-inch squares

1 Cook the rice according to package directions; set aside. Meanwhile, cook the bacon until crisp in a 5- or 6-quart Dutch oven over moderate heat. Drain on paper toweling and pour off all but 1 tablespoon of the drippings.

2 Add the celery, pepper, and onion to the Dutch oven and sauté, stirring occasionally, until limp and golden—about 5 minutes.

3 Add the tomatoes, clam juice, water, white and balsamic vinegars, cinnamon, cloves, salt, and red pepper sauce. Raise the heat to high and bring to a boil. Add the fish, reduce the heat to moderate, cover, and simmer for 8 to 10 minutes or until the fish flakes at the touch of a fork. Stir in the bacon. Place ½ cup of the cooked rice in each bowl and ladle the stew on top. Serves 4.

> Per serving:
> Calories 380; Protein 30 g;
> Carbohydrates 48 g;
> Fat 7 g; Sodium 513 mg;
> Cholesterol 87 mg

25 minutes	20 minutes

Flounder Florentine—flakes of fish on a delicious deep-green sea of spinach and fettuccine

Fish Pie with Mashed Potato Crust

Either leftover or instant mashed potatoes can be used, but if you prefer fresh, use 6 medium-size all-purpose potatoes. You can substitute thawed frozen cod or other lean white fish for the fresh, but drain it well and pat dry with paper toweling.

- 3 cups mashed potatoes
- 2 tablespoons butter or margarine, at room temperature
- 1 large egg, lightly beaten
- 1 tablespoon olive oil
- 1 medium-size sweet green pepper, cored, seeded, and sliced ½ inch thick
- 1 medium-size sweet red pepper, cored, seeded, and sliced ½ inch thick
- 4 cloves garlic, minced
- 2 cans (14½ ounces each) no-salt-added stewed tomatoes with their juice
- ¼ teaspoon salt
- ¼ cup sliced pitted black olives
- 1 pound cod fillets, about ½ inch thick, cut into 1-inch squares
- ⅓ cup coarsely chopped unblanched almonds

Per serving:
Calories 451; Protein 30 g;
Carbohydrates 46 g;
Fat 19 g; Sodium 1,294 mg;
Cholesterol 121 mg

25 minutes | 41 minutes

1 Preheat the oven to 400° F. Combine the potatoes with the butter and egg and spread over the bottom and up the sides of a 9-inch deep-dish pie pan. Bake, uncovered, for 15 minutes while you prepare the filling.

2 Heat the oil in a deep 12-inch skillet over moderate heat for 1 minute. Add the green and red peppers and garlic and sauté, stirring occasionally, until the peppers are crisp-tender—about 8 minutes.

Add the tomatoes, salt, and olives, and cook, uncovered, until the flavors meld and the juices reduce by half—about 7 minutes.

3 Spoon ⅓ of the tomato mixture into the potato crust, lay ½ of the cod on top, and cover with ½ of the remaining tomato mixture. Place the remaining cod on top, then the remaining tomato mixture.

4 Sprinkle the almonds over all and bake, uncovered, for 20 to 25 minutes or until the fish just flakes at the touch of a fork. Serves 4.

A novel combination of ingredients—Fish Pie with Mashed Potato Crust

Baked Fish Sticks with Zucchini and Yams

Any firm-fleshed white fish such as haddock, pollock, or scrod can be used in this recipe.

- 2 tablespoons olive oil
- 1 medium-size yellow onion, finely chopped
- 1 medium-size sweet red pepper, cored, seeded, and cut into 1-inch squares
- 2 large yams, peeled and cut into 1-inch cubes
- ¼ teaspoon each salt and black pepper
- ½ cup dry white wine or vermouth or Basic Chicken Stock (page 333) or canned chicken broth or fish stock (page 254)
- 1 can (28 ounces) crushed tomatoes
- 2 cloves garlic, minced
- ½ teaspoon each dried basil and oregano, crumbled
- 1 large zucchini, cut into 1-inch cubes
- 1 pound cod fillets, cut into 4- by 1½-inch strips
- 1½ cups plain low-fat yogurt
- 1½ cups seasoned dry bread crumbs
- ¼ cup grated Parmesan cheese

1 Preheat the oven to 400° F. Heat the oil in a large saucepan over moderate heat for 1 minute. Add the onion and red pepper and sauté, stirring occasionally, for 5 minutes or until softened. Add the yams, salt, and black pepper. Cook, stirring, for 1 minute.

2 Add the wine, tomatoes, garlic, basil, and oregano. Bring to a boil, adjust the heat so that the mixture bubbles gently, cover, and simmer for 8 minutes, stirring occasionally. Add the zucchini, cover, and simmer for 5 minutes or until the vegetables are just tender.

3 Meanwhile, dip the fish sticks in the yogurt, then coat with the bread crumbs. Place the fish sticks on a lightly greased baking sheet and bake, uncovered, for 8 to 10 minutes or until just firm.

4 Spread the vegetable mixture over the bottom of an ungreased 12″ x 9″ x 2″ flameproof baking dish, top with the fish sticks, and sprinkle with the cheese. Bake, uncovered, for 10 to 15 minutes or until bubbling. Transfer to the broiler and broil 4 inches from the heat for 1 to 2 minutes or until tipped with brown. Serves 4.

Per serving:
Calories 586; Protein 37 g;
Carbohydrates 76 g;
Fat 14 g; Sodium 999 mg;
Cholesterol 60 mg

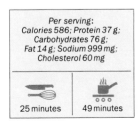

| 25 minutes | 49 minutes |

Fish Steaks with Tomatoes and Mushrooms

This adaptable dish can also be made with 1 pound of shrimp, bay scallops, lobster, or crabmeat.

- 3 tablespoons olive oil
- 4 halibut, salmon, or swordfish steaks (1½ pounds)
- 1 large shallot or scallion (white part only), finely chopped
- 2 large tomatoes, cored, seeded, and coarsely chopped, or 2 cups canned crushed tomatoes
- 10 ounces mushrooms, sliced ¼ inch thick
- ½ cup dry white wine or Basic Chicken Stock (page 333) or canned chicken broth or fish stock (page 254)
- 2 tablespoons minced parsley
- ¼ teaspoon salt
- ⅛ teaspoon black pepper
- 2 cups fine egg noodles
- 1 cup water
- 1 package (10 ounces) frozen green peas, thawed and drained

Per serving:
Calories 440; Protein 43 g;
Carbohydrates 34 g;
Fat 16 g; Sodium 339 mg;
Cholesterol 85 mg

| 20 minutes | 21 minutes |

1 Heat the oil in a deep 12-inch skillet over moderate heat for 1 minute. Pat the fish dry with paper toweling, then add to the skillet and brown lightly—2 to 2½ minutes on each side. Transfer to a plate.

2 Sauté the shallot in the skillet drippings for 2 minutes or until limp. Add the tomatoes, mushrooms, wine, parsley, salt, and pepper, and bring to a simmer.

3 Stir in the noodles and water, cover, and cook for 8 minutes. Add the peas and browned halibut, cover, and simmer 5 minutes more. Serves 4.

Fish Steaks Niçoise Variation

In Step 2, substitute **2 thinly sliced cored and seeded sweet red** or **green peppers** for the mushrooms. In Step 3, substitute **1 pound thinly sliced unpeeled new potatoes** for the noodles and omit the peas. Add ½ **teaspoon crumbled dried thyme** and ½ **cup sliced pitted black olives**. Cover and cook for 10 minutes. Add the browned halibut and simmer 5 minutes more or until the potatoes are tender. Serves 4.

Per serving: Calories 404; Protein 38 g;
Carbohydrates 31 g; Fat 16 g;
Sodium 328 mg; Cholesterol 85 mg

Gingered Swordfish

This Oriental-style dish can also be made with salmon or tuna steaks.

1½ cups water

½ cup dry sherry or ¼ cup each orange juice and Basic Chicken Stock (page 333) or canned chicken broth

½ cup reduced-sodium soy sauce

1 large yellow onion, thinly sliced

1 piece fresh ginger, about 1 inch long, peeled and minced

¼ teaspoon black pepper

½ cup orzo or other small pasta

4 swordfish steaks (1 pound)

2 cups coarsely shredded cabbage

3 large carrots, peeled and coarsely shredded (2 cups)

Per serving:
Calories 416; Protein 42 g;
Carbohydrates 35 g;
Fat 8 g; Sodium 1,561 mg;
Cholesterol 72 mg

20 minutes | 37 minutes

1 Place the water, sherry, soy sauce, onion, ginger, and pepper in a deep 12-inch skillet, and bring to a boil over high heat. Reduce the heat to low, cover, and simmer for 15 minutes.

2 Raise the heat to high and bring the mixture to a rolling boil. Add the orzo and cook, uncovered, for 5 minutes.

3 Arrange the swordfish steaks in a single layer in the skillet, reduce the heat to moderately low, cover, and simmer for 5 minutes. Using a wide spatula, gently turn the steaks over.

4 Sprinkle the cabbage and carrots on top, cover, and simmer for 5 to 8 minutes or until the swordfish flakes when touched with a fork. Place the swordfish on a warm platter. Toss the vegetables and pasta together and spoon around the fish. Serves 4.

Gingered Swordfish—created with Far Eastern flair, served with easy elegance

Salmon Soufflé

Puffy on the outside, pudding soft on the inside, this soufflé is a breeze to make.

- 3 tablespoons unsalted butter or margarine
- 1 tablespoon dry bread crumbs
- 4 scallions, including tops, finely chopped
- 1¾ cups whole milk
- ½ teaspoon plus 1 pinch salt
- ¼ teaspoon black pepper
- 1¼ cups instant mashed potato flakes or buds (not granules)
- ¾ cup shredded Cheddar cheese
- 6 large eggs, separated
- 1 package (10 ounces) frozen green peas, thawed and drained
- 6 dashes hot red pepper sauce
- 1 can (15½ ounces) salmon, drained, skinned, and flaked
- Pinch cream of tartar

Per serving:
Calories 606; Protein 45 g;
Carbohydrates 30 g;
Fat 34 g; Sodium 1,230 mg;
Cholesterol 379 mg

| 20 minutes | 55 minutes |

1 Preheat the oven to 375° F. Using 1 tablespoon of the butter, grease a 1½-quart soufflé dish and a 24- by 2-inch strip of heavy-duty foil. Wrap the foil around the dish, buttered side in, to form a collar that extends 1½ inches above the rim, and secure with cellophane tape.

2 Add the bread crumbs to the dish and tilt it from side to side to coat the bottom and sides evenly. Tap out excess crumbs and set aside.

3 Melt the remaining butter in a medium-size saucepan over moderate heat. Add the scallions and sauté, stirring, until softened.

4 Add the milk, the ½ teaspoon salt, and the pepper, and bring just to a boil; turn off the heat.

5 Mix in the potato flakes and stir until thickened. Add the cheese, stir until melted, then mix in the egg yolks, one at a time. Stir in the peas, red pepper sauce, and salmon.

6 Beat the egg whites with an electric mixer until foamy. Add the pinch of salt and cream of tartar and continue beating to form soft peaks. Stir about ¼ of the beaten whites into the salmon mixture, then gently but thoroughly fold in the balance.

7 Pour into the soufflé dish and bake, uncovered, for 50 minutes or until puffed, golden brown, and softly set. Remove the foil collar and serve at once. Serves 4 to 6.

Salmon Pastry Puff

Here's a delicious way to dress up canned salmon or, if you like, canned tuna.

- 3 sheets (12 by 17 inches each) frozen phyllo pastry, thawed and folded in half
- 1 large yellow onion, finely chopped
- ½ cup finely chopped sweet green pepper
- ½ cup finely chopped celery
- 3 tablespoons melted butter or margarine
- 3 tablespoons all-purpose flour
- 2 tablespoons snipped fresh dill or 1 teaspoon dill weed
- ½ teaspoon salt
- ¼ teaspoon black pepper
- 1 can (15½ ounces) salmon, drained, with liquid reserved
- 1 bottle (8 ounces) clam juice or 1 cup fish stock (page 254)
- ½ cup whole milk
- 1 package (10 ounces) frozen chopped asparagus, thawed and drained
- 1 tablespoon lemon juice

Per serving:
Calories 492; Protein 29 g;
Carbohydrates 31 g;
Fat 28 g; Sodium 1,332 mg;
Cholesterol 57 mg

| 25 minutes | 34 minutes |

1 Stack the folded sheets of phyllo pastry, then invert an ungreased 11″ x 7″ x 2″ baking dish on top of them. Using a sharp paring knife, carefully cut around the dish so that you have 6 single sheets of pastry Lift off the dish and cover the pastry sheets with damp paper toweling.

2 Preheat the oven to 400° F. Sauté the onion, green pepper, and celery in 2 tablespoons of the melted butter in a medium-size saucepan over moderate heat, stirring occasionally, for 5 minutes or until limp.

3 Blend in the flour, dill, salt, and black pepper, gradually add the reserved salmon liquid, clam juice, and milk, and cook, stirring constantly, for 3 to 5 minutes or until thickened.

4 Flake the salmon into the mixture, then stir in the asparagus and lemon juice. Simmer, uncovered, over moderately low heat for 3 minutes. Pour the hot mixture into the baking dish.

5 Lay a sheet of the phyllo pastry on top and lightly brush with a little of the remaining melted butter. Repeat with the remaining 5 sheets, lightly brushing each with the butter. Bake, uncovered, for 20 minutes or until puffed and golden. Serves 4.

Mediterranean Fish Stew

The inspiration for this dish is bouillabaisse (pronounced BOOL-yuh-BAYZ), a classic French stew that we've adapted for American tastes. You can vary the combination of fish and shellfish to suit your preference, but there should be 2 pounds in all.

3 tablespoons olive oil

1 large yellow onion, thinly sliced

1 can (1 pound) tomatoes with their juice, coarsely chopped

2 cups dry white wine or 1 cup clam juice or fish stock (page 254) plus 1 cup Basic Chicken Stock (page 333) or canned chicken broth

1 bottle (8 ounces) clam juice or 1 cup fish stock (page 254)

1 cup water

2 cloves garlic, minced

1 whole bay leaf

1 teaspoon dried basil, crumbled

½ teaspoon dried thyme, crumbled

½ teaspoon grated orange rind

⅛ teaspoon each black pepper and ground red pepper (cayenne)

1 pound white fish fillets (halibut, cod, sea bass, or preferably a combination), cut into 1-inch squares

8 ounces medium-size shrimp, shelled and deveined

12 clams or mussels in the shell

2 medium-size zucchini, sliced ¾ inch thick

12 slices French bread, about ¾ inch thick, toasted

¼ cup olive oil mixed with 1 crushed clove garlic

2 tablespoons minced parsley

Per serving:
Calories 549; Protein 35 g;
Carbohydrates 44 g;
Fat 21 g; Sodium 689 mg;
Cholesterol 100 mg

40 minutes | 38 minutes

1 Heat the oil in a 6-quart Dutch oven over moderate heat for 1 minute. Add the onion and sauté until very soft—about 10 minutes.

2 Stir in the tomatoes, wine, clam juice, water, garlic, bay leaf, basil, thyme, orange rind, and black and red pepper. Bring to a simmer, reduce the heat to low, partially cover, and simmer for 15 minutes.

3 Add the fish, shrimp, clams, and zucchini, cover, and cook for 8 to 10 minutes or until the fish is just opaque and the clams have opened. Discard any unopened clams and remove the bay leaf.

4 Brush the toasted bread with the garlic oil and place 2 slices in the bottom of each of 6 soup bowls. Ladle the fish stew on top and sprinkle with the parsley. Serves 6.

Bring the bounty of the sea to your table with this mouth-watering Mediterranean Fish Stew.

No-Crust Shrimp Pie

Either scallops or crabmeat can be used as a substitute. Sauté the scallops until they're translucent. Add the crabmeat with the collards and corn in Step 2.

2½ tablespoons butter or margarine

12 ounces medium-size shrimp, shelled, deveined, and coarsely chopped

12 ounces collard greens or kale, trimmed and coarsely chopped

1 package (10 ounces) frozen corn kernels, thawed and drained

3 large eggs

⅔ cup all-purpose flour

⅓ cup half-and-half

½ teaspoon salt

¼ teaspoon black pepper

⅛ teaspoon ground nutmeg

Per serving:
Calories 367; Protein 26 g;
Carbohydrates 33 g;
Fat 15 g; Sodium 539 mg;
Cholesterol 303 mg

15 minutes   53 minutes

1 Preheat the oven to 450° F. Grease a 9-inch pie pan with ½ tablespoon of the butter and set aside. Heat the remaining butter in a deep 12-inch skillet over moderate heat until bubbling—about 3 minutes.

2 Add the shrimp and sauté, stirring occasionally, for 3 to 5 minutes or until pink. Stir in the collard greens and corn. Cook, uncovered, stirring occasionally, for 10 minutes or until tender.

3 Meanwhile, beat the eggs until frothy in a medium-size bowl. Add the flour, half-and-half, salt, pepper, and nutmeg, then beat until smooth.

4 Spread the shrimp and vegetables in the bottom of the pie pan and pour the egg mixture on top. Set the pan on a large baking sheet and bake, uncovered, for 35 minutes or until a knife inserted in the center comes out clean. Serves 4.

123

Paella

This classic Spanish one-dish meal is named for the broad, shallow metal pan in which it's cooked, but a Dutch oven works just as well.

- 4 cups Basic Chicken Stock (page 333) or 2 cups canned chicken broth mixed with 2 cups water
- ½ teaspoon crushed saffron threads (optional)
- 8 ounces chorizo or hot Italian sausage, cut into 1-inch lengths
- 1 broiler-fryer (3 pounds), cut into 8 pieces
- ¼ cup olive oil
- 1 large yellow onion, coarsely chopped
- 1 large sweet red pepper, cored, seeded, and coarsely chopped
- 1 large sweet green pepper, cored, seeded, and coarsely chopped
- 4 large tomatoes, cored, seeded, and coarsely chopped, or 4 cups canned crushed tomatoes
- 2 cloves garlic, minced
- 1 teaspoon paprika
- 2 cups long-grain white rice
- ¾ teaspoon salt
- ¼ teaspoon black pepper
- 1 pound medium-size shrimp, shelled and deveined
- 2 cups fresh green peas or 1 package (10 ounces) frozen peas, thawed and drained

Per serving:
Calories 696; Protein 52 g;
Carbohydrates 49 g;
Fat 32 g; Sodium 898 mg;
Cholesterol 188 mg

35 minutes   1 hr. 15 min.

1 Bring half of the stock to a simmer in a small saucepan over low heat. Add the saffron, if desired, cover, and simmer for 10 minutes.

2 Meanwhile, heat a 4-quart Dutch oven over moderately low heat for 1 minute. Add the chorizo and brown—about 10 minutes. Transfer to a plate and discard all but 2 tablespoons of the drippings.

3 Pat the chicken dry, then arrange skin side down in the Dutch oven in a single layer. Brown for 7 to 8 minutes, turn, and brown the other side for 6 to 7 minutes. Transfer to a platter. Pour off the drippings.

4 Add the oil to the Dutch oven and heat for 30 seconds over moderate heat. Add the onion and red and green peppers and sauté for 10 minutes or until lightly browned. Add the tomatoes, garlic, and paprika, bring to a simmer, and cook, uncovered, for 5 minutes.

5 Stir in the rice, the saffron mixture, the remaining stock, and the salt and black pepper, and bring to a simmer. Add the chicken and chorizo, reduce the heat to low, cover, and simmer for 15 minutes.

6 Turn the chicken over and add the shrimp and peas. Cover and simmer for 15 minutes or until the liquid has been absorbed. Serves 8.

Shrimp and Noodles with Beer

Beer lends a wonderfully subtle flavor to shrimp. You can, however, substitute 1 cup clam juice for the beer and still have a delicious dish.

- 2 tablespoons olive oil
- 1 medium-size yellow onion, finely chopped
- 1 medium-size sweet red pepper, cored, seeded, and thinly sliced
- 1 medium-size sweet green pepper, cored, seeded, and thinly sliced
- 2 cloves garlic, minced
- ½ teaspoon salt
- ¼ teaspoon black pepper
- 8 ounces mushrooms, thinly sliced
- 1 can (1 pound) tomatoes with their juice, puréed
- 1 cup light beer
- 1 tablespoon tomato paste
- ½ teaspoon each dried thyme and basil, crumbled
- 4 cups medium-wide egg noodles (8 ounces)
- 1 pound large shrimp, shelled and deveined
- 1 cup frozen corn kernels, thawed and drained
- 3 tablespoons minced fresh basil or parsley

Per serving:
Calories 438; Protein 31 g;
Carbohydrates 52 g;
Fat 11 g; Sodium 636 mg;
Cholesterol 157 mg

30 minutes   36 minutes

1 Heat the oil in a 4-quart Dutch oven over moderate heat for 1 minute. Add the onion, red and green peppers, garlic, salt, and black pepper. Sauté, uncovered, stirring occasionally, for 5 minutes or until the onion is limp. Add the mushrooms and sauté 3 minutes more, stirring occasionally.

2 Add the puréed tomatoes to the Dutch oven, along with the beer, tomato paste, thyme, and dried basil. Simmer, uncovered, stirring occasionally, for 12 to 15 minutes or until sauce is slightly thickened. Meanwhile, cook the noodles according to package directions.

3 Add the shrimp and corn to the Dutch oven and bring to a simmer. Cover and cook for 5 minutes or until the shrimp are cooked through. Stir in the noodles, cover, and cook 5 minutes longer or until heated through. Just before serving, stir in the fresh basil. Serves 4.

Cajun Shrimp Casserole

*A mildly spiced shrimp and rice combination. If you happen to have
2 to 3 cups of leftover rice on hand, use it instead of the uncooked rice. Simply add
it in Step 3 along with the shrimp and proceed as directed.*

¼ cup vegetable oil

2 cloves garlic, minced

1 large yellow onion, coarsely chopped

1 small sweet green pepper, cored, seeded, and coarsely chopped

1 medium-size stalk celery, coarsely chopped

2 large tomatoes, cored and coarsely chopped, or 2 cups canned crushed tomatoes

2 whole bay leaves

½ teaspoon dried thyme, crumbled

½ teaspoon salt

¼ teaspoon ground red pepper (cayenne)

1 cup Basic Chicken Stock (page 333) or canned chicken broth

½ cup water

1 tablespoon Worcestershire sauce

1 cup long-grain white rice

1 package (10 ounces) frozen sliced okra, partially thawed and drained

1 pound medium-size shrimp, shelled and deveined

Per serving:
Calories 463; Protein 28 g;
Carbohydrates 51 g;
Fat 16 g; Sodium 554 mg;
Cholesterol 157 mg

30 minutes   41 minutes

1 Heat the oil in a 6-quart Dutch oven over moderate heat for 1 minute. Add the garlic, onion, green pepper, and celery, and sauté, stirring occasionally, until lightly browned and limp—about 10 minutes.

2 Add the tomatoes, bay leaves, thyme, salt, red pepper, stock, water, and Worcestershire sauce, and bring to a simmer. Stir in the rice, reduce the heat to low, cover, and simmer for 15 minutes.

3 Stir in the okra, cover, and cook for 5 minutes. Stir in the shrimp, cover, and cook for another 8 minutes or until the rice is tender and the shrimp are cooked through. Remove the bay leaves and serve. Serves 4.

*Like many southern dishes, Cajun Shrimp Casserole—
a Louisiana favorite—features okra.*

125

Shrimp Scampi Supreme

An ever-popular Italian dish takes on a new look—and flavor.

1 cup orzo or other small pasta
¼ cup olive oil
1 pound medium-size shrimp, shelled and deveined, or scallops
2 medium-size zucchini, halved lengthwise and sliced ½ inch thick
4 large cloves garlic, minced
½ cup dry white wine or clam juice
2 teaspoons fresh lemon juice
¼ teaspoon black pepper
⅓ cup minced parsley

Per serving:
Calories 435; Protein 25 g;
Carbohydrates 42 g;
Fat 16 g; Sodium 189 mg;
Cholesterol 157 mg

20 minutes | 15 minutes

1 Cook the orzo according to package directions, drain, rinse with hot water, and drain well again.

2 Meanwhile, in a 12-inch skillet, heat 2 tablespoons of the oil over moderately high heat for 1 minute. Add the shrimp and stir-fry for 2 to 3 minutes or until pink and curled. Transfer to a large bowl.

3 Add the zucchini to the skillet and stir-fry for 2 to 3 minutes or until crisp-tender. Transfer to the bowl with the shrimp.

4 Reduce the heat to moderate. Add another tablespoon of the oil to the skillet and heat for 1 minute. Add the garlic, stir-fry for 1 minute, and reduce the heat to low. Add the wine and lemon juice, stirring to loosen any browned bits from the bottom of the skillet, then add the remaining 1 tablespoon oil and bring to a boil.

5 Add the pepper and orzo to the shrimp mixture and toss. Add the shrimp mixture to the skillet and cook, uncovered, for 3 to 5 minutes or until heated through, then stir in the parsley. Serves 4.

Stir-Fried Shrimp and Scallops

A delightful mix of ingredients. If you prefer, asparagus or Italian green beans can be used in place of the snow peas; peeled and seeded cucumber can replace the water chestnuts.

⅔ cup quick-cooking or long-grain white rice
2 tablespoons reduced-sodium soy sauce
2 tablespoons rice vinegar or cider vinegar
5 tablespoons peanut or vegetable oil
1 large sweet red pepper, cored, seeded, and cut into ½-inch squares
1 large carrot, peeled and coarsely shredded
1 can (8 ounces) sliced water chestnuts, drained
3 ounces snow peas, trimmed
1½ teaspoons sugar
12 ounces medium-size shrimp, shelled and deveined
8 ounces whole bay scallops or halved sea scallops
3 scallions, including tops, minced
1 piece fresh ginger, about ¾ inch long, peeled and minced

1 Cook the rice according to package directions. Meanwhile, combine the soy sauce and vinegar in a small bowl and set aside.

2 Heat the oil in a wok or deep 12-inch skillet over moderately high heat for 1 minute. Add the pepper, carrot, water chestnuts, and snow peas, sprinkle with the sugar, and stir-fry for 2 minutes or until glossy.

3 Add the shrimp and scallops and stir-fry for 3 minutes. Add the scallions and ginger and stir-fry 1 minute longer. Add the soy mixture and cook, uncovered, stirring occasionally, about 1 minute or until the mixture is syrupy and the shrimp and scallops are cooked through. Serve over the rice. Serves 4.

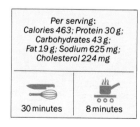

Per serving:
Calories 463; Protein 30 g;
Carbohydrates 43 g;
Fat 19 g; Sodium 625 mg;
Cholesterol 224 mg

30 minutes | 8 minutes

Seafood Risotto

For variations, try substituting any firm-fleshed fish—halibut, salmon, swordfish, or tuna—for the shrimp and scallops. To save time, chop the vegetables in a food processor.

- 2 tablespoons unsalted butter or margarine
- 2 tablespoons olive oil
- 2 cloves garlic, minced
- 8 ounces medium-size shrimp, shelled, deveined, and cut into ½-inch pieces
- 8 ounces bay or sea scallops, cut into ½-inch pieces
- ¼ cup minced parsley
- 1 large yellow onion, finely chopped
- 1½ cups long-grain white rice
- 2 cups Basic Chicken Stock (page 333) or canned chicken broth
- 1 cup water
- ½ teaspoon salt
- ¼ teaspoon black pepper
- 2 medium-size stalks celery, coarsely chopped

- 2 medium-size carrots, peeled and coarsely chopped
- 1 large tomato, cored, peeled, and coarsely chopped, or 1 cup canned crushed tomatoes
- 8 ounces asparagus tips
- ½ cup grated Parmesan cheese (2 ounces)

Per serving:
Calories 580; Protein 34 g;
Carbohydrates 70 g;
Fat 18 g; Sodium 894 mg;
Cholesterol 210 mg

| 40 minutes | 37 minutes |

---

1 Heat the butter and oil for 1 minute in a 6-quart Dutch oven over moderate heat. Add the garlic and sauté for 1 minute. Add the shrimp, scallops, and parsley, and sauté, stirring often, for 3 minutes. With a slotted spoon, transfer the seafood mixture to a plate.

2 In the drippings, sauté the onion until limp—about 5 minutes. Stir in the rice, stock, water, salt, and ⅛ teaspoon of the pepper. Bring to a simmer, reduce the heat to low, cover, and cook for 10 minutes.

3 Add the celery, carrots, and tomato, cover, and simmer for 5 minutes. Lay the asparagus on top, cover, and simmer 5 minutes longer or until the asparagus and rice are tender.

4 Stir in the seafood mixture, cover, and heat to serving temperature—3 to 5 minutes. Stir in the cheese and remaining pepper. Serves 4.

Seafood Risotto—a New World version of an Old World favorite

Seafood Newburg

This recipe was specially created to tempt all shellfish fans. Choose your favorite shellfish or mix two together to equal 1 pound.

- **2 tablespoons unsalted butter or margarine**
- **1 medium-size yellow onion, finely chopped**
- **2 large baking potatoes, peeled and cut into 1-inch cubes**
- **½ teaspoon salt**
- **¼ teaspoon black pepper**
- **2½ cups Basic Chicken Stock (page 333) or canned chicken broth or fish stock (page 254)**
- **1 package (1 pound) frozen mixed vegetables or frozen peas and carrots, thawed and drained**
- **1 pound shellfish (shelled and deveined shrimp, bay or halved sea scallops, or crab or lobster meat, picked over to remove bits of shell and cartilage)**
- **½ cup half-and-half**
- **2 tablespoons cornstarch**
- **2 tablespoons Dijon mustard**
- **2 tablespoons dry sherry (optional)**
- **2 teaspoons lemon juice (freshly squeezed preferred)**
- **¼ teaspoon paprika**

Per serving:
Calories 404; Protein 31 g;
Carbohydrates 44 g;
Fat 12 g; Sodium 752 mg;
Cholesterol 183 mg

20 minutes | 21 minutes

1 Melt the butter in a large saucepan over moderate heat. Add the onion and sauté, stirring occasionally, for 5 minutes or until limp. Add the potatoes, salt, and pepper, and cook, stirring, for 1 minute.

2 Add the stock, cover, and simmer for 5 minutes. Add the vegetables, cover, and simmer for 5 minutes or until the vegetables are just tender.

3 Add the shellfish, bring to a simmer, cover, and cook for 2 minutes or until just firm.

4 In a small bowl, combine the half-and-half and cornstarch, whisk into the saucepan, and cook, stirring constantly, until slightly thickened—1 to 2 minutes. Smooth in the mustard, sherry, if desired, and the lemon juice. Sprinkle with the paprika. Serves 4.

A sublime blend of taste and texture— creamy, comforting Seafood Newburg

128

Meatless Meals

Meatless meals have earned an increasingly
respectable place at America's dinner tables. Once considered strictly
for vegetarians, such fare now appeals to a wide variety of people. Thanks to a
creative combination of fruits, vegetables, pasta, grains, and dairy
products, these dishes are surprisingly rich and robust in flavor. Use them
to round out your diet and enjoy a refreshing change of pace.

Cheddar-Broccoli Bread Pudding

Green chilies pep up this intriguing combination of taste and texture. If you want to vary the recipe, use frozen cut asparagus or French-style green beans.

2 tablespoons vegetable oil
1 medium-size yellow onion, finely chopped
8 ounces mushrooms, thinly sliced
2 cups fresh or 1 package (10 ounces) frozen broccoli florets, unthawed
½ teaspoon salt
¼ teaspoon black pepper
8 slices white or whole wheat bread, crusts removed and each slice halved
2 cups shredded sharp Cheddar cheese (8 ounces)
3 large eggs
1 cup whole milk or evaporated skim milk
1 can (4 ounces) chopped green chilies, drained

1 Preheat the oven to 375° F. Heat the oil in a 9-inch skillet over moderate heat for 1 minute. Add the onion and sauté for 2 to 3 minutes or until slightly soft. Add the mushrooms and sauté, stirring, for 2 to 3 minutes. Add the broccoli, salt, and pepper, cover, and cook for 2 minutes.

2 Line a greased 13″ x 9″ x 2″ baking dish with half the bread, top with half the broccoli mixture, and sprinkle with half the cheese.

3 Combine the eggs, milk, and chilies in a medium-size bowl, pour into the baking dish, then layer in the remaining bread, broccoli mixture, and cheese.

4 Cover with foil and bake for 15 minutes. Uncover and bake 10 to 15 minutes more or until puffed and set like custard. Serves 4.

> *Per serving:*
> *Calories 559; Protein 28 g;*
> *Carbohydrates 37 g;*
> *Fat 34 g; Sodium 967 mg;*
> *Cholesterol 228 mg*

| 25 minutes | 39 minutes |

Cheese and Sweet Pepper Bake

Muenster, Swiss, and Monterey Jack all make good substitutes for Cheddar cheese in this multilayered dish.

2 cups bulgur
2 cups boiling water
2 tablespoons olive oil
2 large yellow onions, coarsely chopped
1 large sweet green pepper, cored, seeded, and coarsely chopped
1 large sweet red pepper, cored, seeded, and coarsely chopped
1 package (10 ounces) frozen corn kernels, thawed and drained
2 cloves garlic, minced
¼ cup reduced-sodium soy sauce
2 tablespoons dry sherry, Basic Chicken Stock (see page 333), or canned chicken broth
¼ teaspoon salt
¼ teaspoon black pepper
2 cups shredded Cheddar cheese, low-fat preferred (8 ounces)
4 large eggs
2½ cups low-fat milk

1 Preheat the oven to 325° F. Place the bulgur in a large heatproof bowl, pour the boiling water over it, and let stand for 15 minutes.

2 Meanwhile, heat the oil in a 12-inch skillet over moderate heat for 1 minute. Add the onions and green and red peppers and sauté, stirring occasionally, for 5 minutes or until tender.

3 Stir in the corn and garlic and sauté for 1 minute. Mix in 1 tablespoon each of the soy sauce and sherry and half the salt and black pepper. Stir the remaining soy sauce, sherry, salt, and black pepper into the bulgur.

4 Spoon the onions and peppers into a lightly greased 13″ x 9″ x 2″ baking dish and top with the bulgur, then with the cheese. In a medium-size bowl, lightly beat the eggs and milk, then pour evenly over the cheese.

5 Bake, uncovered, for 50 minutes or until slightly puffed and tipped with brown. Serves 6.

> *Per serving:*
> *Calories 518; Protein 24 g;*
> *Carbohydrates 72 g;*
> *Fat 16 g; Sodium 1,188 mg;*
> *Cholesterol 162 mg*

| 20 minutes | 57 minutes |

Oriental Omelet

Here's a vegetarian adaptation of a Chinese favorite, Eggs Foo Yung.

3 tablespoons reduced-sodium soy sauce

1 tablespoon dry sherry or rice wine

2 teaspoons Oriental sesame oil

8 ounces firm tofu, cut into 1" x ½" x ½" pieces

½ cup quick-cooking white rice

¼ cup canned straw or button mushrooms with their liquid

1 teaspoon cornstarch

2 tablespoons vegetable oil

1 medium-size sweet red pepper, cored, seeded, and thinly sliced

2 scallions, including tops, cut into 2-inch-long slivers

¾ cup frozen green peas, thawed and drained

4 large eggs

3 tablespoons water

1 Combine the soy sauce, sherry, and sesame oil in a small bowl. Add the tofu, turning to coat, then marinate at room temperature for 20 minutes, tossing occasionally. Meanwhile, cook the rice according to package directions but do not season; set aside.

2 Drain the tofu marinade and the mushroom liquid into a measuring cup, then add enough water to equal ½ cup. Blend in the cornstarch, pour into a 10-inch ovenproof nonstick skillet, and cook, stirring constantly, over moderate heat until thickened and clear—2 to 3 minutes. Transfer to a sauceboat, cover with foil, and keep warm.

3 Preheat the broiler. Quickly wipe the skillet clean with a damp sponge, add the vegetable oil, and heat for 1 minute over moderate heat. Add the pepper and scallions and stir-fry for 5 minutes or until tender. Stir in the cooked rice and the peas and mushrooms, then scatter the tofu on top.

4 In a medium-size bowl, beat the eggs and water until foamy and pour into the skillet. Reduce the heat to moderately low and cook, uncov-

ered, for 5 minutes, lifting the eggs around the edge and tilting the skillet so that the uncooked portion runs underneath.

5 Transfer the skillet to the broiler and broil about 5 inches from the heat for 4 to 6 minutes or until the eggs are set. Cut the omelet into quarters and serve with the sauce. Serves 4.

Per serving:
Calories 369; Protein 20 g;
Carbohydrates 30 g;
Fat 19 g; Sodium 613 mg;
Cholesterol 213 mg

20 minutes   20 minutes

It's sesame oil that gives this savory Oriental Omelet an unforgettable flavor and aroma.

Three-Cheese Calzones

Cooking time for these Italian-style specialties is only 33 minutes, but it takes an additional 25 minutes for the dough to rise beforehand. Enjoy them either piping hot or at room temperature.

1 tablespoon olive oil
1 medium-size yellow onion, coarsely chopped
½ small sweet red pepper, cored, seeded, and coarsely chopped
1 clove garlic, minced
1 teaspoon dried basil, crumbled
1 package (10 ounces) frozen chopped broccoli, unthawed
2 tablespoons water
1 cup part-skim ricotta cheese
¾ cup shredded mozzarella cheese (3 ounces)

¼ cup grated Parmesan cheese
1 large egg
1 pound frozen bread dough, thawed

Per serving:
Calories 582; Protein 31 g;
Carbohydrates 69 g;
Fat 21 g; Sodium 1,205 mg;
Cholesterol 100 mg

45 minutes	33 minutes

1 Heat the oil in a 10-inch skillet over moderate heat for 1 minute. Add the onion, pepper, garlic, and basil, and sauté for 4 minutes or until almost soft. Add the broccoli and water, cover, and cook until the broccoli is tender—8 minutes. Remove from the heat and mix in the ricotta, mozzarella, 3 tablespoons of the Parmesan cheese, and the egg. Set aside.

2 Divide the dough into fourths. Roll 1 portion on a lightly floured surface into a 10- by 7-inch oval, then spoon a scant ¾ cup of the broccoli filling down the center, leaving a 1-inch margin at each end. Fold the dough over lengthwise to enclose the filling and pinch the edges to seal. Transfer to a baking sheet lined with foil. Roll, fill, and fold the remaining calzones the same way, and add to the baking sheet.

3 Cover with a clean cloth and let rise in a warm, dry, draft-free spot for 25 minutes. Meanwhile, preheat the oven to 400° F. Brush the calzones lightly with water and sprinkle with the remaining Parmesan.

4 Bake, uncovered, for 18 to 20 minutes or until golden brown. If the calzones brown too fast, cover loosely with foil during the last 5 minutes of baking. Serves 4.

So mouth-watering to look at,
so satisfying to eat—
Three-Cheese Calzones

Down-Home Cheese and Hominy Casserole

Almost any combination of vegetables can be used in this comforting family fare.

- 5 cups Basic Chicken Stock (page 333), canned chicken broth, or water
- ½ teaspoon salt
- 1 cup quick-cooking hominy grits
- 2 tablespoons unsalted butter or margarine
- 1 large yellow onion, coarsely chopped
- 1 package (1 pound) frozen mixed vegetables, thawed and drained
- 2 large eggs, lightly beaten
- ¼ teaspoon ground red pepper (cayenne)
- 1½ cups shredded Cheddar, Monterey Jack, or mozzarella cheese (6 ounces)

Per serving:
Calories 406; Protein 25 g; Carbohydrates 28 g; Fat 23 g; Sodium 920 mg; Cholesterol 167 mg

 15 minutes 34 minutes

1 Preheat the oven to 400° F. Bring the stock and salt to a boil in a medium-size saucepan over moderate heat. Mix in the grits and cook, stirring, for 2 to 3 minutes or until thick. Remove from the heat.

2 Melt the butter in a 9-inch skillet over moderate heat. Add the onion and sauté, stirring, for 1 minute. Add the vegetables and cook, uncovered, stirring often, for 2 minutes.

3 Transfer the skillet mixture to a large heatproof bowl. Add the grits, eggs, red pepper, and all but ¼ cup of the cheese, then mix well.

4 Transfer the mixture to a greased 13" x 9" x 2" baking dish and sprinkle with the remaining cheese. Bake, uncovered, for 20 to 25 minutes or until bubbling. Serves 4.

Hash Brown Potato Melt

A perennial breakfast favorite becomes a lovely lunch when enhanced with Cheddar cheese and green peppers.

- ⅓ cup vegetable oil
- 1 large yellow onion, finely chopped
- 2 medium-size sweet green peppers, cored, seeded, and coarsely chopped
- 3 cups frozen hash brown potatoes (from a 20-ounce package)
- 1 cup milk
- 2 cups shredded medium-sharp low-fat Cheddar cheese (8 ounces)
- ⅛ teaspoon each salt and black pepper

Per serving:
Calories 601; Protein 18 g; Carbohydrates 44 g; Fat 42 g; Sodium 1,087 mg; Cholesterol 33 mg

 15 minutes 36 minutes

1 Preheat the oven to 350° F. Heat 1 tablespoon of the oil in a 12-inch ovenproof skillet over moderate heat for 1 minute. Add the onion and green peppers and sauté, stirring occasionally, for 5 minutes or until limp.

2 Stir in the potatoes and add the remaining oil, then flatten the mixture to a uniform thickness. Reduce the heat to moderately low and cook, uncovered, without stirring, for 5 minutes.

3 Mix the milk, cheese, salt, and black pepper in a small bowl, pour over the potato mixture, and transfer to the oven.

4 Bake, uncovered, for 20 to 25 minutes or until the potatoes are tender, bubbling, and tipped with brown. Serves 4.

Whipped Sweet Potato Pie

In this modern version of an old-time favorite, spinach teams up with sweet potatoes to make a tempting casserole.

2 teaspoons olive oil
1 medium-size yellow onion, finely chopped
2 cloves garlic, minced
1 package (10 ounces) frozen chopped spinach, thawed, drained, and squeezed dry
½ teaspoon dried thyme, crumbled
2 cups diced cooked sweet potatoes (fresh or canned)
1½ cups low-fat or whole milk
2 large eggs
½ teaspoon salt
1½ cups shredded Cheddar cheese (6 ounces)

Per serving:
Calories 358; Protein 20 g;
Carbohydrates 26 g;
Fat 20 g; Sodium 676 mg;
Cholesterol 155 mg

20 minutes   31 minutes

1 Preheat the oven to 375° F. Heat the oil in a 10-inch skillet over moderately low heat for 1 minute. Add the onion and garlic and sauté, stirring occasionally, for 7 minutes or until very soft. Mix in the spinach and thyme and cook, uncovered, for 3 minutes.

2 In a food processor or an electric blender, purée the sweet potatoes with the milk, eggs, and salt for 30 seconds. Spread half the mixture in the bottom of a greased 9-inch pie pan. Sprinkle with half of the cheese, cover with the spinach mixture, then top with the remaining sweet potatoes and cheese.

3 Bake, uncovered, for 20 minutes or until the pie is set and very lightly tipped with brown. Serve either hot or at room temperature. Serves 4.

Tomato-Eggplant Tarts

This recipe makes two shallow tarts that are perfect for one delicious meal. You can serve them hot, warm, or at room temperature.

2 tablespoons olive oil
1 medium-size yellow onion, finely chopped
1 medium-size sweet green pepper, cored, seeded, and finely chopped
1 small eggplant, diced (2½ cups)
1 can (14½ ounces) tomatoes, drained and chopped
2 cloves garlic, minced
½ teaspoon salt
½ teaspoon each dried thyme and basil, crumbled
3 large eggs plus 1 large egg white
1 cup whole milk
2 frozen 9-inch pie shells, unthawed
¼ cup grated Parmesan cheese

Per serving:
Calories 608; Protein 17 g;
Carbohydrates 50 g;
Fat 38 g; Sodium 1,294 mg;
Cholesterol 173 mg

25 minutes   50 minutes

1 Preheat the oven to 375° F. Heat the oil in a 12-inch nonstick skillet over moderate heat for 1 minute. Add the onion and pepper and sauté for 3 minutes or until slightly soft.

2 Add the eggplant to the skillet and sauté, stirring, for 2 minutes. Add the tomatoes, garlic, salt, thyme, and basil. Cook, uncovered, stirring often, for 5 minutes or until the mixture is dry. Let cool for 10 minutes.

3 Meanwhile, in a large bowl, lightly beat the eggs with the milk just enough to combine. Stir in the cooled skillet mixture and the cheese, then pour into the pie shells.

4 Place the tarts on a baking sheet in the lower third of the oven and bake, uncovered, for 35 to 40 minutes or until the filling is puffed and set like custard. Serves 4 to 6.

Vegetarian Shepherd's Pie

*A true original, this shepherd's pie is made with
pinto beans, black beans, chick peas, and zucchini. If you plan
to serve mashed potatoes earlier in the week, make 3 extra cups (about
3 large potatoes) so that you'll have leftovers on hand.*

Whip up this Vegetarian Shepherd's Pie for
a hearty meatless meal.

1	tablespoon olive oil
5	cloves garlic, crushed
1	small sweet red pepper, cored, seeded, and coarsely chopped
1	small sweet green pepper, cored, seeded, and coarsely chopped
2	medium-size zucchini, thinly sliced
1	cup canned crushed tomatoes
¼	teaspoon salt
⅛	teaspoon black pepper
1⅓	cups cooked or canned pinto beans, drained and rinsed
1⅓	cups cooked or canned black beans, drained and rinsed
1⅓	cups cooked or canned chick peas, drained and rinsed
3	cups mashed potatoes
¼	teaspoon paprika (optional garnish)

*Per serving:
Calories 459; Protein 21 g;
Carbohydrates 84 g;
Fat 7 g; Sodium 720 mg;
Cholesterol 3 mg*

 25 minutes   34 minutes

1 Preheat the oven to 375° F. Heat 2 teaspoons of the oil in a 10-inch skillet over moderate heat for 1 minute. Add 2 cloves of the garlic and sauté for 1 minute.

2 Add the red and green peppers and zucchini and sauté, stirring occasionally, for 4 minutes or until crisp-tender. Add ¾ cup of the crushed tomatoes and the salt and black pepper and cook, uncovered, 3 minutes longer.

3 Place the pinto beans, black beans, chick peas, and the remaining oil, garlic, and tomatoes in a food processor or an electric blender, and purée until smooth—about 30 seconds.

4 Spoon the purée into a lightly greased 9-inch pie pan, top with the skillet mixture, then spoon the mashed potatoes on top.

5 Bake, uncovered, for 25 minutes or until the potatoes are lightly browned. Sprinkle with paprika if desired. Serves 4.

135

Eggplants with Raisin-Couscous Stuffing

In this savory recipe, you save time by preparing the stuffing while the eggplants bake. For a party buffet, try it with baby eggplants.

- 2 medium-size eggplants (1 pound each), halved lengthwise
- ¾ cup couscous or ⅔ cup long-grain or quick-cooking white rice
- 1½ cups cooked or canned chick peas, drained and rinsed
- 1¼ cups cherry tomatoes, stemmed and halved
- 1 cup plain low-fat yogurt
- 4 ounces feta cheese, crumbled
- ½ cup raisins

- ¼ cup minced fresh basil or 1 teaspoon dried basil, crumbled
- ½ teaspoon salt
- ¼ teaspoon black pepper
- 2 tablespoons pine nuts or toasted slivered almonds (see page 86)
- 2 tablespoons olive oil

Per serving:
Calories 563; Protein 22 g;
Carbohydrates 83 g;
Fat 18 g; Sodium 650 mg;
Cholesterol 29 mg

10 minutes   40 minutes

1 Preheat the oven to 400° F. Prick the eggplant skins with a fork, then wrap each half in foil. Place on a baking sheet and bake for 25 minutes or until soft; cool until easy to handle. Meanwhile, prepare the couscous according to package directions.

2 Mix the couscous, chick peas, cherry tomatoes, yogurt, cheese, raisins, basil, salt, pepper, and pine nuts in a large bowl.

3 With a spoon, gently scoop out the eggplant flesh, leaving the shells intact. Chop the flesh coarsely and stir into the couscous mixture. Mound into the eggplant shells.

4 Arrange the stuffed eggplants in an ungreased 13″ x 9″ x 2″ baking pan, drizzle with the olive oil, and bake, uncovered, for 15 minutes or until piping hot. Serves 4.

These elegant Eggplants with Raisin-Couscous Stuffing are fine fare for family or when company's coming to dinner.

136

Kasha Casserole

*The peanuts in this recipe complement the nutlike flavor of
the crushed buckwheat kernels called kasha. If you prefer, you can use
1 cup long-grain brown rice in place of the kasha.*

- 1 cup kasha
- 1 large egg, lightly beaten
- 2 tablespoons vegetable oil
- 2 medium-size carrots, peeled and thickly sliced
- 1 medium-size yellow onion, finely chopped
- 8 ounces mushrooms, thinly sliced
- ½ teaspoon salt
- ½ teaspoon dried thyme, crumbled
- 1½ cups Basic Chicken Stock (page 333), canned chicken broth, or water
- 1 medium-size yellow squash, sliced 1 inch thick
- 1 medium-size zucchini, sliced 1 inch thick
- 1 cup unsalted dry-roasted peanuts
- ½ cup grated Parmesan cheese (2 ounces)

1 In a small bowl, mix the kasha with the egg. Spoon into a 9-inch skillet and cook, stirring, over moderate heat until dry—about 2 minutes. Remove from the heat and set aside.

2 Heat the oil for 1 minute in a 4-quart flameproof casserole over moderate heat. Add the carrots and onion and sauté for 1 minute. Add the mushrooms, salt, and thyme, and sauté, stirring often, for 2 to 3 minutes.

3 Add the stock to the casserole, bring to a boil, then stir in the kasha mixture. Cover, reduce the heat to moderately low, and cook for 20 minutes.

4 Scatter the yellow squash and zucchini on top of the kasha, cover, and cook for 10 minutes or until the kasha and squash are tender. Stir in the peanuts and cheese. Serves 4.

Per serving:
Calories 475; Protein 23 g;
Carbohydrates 31 g;
Fat 31 g; Sodium 665 mg;
Cholesterol 64 mg

25 minutes | 39 minutes

Tofu Stir-Fry with Peanut Sauce

*A rich source of protein, tofu sets the stage for an attractive
dish that stars a delectable sauce.*

- ½ cup water
- 2 medium-size carrots, peeled and cut into matchstick strips
- 1 cup coarsely shredded green cabbage
- 1 cup coarsely shredded red cabbage
- 2 cups fresh or canned bean sprouts, drained
- 1 pound firm tofu, cut into ¾-inch cubes
- 2 tablespoons vegetable oil
- 1 clove garlic, minced
- 8 scallions, including tops, sliced diagonally into 1-inch lengths
- 1 vegetable bouillon cube dissolved in ⅓ cup water
- ¼ cup cream-style peanut butter
- 2 tablespoons reduced-sodium soy sauce
- 1 tablespoon cider vinegar
- 1 tablespoon sugar
- 1 can (3 ounces) chow mein noodles

1 In a deep 12-inch skillet over high heat, bring the water to a boil. Layer in the carrots, green and red cabbage, and bean sprouts. Reduce the heat to moderate, cover, and boil for 2 minutes.

2 Add the tofu, cover, and cook for 3 minutes or until the vegetables are crisp-tender and the tofu is hot. Drain off all the liquid, transfer the vegetable mixture to a large heatproof bowl, and cover loosely with foil.

3 Add the oil to the skillet and heat for 1 minute over moderate heat. Add the garlic and scallions and stir-fry for 2 minutes or until crisp-tender. Transfer to the bowl.

4 In the same skillet, combine the vegetable bouillon, peanut butter, soy sauce, vinegar, and sugar. Simmer over low heat, whisking often, until smooth—about 2 minutes. Mix the sauce into the vegetable mixture in the bowl. Add half of the noodles and toss until coated. Transfer to a platter and sprinkle the remaining noodles on top. Serves 4.

Per serving:
Calories 487; Protein 29 g;
Carbohydrates 34 g;
Fat 30 g; Sodium 671 mg;
Cholesterol 2 mg

25 minutes | 10 minutes

137

Hoppin' John

*An update of the southern classic that's customarily
served on New Year's Day for good luck.*

2 tablespoons olive oil

3 medium-size yellow onions,
   coarsely chopped

1 large sweet green pepper,
   cored, seeded, and cut into ¾-
   inch squares

1 large sweet red pepper, cored,
   seeded, and cut into ¾-inch
   squares

3 cloves garlic, minced

1¾ cups water

¾ cup quick-cooking white rice

2 packages (10 ounces each)
   frozen black-eyed peas,
   unthawed

1½ teaspoons salt

¼ teaspoon black pepper

¼ teaspoon red pepper flakes

2 teaspoons prepared mustard

2 teaspoons red wine vinegar

1 pound firm tofu, cut into ¾-
   inch cubes

1 Heat the oil in a 10-inch skillet over moderate heat for 1 minute. Add the onions, green and red peppers, and garlic, and sauté, stirring occasionally, for 5 minutes or until soft. Transfer to a bowl and set aside.

2 Pour ¾ cup of the water into the skillet and bring to a boil over high heat. Add the rice, cover, and remove from the heat; let stand for 5 minutes, then transfer to the bowl. Pour the remaining water into the skillet and bring to a boil over moderate heat. Add the peas, salt, black pepper, and red pepper flakes, then return to a boil. Reduce the heat to low, cover, and simmer for 35 minutes or until the peas are almost tender.

3 Stir in the mustard, vinegar, tofu, and reserved vegetables and rice. Cover and simmer for 5 minutes or until the peas are tender and the tofu is heated through. Serves 4.

Per serving:
Calories 584; Protein 34 g;
Carbohydrates 77 g;
Fat 18 g; Sodium 860 mg;
Cholesterol 0 mg

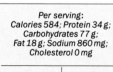

25 minutes	53 minutes

Meatless Chili

*Barley, rice, and corn take the place of meat in this chili. Top it with
chopped onion and plain yogurt or sour cream if desired.*

2 teaspoons vegetable oil

½ cup medium pearl barley

2¾ cups water

1 cup quick-cooking brown rice

1 tablespoon chili powder

1 can (15 ounces) tomato sauce

1 can (8 ounces) no-salt-added
   stewed tomatoes with their
   juice

1 can (1 pound) red kidney
   beans, drained and rinsed

1 package (10 ounces) frozen
   corn kernels, thawed and
   drained

⅛ to ¼ teaspoon ground red
   pepper (cayenne)

¾ cup shredded medium-sharp
   Cheddar cheese (3 ounces)

2 tablespoons pumpkin seeds
   (optional)

1 Heat the oil in a large saucepan over moderate heat for 1 minute. Stir in the barley and cook, uncovered, stirring often, for 2 minutes. Add the water and bring to a boil, then adjust the heat so that the water bubbles gently, cover, and cook for 15 minutes.

2 Raise the heat to moderate and add the rice and chili powder. Return to a boil, cover, and cook for 5 minutes.

3 Stir in the tomato sauce, tomatoes, beans, corn, and red pepper, and bring to a boil again. Adjust the heat so that the mixture bubbles gently, cover, and cook for 10 minutes or until the rice and barley are tender. Sprinkle each serving with the cheese and, if desired, the pumpkin seeds. Serves 4.

Per serving:
Calories 479; Protein 20 g;
Carbohydrates 79 g;
Fat 12 g; Sodium 1,177 mg;
Cholesterol 22 mg

10 minutes	37 minutes

Paella with Tofu

*You can substitute tomato juice for the chicken stock, kidney or black beans for the chick peas,
or brown rice for the white. For a more traditional paella recipe, turn to page 124.*

2 tablespoons olive oil

1 large yellow onion, coarsely chopped

1 large sweet red pepper, cored, seeded, and coarsely chopped

2 cloves garlic, minced

1 can (14½ ounces) tomatoes, drained and chopped

½ teaspoon salt

½ teaspoon ground turmeric

½ teaspoon each dried basil and thyme, crumbled

3½ cups Basic Chicken Stock (page 333) or canned chicken broth

1 can (1 pound 3 ounces) chick peas, drained and rinsed

2 cups long-grain white rice

1 pound firm tofu, drained and cut into 1-inch cubes

½ cup toasted slivered almonds (see page 86), optional garnish

*Per serving:
Calories 862; Protein 44 g;
Carbohydrates 130 g;
Fat 21 g; Sodium 693 mg;
Cholesterol 0 mg*

20 minutes | 39 minutes

1 Preheat the oven to 350° F. Heat the oil in a 3-quart flameproof casserole over moderate heat for 1 minute. Add the onion, pepper, and garlic, and sauté, stirring, for 1 minute or until slightly softened.

2 Mix in the tomatoes, salt, turmeric, basil, and thyme. Cook, uncovered, stirring often, for 3 to 4 minutes or until thick.

3 Stir in the stock and chick peas, bring to a boil, then stir in the rice. Bring the liquid back to a boil, stirring often, then scatter the tofu on top.

4 Cover and bake for 25 to 30 minutes or until the rice is tender. Let stand at room temperature, covered, for 10 minutes. Sprinkle the paella with the almonds if desired. Serves 4.

Light, simple, and delicious, Paella with Tofu—garnished here with sprigs of basil and thyme—is hard to beat.

Rice and Beans, Spanish Style

Orange slices add a colorful touch to this ever-popular Spanish dish.

2 tablespoons vegetable oil

1 medium-size yellow onion, finely chopped

1 medium-size sweet green pepper, cored, seeded, and cut into 1-inch squares

1 medium-size sweet red pepper, cored, seeded, and cut into 1-inch squares

½ teaspoon salt

2 cups water

2 cups quick-cooking white rice

1 can (1 pound) black beans, drained and rinsed

2 hard-boiled eggs, peeled and coarsely chopped

2 medium-size navel oranges, peeled and sliced ½ inch thick

1 Heat the oil in a large saucepan over moderate heat for 1 minute. Add the onion and green and red peppers and sauté, stirring often, for 1 minute. Add the salt and water, bring to a boil, and stir in the rice. Remove from the heat, cover, and let stand for 5 minutes.

2 Stir the beans into the rice mixture, cover, and warm over low heat for 2 minutes. Transfer to a serving dish, top with the chopped eggs, and surround with the orange slices. Serves 4.

Per serving:
Calories 642; Protein 21 g;
Carbohydrates 114 g;
Fat 11 g; Sodium 311 mg;
Cholesterol 137 mg

 25 minutes | 11 minutes

*Rice and Beans,
Spanish Style — almost
too beautiful to eat*

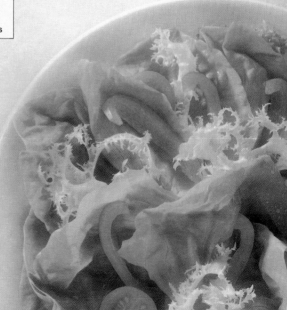

Rice and Beans, Italian Style

*Gorgonzola, a creamy Italian cheese, adds a
tangy flavor to this bean dish. You can, however, substitute ¼ cup
grated Parmesan mixed with 4 ounces shredded mozzarella, or blend
3 ounces of blue cheese with 3 ounces of cream cheese.*

1 tablespoon olive oil
1 medium-size yellow onion, coarsely chopped
1 clove garlic, minced
1 cup long-grain white rice
½ teaspoon dried basil, crumbled
2 vegetable bouillon cubes dissolved in 2 cups water
1 package (9 ounces) frozen Italian green beans, thawed and drained
6 ounces gorgonzola cheese, coarsely crumbled
½ cup half-and-half or ¼ cup each half-and-half and low-fat or whole milk
¼ teaspoon salt
½ teaspoon white pepper
1 can (1 pound) cannellini (white kidney beans), drained and rinsed
2 tablespoons minced flat-leaf parsley (optional)

1 Heat the oil in a large saucepan over moderate heat for 1 minute. Add the onion and garlic and sauté for 5 minutes or until limp.

2 Add the rice and basil and cook, stirring, for 1 minute. Add the vegetable bouillon, bring to a simmer, cover, and cook for 15 minutes.

3 Stir in the green beans, cheese, and ¼ cup of the half-and-half. Cover and cook for 5 minutes or until the beans are tender. Stir in the salt, pepper, cannellini, and remaining half-and-half, reduce the heat to low, and cook until heated through—about 3 minutes more. Sprinkle with parsley if desired. Serves 4 to 6.

*Per serving:
Calories 515; Protein 21 g;
Carbohydrates 62 g;
Fat 20 g; Sodium 1,542 mg;
Cholesterol 43 mg*

15 minutes | 30 minutes

Rice and Beans, Southern Style

*Kale, peas, and green pepper turn red beans and rice,
a Louisiana specialty, into a well-balanced one-dish meal. Although
dried mushrooms aren't essential, they add extra flavor.*

½ ounce dried mushrooms (optional)
2 cups hot water
1½ tablespoons olive oil
1 large yellow onion, finely chopped
3 cloves garlic, crushed
1 large sweet green pepper, cored, seeded, and coarsely chopped
1 cup long-grain white rice
2 cups canned crushed tomatoes
1 teaspoon dried marjoram, crumbled
¼ teaspoon salt
⅛ teaspoon ground red pepper (cayenne)
8 ounces kale, coarsely shredded
1¼ cups frozen green peas, thawed and drained
1 can (1 pound) red kidney beans, drained and rinsed

1 Soak the mushrooms, if using, in the hot water for 20 minutes. Meanwhile, heat the oil in a large saucepan over moderately low heat for 1 minute. Add the onion and garlic and sauté stirring occasionally for 5 minutes, or until limp. Add the green pepper and sauté, stirring now and then, 3 minutes longer.

2 Add the rice to the saucepan and stir to coat, then lift the mushrooms from their soaking liquid and add to the pan. Strain the mushroom soaking liquid through a fine sieve into the saucepan and bring all to a boil. If you omit the mushrooms, use 2 cups water in place of the soaking liquid. Adjust the heat so that the mixture bubbles gently, then cover and cook for 5 minutes.

3 Stir in the tomatoes, marjoram, salt, and red pepper. Cover and cook for 12 to 14 minutes or until the rice is almost tender. Stir in the kale, peas, and beans, cover, and cook 5 minutes longer or until the rice is tender and the vegetables are heated through. Serves 4.

*Per serving:
Calories 417; Protein 15 g;
Carbohydrates 76 g;
Fat 7 g; Sodium 759 mg;
Cholesterol 0 mg*

20 minutes | 35 minutes

Rice and Beans, Mexican Style

In this recipe, tortillas are wrapped around rice and beans to make burritos. For a spicier dish, add ½ teaspoon chili powder.

- ⅓ cup long-grain brown rice
- 1 large yellow onion, coarsely chopped
- 1 large sweet green pepper, cored, seeded, and coarsely chopped
- 1 large sweet red pepper, cored, seeded, and coarsely chopped
- 2 cloves garlic, minced
- 8 flour tortillas, 6 to 7 inches in diameter
- 1 cup cooked or canned black beans, drained and rinsed
- 1 cup cooked or canned pinto beans, drained and rinsed
- 1 teaspoon ground cumin
- ¼ teaspoon hot red pepper sauce
- 1 cup shredded Monterey Jack cheese (4 ounces)
- 1 cup bottled salsa or Basic Salsa (page 339)

1 Preheat the oven to 350° F. Cook the rice according to package directions, mixing in the onion, green and red peppers, and garlic after 30 minutes. Cook, uncovered, 10 minutes more or until the rice is tender.

2 Meanwhile, wrap the tortillas in foil and warm in the oven for 5 to 10 minutes or until flexible.

3 Stir the black beans, pinto beans, cumin, and red pepper sauce into the rice mixture, and cook, uncovered, until all the liquid is absorbed—2 to 3 minutes more.

4 Spoon a scant ½ cup of the mixture down the center of each tortilla. Roll up and place seam side down in a lightly greased 13" x 9" x 2" baking dish.

5 Sprinkle with the cheese, then bake, uncovered, for 10 minutes or until the cheese melts. Meanwhile, heat the salsa to serving temperature in a small uncovered saucepan. Ladle over the burritos. Serves 4.

Per serving:
Calories 486; Protein 22 g; Carbohydrates 71 g; Fat 15 g; Sodium 380 mg; Cholesterol 0 mg

25 minutes	53 minutes

Lentil and Carrot Stew with Yogurt Topping

For a creamier topping, you can drain the yogurt. Simply spoon it into a sieve lined with cheesecloth or a coffee filter, set over a bowl, and let stand at room temperature for 2 hours or refrigerate overnight. Then discard the liquid and stir until smooth.

- 2 tablespoons olive oil
- 3 large yellow onions, coarsely chopped
- 1 cup dried lentils, sorted and rinsed
- ¾ cup long-grain brown rice
- 3½ cups water
- 2 cloves garlic, crushed
- ½ teaspoon ground cinnamon
- ¼ teaspoon ground cloves
- ⅛ teaspoon ground red pepper (cayenne)
- 3 large carrots, peeled and coarsely chopped (2 cups)
- 2 cups plain low-fat yogurt (drained if desired) or 1 cup sour cream

1 Heat the oil in a 4-quart Dutch oven over moderate heat for 1 minute. Add the onions and sauté, stirring often, for 12 to 15 minutes or until dark brown. Transfer half of the onions to a plate and set aside.

2 Add the lentils and rice to the onions remaining in the Dutch oven, and cook, stirring, for 1 minute. Add the water, garlic, cinnamon, cloves, and red pepper, and cook, uncovered, for 20 minutes. Add the carrots and cook, uncovered, 20 to 25 minutes more or until the rice and carrots are tender.

3 Spoon into a large serving bowl and scatter the reserved onions on top. For the topping, spoon the yogurt into a serving bowl and pass separately. Serves 4.

Per serving:
Calories 389; Protein 20 g; Carbohydrates 57 g; Fat 10 g; Sodium 107 mg; Cholesterol 7 mg

15 minutes	1 hr. 2 min.

Spicy Red Lentils and Rice

The yogurt and sesame topping are refreshing touches.

1½ tablespoons vegetable oil

6 scallions, including tops, thinly sliced

3 cloves garlic, thinly sliced

2 medium-size carrots, peeled and thinly sliced

8 ounces mushrooms, quartered

1 cup long-grain white rice

1 cup dried red lentils, sorted and rinsed

1½ teaspoons salt

1 teaspoon each ground coriander, cumin, ginger, and turmeric

4 cups water

8 ounces kale or spinach, coarsely shredded, or 1 package (10 ounces) frozen chopped spinach or kale, thawed and drained

1 cup plain low-fat yogurt

2 tablespoons sesame seeds (optional)

Per serving:
Calories 466; Protein 22 g;
Carbohydrates 81 g;
Fat 7 g; Sodium 881 mg;
Cholesterol 4 mg

 25 minutes   28 minutes

1 Heat 1 tablespoon of the oil in a large saucepan over moderate heat for 1 minute. Add the scallions and garlic and sauté, stirring occasionally, for 3 minutes or until slightly softened.

2 Add the remaining oil to the saucepan along with the carrots and mushrooms and sauté, stirring occasionally, for 5 minutes or until the carrots are crisp-tender.

3 Add the rice, lentils, salt, coriander, cumin, ginger, and turmeric, and stir to coat. Add the water and bring to a boil over high heat. Adjust the heat so that the mixture bubbles gently, cover, and cook for 15 minutes.

4 Stir in the kale, cover, and cook for 2 minutes or just until the kale is slightly wilted. Top each portion with ¼ cup of the yogurt and, if desired, the sesame seeds. Serves 4.

A dish full of goodness with a rich golden hue — Spicy Red Lentils and Rice

"Meatballs" and Spaghetti

Chick peas and Parmesan cheese make a good alternative to traditional meatballs.

1 can (1 pound 3 ounces) chick peas, drained and rinsed
1 clove garlic
1 large egg
1 large egg white
⅓ cup fine dry bread crumbs
⅓ cup grated Parmesan cheese
2 cans (14½ ounces each) no-salt-added stewed tomatoes, with their juice
1½ tablespoons tomato paste
8 ounces spaghetti or long fusilli
1¼ cups frozen green peas, thawed and drained

Per serving:
Calories 586; Protein 32 g;
Carbohydrates 99 g;
Fat 9 g; Sodium 383 mg;
Cholesterol 60 mg

 10 minutes   21 minutes

1 In a food processor or an electric blender, purée the chick peas with the garlic, egg, egg white, bread crumbs, and cheese for about 30 seconds or until the mixture forms a ball. Set the processor work bowl or blender container in the freezer for 10 minutes to quick-chill the mixture.

2 Meanwhile, combine the tomatoes and tomato paste in a 12-inch skillet and cook, uncovered, for 5 minutes over moderate heat.

3 Shape the chick pea mixture into 16 balls about 1½ inches in diameter. Add the balls to the tomato mixture, handling them carefully because they are fragile. Bring the tomato mixture to a boil, reduce the heat to low, cover, and simmer for 10 minutes. After 5 minutes, begin cooking the pasta according to package directions.

4 Add the green peas to the skillet, cover, and simmer for 5 to 6 minutes or until the peas are done. Serve the meatballs and tomato sauce over the pasta. Serves 4.

Warmed pita bread and fresh fruit complement tangy Falafel Casserole.

Falafel Casserole

To blanch shelled pistachios, put them in a heatproof colander, immerse in a saucepan of boiling water for 45 seconds, let cool, then remove the skins.

- 1 package (10 ounces) falafel mix
- 1⅓ cups water
- 6 tablespoons vegetable oil
- 1 medium-size yellow onion, finely chopped
- 2 packages (10 ounces each) frozen chopped spinach, thawed, drained, and squeezed dry
- ½ teaspoon salt
- 2 cups plain yogurt
- 2 tablespoons all-purpose flour
- ½ cup pistachios, shelled and blanched
- ¼ cup minced fresh coriander (cilantro) or flat-leaf parsley

Per serving:
Calories 767; Protein 24 g;
Carbohydrates 51 g;
Fat 56 g; Sodium 656 mg;
Cholesterol 15 mg

15 minutes	32 minutes

1 Preheat the oven to 400° F. Combine the falafel mix and water in a medium-size bowl and let stand, uncovered, for 15 minutes; then shape the falafel into 8 patties.

2 Meanwhile, heat 2 tablespoons of the oil in a 12-inch nonstick skillet over moderate heat for 1 minute. Add the onion and sauté for 1 minute or until slightly soft. Add the spinach and salt and cook, stirring, for 2 minutes or until the mixture is very dry.

3 Whisk the yogurt and flour together in a small bowl, then stir into the spinach mixture. Transfer to an ungreased shallow 2-quart casserole.

4 Heat the remaining oil in the skillet over moderate heat for 1 to 2 minutes or until ripples show on the skillet bottom. Add the falafel patties and brown for 2 to 3 minutes on each side or until golden. Arrange in the casserole on top of the spinach.

5 Bake, uncovered, for 15 to 20 minutes or until the spinach mixture is bubbling. Sprinkle the pistachios and coriander on top of the falafel patties before serving. Serves 4.

Chick Pea and Barley Pilaf

This recipe can also be served cold as a main-dish salad. Just toss with a little vinegar and olive oil; if you like extra crunch, add ½ cup diced celery.

1 tablespoon olive oil
1 large yellow onion, finely chopped
3 cloves garlic, crushed
1 cup medium pearl barley
1 teaspoon salt
¾ teaspoon each ground cinnamon, coriander, and cumin
¼ teaspoon black pepper
4½ cups water
4 medium-size carrots, peeled and sliced diagonally ½ inch thick

2 medium-size zucchini, cut into ½ inch cubes
2 cans (1 pound each) chick peas, drained and rinsed
½ cup raisins
⅔ cup unsalted roasted cashews or peanuts

Per serving:
Calories 859; Protein 34 g;
Carbohydrates 144 g;
Fat 20 g; Sodium 599 mg;
Cholesterol 0 mg

15 minutes | 53 minutes

1 Heat the oil in a large saucepan over moderate heat for 1 minute. Add the onion and garlic and sauté, stirring occasionally, for 5 minutes or until limp.

2 Add the barley, salt, cinnamon, coriander, cumin, and pepper, and stir to coat. Add the water and bring to a boil. Adjust the heat so that the water bubbles gently, cover, and cook for 30 minutes.

3 Add the carrots, cover, and cook for 10 minutes more. Add the zucchini, chick peas, and raisins, cover, and cook 5 minutes longer, then stir in the cashews. Serves 4.

Chick Pea and Barley Pilaf— a marvelous mélange with just a hint of sweetness

Pasta and Pizza

Luscious layers of lasagne . . . veal and peppers
dressed up with little bow ties . . . a pizza sandwich filled with ham,
cheese, apples, and walnuts. These are just a few of the mouth-watering dishes
waiting to be savored in this chapter. Today pasta comes in an amazing
array of shapes, sizes, and colors (see page 16), but one rule applies to all: pasta
tastes best when it's cooked *al dente*—firm and chewy.

Spaghetti with Chunky Meat Sauce

This quick sauce is good over any kind of pasta.

- 2 teaspoons olive oil
- 1 large red onion, coarsely chopped
- 2 medium-size carrots, peeled, halved lengthwise, and sliced ¼ inch thick
- 4 ounces sweet Italian-style sausage or turkey sausage, casings removed and crumbled
- 12 ounces lean ground beef or turkey
- 1 can (1 pound 12 ounces) crushed tomatoes in tomato purée
- 10 ounces spaghetti, penne, or wagon-wheel pasta
- 1 cup frozen Italian green beans, thawed and drained
  Grated Parmesan cheese (optional)

1 Heat the oil in a large saucepan over moderately low heat for 1 minute. Add the onion and carrots and sauté, stirring frequently, for 5 minutes or until tender.

2 Push the vegetables to one side of the pan and add the sausage and beef. Raise the heat to moderately high and sauté, stirring constantly, until the beef is browned—about 5 minutes; drain off excess fat.

3 Add the tomatoes and bring to a boil, then reduce the heat to low, cover, and simmer for 15 minutes. Meanwhile, cook the pasta according to package directions.

4 Add the beans to the sauce, cover, and cook over low heat until tender—5 to 7 minutes longer. Drain the pasta, mound on a platter, and top with the sauce. Pass the Parmesan cheese if desired. Serves 4.

Per serving:
Calories 611; Protein 44 g;
Carbohydrates 70 g;
Fat 16 g; Sodium 668 mg;
Cholesterol 99 mg

| 15 minutes | 33 minutes |

Spicy Beef and Spaghetti Pie

This dish has a delicious Oriental flavor and can be served hot or at room temperature. To save time, prepare the vegetables while the spaghetti cooks.

- 8 ounces spaghetti
- 1 tablespoon vegetable oil
- 2 medium-size carrots, peeled and coarsely shredded
- 2 small zucchini or yellow squash, halved lengthwise and thinly sliced
- 1¼ pounds lean ground beef
- 4 scallions, including tops, thinly sliced
- ¼ cup bottled chili sauce
- 3 tablespoons dry sherry (optional)
- 1 tablespoon reduced-sodium soy sauce
- 1 tablespoon cornstarch
- 3 cloves garlic, minced
- 1 teaspoon ground ginger

1 Preheat the oven to 400° F. Cook the spaghetti according to package directions. Meanwhile, brush the bottom and sides of a 9-inch pie pan with the oil.

2 Drain the spaghetti and place in a medium-size bowl. Add the carrots and zucchini and toss well, then spoon into the pie pan and smooth the top. Bake, uncovered, for 15 minutes.

3 Meanwhile, combine the beef, scallions, chili sauce, sherry, if using, soy sauce, cornstarch, garlic, and ginger in a medium-size bowl. Spread the mixture evenly over the pasta. Bake, uncovered, 20 minutes longer or until the meat is cooked through. Serves 4.

Per serving:
Calories 567; Protein 54 g;
Carbohydrates 55 g;
Fat 13 g; Sodium 498 mg;
Cholesterol 129 mg

| 15 minutes | 45 minutes |

Bow-Tie Pasta with Veal and Sweet Peppers

Veal and peppers — a classic Italian duo — here mixed with green peas and served over bow-tie pasta.

- 2 tablespoons all-purpose flour
- 1 teaspoon dried sage, crumbled
- ¼ teaspoon dried marjoram, crumbled
- ¾ cup Basic Beef Stock (page 332) or canned beef broth
- ¼ cup Marsala, dry white wine, or beef stock
- 2 teaspoons cornstarch
- 8 ounces bow-tie pasta or ziti
- 1 medium-size sweet red pepper, cored, seeded, and cut into ¾-inch squares

- 1 medium-size sweet yellow or green pepper, cored, seeded, and cut into ¾-inch squares
- 1 cup frozen green peas, unthawed
- 2 tablespoons vegetable oil
- 12 ounces veal scaloppine, cut crosswise into strips ½ inch wide
- 1 tablespoon heavy cream or 2 tablespoons half-and-half

Per serving:
Calories 539; Protein 33 g;
Carbohydrates 54 g;
Fat 18 g; Sodium 163 mg;
Cholesterol 92 mg

20 minutes | 10 minutes

1 Combine the flour, ½ teaspoon of the sage, and the marjoram in a small paper bag and set aside. In a 1-pint measuring cup, blend the stock with the Marsala, cornstarch, and remaining sage and set aside.

2 Cook the pasta according to package directions, adding the peppers and peas during the last 4 minutes.

3 Meanwhile, heat the oil in a 10-inch skillet over moderately high heat for 1 minute. Quickly shake the veal in the flour mixture in the bag, add to the skillet, and brown for 6 minutes, stirring occasionally. Using a slotted spoon, arrange the veal around the edge of a large, deep platter.

4 As soon as the pasta, peppers, and peas are tender, drain well, mound in the middle of the platter, and cover with foil.

5 Stir the stock mixture, add to the skillet, and bring to a boil, scraping up any browned bits. Boil, uncovered, for 1 minute, smooth in the cream, and spoon over the pasta and veal. Serves 4.

Set aside a few sliced vegetables for decorating the top of Spicy Beef and Spaghetti Pie.

149

Oriental Pork and Pasta

An adaptation of the traditional Chinese lo mein. If you'd prefer chicken or turkey lo mein, substitute 12 ounces chicken or turkey cutlets for the pork tenderloin. You'll find that meat and poultry are much easier to slice if partially frozen—45 minutes will do.

12 ounces pork tenderloin, trimmed of fat and cut into thin 2-inch strips

1 clove garlic, minced

1 teaspoon ground ginger

3 tablespoons reduced-sodium soy sauce

2 tablespoons cornstarch

1 cup Basic Chicken Stock (page 333) or water

¼ teaspoon hot red pepper sauce

1 tablespoon Oriental sesame oil (optional)

8 ounces thin spaghetti

2 tablespoons vegetable oil

4 ounces mushrooms, thinly sliced, or 1 can (6 ounces) button mushrooms, drained

1 large carrot, peeled and coarsely shredded

1 package (9 ounces) frozen snow peas, thawed and drained

Per serving:
Calories 511; Protein 39 g;
Carbohydrates 60 g;
Fat 12 g; Sodium 646 mg;
Cholesterol 79 mg

20 minutes   10 minutes

1 Place the pork in a small bowl and add the garlic, ginger, and 1 tablespoon each of the soy sauce and cornstarch. Toss well and set aside. In a second small bowl, combine the stock, red pepper sauce, remaining soy sauce and cornstarch, and, if you like, the sesame oil; set aside.

2 Cook the spaghetti according to package directions. Meanwhile, heat the vegetable oil in a 12-inch skillet over moderate heat for 1 minute. Add the pork mixture and stir-fry for 5 minutes. Add the mushrooms and carrot, then quickly stir the reserved stock mixture and pour it into the skillet. Bring to a boil, then cook and stir for 1 minute. Stir in the snow peas and cook, uncovered, for 1 minute; remove from the heat.

3 Drain the spaghetti well, mound on a large, deep platter, ladle the skillet mixture on top, and serve hot or at room temperature. Serves 4.

With Oriental Pork and Pasta, East meets West with great success.

Sesame Noodles with Pork and Snow Peas

Since this dish should chill for at least an hour before serving, it's a great make-ahead.

8   ounces thin whole wheat or regular spaghetti
1   pound boned pork blade chops or pork sirloin cutlets, cut ¼ inch thick, or 1 pound skinned and boned chicken breasts
2   large carrots, peeled and coarsely shredded
1   cup frozen snow peas or sugar snap peas, unthawed
2   tablespoons Oriental sesame or vegetable oil
¼   cup water
¼   cup cream-style peanut butter
3   tablespoons reduced-sodium soy sauce
3   tablespoons white vinegar
1   tablespoon honey
¾   teaspoon ground ginger
½   clove garlic

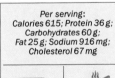

Per serving:
Calories 615; Protein 36 g;
Carbohydrates 60 g;
Fat 25 g; Sodium 916 mg;
Cholesterol 67 mg

15 minutes | 8 minutes

1 Cook the spaghetti according to package directions in a large kettle of boiling water and let the pork simmer along with it—both will be done at the same time. Add the carrots and snow peas to the kettle for the final 2 minutes of cooking.

2 Skim the froth from the spaghetti cooking water, then, using a slotted spoon, transfer the pork to paper toweling to drain.

3 Drain the spaghetti, carrots, and peas well, and place in a large serving bowl. Add the oil and toss. Cut the pork into thin strips, add to the bowl, and toss well. Cover and refrigerate for 1 to 2 hours.

4 Whirl the water, peanut butter, soy sauce, vinegar, honey, ginger, and garlic in a food processor or an electric blender at high speed until smooth—about 1 minute. Transfer to a small bowl, cover, and refrigerate.

5 When ready to serve, add the peanut sauce to the pork and spaghetti and toss well. Serve cold or let stand at room temperature about 30 minutes before serving. Serves 4.

Noodles with Ham and Walnuts, Hawaiian Style

Here's a recipe that evokes the ambience of our island state. It is equally good prepared with either chicken or shrimp.

1   can (8 ounces) pineapple chunks, drained, with ½ cup juice reserved
⅓   cup cider vinegar
2   tablespoons reduced-sodium soy sauce
1   tablespoon ketchup
1   tablespoon cornstarch
8   ounces fine egg noodles
2   tablespoons vegetable oil
1   medium-size yellow onion, halved, then thinly slivered
2   large sweet peppers (green, red, or a combination), cored, seeded, and cut into ¾-inch squares
¾   cup coarsely chopped walnuts
1   clove garlic, minced
8   ounces baked or boiled ham, cut into ½-inch cubes

Per serving:
Calories 601; Protein 22 g;
Carbohydrates 65 g;
Fat 30 g; Sodium 1,135 mg;
Cholesterol 32 mg

20 minutes | 18 minutes

1 Combine the pineapple juice, vinegar, soy sauce, ketchup, and cornstarch in a small bowl and set aside. Begin cooking the noodles according to package directions.

2 Meanwhile, heat the oil in a 12-inch skillet over moderate heat for 1 minute. Add the onion, peppers, and walnuts, cover, and cook for 8 minutes, stirring occasionally. Stir in the garlic and ham, cover, and cook 4 minutes more.

3 As soon as the noodles are tender, drain well, mound on a large, deep platter, and cover with foil to keep warm.

4 Stir the pineapple juice—cornstarch mixture and add to the skillet along with the pineapple chunks. Bring to a boil over moderate heat and cook, stirring constantly, until the sauce is thickened and clear—about 3 minutes. Ladle over the pasta and serve. Serves 4.

Linguine with Ham, Peas, and Mushrooms

For busy days, try this quick and easy supper-in-a-skillet.

- 8 ounces linguine
- 2 tablespoons olive oil
- 4 scallions, including tops, thinly sliced
- 3 cloves garlic, minced
- 8 ounces mushrooms, thinly sliced
- 4 ounces baked or boiled ham, cut into matchstick strips
- 1¼ cups frozen green peas, thawed and drained
- 1½ cups Basic Chicken Stock (page 333) or canned chicken broth
- ⅛ teaspoon black pepper
- 1 tablespoon butter or margarine
- ⅓ cup grated Parmesan cheese

1 Cook the linguine according to package directions. Meanwhile, heat 1 tablespoon of the oil in a deep 12-inch skillet over moderate heat for 1 minute. Add the scallions and garlic and sauté for 3 minutes. Add the mushrooms and the remaining oil and sauté 3 minutes longer.

2 Add the ham and sauté, stirring, for 1 minute. Add the peas, stock, and pepper, raise the heat to high, and boil, uncovered, for 3 minutes or until the liquid is slightly reduced.

3 Remove from the heat and swirl in the butter. Drain the linguine and add to the skillet along with the cheese and toss lightly. Serve with additional Parmesan cheese on the side if desired. Serves 4.

Per serving:
Calories 452; Protein 21 g; Carbohydrates 54 g; Fat 16 g; Sodium 699 mg; Cholesterol 30 mg

15 minutes | 11 minutes

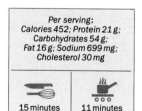

Chicken Fettuccine with Broccoli

Cooking the broccoli with the pasta saves time—and simplifies cleanup.

- 1 tablespoon olive oil
- 1 medium-size yellow onion, coarsely chopped
- 1 medium-size sweet red pepper, cored, seeded, and cut lengthwise into thin strips
- ¼ teaspoon each dried rosemary and thyme, crumbled
- 8 ounces fettuccine or linguine
- 1½ cups frozen broccoli florets, unthawed
- 12 ounces skinned and boned chicken breasts, cut crosswise into strips ½ inch wide
- ¼ cup dry white wine, dry vermouth, or water
- 2 teaspoons instant chicken bouillon granules
- ½ teaspoon black pepper
- ½ cup half-and-half
- ¼ cup grated Parmesan cheese

1 Heat the oil in a 12-inch skillet over moderate heat for 1 minute. Add the onion, red pepper, rosemary, and thyme; cover and cook, stirring occasionally, for 8 minutes or until soft.

2 Meanwhile, cook the fettuccine according to package directions, adding the broccoli during the last 4 minutes.

3 Drain the fettuccine and broccoli well, place in a large serving dish, cover with foil, and keep warm.

4 Raise the heat under the skillet to moderately high and stir in the chicken, wine, bouillon granules, and black pepper. Cook, uncovered, stirring often, until the chicken is no longer pink on the inside—about 5 minutes.

5 Add the half-and-half, lower the heat to moderate, and cook, stirring, 1 to 2 minutes more—just until it reaches serving temperature. Ladle over the fettuccine and broccoli and sprinkle with the cheese. Serves 4.

Per serving:
Calories 446; Protein 33 g; Carbohydrates 50 g; Fat 11 g; Sodium 634 mg; Cholesterol 65 mg

20 minutes | 16 minutes

Fusilli with Chicken and Roasted Vegetables

*This colorful combination of zucchini, yellow squash, and sweet red peppers can also be served as a salad—
just add 1½ tablespoons of balsamic or red wine vinegar and serve at room temperature .*

- 1 **pound skinned and boned chicken thighs or turkey drumsticks, cut into 1½-inch cubes**
- 1 **medium-size zucchini, cut into 1½-inch cubes**
- 1 **medium-size yellow squash, cut into 1½-inch cubes**
- 2 **medium-size sweet red peppers, cored, seeded, and cut into 1½-inch squares**
- ½ **teaspoon each salt and black pepper**
- ½ **teaspoon each crushed fennel seeds and dried rosemary, crumbled**
- 2 **cloves garlic, minced**
- ¼ **cup olive oil**
- 1 **pound fusilli, rotelle, or penne**
- ¼ **cup minced fresh basil or flat-leaf parsley**
- **Grated Parmesan cheese**

Per serving:
Calories 780; Protein 41 g;
Carbohydrates 91 g;
Fat 26 g; Sodium 361 mg;
Cholesterol 94 mg

25 minutes   23 minutes

1 Preheat the oven to 450° F. Mix the chicken, zucchini, yellow squash, red peppers, salt, black pepper, fennel seeds, rosemary, garlic, and oil in an ungreased 15" x 12" x 2" baking pan, then spread in a single layer.

2 Bake, uncovered, for 15 to 20 minutes or until the vegetables are tender and the chicken is no longer pink on the inside.

Fusilli with Chicken and Roasted Vegetables is garnished with a sprig of fresh rosemary that echoes the flavor of the sauce.

3 Meanwhile, cook the fusilli according to package directions, drain well, and transfer to a large bowl.

4 As soon as the chicken and vegetables are done, transfer to the broiler and broil 4 inches from the heat for 2 to 3 minutes or until lightly browned. Add to the fusilli along with all the pan juices and toss to mix. Sprinkle with the basil and serve with the cheese. Serves 4.

Tex-Mex Pasta

Italy meets the Southwest in this colorful mix of chicken, avocado, and salsa.

8 ounces spinach or regular fettuccine

1 pound skinned and boned chicken breasts

2 medium-size yellow squash, sliced ¼ inch thick

1 medium-size sweet red pepper, cored, seeded, and coarsely chopped

1 jar (1 pound) mild salsa or 2 cups Basic Salsa (page 339)

¼ cup minced fresh coriander (cilantro) or flat-leaf parsley

1 teaspoon each chili powder and ground cumin

½ teaspoon dried oregano, crumbled

⅛ teaspoon ground red pepper (cayenne)

1 large avocado, pitted, peeled, and cut into ½-inch cubes

1 tablespoon lemon juice

1 cup shredded Monterey Jack cheese (optional)

Per serving:
Calories 515 g; Protein 38 g;
Carbohydrates 66 g;
Fat 15 g; Sodium 871 mg;
Cholesterol 66 mg

20 minutes   15 minutes

1 Cook the fettuccine according to package directions in a large kettle but add the chicken breasts and let them simmer along with it—both will be done in about 10 minutes.

2 Meanwhile, boil the squash and sweet red pepper in a large covered saucepan until tender—3 minutes. Drain, transfer to a bowl, and cover with foil. Add the salsa, coriander, chili powder, cumin, oregano, and ground red pepper to the saucepan, and simmer, stirring occasionally, for 5 minutes.

3 Drain the chicken and fettuccine well, reserving 1 cup of the cooking water. Transfer the chicken to a cutting board, then return the fettuccine to the kettle, cover, and keep warm. Cut the chicken into thin strips. In a small bowl, toss the avocado with the lemon juice and set aside.

4 Add the chicken, squash mixture, and avocado to the salsa mixture and simmer, uncovered, stirring occasionally, for 5 minutes. If the sauce seems too thick, add some of the pasta water. Pour the sauce over the fettuccine and toss. Sprinkle the cheese on top if desired. Serves 4.

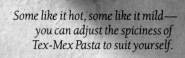

Some like it hot, some like it mild—you can adjust the spiciness of Tex-Mex Pasta to suit yourself.

Chicken Pesto

Traditionally, pesto is made with fresh basil, which is not available all year round, so this recipe uses parsley instead.

12 ounces spaghetti
1 pound skinned and boned chicken breasts
1¾ cups loosely packed flat-leaf parsley leaves
½ cup olive oil
½ cup coarsely chopped walnuts
⅓ cup grated Parmesan cheese
2 cloves garlic
½ cup plus 1 tablespoon Basic Chicken Stock (page 333) or canned chicken broth
½ teaspoon salt
2 jars (7 ounces each) roasted sweet red peppers or pimientos, drained and thinly sliced
Grated Parmesan cheese (optional)

1 Cook the spaghetti according to package directions but add the chicken breasts and let them simmer along with it—both will be done at the same time—about 10 minutes.

2 Meanwhile, whirl the parsley, oil, walnuts, cheese, garlic, stock, and salt in a food processor or an electric blender until smooth.

3 Drain the chicken and spaghetti well. Cut the chicken into thin strips and place in a large bowl. Add the spaghetti, red peppers, and parsley mixture, and toss lightly. Serve with extra Parmesan if desired. Serves 4.

Per serving:
Calories 853; Protein 45 g;
Carbohydrates 74 g;
Fat 42 g; Sodium 545 mg;
Cholesterol 72 mg

5 minutes   10 minutes

Turkey Fettuccine

Carrots, zucchini, and turkey in a creamy sauce— pour over pasta for a delightful dinner.

2 tablespoons unsalted butter or margarine
1 pound turkey or chicken cutlets, cut into 2½" x ¼" x ¼" strips
½ teaspoon salt
12 ounces fettuccine
1 medium-size yellow onion, finely chopped
2 medium-size carrots, peeled and cut into matchstick strips
⅓ cup dry white wine or ¼ cup Basic Chicken Stock (page 333) or canned chicken broth
1 medium-size zucchini, cut into matchstick strips
1 jar (12 ounces) chicken gravy
½ cup half-and-half or whole milk
¼ cup minced fresh chives or scallion tops
Grated Parmesan cheese (optional)

1 Heat 1 tablespoon of the butter in a 12-inch nonstick skillet over moderate heat for 1 minute. Add the turkey and ¼ teaspoon of the salt and stir-fry for 1 minute or until no longer pink. Transfer to a bowl and set aside.

2 Cook the fettuccine according to package directions. Meanwhile, add the remaining butter and the onion to the skillet and stir-fry for 1 minute. Add the carrots and stir-fry 1 minute more. Add the wine, bring to a simmer, cover, and cook for 3 minutes.

3 Add the zucchini and cook and stir for 1 minute. Add the gravy, half-and-half, and remaining salt, and bring to a simmer. Cover and cook for 2 minutes. Return the turkey to the skillet and bring to serving temperature—1 to 2 minutes.

4 As soon as the fettuccine is tender, drain well and place in a large bowl. Add the turkey mixture and toss well. Mound on a large, deep platter and sprinkle with the chives. Accompany, if you like, with the cheese. Serves 4.

Per serving:
Calories 625; Protein 29 g;
Carbohydrates 76 g;
Fat 20 g; Sodium 839 mg;
Cholesterol 73 mg

20 minutes   14 minutes

155

Linguine with Turkey Sausage

*An intriguing mix of ingredients. If you like your food spicy,
use hot Italian sausage in place of the turkey sausage.*

12 ounces turkey sausage
8 ounces linguine or spaghetti
2 tablespoons olive oil
1 large yellow onion, coarsely chopped
1 medium-size zucchini or yellow squash, coarsely shredded (12 ounces)
3 cloves garlic, minced
⅓ cup plain low-fat yogurt
¼ teaspoon black pepper
1 cup shredded low-fat Cheddar cheese (4 ounces)

Per serving:
Calories 564; Protein 34 g;
Carbohydrates 53 g;
Fat 24 g; Sodium 1,027 mg;
Cholesterol 82 mg

20 minutes   20 minutes

1 Prick each sausage once with a fork, place in a heatproof colander, and lower into a large kettle of boiling water. Cover and cook for 3 minutes. Raise the colander to allow the sausage to drain, then transfer the sausage to paper toweling. When cool enough to handle, slice the sausage ½ inch thick and set aside.

2 Return the water in the kettle to a boil and cook the linguine according to package directions.

3 Meanwhile, heat the oil in a deep 12-inch skillet over moderately high heat for 1 minute. Add the sausage and onion and sauté, stirring occasionally, for 3 minutes. Add the zucchini and garlic and sauté, stirring occasionally, for 3 to 5 minutes or until the zucchini is tender. Stir in the yogurt and pepper and turn the heat under the skillet to the lowest setting.

4 Drain the linguine and return it to the kettle. Add the cheese, toss lightly, and cover for 1 minute, so that the cheese melts and coats the linguine. Pour the sausage mixture over the linguine and toss well to mix. Serves 4.

Tuna Noodle Niçoise

*This layered variation of the famed salad can be served at room temperature
or chilled. Use a clear glass bowl to show off the colorful tiers.*

1 package (9 ounces) frozen French-style green beans, unthawed
8 ounces broad egg noodles
½ cup olive oil
⅓ cup white wine vinegar or cider vinegar
¼ cup plain low-fat yogurt
2 tablespoons Dijon mustard
2 tablespoons reduced-calorie mayonnaise
1½ tablespoons capers, drained
1½ teaspoons sugar
½ teaspoon salt
½ teaspoon black pepper
1 can (6 ounces) solid-pack white tuna in water, drained and flaked
2 large ripe tomatoes, cored and thinly sliced
½ cup pitted black olives, halved

Per serving:
Calories 594; Protein 22 g;
Carbohydrates 54 g;
Fat 34 g; Sodium 690 mg;
Cholesterol 19 mg

15 minutes   11 minutes

1 Place the beans in a heatproof colander and lower into a large kettle of boiling water. Cover and cook for 3 minutes. Raise the colander to allow the beans to drain, then transfer to a small bowl.

2 Return the water in the kettle to a boil, add the noodles, and cook according to package directions. Drain, rinse under hot water, and return to the kettle. Cover and keep warm.

3 In a small bowl, whisk the oil with the vinegar, yogurt, mustard, mayonnaise, 1 tablespoon of the capers, the sugar, salt, and pepper. Spoon ⅓ of the mixture onto the noodles and toss well.

4 Place half the noodles in a 2-quart glass bowl, layer half the tuna on top, then half each of the beans, tomatoes, and olives. Pour another third of the dressing evenly over all. Repeat the layering once more and top with the remaining dressing. Sprinkle the remaining ½ tablespoon of capers over all. Serves 4.

Fish and Pasta Pronto

This elegant but easy recipe lends itself to many variations.
Substitute shrimp, scallops, lobster, or crabmeat for the fish. Or use
diced carrots or chopped broccoli instead of the corn.

2 tablespoons olive oil

3 medium-size stalks celery, thinly sliced

2 cloves garlic, minced

1 can (14½ ounces) tomatoes with their juice

2 cups fish stock (page 254) or Basic Chicken Stock (page 333) or canned chicken broth

½ teaspoon salt

½ teaspoon each dried basil and oregano, crumbled

6 ounces medium-size pasta shells, cavatelli, or elbow macaroni

1 package (10 ounces) frozen corn kernels, thawed and drained

1 pound flounder, haddock, cod, or other lean white fish fillets, cut into 1-inch pieces

3 tablespoons minced parsley

1 Heat the oil in a medium-size saucepan over moderate heat for 1 minute. Add the celery and garlic and sauté for 1 minute, stirring often. Add the tomatoes, stock, salt, basil, and oregano, and bring to a boil.

2 Add the pasta, cover, and simmer, stirring occasionally, for 8 minutes or until the pasta is almost tender.

3 Add the corn and fish, cover, and simmer, stirring occasionally, for 3 to 4 minutes or until the fish just flakes when touched with a fork. Sprinkle with the parsley. Serves 4.

Per serving:
Calories 382; Protein 26 g;
Carbohydrates 52 g;
Fat 8 g; Sodium 552 mg;
Cholesterol 57 mg

15 minutes

15 minutes

Tuna Noodle Niçoise — simple but splendid

157

Salmon and Shells

*With either curry or mustard, you can change the flavor
of this easy pasta sauce to suit your taste.*

- 2 tablespoons unsalted butter or margarine
- 1 medium-size yellow onion, finely chopped
- 1 tablespoon curry powder or Dijon mustard
- 3 cups Basic Chicken Stock (page 333) or canned chicken broth
- ½ teaspoon salt
- 6 ounces small pasta shells, cavatelli, or elbow macaroni
- 1 package (10 ounces) frozen cut asparagus or green beans, thawed and drained
- ½ cup plain yogurt
- 2 teaspoons all-purpose flour
- 1 can (7½ ounces) red salmon or tuna, drained and flaked
- 1 jar (6 ounces) roasted sweet red peppers, drained and finely chopped

> Per serving:
> Calories 367; Protein 24 g;
> Carbohydrates 43 g;
> Fat 11 g; Sodium 771 mg;
> Cholesterol 19 mg

10 minutes 21 minutes

1 Melt the butter in a medium-size saucepan over moderate heat. Add the onion and sauté for 1 minute, stirring often. Blend in the curry powder and cook and stir 1 minute more. Mix in the stock and salt and bring to a boil.

2 Add the pasta, cover, and boil for 9 minutes. Add the asparagus, cover, and boil 3 minutes more or until the pasta and asparagus are just tender.

3 Quickly combine the yogurt and flour in a small bowl, blend into the saucepan liquid, and cook, stirring constantly, until slightly thickened—about 2 minutes.

4 Fold in the salmon and peppers and simmer, uncovered, stirring occasionally, just until heated through—about 2 minutes more. Serves 4.

As light and refreshing as a sea breeze: Lemon-Flavored Shrimp and Ziti

Lemon-Flavored Shrimp and Ziti

You can vary the flavor of this recipe by substituting orange rind for lemon and oregano for basil.

12	ounces ziti
2	tablespoons vegetable oil
1½	cups small broccoli florets
1	medium-size sweet yellow or red pepper, cored, seeded, and cut into strips ½ inch wide
2	scallions, including tops, thinly sliced
½	teaspoon dried basil, crumbled
1	pound medium-size shrimp, shelled and deveined
2	teaspoons grated lemon rind
1	clove garlic, minced
½	teaspoon salt
¾	teaspoon ground ginger
½	cup half-and-half or light cream

Per serving:
Calories 538; Protein 34 g;
Carbohydrates 67 g;
Fat 13 g; Sodium 456 mg;
Cholesterol 168 mg

20 minutes | 25 minutes

1 Cook the ziti according to package directions. Drain well, place in a large serving dish, cover with foil, and keep warm.

2 In a 12-inch skillet, heat the oil over moderate heat for 1 minute. Add the broccoli, pepper, scallions, and basil, cover, and cook, stirring occasionally, for 8 minutes or until soft.

3 Stir in the shrimp, lemon rind, garlic, salt, and ginger, and cook, uncovered, for 4 minutes or just until the shrimp turn pink.

4 Stir in the half-and-half and bring to a boil, then cook, uncovered, for 2 minutes. Spoon over the ziti and toss well. Serves 4.

Spaghetti and Shrimp in Mustard Sauce

This creamy sauce is made with cottage cheese, so it's nutritious as well as tasty.

- 8 ounces spaghetti
- 1 cup cream-style cottage cheese
- 2 tablespoons vegetable oil
- 12 ounces medium-size shrimp, shelled and deveined, or bay scallops
- 12 ounces asparagus, cut diagonally into 1-inch lengths, or 1 package (10 ounces) frozen cut asparagus, thawed
- 2 large shallots or 1 small yellow onion, thinly slivered
- 1 can (8 ounces) sliced water chestnuts, drained
- 3 tablespoons Dijon mustard
- 2 tablespoons dry white wine, dry vermouth, or chicken broth
- ½ teaspoon salt
- ¼ teaspoon black pepper

1 Cook the spaghetti according to package directions. Meanwhile, purée the cottage cheese by whirling in a food processor or an electric blender for 1 minute.

2 Heat 1 tablespoon of the oil in a deep 12-inch skillet over moderately high heat for 1 minute. Add the shrimp and stir-fry for 3 minutes or until pink; transfer to a plate and set aside.

3 Reduce the heat to moderate. Add the remaining oil to the skillet and heat for 1 minute. Add the asparagus and shallots and stir-fry until the asparagus is almost tender—5 to 7 minutes.

4 Drain the cooked spaghetti, rinse under hot water, and drain well again. Place in a large serving bowl, cover, and keep warm.

5 Add the water chestnuts to the skillet and stir-fry for 1 to 2 minutes. Reduce the heat to low and blend in the cottage cheese, mustard, wine, salt, and pepper. Stir in the shrimp and heat just to serving temperature—2 to 3 minutes.

6 Remove the skillet from the heat, transfer the contents to the bowl with the spaghetti, and toss lightly. Serves 4.

Per serving:
Calories 487; Protein 34 g;
Carbohydrates 58 g;
Fat 12 g; Sodium 787 mg;
Cholesterol 126 mg

20 minutes | 14 minutes

Scallops and Linguine in Spicy Tomato Sauce—a seafood and pasta combination that's sure to win compliments.

Scallops and Linguine in Spicy Tomato Sauce

Hot red pepper, vinegar, and a touch of orange rind add zing to a quick tomato sauce. If you want to change this to a poultry recipe, use 1 pound chicken or turkey cutlets cut into matchstick strips.

- 1 tablespoon vegetable oil
- 1 small red onion, coarsely chopped
- 1 small yellow squash or zucchini, cut into ½-inch cubes
- ⅛ to ¼ teaspoon red pepper flakes
- 12 ounces linguine or spaghettini
- 1 pound bay scallops or medium-size shrimp, shelled and deveined
- 1 can (1 pound 12 ounces) whole tomatoes in tomato purée
- 1 tablespoon light brown sugar
- 2 teaspoons red wine vinegar or cider vinegar
- 2 teaspoons grated orange rind

1 Heat the oil in a deep 12-inch skillet over moderate heat for 1 minute. Add the onion, squash, and pepper flakes; cover and cook, stirring occasionally, for 5 minutes or until almost soft. Meanwhile, cook the linguine according to package directions.

2 Add the scallops to the skillet and cook, uncovered, until opaque—1 to 2 minutes. Mix in the tomatoes with their purée, breaking them up with a spoon, and the sugar, vinegar, and orange rind. Heat just until the sauce simmers—2 minutes—then turn off the heat.

3 When the linguine is done, drain and transfer it to a serving dish. Bring the sauce to serving temperature over low heat, then ladle over the linguine. Serves 6.

Per serving:
Calories 336; Protein 21 g;
Carbohydrates 54 g;
Fat 4 g; Sodium 411 mg;
Cholesterol 142 mg

10 minutes | 10 minutes

Crab Bake, Mexican Style

This recipe features a special time-saving bonus: the noodles are cooked right in the sauce. Canned salmon or tuna works just as well as crabmeat in this south-of-the-border casserole.

- 2 tablespoons vegetable oil
- 1 medium-size yellow onion, finely chopped
- 2 tablespoons all-purpose flour
- ½ teaspoon each chili powder and ground cumin
- 3 cups Basic Chicken Stock (page 333) or canned chicken broth
- ½ cup sour cream
- 5 ounces medium-wide egg noodles
- 12 ounces fresh, frozen, or canned crabmeat, picked over to remove bits of shell and cartilage
- 1 package (10 ounces) frozen succotash, thawed and drained
- 1 can (4 ounces) chopped green chilies, drained
- ½ teaspoon salt
- ½ cup crushed tortilla chips

1 Preheat the oven to 400° F. Heat the oil in a medium-size saucepan over moderate heat for 1 minute. Add the onion and sauté, stirring, for 1 minute. Blend in the flour, chili powder, and cumin, and cook and stir 1 minute more. Whisk in the stock and cook, stirring constantly, until slightly thickened—3 to 5 minutes.

2 Mix in the sour cream, noodles, crabmeat, succotash, chilies, and salt. Pour into an ungreased 1½-quart flameproof casserole, scatter the tortilla chips on top, set over moderate heat, and bring just to a simmer.

3 Transfer to the oven and bake, uncovered, for 20 to 25 minutes or until the pasta is tender and the top is lightly browned. Serves 4.

Per serving:
Calories 538; Protein 29 g;
Carbohydrates 61 g;
Fat 20 g; Sodium 755 mg;
Cholesterol 98 mg

15 minutes | 35 minutes

Last-Minute Lasagne

The rich taste in this meatless low-fat lasagne comes from caponata, the tasty Italian eggplant appetizer. Most supermarkets carry it in the Italian specialties section.

6 lasagne noodles
2 teaspoons olive oil
1¼ cups part-skim ricotta cheese
½ cup plus 2 tablespoons grated Parmesan cheese
¾ cup low-fat milk
2 large eggs, lightly beaten
¼ teaspoon salt
1 package (10 ounces) frozen chopped spinach, thawed and drained
2 cans (7½ ounces each) caponata

1 Preheat the oven to 400° F. Cook the noodles according to package directions. Meanwhile, brush the bottom and sides of a 9" x 5" x 3" loaf pan with the olive oil and set aside.

2 Combine the ricotta and ½ cup of the Parmesan cheese with the milk, eggs, and salt in a medium-size bowl. Drain the noodles well, then lay 2 on the bottom of the pan, trimming off any overhang so that they fit exactly.

3 Spread ⅓ of the cheese mixture on top of the noodles, followed by ½ of the spinach and ½ of the caponata. Add 2 more noodles, again trimming to fit, and repeat the cheese, spinach, and caponata layers. Top with the remaining 2 noodles, followed by the remaining cheese mixture.

4 Sprinkle with the 2 tablespoons Parmesan cheese. Bake, uncovered, for 25 minutes or until set and lightly golden. Serves 4.

Per serving:
Calories 542; Protein 30 g;
Carbohydrates 49 g;
Fat 23 g; Sodium 1,048 mg;
Cholesterol 145 mg

7 minutes | 35 minutes

Cheese Tortellini with Mushroom Sauce

An ideal recipe for an extra-busy day.

1 tablespoon olive oil
1 large red onion, finely chopped
2 cloves garlic, minced
1 sweet red pepper, cored, seeded, and diced
10 ounces mushrooms, thinly sliced
1 pound cheese tortellini or ravioli
1¼ cups Basic Chicken Stock (page 333) or canned chicken broth
¼ teaspoon each salt and black pepper
1 cup frozen Italian green beans, thawed and drained
1 tablespoon unsalted butter or margarine

1 Heat the oil in a 12-inch skillet over moderately low heat for 1 minute. Add the onion and sauté until limp—5 minutes. Add the garlic and sauté 1 minute longer. Add the red pepper and mushrooms, toss to mix, and sauté for 5 minutes or until the mushrooms start to release their liquid.

2 Meanwhile, cook the tortellini according to package directions. Add the stock, salt, black pepper, and beans to the skillet. Raise the heat to high and cook, uncovered, for 5 to 7 minutes or until the sauce is slightly thickened. Remove from the heat and swirl in the butter. Drain the tortellini and toss lightly with the sauce. Serves 4.

Per serving:
Calories 447; Protein 23 g;
Carbohydrates 63 g;
Fat 12 g; Sodium 726 mg;
Cholesterol 70 mg

15 minutes | 19 minutes

Ravioli with Herbed Tomato Sauce

You can mix and match the ingredients in this recipe almost any way you choose. Omit the beans, for example, and use frozen cut asparagus or broccoli florets. Or substitute frozen meat ravioli or tortellini for the cheese ravioli.

1 package (9 ounces) frozen Italian green beans, unthawed

2 packages (8 ounces each) frozen regular or mini cheese ravioli, unthawed

2 tablespoons olive oil

2 large yellow onions, cut into ¾-inch pieces

1 teaspoon fennel seeds, finely crushed, or ground fennel, or ½ teaspoon each dried basil and oregano, crumbled

3 cloves garlic, minced

2 cups prepared spaghetti sauce

½ cup thinly sliced pitted black olives (optional)

Grated Parmesan cheese (optional)

Per serving:
Calories 598; Protein 23 g;
Carbohydrates 63 g;
Fat 30 g; Sodium 1,216 mg;
Cholesterol 94 mg

15 minutes   35 minutes

1 Place the beans in a heatproof colander and lower into a large kettle of boiling water. Cover and cook for 3 to 5 minutes or until crisp-tender. Raise the colander to allow the beans to drain, transfer to a large bowl, cover, and keep warm.

2 Return the water in the kettle to a boil, add the ravioli, and cook according to package directions. Drain, rinse under hot water, and add to the bowl of beans. Cover and keep warm.

3 Quickly rinse and dry the kettle, add the oil, and heat for 1 minute over moderate heat. Add the onions and fennel seeds and sauté, stirring occasionally, for 8 to 10 minutes or until lightly browned. Add the garlic and sauté, stirring occasionally, 2 minutes more.

4 Stir in the spaghetti sauce, bring to a boil, stirring occasionally, and cook, uncovered, for 3 to 5 minutes or until slightly thickened.

5 Mix in the olives, if using, the ravioli, and beans, and heat, uncovered, tossing now and then, just to serving temperature—3 to 5 minutes. Accompany with the cheese if you like. Serves 4.

Ravioli with Herbed Tomato Sauce: fennel turns an everyday dish into a knockout.

Manicotti with Garden Vegetables

A marvelous mélange of vegetables creates a refreshing sauce for manicotti.

1/4 cup olive oil

1 medium-size yellow onion, finely chopped

1 medium-size sweet red pepper, cored, seeded, and cut into 1/2-inch squares

1 small eggplant (8 ounces), cut into 1/2-inch cubes

1/4 teaspoon salt

1/2 teaspoon each dried thyme and basil, crumbled

2 cloves garlic, minced

1 medium-size zucchini, halved lengthwise and thickly sliced

1/4 cup minced fresh basil or 1 1/2 teaspoons dried basil, crumbled

2 packages (12 ounces each) frozen spinach or regular manicotti, thawed

1/3 cup Basic Beef Stock (page 332) or canned beef broth

1/4 cup grated Parmesan cheese

1 Preheat the oven to 400° F. Heat the oil in a 12-inch nonstick skillet over moderate heat for 1 minute. Add the onion and pepper and sauté, stirring occasionally, until softened—3 minutes.

2 Add the eggplant, salt, thyme, and dried basil, and sauté, stirring now and then, for 2 minutes. Add the garlic and zucchini and sauté, stirring occasionally, 3 to 5 minutes more or until all the vegetables are crisp-tender. Add the fresh basil and toss to mix.

3 Arrange the manicotti in a lightly greased 13" x 9" x 2" baking dish and cover with the sautéed vegetables. Pour the stock evenly over all and sprinkle with the cheese.

4 Cover with foil and bake until the manicotti and vegetables are heated through—15 to 20 minutes. Serves 4.

Per serving:
Calories 725; Protein 33 g;
Carbohydrates 59 g;
Fat 41 g; Sodium 1,152 mg;
Cholesterol 144 mg

 20 minutes 31 minutes

Shells Stuffed with Ricotta and Broccoli

Caponata, a canned Italian eggplant appetizer, makes a quick and zesty topping for pasta. If you prefer, you can substitute 2 cups of your favorite spaghetti sauce.

8 ounces large pasta shells

2 cups part-skim ricotta cheese

2 cloves garlic, minced

1 package (10 ounces) frozen chopped broccoli, thawed and drained

1/4 cup chopped roasted sweet red pepper (from a 5-ounce jar), well drained

1 large egg, lightly beaten

1/4 teaspoon salt

1/3 cup plus 2 tablespoons grated Parmesan cheese

2 cans (7 1/2 ounces each) caponata (eggplant appetizer)

1/4 cup Basic Chicken Stock (page 333), canned chicken broth, or water

3 tablespoons minced fresh basil or 1 1/2 teaspoons dried basil, crumbled

1 Preheat the oven to 350° F. Cook the pasta shells according to package directions. Meanwhile, combine the ricotta cheese, garlic, broccoli, red pepper, egg, salt, and 1/3 cup of the Parmesan cheese in a medium-size bowl.

2 As soon as the shells are firm-tender, drain well and let cool until easy to handle. Stuff the shells with the ricotta mixture, dividing the total amount evenly.

3 Arrange the stuffed shells in a single layer in a greased shallow 2-quart baking dish. Quickly combine the caponata, stock, and basil in a small bowl, and spoon evenly over the shells.

4 Sprinkle the remaining 2 tablespoons of Parmesan cheese on top and bake, uncovered, for 20 to 25 minutes or until bubbling and lightly browned. Serves 4.

Per serving:
Calories 593; Protein 33 g;
Carbohydrates 62 g;
Fat 22 g; Sodium 961 mg;
Cholesterol 100 mg

10 minutes 33 minutes

Penne with Three Peppers and Mozzarella

You can use many different pasta shapes in this recipe with equal success: penne (quill-shaped pasta), rotelle, wagon wheels, radiatori, even elbow macaroni.

3 large sweet peppers (preferably 1 each of green, red, and yellow), cored, seeded, and cut into thin strips

8 ounces penne

2 tablespoons olive oil

1 large yellow onion, thinly sliced

½ teaspoon each dried oregano and basil, crumbled

½ teaspoon salt

¼ teaspoon black pepper

2 cloves garlic, minced

2 cups shredded part-skim mozzarella cheese (8 ounces)

⅓ cup grated Parmesan cheese

Per serving:
Calories 486; Protein 26 g; Carbohydrates 51 g; Fat 19 g; Sodium 693 mg; Cholesterol 39 mg

23 minutes	16 minutes

1 Place the peppers in a heatproof colander, lower into a large kettle of boiling water, and cook, uncovered, for 5 minutes. Raise the colander to allow the peppers to drain, then transfer the peppers to paper toweling. Or place the peppers in a vegetable steamer, cover, and steam for 8 minutes, then drain them on paper toweling.

2 Return the water in the kettle to a boil, add the penne, and cook according to package directions. Meanwhile, heat the oil in a 12-inch skillet over moderately high heat for 1 minute. Add the onion, drained peppers, oregano, basil, salt, and black pepper, and sauté, stirring occasionally, for 5 minutes or until the onion is limp. Add the garlic and sauté, stirring occasionally, 2 minutes more.

3 Drain the penne and return to the kettle. Add the mozzarella cheese, toss lightly, and cover for 1 minute, so that the cheese melts and coats the penne. Add the skillet mixture to the pasta and toss lightly. Sprinkle with the Parmesan cheese. Serves 4.

Manicotti with Garden Vegetables: you'll want to use this superb sauce on other pastas too!

Rotelle with Black Beans and Tomatoes

*Pasta and beans team up with kale to make a hearty meatless meal that's very high in protein.
For a stronger cheese flavor, use Cheddar in place of the Monterey Jack.*

8 ounces rotelle, ziti, or wagon-
wheel pasta

2 tablespoons olive oil

1 large yellow onion, coarsely
chopped

1 large sweet green pepper,
cored, seeded, and coarsely
chopped

3 cloves garlic, minced

2 cups shredded Monterey Jack
cheese (8 ounces)

4 large tomatoes, cored and
coarsely chopped

1 can (1 pound 4 ounces) black
beans, drained and rinsed

1 package (10 ounces) frozen
chopped kale, thawed and
drained

⅓ cup minced fresh coriander
(cilantro) or flat-leaf parsley

1 teaspoon salt

1 teaspoon lemon juice

½ teaspoon black pepper

Per serving:
Calories 747; Protein 38 g;
Carbohydrates 92 g;
Fat 26 g; Sodium 870 mg;
Cholesterol 56 mg

25 minutes 19 minutes

---

1 Cook the rotelle according to package directions. Meanwhile, heat the oil in a deep 12-inch skillet over moderate heat for 1 minute. Add the onion and green pepper and sauté, uncovered, stirring occasionally, until limp—5 minutes. Add the garlic and sauté 2 minutes more.

2 Drain the rotelle and return to its pan. Add the cheese and toss until combined. Cover and keep warm.

3 Stir the tomatoes into the skillet along with the beans, kale, and coriander, and simmer, uncovered, stirring occasionally, for 5 to 8 minutes or until the tomatoes start to soften slightly.

4 Mix in the salt, lemon juice, and black pepper, add the pasta and cheese mixture, and toss well to mix. Cook, uncovered, over low heat until warmed through. Serves 4.

Noodle and Cottage Cheese Casserole

A savory main-course version of kugel, a popular Middle European dessert.

2 cups thickly sliced cabbage
6 ounces broad egg noodles
1 cup frozen chopped broccoli, unthawed
1 cup frozen sliced carrots, unthawed
1 tablespoon butter or margarine
1 cup low-fat cottage cheese
3 large eggs
½ cup low-fat milk

½ cup reduced-fat sour cream
¾ teaspoon salt
¾ teaspoon caraway seeds
¼ teaspoon dried thyme, crumbled
¼ teaspoon black pepper
¼ cup grated Parmesan cheese

Per serving:
Calories 365; Protein 23 g;
Carbohydrates 42 g;
Fat 12 g; Sodium 880 mg;
Cholesterol 176 mg

10 minutes | 1 hour

1 Preheat the oven to 350° F. Bring a 5-quart flameproof casserole of water to a boil. Add the cabbage, cover, and cook over moderate heat for 4 minutes.

2 Add the noodles and cook according to package directions, adding the broccoli and carrots during the last 4 minutes. Drain all well and transfer to a large bowl.

3 Lightly coat the casserole with nonstick cooking spray. Return the noodles and vegetables to the casserole, add the butter, and toss to mix. Combine the cottage cheese, eggs, milk, sour cream, salt, caraway seeds, thyme, and pepper, pour over the noodle mixture, toss well, then smooth the surface.

4 Sprinkle the Parmesan on top, cover, and bake for 45 minutes or until set. Remove from the oven and let stand, uncovered, for 10 minutes before serving. Serves 4.

Red Cabbage and Beet Variation

Substitute **red cabbage** for green in Step 1 and add **2 teaspoons white vinegar** to the cooking water. In Step 2, omit the broccoli and proceed as directed. In Step 3, arrange **1 cup drained diced canned beets** on the bottom of the casserole, then layer the noodle-vegetable mixture on top. Follow Step 4 as directed. Serves 4.

Per serving: Calories 356; Protein 22 g;
Carbohydrates 41 g; Fat 11 g;
Sodium 1,005 mg; Cholesterol 176 mg

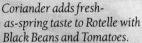

Coriander adds fresh-as-spring taste to Rotelle with Black Beans and Tomatoes.

167

Pita-Bread Pizza

Pita bread is a ready-made crust for pizza. For variety, you can use zucchini or yellow squash in place of the eggplant.

- 2 tablespoons olive oil
- 1 medium-size yellow onion, finely chopped
- 1 medium-size sweet green or red pepper, cored, seeded, and thinly sliced
- ½ teaspoon salt
- ½ teaspoon each dried basil and oregano, crumbled
- 4 ounces mushrooms, thinly sliced
- 8 ounces eggplant, cut into 1-inch cubes
- 1 can (14½ ounces) tomatoes with their juice
- 2 cloves garlic, minced
- 2 pita breads, 9 inches in diameter, split in half horizontally
- 2 cups shredded part-skim mozzarella or fontina cheese (8 ounces)

1 Preheat the oven to 425° F. Heat the oil in a 12-inch nonstick skillet over moderate heat for 1 minute. Add the onion, pepper, salt, basil, and oregano, and sauté, stirring often, for 2 minutes or until slightly softened. Add the mushrooms and sauté, stirring, 2 minutes more. Add the eggplant and cook and stir for 3 minutes.

2 Meanwhile, purée the tomatoes and their juice by whirling in a food processor or an electric blender for 1 minute. Add to the skillet along with the garlic and simmer, uncovered, stirring occasionally, for 4 to 5 minutes or until almost all of the liquid has evaporated.

3 Arrange the pita rounds, cut sides up, on an ungreased baking sheet, and top with the vegetable mixture, dividing the total amount evenly. Sprinkle with the cheese and bake, uncovered, for 10 minutes or until the cheese melts and the topping is bubbling. Serves 4.

Per serving:
Calories 333; Protein 16 g;
Carbohydrates 25 g;
Fat 20 g; Sodium 759 mg;
Cholesterol 45 mg

20 minutes | 23 minutes

Pizza Surprise

Discover a luscious filling of ham, cheese, spinach, apple, and walnuts inside this double-crust pizza pie.

- 1 tablespoon cornmeal
- 2 packages (10 ounces each) refrigerated pizza dough
- 2½ cups shredded Monterey Jack cheese (10 ounces)
- 1 package (10 ounces) frozen chopped spinach, thawed, drained, and squeezed dry
- ¼ cup coarsely chopped walnuts (optional)
- 1 medium-size sweet apple (Red or Golden Delicious), cored and coarsely chopped
- 4 ounces thinly sliced boiled or baked ham

Per serving:
Calories 728; Protein 37 g;
Carbohydrates 76 g;
Fat 29 g; Sodium 1,497 mg;
Cholesterol 85 mg

25 minutes | 10 minutes

1 Place the oven rack in the lowest position and preheat the oven to 500° F. Sprinkle a large baking sheet with the cornmeal, center half the dough on top, and pat into an 11-inch round. Leaving a 1-inch border, sprinkle with half of the cheese.

2 Spread the spinach over the cheese, scatter with the walnuts, if using, and the apple, then top with the ham. Sprinkle with the remaining cheese.

3 Pat the remaining dough into a 12-inch round on a sheet of wax paper. Dip a pastry brush in water and brush a 1-inch border all around the dough. Invert on top of the pizza, peel off the wax paper, then crimp the top and bottom crusts together, forming a decorative edge.

4 Bake the pizza, uncovered, for 10 minutes or until crisp and lightly browned. Serves 4.

Pizza with the Works

Here's pizza that has it all—cheese, pepperoni, onions, peppers, and mushrooms. You can buy prepared dough at the supermarket or your local pizzeria. Serve with a crisp green salad.

1 tablespoon cornmeal

2 packages (10 ounces each) refrigerated pizza dough

2 medium-size yellow onions, halved and thinly sliced

2 medium-size sweet red or green peppers, cored, seeded, and thinly sliced

8 ounces mushrooms, thickly sliced

2 teaspoons dried oregano, crumbled

2 tablespoons olive oil

3 cups shredded part-skim mozzarella cheese (12 ounces)

3 ounces thinly sliced pepperoni

2 tablespoons grated Parmesan cheese

Per serving:
Calories 832; Protein 37 g;
Carbohydrates 77 g;
Fat 40 g; Sodium 1,497 mg;
Cholesterol 69 mg

25 minutes | 12 minutes

1 Place the oven rack on the lowest shelf and preheat the oven to 500° F. Sprinkle 2 large baking sheets with the cornmeal, then place half of the dough on each one and flatten into 12-inch rounds; set aside.

2 Mix the onions, peppers, mushrooms, oregano, and oil in a large bowl. Leaving a 1-inch border, sprinkle each round of dough with half of the mozzarella cheese, followed by half the pepperoni, half the vegetable mixture, and 1 tablespoon of the Parmesan. Bake, uncovered, for 12 minutes or until the crust is crisp and the cheese has melted. Serves 4 to 6.

Pizza Surprise—a pie you can eat like a sandwich

169

Torta Rustica

*Everyone loves deep-dish pizza, especially children. This one is even
good for picnics because it's served at room temperature.*

2 teaspoons olive oil

1 package (10 ounces) refrigerated pizza dough

2 cups part-skim or whole-milk ricotta cheese

½ cup grated Parmesan cheese (2 ounces)

1 package (10 ounces) frozen chopped spinach, thawed, drained, and squeezed dry

3 large eggs

3 tablespoons chopped fresh basil or 1 teaspoon dried basil, crumbled

1 clove garlic, minced

⅛ teaspoon black pepper

1 jar (7 ounces) pimientos, drained and cut into strips ½ inch wide

3 tablespoons pine nuts (optional)

4 ounces baked or boiled ham, thinly sliced

Per serving:
Calories 570; Protein 38 g;
Carbohydrates 47 g;
Fat 25 g; Sodium 1,208 mg;
Cholesterol 233 mg

13 minutes | 35 minutes

1 Place the oven rack in the lowest position and preheat the oven to 400° F. Brush a 9-inch deep-dish pie pan with the olive oil. On a lightly floured board, roll the pizza dough into a 13-inch round and press into the pan so that it covers the bottom and comes up the sides; set aside.

2 Combine the ricotta cheese, Parmesan, spinach, eggs, basil, garlic, and pepper in a large bowl. Fold in the pimientos and, if desired, the pine nuts. Cover the crust with half the ricotta mixture, arrange the ham on top, and spoon the remaining ricotta mixture over all.

3 Bake, uncovered, for 30 to 35 minutes, or until the filling is set and the crust is crisp. Let cool to room temperature before serving. Serves 4.

Torta Rustica—the perfect one-dish meal for an impromptu get-together

Main-Dish Salads

Though usually served as a side dish, salads
are equally worthy of center stage. Indeed, few meals are as quick to
prepare, as pretty to look at, or as accommodating to so many combinations
of ingredients. If you thought salad meant lettuce and tomatoes,
wait till you try our Steak and Potatoes, Jambalaya Salad, and Chicken
Salad Olé—just to name a few. And calorie counters will love
the choice of yogurt- and buttermilk-based dressings.

Chicken Salad with Pecans

This salad owes its great flavor to two very different foreign ingredients: sesame oil—available at Oriental specialty stores and in the Oriental section of most supermarkets—and spaetzle, teardrop-shaped German noodles.

6½ **cups water**

1 **pound skinned and boned chicken breasts**

½ **cup chopped pecans or walnuts**

1¾ **cups spaetzle or orzo (rice-shaped pasta)**

1 **package (9 ounces) frozen cut green beans, unthawed**

1 **large sweet red pepper, cored, seeded, and coarsely chopped**

For the dressing:

3 **tablespoons Oriental sesame oil**

3 **tablespoons vegetable oil**

2 **tablespoons rice wine vinegar or white vinegar**

1 **tablespoon orange juice**

1½ **teaspoons ground sage**

½ **teaspoon salt**

½ **teaspoon black pepper**

Pinch sugar

Per serving:
Calories 725; Protein 35 g;
Carbohydrates 75 g;
Fat 32 g; Sodium 347 mg;
Cholesterol 66 mg

15 minutes   32 minutes

1 Preheat the oven to 350° F. Pour 6 cups of the water into a large saucepan and bring to a simmer over moderate heat. Add the chicken and bring to a boil. Adjust the heat so that the water bubbles gently, cover, and cook the chicken for 8 to 10 minutes or until no longer pink on the inside.

2 Meanwhile, spread the pecans in a pie pan. Place, uncovered, in the oven, and toast until lightly browned—8 to 10 minutes. Set aside.

3 When the chicken is done, transfer to a cutting board and let cool. Meanwhile, return the water to a boil over high heat. Add the spaetzle, reduce the heat to low, and simmer, uncovered, for 10 minutes or until tender. Using a slotted spoon, transfer to a large bowl; set aside.

4 Add the remaining ½ cup water and the beans to the water in the saucepan and bring to a boil over high heat. Adjust the heat so that the water bubbles gently, cover, and cook until the beans are crisp-tender—3 to 5 minutes. Drain and add to the bowl with the spaetzle. Dice the chicken and add to the bowl along with the pecans and red pepper.

5 *For the dressing:* In a small bowl, whisk the sesame and vegetable oils with the vinegar, orange juice, sage, salt, black pepper, and sugar until smooth. Pour evenly over the chicken mixture and toss well. Serves 4 to 6.

Chicken Salad with Pecans—easy to make, a pleasure to taste

Curried Chicken and Rice Salad

If you have leftover cooked chicken, use ½ cup diced cooked chicken per person.

2 cups Basic Chicken Stock (page 333) or canned chicken broth

1 pound skinned and boned chicken breasts

8 ounces snow peas, trimmed, or 1 package (10 ounces) frozen snow peas, unthawed

¾ cup long-grain white rice

4 large carrots, peeled and coarsely shredded

6 scallions, including tops, thinly sliced

½ cup raisins

1 cup plain low-fat yogurt

2 tablespoons mayonnaise

¼ cup low-fat milk

1 teaspoon curry powder

¼ teaspoon salt

⅛ teaspoon black pepper

4 to 6 large lettuce leaves, preferably romaine

¼ cup toasted slivered almonds (page 86)

Per serving:
Calories 546; Protein 42 g;
Carbohydrates 68 g;
Fat 12 g; Sodium 458 mg;
Cholesterol 73 mg

| 20 minutes | 30 minutes |

---

1 Bring the stock to a simmer in a large saucepan over moderate heat. Add the chicken, reduce the heat to moderately low, cover, and simmer until the chicken is no longer pink on the inside—8 to 10 minutes.

2 Meanwhile, cook the snow peas, uncovered, in a large saucepan of boiling water for 1 minute or until crisp-tender. Drain, then set aside. If using frozen snow peas, cook according to package directions.

3 Using a slotted spoon, remove the cooked chicken from the stock and transfer to a plate to cool. Bring the stock to a boil over moderate heat, add the rice, cover, and cook for 20 minutes or until the rice is tender. Let cool to room temperature.

4 Meanwhile, slice the snow peas crosswise 1 inch wide, then cut the chicken crosswise into thin strips. Place both in a large bowl along with the carrots, scallions, raisins, and rice.

5 In a small bowl, whisk the yogurt with the mayonnaise, milk, curry powder, salt, and pepper until smooth. Pour over the chicken mixture and toss well to mix. Cover and chill for 1 hour or overnight.

6 When ready to serve, line a large platter with the lettuce, mound the salad on top, and sprinkle with the almonds. Serves 4.

Chicken Salad Olé

Crispy hot chicken nuggets are simple to prepare. To reduce fat and calories, substitute diced cooked chicken or turkey.

1 package (12 ounces) refrigerated breaded chicken nuggets

4 cups bite-size pieces lettuce (any kind)

2 cups coarsely crushed tortilla or corn chips

1 small avocado, peeled, pitted, and thinly sliced

2 medium-size tomatoes, cored, seeded, and chopped but not peeled

1 can (4 ounces) chopped green chilies, drained

½ cup thinly sliced pitted black olives

For the dressing:

½ cup sour cream or plain low-fat yogurt

2 tablespoons olive oil

1 tablespoon lime or lemon juice

1 small clove garlic, minced

½ teaspoon ground cumin

⅛ teaspoon black pepper

1 Preheat the oven to 400° F. Spread the chicken nuggets on a baking sheet and bake, uncovered, for 7 minutes or until crisp and lightly browned.

2 Meanwhile, arrange the lettuce in an even layer on a large platter. Layer the tortilla chips, avocado, tomatoes, chilies, and olives on top.

3 *For the dressing:* In a small bowl, whisk the sour cream with the oil, lime juice, garlic, cumin, and pepper until smooth. Pour the dressing over the salad, then arrange the hot chicken nuggets on top. Serves 4.

Jicama-Salsa Variation

Follow Step 1 as directed. In Step 2, substitute **2 cups thinly sliced peeled jicama or cucumbers** for the tomatoes. In Step 3, omit all of the dressing ingredients and prepare the salsa instead. Place **2 large tomatoes, cored and finely chopped, ¼ cup each minced fresh coriander (cilantro) and scallions (including tops), 2 tablespoons olive oil, 1 tablespoon lime juice, 1 minced clove garlic, and ⅛ teaspoon black pepper** in a medium-size bowl and mix well. Pour over the salad, then proceed as directed. Serves 4.

Per serving: Calories 518; Protein 19 g; Carbohydrates 28 g; Fat 37 g; Sodium 1,230 mg; Cholesterol 12 mg

Per serving:
Calories 580; Protein 20 g;
Carbohydrates 29 g;
Fat 43 g; Sodium 1,247 mg;
Cholesterol 24 mg

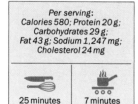

25 minutes   7 minutes

Chinese Chicken and Noodles

Peanut butter and soy sauce flavor this wonderful dressing, which can be made several days in advance and refrigerated.

1½ pounds skinned and boned chicken breasts

8 ounces linguine

½ cup cream-style peanut butter

½ cup water

3 tablespoons reduced-sodium soy sauce

3 tablespoons cider vinegar

1 tablespoon sugar

1 tablespoon vegetable oil

4 cups coarsely shredded cabbage or 1 package (10 ounces) coleslaw mix

6 scallions, including tops, thinly sliced

Optional garnishes:

1 scallion, including top, coarsely chopped

2 tablespoons coarsely chopped dry-roasted peanuts

1 Place the chicken in a large saucepan of water and bring to a boil over moderate heat. Reduce the heat to low and simmer, uncovered, until no longer pink on the inside— about 10 minutes. Meanwhile, cook the linguine according to package directions.

2 Whirl the peanut butter, water, soy sauce, vinegar, sugar, and oil in a food processor or electric blender at high speed for about 30 seconds or until smooth, then transfer to a large bowl. Drain the chicken breasts and let cool on paper toweling. Drain the linguine, rinse well, and add to the bowl with the peanut mixture.

3 Using your fingers, pull the chicken into long, thin shreds and add to the bowl along with the cabbage and sliced scallions. Toss well to mix, then sprinkle, if you like, with the chopped scallion and peanuts. Serves 6.

Per serving:
Calories 440; Protein 39 g;
Carbohydrates 38 g;
Fat 15 g; Sodium 528 mg;
Cholesterol 66 mg

15 minutes   12 minutes

Creamy Chicken Waldorf Salad

If you don't have cooked chicken (or turkey), place 3 skinned and boned chicken breasts in a medium-size saucepan, add enough water to cover, and bring to a simmer over moderate heat—about 3 minutes. Adjust the heat so that the water bubbles gently and cook until no longer pink on the inside—6 to 8 minutes longer. Drain, cool, and dice.

4 slices cinnamon raisin bread, cut into ¾-inch cubes

8 ounces sugar snap peas or snow peas, trimmed

2 medium-size bunches watercress, stems removed

3 cups diced cooked chicken or turkey

2 large Granny Smith or other tart apples, cored and diced but not peeled

2 cups seedless red grapes

3 stalks celery, diced

½ cup coarsely chopped walnuts

For the dressing:

1 cup plain low-fat yogurt

⅔ cup buttermilk

2 tablespoons sugar

1 tablespoon lemon juice

1 tablespoon snipped fresh dill or ½ teaspoon dill weed

⅛ teaspoon each salt and black pepper

1 Preheat the oven to 350° F. Spread the bread cubes on a baking sheet and toast, uncovered, in the oven for 10 minutes or until lightly browned.

2 Meanwhile, in a large saucepan of boiling water, cook the peas, uncovered, for 1 minute. Drain, rinse under cool water, and drain well again.

3 In a large bowl, add the watercress, chicken, bread cubes, peas, apples, grapes, celery, and walnuts.

4 *For the dressing:* In a small bowl, combine the yogurt, buttermilk, sugar, lemon juice, dill, salt, and pepper; add to salad and toss. Serves 4.

A low-calorie dressing complements this classic Creamy Chicken Waldorf Salad.

Per serving:
Calories 551; Protein 46 g;
Carbohydrates 59 g;
Fat 16 g; Sodium 365 mg;
Cholesterol 94 mg

35 minutes

10 minutes

Chutney, Chicken, and Pasta Salad

If you don't care for curry, substitute 2 teaspoons of Dijon mustard.

1 **pound spinach fettuccine or regular spaghetti**

12 **ounces fresh or 1 package (10 ounces) frozen broccoli florets, thawed and drained**

3 **cups diced cooked chicken (if using uncooked chicken, see page 175)**

1 **medium-size sweet red pepper, cored, seeded, and diced**

1 **medium-size red onion, finely chopped**

3 **tablespoons vegetable oil**

Optional garnishes:

2 **tablespoons toasted slivered almonds (see page 86)**

2 **tablespoons minced fresh coriander (cilantro) or flat-leaf parsley**

For the dressing:

½ **cup plain low-fat yogurt**

½ **cup sour cream**

2 **tablespoons white wine vinegar or cider vinegar**

2 **teaspoons curry powder**

2 **to 3 tablespoons finely chopped chutney, or to taste**

½ **teaspoon salt**

¼ **teaspoon black pepper**

1 Cook the fettuccine according to package directions, adding the broccoli during the last 3 minutes. Drain well, rinse under cool water, drain again, and transfer to a large serving bowl.

2 Add the chicken, red pepper, onion, and oil, and toss well. Sprinkle with the almonds and coriander if desired.

3 *For the dressing:* In a small bowl, whisk the yogurt with the sour cream, vinegar, curry powder, chutney, salt, and black pepper, then pour into a cruet. Pass the salad and the dressing separately. Serves 4.

Per serving:
Calories 811; Protein 52 g;
Carbohydrates 98 g;
Fat 22 g; Sodium 468 mg;
Cholesterol 104 mg

 30 minutes 10 minutes

Bread Salad with Diced Chicken

A basil vinaigrette drenches this luscious Italian-style salad in garden-fresh flavor.

4 **cups ½-inch cubes Italian or French bread**

½ **cup olive oil**

⅓ **cup balsamic or red wine vinegar**

⅓ **cup firmly packed fresh basil leaves or 1 teaspoon dried basil, crumbled**

2 **cloves garlic**

4 **flat anchovy fillets**

¼ **teaspoon salt**

4 **cups diced cooked chicken (if using uncooked chicken, see page 175)**

2 **pounds tomatoes, peeled, cored, seeded, and cut into ½-inch cubes**

1 **large cucumber, peeled, seeded, and cut into ½-inch cubes**

12 **leaves romaine or other lettuce**

4 **small sprigs fresh basil (optional garnish)**

1 Preheat the oven to 350° F. Spread the bread cubes in a large shallow baking pan; place, uncovered, in the oven and toast for 12 to 15 minutes or until crisp and pale golden.

2 Meanwhile, whirl the oil, vinegar, basil, garlic, anchovies, and salt in a food processor or an electric blender at high speed until the basil is coarsely chopped—about 30 seconds. Transfer to a large bowl.

3 Add the bread cubes, chicken, tomatoes, and cucumber, and toss well to mix. Let stand for 5 minutes to allow the bread to soften slightly. Divide the lettuce leaves among 4 plates, mound the bread mixture on top, and garnish, if desired, with the basil sprigs. Serves 4 to 6.

Per serving:
Calories 629; Protein 51 g;
Carbohydrates 33 g;
Fat 33 g; Sodium 561 mg;
Cholesterol 119 mg

 25 minutes 15 minutes

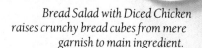

Bread Salad with Diced Chicken raises crunchy bread cubes from mere garnish to main ingredient.

Turkey-Spinach Salad

*The crunchy goodness of toasted almond slivers adds
a superb touch to this healthy salad.*

- 4 medium-size new potatoes, thinly sliced but not peeled
- ¼ cup slivered almonds
- 8 ounces fresh spinach, trimmed and rinsed
- 8 ounces mushrooms, thinly sliced
- 1 cup frozen green peas, thawed and drained
- 6 large radishes, thinly sliced
- 4 scallions, including tops, thinly sliced
- 8 ounces thinly sliced roast turkey or turkey cold cuts, cut into strips about ½ inch wide

For the dressing:

- 2 cups plain low-fat yogurt or sour cream or mixture of both
- ⅓ cup skim or low-fat milk
- 4 teaspoons cider vinegar
- ¾ teaspoon dill weed
- ⅛ teaspoon black pepper
- Pinch dried oregano, crumbled

1 Preheat the oven to 400° F. Cook the potatoes, uncovered, in a large saucepan of boiling water over moderate heat until tender—about 10 minutes; drain and let cool. Meanwhile, toast the almonds, uncovered, in a pie pan in the oven for 8 to 10 minutes or until lightly browned; let cool.

2 Tear the spinach into pieces and place in a large bowl. Add the mushrooms, peas, radishes, scallions, turkey, potatoes, and almonds. Toss well; divide among 4 plates.

3 *For the dressing:* In a small bowl, whisk the yogurt with the milk, vinegar, dill weed, pepper, and oregano. Spoon over each salad. Serves 4.

Per serving:
Calories 390; Protein 33 g;
Carbohydrates 49 g;
Fat 8 g; Sodium 217 mg;
Cholesterol 47 mg

 30 minutes 10 minutes

Turkey and Stuffing Salad

For best results, use a crouton-type mix rather than one made of crumbs.

- 1 cup plain low-fat yogurt
- ¼ cup reduced-calorie mayonnaise
- 1 tablespoon Oriental sesame oil or vegetable oil
- 1 tablespoon finely chopped chutney
- ¼ teaspoon black pepper
- 2 cups diced cooked turkey (if using uncooked turkey, see page 175)
- 2 cups packaged stuffing mix
- 1 large sweet red pepper, cored, seeded, and coarsely chopped
- 1 large sweet green pepper, cored, seeded, and coarsely chopped
- 1 large red onion, coarsely chopped
- ½ medium-size bunch watercress, stems removed

1 In a large bowl, whisk together the yogurt, mayonnaise, oil, chutney, and black pepper until smooth.

2 Add the turkey, stuffing mix, red and green peppers, onion, and watercress; toss well. Serves 4.

Per serving:
Calories 303; Protein 27 g;
Carbohydrates 23 g;
Fat 11 g; Sodium 322 mg;
Cholesterol 57 mg

 20 minutes None

177

Turkish Turkey Salad

Here's a salad that's quick and easy to assemble. It's versatile too—you can enjoy it as soon as you've made it or the next day, after it's marinated and chilled.

¾ cup bulgur

1 cup boiling water

3 cups diced cooked turkey (if using uncooked turkey, see page 175)

2 medium-size tomatoes, cored, seeded, and chopped

1 cup canned corn kernels, drained

For the dressing:

2 cloves garlic

2 tablespoons minced fresh basil or 2 teaspoons dried basil, crumbled

1 tablespoon minced fresh mint or 2 teaspoons mint flakes, crumbled

¼ cup olive oil

3 tablespoons red wine vinegar or cider vinegar

¾ teaspoon salt

¼ teaspoon black pepper

1 At least 1½ hours before serving, place the bulgur in a large heatproof bowl, add the boiling water, and let stand, uncovered, for 20 minutes or until the bulgur is tender. Drain well, cover, and refrigerate for at least 1 hour. Mix in the turkey, tomatoes, and corn.

2 *For the dressing:* Place the garlic, basil, mint, oil, vinegar, salt, and pepper in a food processor or an electric blender, and whirl at high speed until smooth—about 30 seconds.

3 Pour the dressing evenly over all, and toss well. Serve immediately or let marinate in the refrigerator for up to 24 hours before serving. Serves 4.

Per serving:
*Calories 450; Protein 36 g;
Carbohydrates 38 g;
Fat 18 g; Sodium 591 mg;
Cholesterol 73 mg*

15 minutes | None

Turkey, Rice, and Olive Salad

Here's a hearty warm salad that you can consider serving chilled if a heat wave hits.

1 cup long-grain white rice

3 cups diced cooked turkey breast (if using uncooked turkey, see page 175)

1 large sweet green pepper, cored, seeded, and chopped

1 cup pitted black olives, halved

2 large carrots, peeled and coarsely shredded

2 stalks celery, diced

1 medium-size red onion, coarsely chopped

2 ounces salami, diced

2 teaspoons capers, drained

For the dressing:

1 large clove garlic, minced

¼ cup olive oil

2 tablespoons white wine vinegar or cider vinegar

1 teaspoon lemon juice

¼ teaspoon black pepper

⅛ teaspoon sugar

1 Cook the rice according to package directions. Meanwhile, place the turkey, green pepper, olives, carrots, celery, onion, salami, and capers in a large bowl, toss, and set aside.

2 *For the dressing:* In a small bowl, whisk the garlic with the oil, vinegar, lemon juice, black pepper, and sugar until smooth.

3 Add the rice to the turkey mixture, pour the dressing evenly over all, toss well, and serve warm. Serves 4 to 6.

Per serving:
*Calories 552; Protein 38 g;
Carbohydrates 48 g;
Fat 24 g; Sodium 421 mg;
Cholesterol 81 mg*

35 minutes | 20 minutes

Turkey, Rice, and Olive Salad has a distinctly Mediterranean flavor.

Club Salad with Blue Cheese Dressing

If you're in a hurry, you can use store-bought blue cheese dressing.

1 pound small new potatoes, sliced ¼ inch thick but not peeled

4 slices bacon

1 medium-size head romaine or other lettuce, torn into bite-size pieces

3 cups diced cooked turkey or chicken (if using uncooked poultry, see page 175)

1 large sweet green pepper, cored, seeded, and diced

2 large tomatoes, cored, seeded, and diced

For the dressing:

4 ounces blue cheese

¾ cup plain low-fat yogurt

2 tablespoons white wine vinegar or cider vinegar

1 clove garlic, minced

¼ teaspoon black pepper

Per serving:
Calories 462; Protein 46 g;
Carbohydrates 34 g;
Fat 16 g; Sodium 617 mg;
Cholesterol 102 mg

 25 minutes

 12 minutes

1 In a large saucepan of boiling water, cook the potatoes, uncovered, over moderate heat until tender—10 to 12 minutes.

2 Meanwhile, cook the bacon in an 8-inch skillet over moderate heat for 4 to 5 minutes or until crisp and brown. Drain on paper toweling and discard the drippings.

3 Drain the potatoes well and let cool for 10 minutes. Meanwhile, cover the bottom of a large platter with the lettuce. Arrange the potatoes in a broad band across the middle, then make rows of the turkey, green pepper, and tomatoes on either side of the potatoes, alternating the colors. Crumble the bacon evenly over all.

4 *For the dressing:* In a food processor or an electric blender, whirl the cheese, yogurt, vinegar, garlic, and black pepper for 1 minute or until smooth. Pour into a sauceboat and pass at the table. Serves 4.

Steak and Potatoes

Here's a popular combination that makes a superb salad. Be sure to allow an extra 30 to 60 minutes for the marinating time.

⅓ cup prepared salsa or Basic Salsa (page 339)

3 tablespoons cider vinegar

1 tablespoon Worcestershire sauce

1 tablespoon firmly packed light brown sugar

1 clove garlic, minced

1 pound flank steak, trimmed and quartered

1 pound small new potatoes (about 8), halved and sliced ¼ inch thick but not peeled

2 large sweet red and/or green peppers, cored, seeded, and cut into thin strips

2 tablespoons olive or vegetable oil

Per serving:
Calories 416; Protein 37 g;
Carbohydrates 32 g;
Fat 16 g; Sodium 178 mg;
Cholesterol 103 mg

---

 20 minutes | 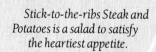 19 minutes

1 Combine the salsa, vinegar, Worcestershire sauce, sugar, and garlic in a self-sealing plastic food storage bag. Add the steak, push out all the air, and seal the bag. Let the meat marinate at room temperature for 30 to 60 minutes.

2 Meanwhile, in a 10-inch skillet of boiling water, cook the potatoes and peppers, uncovered, until just tender—10 to 12 minutes. Drain well, place in a large bowl, and set aside.

3 Heat the oil in the skillet over moderate heat for 1 minute. Lift the meat from the marinade, add to the skillet, and sauté for 2 to 3 minutes on each side for rare, 4 for medium (do not overcook or the steak will be tough). Transfer the steak to a cutting board and let stand for 5 minutes.

4 Meanwhile, add the steak marinade to the skillet, bring to a boil, and cook and stir for 1 minute. Spoon over the potato mixture, tossing well to mix.

5 Slice the steak at an angle across the grain about ¼ inch thick, arrange on a large, deep platter, surround with the potato mixture, and spoon any juices over all. Serve warm or at room temperature. Serves 4.

Steak and Pasta Variation

In Step 1, omit the salsa, Worcestershire sauce, and sugar. To the cider vinegar and garlic, add *¼ cup ketchup, ¼ cup reduced-sodium soy sauce, 1 teaspoon ground ginger,* and *⅛ teaspoon ground red pepper (cayenne)* and proceed as directed. In Step 2, omit the potatoes and peppers. Cook *8 ounces penne (quill-shaped pasta) or ziti* according to package directions in a large kettle of boiling water, adding *1 pound asparagus cut into 3-inch lengths* and *1 halved medium-size red onion* during the last 6 minutes of cooking, then proceed as directed. Follow Step 3 as directed. In Step 4, proceed as directed, then pour the marinade over the pasta mixture and toss to coat. Follow Step 5 as directed, arranging the pasta mixture around the steak. If desired, sprinkle *2 tablespoons sesame seeds* over all. Serve warm or at room temperature. Serves 4.

Per serving: Calories 556; Protein 46 g;
Carbohydrates 56 g; Fat 16 g;
Sodium 908 mg; Cholesterol 103 mg

Stick-to-the-ribs Steak and Potatoes is a salad to satisfy the heartiest appetite.

Corned Beef and Two-Cabbage Combo

A light, cool rendition of an old-time favorite.

- **1** pound all-purpose potatoes (about 3)
- **½** cup sour cream or ¼ cup each sour cream and plain low-fat yogurt
- **2** tablespoons cider vinegar
- **1** tablespoon prepared horse-radish (red or white), drained
- **2** teaspoons prepared mustard
- **3** cups coarsely shredded red cabbage

- **3** cups coarsely shredded green cabbage
- **12** ounces thinly sliced cooked corned beef, halved lengthwise

Per serving:
Calories 408; Protein 28 g;
Carbohydrates 32 g;
Fat 19 g; Sodium 1,101 mg;
Cholesterol 86 mg

20 minutes | 20 minutes

1 Cook the potatoes, uncovered, in a large saucepan of boiling water until tender—about 20 minutes. Drain and let cool until easy to handle, then peel and cut into 2-inch wedges.

2 Meanwhile, in a large bowl, whisk together the sour cream, vinegar, horseradish, and mustard, and set aside.

3 Add the potatoes to the sour cream mixture along with the red and green cabbage and the corned beef and toss gently to mix. Serves 4.

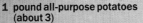

Roast Beef Salad

To save time, you can use your favorite dressing.

- 8 ounces medium-size pasta shells, elbow macaroni, ziti, or bow-tie pasta
- 8 ounces green beans, trimmed and cut into 1-inch lengths
- ¼ cup olive oil
- 2 tablespoons red wine vinegar
- 1 clove garlic, minced
- ¼ cup minced fresh basil or 1 teaspoon dried basil, crumbled
- ¼ teaspoon salt
- ⅛ teaspoon black pepper
- 8 ounces sliced roast beef, cut crosswise into strips ½-inch wide
- 1 medium-size red onion, coarsely chopped
- 1 pint cherry tomatoes, halved

1 Cook the pasta and beans, uncovered, in a large kettle of boiling water until both are firm-tender—about 8 minutes. Drain, rinse under cool water, and drain again.

2 In a large bowl, whisk the oil with the vinegar, garlic, basil, salt, and pepper until smooth. Add the pasta, beans, beef, and onion, toss well, then stir in the tomatoes. Serves 4.

Per serving:
Calories 506; Protein 27 g;
Carbohydrates 54 g;
Fat 20 g; Sodium 183 mg;
Cholesterol 51 mg

 25 minutes | 8 minutes

Russian Potato Salad

A lovely combination of vegetables and ham enveloped in a light and creamy dill dressing.

- 1 pound all-purpose potatoes (about 3), peeled and cut into ½-inch cubes
- ⅓ cup mayonnaise
- ⅓ cup plain low-fat yogurt
- 3 scallions, including tops, thinly sliced
- 3 tablespoons snipped fresh dill or minced parsley
- ¼ teaspoon salt
- ⅛ teaspoon black pepper
- 8 ounces boiled or baked ham, cut into ½-inch cubes
- 1½ cups frozen green peas, thawed and drained
- 2 medium-size cooked or canned beets, peeled and cut into ½-inch cubes, or 4 medium-size carrots, peeled and thinly sliced
- 12 romaine or leaf lettuce leaves, rinsed and dried
- 2 ripe tomatoes, cored and cut into 12 wedges

1 Cook the potatoes, uncovered, in a large saucepan of boiling water over moderate heat until tender—12 minutes. (If you are using carrots instead of beets, add them to the saucepan for the last 5 minutes of cooking time.)

2 Meanwhile, combine the mayonnaise, yogurt, scallions, dill, salt, and pepper in a large mixing bowl.

3 Drain the potatoes (and the carrots, if using). Add the ham, potatoes, peas, and beets or carrots to the yogurt mixture and toss gently until well coated. Serve on a bed of lettuce leaves and circle with the tomato wedges. Serves 4.

Per serving:
Calories 467; Protein 21 g;
Carbohydrates 48 g;
Fat 22 g; Sodium 1,109 mg;
Cholesterol 44 mg

 20 minutes | 12 minutes

*Ham and Pasta Salad—
a meal even fussy
eaters will enjoy*

Ham and Pasta Salad

*Ever-popular pistachio nuts
are the surprise ingredient in this recipe.*

8 ounces rotelle (corkscrew-shaped pasta) or penne (quill-shaped pasta)
1 cup buttermilk
¼ cup mayonnaise
1 teaspoon dried tarragon
12 ounces boiled or baked ham, cut into ½-inch cubes
1 cup cherry tomatoes, halved
½ cup shelled blanched pistachios or blanched almonds, coarsely chopped (see page 145)
⅛ teaspoon black pepper
1 teaspoon minced fresh tarragon (optional garnish)
8 ounces spinach, trimmed, rinsed, and drained well

1 Cook the rotelle according to package directions. Meanwhile, whisk the buttermilk with the mayonnaise and dried tarragon in a large bowl until smooth and set aside.

2 Drain the pasta well, then add to the buttermilk mixture in the bowl and toss until well coated.

3 Add the ham, tomatoes, pistachios, and pepper, toss well again, and sprinkle with the fresh tarragon, if desired. Serve over a bed of spinach leaves. Serves 4.

> **Per serving:**
> *Calories 606; Protein 28 g;*
> *Carbohydrates 56 g;*
> *Fat 30 g; Sodium 1,310 mg;*
> *Cholesterol 58 mg*

20 minutes	10 minutes

German Potato and Knockwurst Salad

On a frosty day, this warm, spicy dish hits the spot.

1¾ pounds new potatoes, peeled and cut into 1-inch cubes
1 package (10 ounces) frozen green peas, thawed and drained
4 medium-size knockwurst or 6 frankfurters, pricked with a fork
2 tablespoons vegetable oil
1 medium-size sweet red pepper, cored, seeded, and diced
1 medium-size yellow onion, finely chopped
⅓ cup white wine vinegar or cider vinegar
⅓ cup Basic Chicken Stock (page 333) or canned chicken broth
2 tablespoons Dijon mustard, or to taste
1 teaspoon caraway seeds
½ teaspoon salt
¼ teaspoon black pepper
1 tablespoon snipped fresh dill (optional)

1 Cook the potatoes, partially covered, in a medium-size saucepan of boiling water until almost tender —10 to 12 minutes—adding the peas during the last 3 minutes.

2 Meanwhile, in a 10-inch non-stick skillet over moderate heat, bring ¼ cup water to a simmer. Add the knockwurst, cover, and cook, shaking the skillet occasionally, for 5 minutes or until almost all of the water has evaporated. Remove the lid, turn the knockwurst, and cook 1 minute more.

3 Transfer the knockwurst to a cutting board and slice them ½ inch thick; transfer to a large bowl. Drain the potatoes and peas, add to the bowl, and toss lightly.

4 Add the oil to the skillet and heat for 1 minute over moderate heat. Add the red pepper and onion and sauté for 2 minutes, stirring often, or until slightly soft.

5 Add the vinegar, stock, mustard, caraway seeds, salt, and black pepper to the skillet. Bring to a simmer, stirring constantly. Pour over the potato mixture and toss gently. Sprinkle, if you like, with the dill. Serves 4.

> **Per serving:**
> *Calories 525; Protein 17 g;*
> *Carbohydrates 57 g;*
> *Fat 27 g; Sodium 1,149 mg;*
> *Cholesterol 39 mg*

20 minutes	16 minutes

Tomatoes Stuffed with Rice and Black-Eyed Peas

For a festive look, place each of the stuffed tomatoes on celery or lettuce leaves and arrange the extra filling around the sides.

8 ounces hot or sweet Italian sausage, casings removed

1 medium-size red onion, finely chopped

1 clove garlic

2 cups water

1 package (10 ounces) frozen black-eyed peas, unthawed

¾ cup long-grain white rice

½ teaspoon salt

4 large tomatoes (about 2 pounds)

3 medium-size carrots, peeled and coarsely shredded

½ cup minced fresh parsley or basil

3 tablespoons olive oil

3 tablespoons lemon juice

Per serving:
Calories 557; Protein 22 g;
Carbohydrates 60 g;
Fat 26 g; Sodium 832 mg;
Cholesterol 44 mg

25 minutes | 40 minutes

---

1 In a medium-size saucepan over moderate heat, sauté the sausage, onion, and garlic for 8 minutes, crumbling the meat as it cooks. With a slotted spoon, transfer the mixture to paper toweling. Pour off all the drippings.

2 Add the water and peas to the saucepan, cover, and bring to a boil over moderate heat. Adjust the heat so that the water bubbles gently and simmer for 10 minutes. Stir in the rice and salt, cover, and simmer 20 minutes more.

3 Meanwhile, cut the tops off the tomatoes and discard, then hollow out the tomatoes with a large spoon and discard the pulp. Invert the shells on paper toweling to drain.

4 When the rice is done, stir in the sausage mixture, carrots, parsley, oil, and lemon juice. Let cool, then fill each tomato with ½ cup of the mixture. Place the remaining rice mixture in a bowl and serve on the side. Serves 4.

Serve Tomatoes Stuffed with Rice and Black-Eyed Peas when tomatoes are at their peak ripeness.

French-Style Flaked Tuna Salad

Surrounding the tuna with a stunning assortment of vegetables creates a beautiful salad.

1 pound small new potatoes (about 8), sliced ¼ inch thick but not peeled

8 ounces green beans, trimmed

1 large head Boston lettuce or ½ small head iceberg lettuce, separated into leaves

1 pint cherry tomatoes

2 cans (6½ ounces each) light or white tuna in water, drained and flaked

½ cup pitted black olives

4 large scallions, including tops, finely chopped

1 can (1 pound) artichoke hearts, drained and halved

2 tablespoons capers, drained (optional)

For the dressing:

3 tablespoons red wine vinegar or tarragon vinegar

2 teaspoons Dijon mustard

¼ teaspoon salt

¼ teaspoon black pepper

⅓ cup olive oil

1 In a large saucepan of boiling water, cook the potatoes, covered, over moderate heat for 7 minutes. Add the beans, cover, and cook 5 minutes more or until both the potatoes and beans are tender. Drain well, rinse under cool water, then drain again.

2 Line a large shallow bowl with the lettuce and arrange the potatoes, beans, tomatoes, tuna, olives, scallions, and artichoke hearts on top. Scatter the capers over all.

3 *For the dressing:* In a small bowl, whisk the vinegar with the mustard, salt, and pepper until smooth. Add the oil in a fine stream, whisking continuously until the mixture thickens slightly. Pass the salad and the dressing separately. Serves 4.

Per serving:
Calories 492; Protein 35 g;
Carbohydrates 46 g;
Fat 21 g; Sodium 639 mg;
Cholesterol 33 mg

| 30 minutes | 12 minutes |

Tuna and Chick Pea Salad

This salad travels well, so it's great for a picnic. It's also a flexible recipe. You can substitute cannellini, red kidney beans, or even black beans for the chick peas.

¼ cup olive oil

3 tablespoons lemon juice

½ teaspoon dried oregano, crumbled

⅛ teaspoon black pepper

2 cans (1 pound 3 ounces each) chick peas or Great Northern beans, drained and rinsed

2 cans (6½ ounces each) light or white tuna in water, drained and flaked

4 medium-size stalks celery, thinly sliced

2 large tomatoes, cored, seeded, and diced but not peeled

10 radishes, thinly sliced

1 small red onion, coarsely chopped

4 cups bite-size pieces of lettuce (any kind)

1 Combine the oil, lemon juice, oregano, and pepper in a large bowl. Add the chick peas, tuna, celery, tomatoes, radishes, and onion, and toss well to mix.

2 Arrange the lettuce in a large shallow bowl and mound the tuna mixture on top. Serves 4.

Per serving:
Calories 543; Protein 41 g;
Carbohydrates 53 g;
Fat 19 g; Sodium 1,150 mg;
Cholesterol 33 mg

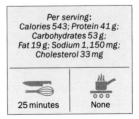

| 25 minutes | None |

Creamy Tuna and Pasta Salad

This salad is also delicious made with canned salmon.

For the dressing:

- 1 can (1 pound) cannellini (white kidney beans), drained and rinsed
- 1 cup plain low-fat yogurt
- 3 tablespoons olive oil
- 3 cloves garlic
- 2 teaspoons lemon juice
- ¼ teaspoon salt

For the salad:

- 12 ounces tricolor rotelle (corkscrew-shaped pasta), macaroni, or pasta shells
- 1 package (10 ounces) frozen Italian green beans, thawed and drained
- 1 can (6½ ounces) light or white tuna in water, drained and flaked
- 1 medium-size red onion, halved and thinly sliced
- 2 tablespoons minced parsley

1 *For the dressing:* Purée the cannellini with the yogurt, oil, garlic, lemon juice, and salt in a food processor or in an electric blender at high speed until smooth—about 1 minute. Transfer to a large bowl and set aside.

2 *For the salad:* Cook the rotelle according to package directions, adding the green beans during the last 4 minutes.

3 Drain and rinse the rotelle and beans, then add to the bowl of dressing along with the tuna and onion. Toss gently to mix and sprinkle with the parsley. Serves 4.

The peppy dressing for Creamy Tuna and Pasta Salad is a smooth blend of white beans and yogurt with plenty of garlic.

Per serving:
Calories 623; Protein 35 g;
Carbohydrates 90 g;
Fat 13 g; Sodium 709 mg;
Cholesterol 24 mg

10 minutes | 10 minutes

Scandinavian Herring Salad

A colorful salad, handsomely presented.

- 8 small new potatoes
- 4 large eggs
- 1 cup sour cream or plain low-fat yogurt
- 2 tablespoons prepared horseradish
- 1 teaspoon dill weed
- ⅛ teaspoon black pepper
- 1 head Boston lettuce, separated into leaves
- 1 jar (8 ounces) pickled herring or sardines, drained
- 2 cans (1 pound each) sliced beets, drained
- 1 small red onion, thinly sliced

Per serving:
Calories 533; Protein 21 g;
Carbohydrates 51 g;
Fat 28 g; Sodium 1,316 mg;
Cholesterol 246 mg

10 minutes   20 minutes

1 Cook the potatoes and eggs, uncovered, in a medium-size saucepan of boiling water over moderate heat for 10 minutes. Remove the eggs and plunge into cold water to cool. Continue boiling the potatoes until tender—about 10 minutes more. Drain the potatoes, slice ¼ inch thick, and place in a medium-size bowl. Peel and quarter the eggs, then set aside.

2 Meanwhile, combine the sour cream, horseradish, dill weed, and pepper in a small bowl. Spoon half of the dressing over the potatoes and toss until lightly coated.

3 Arrange the lettuce leaves on a large platter and mound the remaining sauce in the center. Arrange the potatoes, herring, eggs, and beets decoratively around the sauce. Separate the onion into rings and scatter over all. Serves 4.

Tropical Shrimp and Bow-Tie Salad

Here's a delightfully tart seafood salad with a sweet accent.

- 2 cups medium-size bow-tie pasta
- 1 package (9 ounces) frozen Italian green beans, unthawed
- 1 cup plain low-fat yogurt
- 3 tablespoons reduced-calorie mayonnaise
- ¾ teaspoon curry powder
- ¼ teaspoon grated lime rind
- 1 teaspoon lime juice
- ¼ teaspoon sugar
- 1 pound cooked shelled and deveined shrimp
- 1 large mango or 2 medium-size peaches or oranges, peeled, pitted or seeded, and cut into ½-inch cubes
- ¾ cup toasted sliced almonds (see page 86)

Per serving:
Calories 575; Protein 39 g;
Carbohydrates 66 g;
Fat 17 g; Sodium 306 mg;
Cholesterol 229 mg

17 minutes   15 minutes

1 Cook the pasta according to package directions, adding the beans during the last 5 minutes.

2 Whisk the yogurt with the mayonnaise, curry powder, lime rind, lime juice, and sugar in a large bowl until smooth; set aside.

3 Drain the pasta and beans well, then add to the yogurt mixture along with the shrimp, mango, and almonds. Toss well. Serves 4.

Red, White, and Green Salad

Red peppers, rice, and green peas
join shrimp in a perfect-for-summer salad.

2 tablespoons olive or vegetable oil

1 medium-size yellow onion, finely chopped

2 cups long-grain white rice

3 cups Basic Chicken Stock (page 333) or canned chicken broth

½ teaspoon each salt and black pepper

1 pound large shrimp, shelled and deveined, or sea scallops, halved

1 jar (7 ounces) roasted red peppers, drained and coarsely chopped

4 scallions, including tops, finely chopped

1 package (10 ounces) frozen green peas, thawed and drained

For the dressing:

3 tablespoons lemon juice

2 tablespoons balsamic or red wine vinegar

1 teaspoon Dijon mustard, or to taste

¼ cup olive or vegetable oil

¼ cup snipped fresh dill or ½ teaspoon dill weed

1 Heat the oil for 1 minute in a medium-size saucepan over moderate heat. Add the onion and sauté for 1 to 2 minutes or until slightly softened. Stir in the rice, then add the stock, salt, and black pepper. Bring to a boil, then adjust the heat so that the mixture bubbles gently. Cover and simmer for 10 minutes.

2 Place the shrimp on top of the rice, cover, and simmer for 10 minutes. Stir in the roasted red peppers, scallions, and peas, cover, and cook for 2 minutes. Remove from the heat and let stand, covered, for 5 minutes.

3 *For the dressing:* In a small bowl, whisk the lemon juice with the vinegar and mustard until smooth. Add the oil in a fine stream, whisking vigorously, then stir in the dill.

4 Transfer the shrimp mixture to a large bowl, pour the dressing over all, and toss well. Serves 4.

Per serving:
Calories 727; Protein 36 g;
Carbohydrates 93 g;
Fat 23 g; Sodium 707 mg;
Cholesterol 157 mg

25 minutes | 27 minutes

Shrimp Salad with Sugar Snap Peas

Suitable for hot weather or cool, this salad can
be served either warm or chilled.

1¼ pounds small new potatoes (about 10), cut into ¾-inch cubes but not peeled

1 pound medium-size shrimp, shelled and deveined

1 package (8 ounces) frozen sugar snap peas, thawed and drained

1 medium-size sweet red pepper, cored, seeded, and cut into ½-inch squares

2 medium-size stalks celery, diced

For the dressing:

½ cup reduced-fat sour cream or ¼ cup mayonnaise mixed with ¼ cup plain low-fat yogurt

¼ cup lemon juice (freshly squeezed preferred)

2 tablespoons snipped fresh dill or ½ teaspoon dill weed

2 teaspoons Dijon mustard

½ teaspoon salt

6 to 8 drops hot red pepper sauce

1 In a large saucepan of boiling water, cook the potatoes, uncovered, over moderate heat for 10 minutes. Add the shrimp, peas, and pepper, and cook, uncovered, 3 minutes more. Drain well in a colander. Place the celery on top.

2 *For the dressing:* Combine the sour cream, lemon juice, dill, mustard, salt, and red pepper sauce in a large serving bowl.

3 Add the drained potato-shrimp mixture and toss well to mix. Serves 4.

Per serving:
Calories 346; Protein 29 g;
Carbohydrates 41 g;
Fat 7 g; Sodium 523 mg;
Cholesterol 157 mg

30 minutes | 15 minutes

Shrimp, Corn, and Avocado Salad

Here's a spicy summer meal that's best served on a bed of radicchio or shredded lettuce and sprinkled with chopped scallions. It also has make-ahead possibilities — after Step 1, you can refrigerate the ingredients for up to 24 hours.

- 8 ounces ditalini (tube-shaped pasta) or orzo (rice-shaped pasta)
- 1 pound medium-size shrimp, shelled and deveined
- 1 cup frozen corn kernels, thawed and drained
- 1 large avocado, peeled, pitted, and cut into ½-inch cubes
- 3 tablespoons white wine vinegar or cider vinegar
- ⅓ cup bottled chili sauce
- 3 tablespoons olive or vegetable oil
- 1 tablespoon prepared horseradish
- ¼ teaspoon salt
- 6 drops hot red pepper sauce
- 1 cup slivered radishes
- 3 scallions, including tops, thinly sliced

Per serving:
*Calories 563; Protein 31 g;
Carbohydrates 61 g;
Fat 22 g; Sodium 662 mg;
Cholesterol 157 mg*

 25 minutes   15 minutes

1 Cook the ditalini according to package directions, adding the shrimp and corn during the last 3 minutes. Drain, rinse under cool water, and drain again.

2 Meanwhile, toss the avocado with 1 tablespoon of the vinegar in a medium-size serving bowl. Using a slotted spoon, transfer the avocado to a plate and set aside.

3 Add the remaining 2 tablespoons vinegar to the serving bowl along with the chili sauce, oil, horseradish, salt, and red pepper sauce, and blend well. Add the pasta mixture, radishes, and scallions, and toss. Gently mix in the avocado. Serves 4.

Shrimp, Corn, and Avocado Salad may not look it, but it has a real bite.

Jambalaya Salad

A Creole favorite translated into a delicious salad.

- 3 tablespoons olive oil
- 1 large yellow onion, finely chopped
- 2 cloves garlic, minced
- 1 cup long-grain white or brown rice
- 2½ cups water
- ¾ teaspoon dried oregano, crumbled
- ¾ teaspoon salt
- ⅛ teaspoon ground red pepper (cayenne)
- 6 ounces boiled or baked ham, cubed
- 1 large tomato, cored, seeded, and chopped, or 1 cup canned crushed tomatoes
- 12 ounces fresh or 1 package (10 ounces) frozen asparagus spears, thawed and drained, halved
- 1 can (6 ounces) crabmeat, drained and picked over for bits for shell and cartilage
- 1 tablespoon red wine vinegar

1 Heat 1 tablespoon of the oil in a medium-size saucepan over moderate heat for 1 minute. Add the onion and garlic and sauté, stirring frequently, until limp—5 minutes. Stir in the rice and cook for 1 minute. Add the water, oregano, salt, red pepper, and ham, and bring to a boil.

2 Reduce the heat to low, cover, and simmer for 10 minutes for white rice, 30 for brown. Add the tomato, cover, and cook 10 minutes longer or until the rice is almost tender. Lay the asparagus on top, cover, and cook for 5 minutes or until the asparagus and rice are tender. Transfer all to a large serving bowl.

3 Stir in the crabmeat, the remaining 2 tablespoons oil, and the vinegar, and toss lightly. Serve at room temperature. Serves 4.

Per serving:
Calories 421; Protein 22 g;
Carbohydrates 48 g;
Fat 16 g; Sodium 1,110 mg;
Cholesterol 62 mg

25 minutes | 34 minutes

Creamy Crab and Pasta Salad

Try this dish with tuna for a quick, inexpensive meal. It should be refrigerated for an hour before serving to let the flavors blend.

- 8 ounces small pasta shells or elbow macaroni
- 1 pound green beans, trimmed, or 1 package (10 ounces) frozen green beans, unthawed
- ¼ cup mayonnaise
- 1 cup plain low-fat yogurt
- ¼ cup bottled chili sauce
- 1 teaspoon Worcestershire sauce
- 2 or 3 drops hot red pepper sauce
- 8 ounces fresh or canned crabmeat, drained and picked over for bits of shell and cartilage
- 2 medium-size sweet red peppers, cored, seeded, and finely chopped
- 8 scallions, including tops, coarsely chopped

1 In a large saucepan of boiling water, cook the pasta and beans, uncovered, stirring occasionally, until firm-tender—about 8 minutes. Drain, rinse under cool water, and drain well again.

2 Meanwhile, combine the mayonnaise, yogurt, chili sauce, Worcestershire sauce, and red pepper sauce in a large bowl. Add the pasta, beans, crabmeat, peppers, and scallions, and toss lightly to mix. Chill for 1 hour. Serves 4.

Per serving:
Calories 445; Protein 23 g;
Carbohydrates 58 g;
Fat 13 g; Sodium 811 mg;
Cholesterol 35 mg

20 minutes | 8 minutes

Deviled Crab Salad

A piquant dressing makes a marvelous counterpoint to the crabmeat.

8 ounces asparagus, cut into 1-inch lengths, or 1 package (10 ounces) frozen cut asparagus, unthawed

1 pound fresh, canned, or frozen crabmeat, thawed if frozen, drained, and picked over for bits of shell and cartilage

1 can (14 ounces) whole baby corn, drained and rinsed

1 cup plain croutons

1 large sweet green pepper, cored, seeded, and coarsely chopped

1 large sweet red pepper, cored, seeded, and coarsely chopped

3 scallions, including tops, coarsely chopped

For the dressing:

¼ cup olive or vegetable oil

1 tablespoon lemon juice

1 tablespoon Dijon mustard

⅛ teaspoon black pepper

3 drops hot red pepper sauce
Pinch ground red pepper (cayenne), sugar, and salt

1 In a medium-size saucepan over moderate heat, cook the asparagus, covered, in ½ cup boiling water until crisp-tender—about 5 minutes. Drain well and transfer to a large serving bowl.

2 Add the crab, corn, croutons, green and red peppers, and scallions and set aside.

3 *For the dressing:* In a small bowl, whisk the oil with the lemon juice, mustard, black pepper, red pepper sauce, ground red pepper, sugar, and salt until well blended. Serve with the salad. Serves 4.

Per serving:
Calories 352; Protein 27 g; Carbohydrates 29 g; Fat 16 g; Sodium 1,433 mg; Cholesterol 47 mg

30 minutes	5 minutes

Deviled Crab Salad guarantees that your luncheon will be a success.

191

Broccoli-Cheddar Salad

Cheese and vegetables are delightfully combined with pasta to produce a salad with a special taste.

- 8 ounces medium-size pasta shells or macaroni
- 4 cups broccoli florets
- 1 medium-size sweet red pepper, cored, seeded, and diced
- ¼ cup vegetable or olive oil
- ½ cup coarsely chopped walnuts
- 1 teaspoon dried basil, crumbled
- 1 teaspoon sugar
- ¼ teaspoon salt
- 3 tablespoons cider vinegar
- 3 tablespoons lemon juice
- 3 scallions, including tops, cut into 1-inch lengths
- 12 ounces sharp low-fat Cheddar, Muenster, or Jarlsberg cheese, cubed

1 Cook the pasta shells according to package directions, adding the broccoli and red pepper during the last 6 minutes.

2 Meanwhile, heat 1 tablespoon of the oil in a 10-inch nonmetallic skillet over moderate heat for 1 minute. Add the walnuts and sauté, stirring often, for 2 to 3 minutes or until lightly browned. Remove from the heat and stir in the remaining oil and the basil, sugar, salt, vinegar, and lemon juice. Set aside.

3 When the pasta is firm-tender, add the scallions to the boiling water, then remove from the heat and drain well. Transfer the pasta and vegetables to a large bowl, add the walnut mixture, and toss to mix. Scatter the cheese evenly over all. Serve warm or at room temperature. Serves 4 to 6.

Per serving:
Calories 681; Protein 30 g;
Carbohydrates 62 g;
Fat 36 g; Sodium 1,122 mg;
Cholesterol 36 mg

 25 minutes | 15 minutes

Three-Bean Salad

Almost any cheese can be substituted for the Muenster, but Cheddar, Swiss, Monterey Jack, and mozzarella are especially good. If you're watching calories or cholesterol, use low-fat varieties.

- 1 package (10 ounces) frozen baby lima beans, unthawed
- 1 package (10 ounces) frozen cut green beans, unthawed
- 1 can (1 pound 3 ounces) red kidney beans, drained and rinsed
- 8 ounces Muenster cheese, cut into thin strips
- 1 can (8 ounces) sliced water chestnuts, drained
- 1 cup thinly sliced radishes

For the dressing:
- ⅓ cup olive oil
- 2 tablespoons white vinegar
- 1 tablespoon prepared mustard
- ¼ teaspoon each salt and black pepper

1 In a large saucepan, cook the lima beans according to package directions, adding the green beans during the last 5 minutes.

2 Meanwhile, place the kidney beans, cheese, water chestnuts, and radishes in a large bowl and set aside.

3 *For the dressing:* In a small bowl, whisk the oil with the vinegar, mustard, salt, and pepper until smooth, then pour over the kidney bean mixture.

4 When the lima beans and green beans are done, drain well, rinse under cool water, and drain again. Add to the kidney bean mixture and toss well. Serves 4 to 6.

Per serving:
Calories 609; Protein 27 g;
Carbohydrates 47 g;
Fat 36 g; Sodium 815 mg;
Cholesterol 55 mg

 15 minutes | 17 minutes

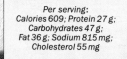

Special Macaroni and Cheese Salad

Roasted red peppers add a splash of color to this old favorite.

- 12 ounces elbow macaroni
- ¼ cup firmly packed flat-leaf parsley leaves
- ⅓ cup olive oil
- 3 tablespoons lime or lemon juice
- 6 dashes hot red pepper sauce
- 1 pound feta, mozzarella, or Monterey Jack cheese, cubed
- 2 jars (7 ounces each) roasted red peppers, drained and thickly sliced
- ½ cup pitted black olives, halved
- Parsley sprigs (optional garnish)

1 Cook the macaroni according to package directions until firm-tender. Meanwhile, purée the parsley, oil, lime juice, and red pepper sauce in a food processor or in an electric blender at high speed until smooth—about 30 seconds; transfer to a large bowl.

2 Drain the macaroni, rinse well, and add to the bowl along with the cheese, peppers, and olives. Toss well to mix and garnish, if desired, with the parsley sprigs. Serves 4.

Per serving:
Calories 820; Protein 28 g;
Carbohydrates 75 g;
Fat 45 g; Sodium 1,333 mg;
Cholesterol 101 mg

 10 minutes 10 minutes

Minted Barley with Peas

To prepare this salad ahead of time, after Step 2, simply cover and refrigerate the ingredients for up to 4 to 6 hours.

- ¾ cup medium pearl barley
- 1 package (10 ounces) frozen petite green peas, unthawed
- 1 small red onion, finely diced
- 2 medium-size stalks celery, finely diced
- ¼ cup olive or vegetable oil
- 3 tablespoons red wine vinegar
- 1 tablespoon minced fresh mint
- ¼ teaspoon each salt and black pepper
- 2 cups cubed Cheddar cheese
- ¾ cup coarsely chopped roasted peanuts or walnuts
- 2 medium-size tomatoes, seeded, drained, and diced
- 4 sprigs mint (optional garnish)

1 Cook the barley according to package directions in a large saucepan over moderate heat, adding the peas, onion, and celery during the last 3 minutes. Drain all well.

2 Place the barley and vegetables in a large bowl, add the oil, vinegar, chopped mint, salt, and pepper, and toss well.

3 Add the cheese, peanuts, and tomatoes and toss well again. Garnish with the mint if desired. Serve cold or at room temperature on a bed of lettuce. Serves 4.

Per serving:
Calories 714; Protein 29 g;
Carbohydrates 51 g;
Fat 47 g; Sodium 580 mg;
Cholesterol 61 mg

 20 minutes 45 minutes

Minted Barley with Peas—crisp, cool, and perfect for a summer day

Roasted Vegetable Salad

Because this salad needs to marinate, prepare it at least several hours in advance.

- 1 medium-size eggplant, cut into 8 thick slices
- 2 medium-size zucchini, quartered lengthwise
- 2 medium-size yellow squash, quartered lengthwise
- 2 large sweet red peppers, cored, seeded, and quartered
- 1 teaspoon each dried thyme and basil, crumbled
- ½ teaspoon each salt and black pepper
- 1 clove garlic, minced
- 3 tablespoons olive oil
- 3 tablespoons balsamic or red wine vinegar

- 8 slices French or Italian bread, lightly toasted
- 8 ounces part-skim mozzarella cheese, thinly sliced

For the dressing:
- 3 tablespoons reduced-calorie mayonnaise
- 2 tablespoons olive or vegetable oil
- 2 teaspoons Dijon mustard
- 4 small sprigs each fresh basil and thyme (optional garnish)

Per serving:
Calories 588; Protein 24 g;
Carbohydrates 53 g;
Fat 33 g; Sodium 960 mg;
Cholesterol 36 mg

30 minutes   25 minutes

1 In an 11″ x 9″ x 2″ flameproof baking dish, arrange the eggplant, zucchini, yellow squash, and red peppers in a single layer, then sprinkle with the thyme, basil, salt, black pepper, and garlic. Drizzle with the oil and vinegar, cover, place in the refrigerator, and marinate for 2 to 3 hours or overnight, turning once.

2 Preheat the oven to 550° F. Drain the vegetables, reserving the marinade, and return to the baking dish. Bake, uncovered, for 15 minutes. Transfer to the broiler, and broil 4 inches from the heat for 2 to 3 minutes or until tipped with brown. Divide the roasted vegetables among 4 dinner plates and set aside. Return the oven temperature to 550° F.

3 Arrange the bread on a baking sheet, top each slice with cheese, and bake, uncovered, just until the cheese melts—5 to 7 minutes.

4 *For the dressing:* In a food processor or an electric blender, whirl the reserved marinade with the mayonnaise, oil, and mustard at high speed for 30 seconds or until smooth.

5 Tuck 2 pieces of the cheese toast onto each plate of roasted vegetables, pour the dressing over the vegetables, and garnish with sprigs of basil and thyme if desired. Serves 4.

Roasted Vegetable Salad— a treat for the eye as well as the taste buds

194

Brunches and Lunches

The family wants something really special for Sunday breakfast. It's your turn to host a luncheon for the bridge club. The neighbors are coming over to watch a football game. Whatever the occasion, you're sure to find a recipe here that's made to order. It might be Easy Eggs Benedict, Asparagus Quiche, Smoked Turkey Sandwich with Cranberry Butter, or some equally enticing entrée that's perfect for an impromptu or odd-time-of-day meal. When it's too late for breakfast or not quite late enough for dinner, it's time for one of these light, low-fuss lunches or brunches.

Fruit Cobbler with Oatmeal Biscuits

This delectable blend of fruits makes a great way to start the day. To save time, soak the apricots and raisins while you prepare the other ingredients. If you prefer to make the biscuits with whole milk instead of yogurt, omit the baking soda and increase the baking powder to 1½ teaspoons.

For the filling:
- ⅓ cup chopped dried apricots
- ¼ cup raisins
- ¾ cup apple cider or apricot, pear, or grape juice
- 1 pound Golden Delicious apples, peeled, cored, and thinly sliced
- 12 ounces ripe Bartlett or Bosc pears, peeled, cored, and thinly sliced
- 2 teaspoons lemon juice, (freshly squeezed preferred)
- ¼ cup water
- ½ cup coarsely chopped walnuts

For the topping:
- ½ cup unsifted all-purpose flour
- ½ cup old-fashioned rolled oats or all-purpose flour
- 2 tablespoons sugar
- 1 teaspoon baking powder
- ½ teaspoon baking soda
- ½ teaspoon salt
- ¼ cup (½ stick) unsalted butter or margarine, chilled and cut into bits
- ½ cup plain low-fat yogurt or buttermilk
- 2 cups plain low-fat yogurt or light cream
- Ground cinnamon (optional garnish)

1 For the filling: Mix the apricots, raisins, and cider in a 12-inch ovenproof skillet and let stand for 30 minutes at room temperature.

2 Add the apples, pears, lemon juice, and water to the skillet, and bring to a boil over moderate heat. Cover, reduce the heat to moderately low, and simmer until the fruit is tender—10 to 20 minutes depending on the ripeness of the fruit. If the mixture starts to boil dry, add a little more fruit juice and water. When the fruit has finished cooking, stir in the walnuts. Meanwhile, prepare the topping.

3 For the topping: Preheat the oven to 425° F. Mix the flour, oats, sugar, baking powder, soda, and salt in a medium-size bowl. Using a pastry blender or 2 knives, cut in the butter until the mixture resembles coarse meal. Add the ½ cup of yogurt and stir just enough to combine.

4 Place the dough on a lightly floured surface and, with floured hands, pat out to a thickness of ½ inch. With a floured 2-inch round biscuit cutter, cut out 8 rounds. Arrange the rounds on top of the fruit mixture in the skillet, set in the oven, and bake, uncovered, for 20 minutes or until the biscuits are golden brown. Top each portion with yogurt and a sprinkling of cinnamon if desired. Serves 4.

Fruit Cobbler with Oatmeal Biscuits, served piping hot and topped with a dollop of yogurt

Per serving:
Calories 596; Protein 14 g;
Carbohydrates 87 g;
Fat 24 g; Sodium 561 mg;
Cholesterol 40 mg

30 minutes | 42 minutes

Waffles with Ham and Apples

Serve this sweet and savory brunch dish with a drizzle of maple syrup or a sprinkling of confectioners sugar. Allow an extra half-hour preparation time for the milk to soak into the waffles.

- 2 cups low-fat milk
- 2 large eggs
- 1 large egg white
- ⅓ cup maple syrup
- ½ teaspoon vanilla extract
- ¼ teaspoon salt
- 1 package (10 ounces) frozen waffles (8 4-inch waffles), unthawed
- 2 medium-size sweet apples, 1 cored, peeled, and chopped, 1 cored and sliced
- 4 ounces baked or boiled ham, diced
- ½ cup shredded low-fat Cheddar cheese (2 ounces)

1 Whisk the milk, eggs, egg white, syrup, vanilla, and salt in a large bowl until blended.

2 Arrange 4 of the waffles side by side in a lightly greased 9″ x 9″ x 2″ baking pan. Sprinkle evenly with the chopped apple and ham, then top with the remaining 4 waffles. Pour the milk mixture over all, cover with foil, and let stand for 30 minutes at room temperature.

3 Preheat the oven to 375° F. Set the foil-covered baking pan on the top rack and bake for 15 minutes. Remove the foil, sprinkle the cheese on top, and bake 10 minutes more or until the cheese is melted. Garnish with the remaining sliced apple. Serves 4.

Per serving:
Calories 496; Protein 20 g;
Carbohydrates 69 g;
Fat 16 g; Sodium 1,354 mg;
Cholesterol 134 mg

10 minutes | 25 minutes

Sunnyside Sausage Skillet

An easy one-skillet meal combines some great breakfast favorites.

- 8 ounces pork sausages
- ¼ cup vegetable oil
- 1 medium-size yellow onion, finely chopped
- 6 cups frozen hash brown potatoes, unthawed
- ½ teaspoon salt
- ¼ teaspoon black pepper
- 1 cup frozen green peas, unthawed
- 6 large eggs

Per serving:
Calories 663; Protein 20 g;
Carbohydrates 50 g;
Fat 44 g; Sodium 807 mg;
Cholesterol 245 mg

5 minutes | 50 minutes

1 Place the sausages in a 12-inch skillet, pour in ½ inch of water, cover, and bring to a boil over moderate heat. Cook for 10 minutes, then pour off the water and cook, uncovered, 10 minutes more or until nicely browned. Remove the sausages from the skillet, cut into thin slices, and set aside.

2 Wipe out the skillet, add the oil, and set over moderate heat for 1 minute. Add the onion and sauté, stirring occasionally, for 5 minutes or until tender.

3 Add the potatoes, cover, and cook, stirring occasionally, until they begin to brown—5 to 10 minutes. Remove the cover and sprinkle with the salt and pepper. Continue cooking, uncovered, stirring occasionally, until the potatoes are golden and tender—about 10 minutes more. Stir in the peas.

4 Break 1 egg into a cup, then ease into the skillet on top of the potatoes. Repeat with the remaining eggs, spacing them evenly. Scatter the sausage slices around the eggs, cover, and cook for 2 to 3 minutes or until the eggs are set. Serves 6.

Easy Eggs Benedict

In this no-fuss version, the eggs are beautifully baked in rice cups — simple to do, sensational to serve.

- 3 tablespoons unsalted butter or margarine
- 1 large yellow onion, finely chopped
- 2 cloves garlic, minced
- ½ cup long-grain brown rice
- 1 cup boiling water
- ½ teaspoon salt
- 4 large eggs
- 1 package (9 ounces) hollandaise sauce mix
- 1 medium-size bunch arugula or 8 ounces spinach, trimmed, rinsed, drained well, and chopped

Per serving:
Calories 433; Protein 16 g;
Carbohydrates 17 g;
Fat 34 g; Sodium 1,033 mg;
Cholesterol 299 mg

21 minutes | 50 minutes

1 Preheat the oven to 350° F. Melt 2 tablespoons of the butter in a 10-inch skillet over moderate heat. Add the onion and sauté, stirring occasionally, for 3 minutes. Add the garlic and rice and sauté, stirring occasionally, 5 minutes more.

2 Transfer the mixture to a lightly greased 10" x 6" x 2" baking dish. Stir in the boiling water and salt, cover with foil, and bake for 30 minutes or until the rice is almost tender and most of the liquid has been absorbed. Remove from the oven.

3 Reduce the oven temperature to 325° F. Using a large spoon, make 4 wells in the rice and break an egg into each one. Cut the remaining tablespoon of butter into 4 equal parts and place a dab of butter on each egg. Bake, uncovered, for 10 minutes or until the eggs are set.

4 Meanwhile, prepare the hollandaise sauce according to package directions. Remove the baking dish from the oven and sprinkle evenly with the arugula. Serve with the hollandaise sauce. Serves 4.

Eggs Florentine

An easy, elegant version of an Italian classic.

- 4 English muffins, split and toasted
- 3 tablespoons unsalted butter or margarine
- 1 medium-size yellow onion, finely chopped
- 1 package (10 ounces) frozen chopped spinach, thawed, drained, and squeezed dry
- 4 large eggs
- 2 large egg whites
- ⅛ teaspoon salt
- ½ teaspoon black pepper
- 1 can (10 ounces) condensed cream of mushroom soup
- ½ cup whole or low-fat milk
- 2 teaspoons Dijon mustard, or to taste
- ½ cup shredded Gruyère, Monterey Jack, or Swiss cheese

Per serving:
Calories 502; Protein 23 g;
Carbohydrates 44 g;
Fat 27 g; Sodium 1,382 mg;
Cholesterol 257 mg

15 minutes | 30 minutes

1 Preheat the oven to 400° F. Arrange the muffins, cut sides up, in a single layer in a greased flameproof 11" x 9" x 2" baking dish.

2 Melt 1 tablespoon of the butter in a 10-inch nonstick skillet over moderate heat. Add the onion and sauté, stirring, for 2 to 3 minutes or until softened. Add the spinach and sauté, stirring, 2 minutes more. Spoon the spinach mixture onto the muffins. Wipe out the skillet with paper toweling.

3 In a small bowl, whisk together the eggs, egg whites, salt, and pepper; set aside. Then melt the remaining 2 tablespoons of butter in the skillet over moderate heat. Add the egg mixture and cook, stirring, until the eggs are just set — 2 to 3 minutes. Spoon the eggs over the spinach.

4 Add the soup and milk to the skillet, then bring to a simmer over moderate heat, stirring often. Add the mustard and all but 2 tablespoons of the cheese, stir until the cheese just melts, then spoon over the eggs and sprinkle with the remaining cheese.

5 Bake, uncovered, for 10 to 15 minutes or until bubbling. Transfer to the broiler and broil 4 inches from the heat for 1 to 2 minutes or until golden brown. Serves 4.

Baked Eggs, Mexican Style

Salsa, refried beans, and cheese make a hearty, spicy breakfast dish.

- 1 cup canned refried beans
- 2 tablespoons water
- 1 package (10 ounces) frozen chopped spinach, thawed, drained, and squeezed dry
- 5 scallions, including tops, chopped
- ⅓ cup sour cream
- 1 cup shredded Monterey Jack cheese (4 ounces)
- 4 large eggs
- ½ cup bottled salsa (mild, medium, or hot) or Basic Salsa (page 339)
- 4 flour tortillas, 7½ to 8 inches in diameter
- 1 cup prepared guacamole
- ⅛ teaspoon black pepper
- Salsa and sour cream (optional toppings)

Per serving:
Calories 517; Protein 25 g;
Carbohydrates 43 g;
Fat 29 g; Sodium 1,099 mg;
Cholesterol 222 mg

15 minutes   20 minutes

1 Preheat the oven to 400° F. Mix the beans and water in a greased 8″ x 8″ x 2″ or 11″ x 7″ x 2″ baking pan then spread over the bottom. Mix the spinach and all but 2 tablespoons of the scallions and spread on top of the beans. Top with the sour cream, then the cheese.

2 Make 4 indentations in the surface and break an egg into each one. Spoon the salsa on top and bake, uncovered, for 20 minutes or until the eggs are set. Heat the tortillas for five minutes before serving.

3 When the eggs are done, spoon ¼ cup of guacamole on top then sprinkle the pepper and remaining scallions over all. Serve with the hot tortillas, the remaining guacamole and, if desired, additional salsa and sour cream. Serves 4.

Rich, soothing, and wonderfully satisfying—Baked Eggs, Mexican Style

Broccoli Potato Frittata

An enticing potato and egg pancake studded with sweet red peppers, black olives, and broccoli.

- 8 ounces (½ head) broccoli florets or 1 package (10 ounces) frozen chopped broccoli, thawed and drained
- 2 tablespoons olive oil
- 2 cups refrigerated, shredded potatoes
- 1 large yellow onion, coarsely chopped
- 1 large sweet red pepper, cored, seeded, and coarsely chopped
- 2 cloves garlic, minced
- 1 teaspoon salt
- 1 teaspoon dried thyme, crumbled

- ¼ teaspoon black pepper
- 6 large eggs
- 3 tablespoons low-fat milk
- ¼ cup (½ stick) unsalted butter or margarine
- ¼ cup sliced black olives

Per serving:
Calories 379; Protein 14 g;
Carbohydrates 23 g;
Fat 27 g; Sodium 680 mg;
Cholesterol 351 mg

15 minutes   44 minutes

1 Preheat oven to 350° F. If using fresh broccoli, steam or boil until tender—about 10 minutes.

2 Meanwhile, heat the oil in a 10-inch ovenproof skillet over moderate heat for 1 minute. Add the potatoes, onion, red pepper, garlic, and half of the salt, thyme, and black pepper. Sauté, stirring occasionally, until the onion and red pepper are very soft—8 to 10 minutes. Transfer to a medium-size bowl, mix in the broccoli, and set aside.

3 In a small bowl, lightly beat the eggs with the milk and the remaining salt, thyme, and black pepper. Heat the butter in the skillet over low heat until hot and bubbling—about 3 minutes. Pour in the egg mixture and cook, stirring occasionally with a fork, until the eggs are set—about 10 minutes.

4 Remove the skillet from the heat and spread the vegetables on top of the eggs. Sprinkle the olives over all and bake, uncovered, for 10 minutes. Serves 4.

A hearty and healthful way to start the day—Broccoli Potato Frittata

Baked Spaghetti Frittata

A scrumptious combination of eggs, pasta, tomatoes, and cheese. Served either hot or at room temperature, it makes a wonderful buffet or picnic dish.

8 ounces spaghetti or linguine

2 tablespoons olive oil

1 large yellow onion, thinly sliced

2 medium-size sweet green peppers, cored, seeded, and thinly sliced

2 large tomatoes, peeled, cored, seeded, and coarsely chopped

6 large eggs

½ cup low-fat milk

¼ teaspoon salt

⅛ teaspoon black pepper

8 ounces part-skim mozzarella cheese, thinly sliced

1 Preheat the oven to 375° F. Cook the spaghetti according to package directions. Meanwhile, heat the oil in a 12-inch ovenproof skillet over moderate heat for 1 minute. Add the onion and green peppers, cover, and cook, stirring occasionally, for 15 minutes or until very soft.

2 Drain the spaghetti and add to the skillet along with the tomatoes. Toss lightly to mix.

3 In a large bowl, beat the eggs with the milk, salt, and black pepper, then pour over the skillet mixture. Arrange the cheese on top and bake, uncovered, just until the eggs are set—15 to 20 minutes. Serves 4.

Per serving:
Calories 578; Protein 33 g;
Carbohydrates 54 g;
Fat 25 g; Sodium 520 mg;
Cholesterol 353 mg

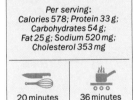

| 20 minutes | 36 minutes |

Sunday Brunch Frittata

Crisp and golden on the outside, moist and fluffy on the inside, this Italian-style omelet is a guaranteed hit.

3 tablespoons vegetable oil

1 medium-size yellow onion, thinly sliced

1 medium-size sweet green pepper, cored, seeded, and diced

2 medium-size all-purpose potatoes, peeled and thinly sliced

8 ounces mushrooms, thinly sliced

4 large eggs

½ cup whole or low-fat milk

⅓ cup grated Parmesan or shredded Gruyère cheese

½ teaspoon each salt and black pepper

½ cup sour cream or plain low-fat yogurt

¼ cup finely chopped sweet pepper (red, green, or mixed)

Per serving:
Calories 372; Protein 15 g;
Carbohydrates 23 g;
Fat 25 g; Sodium 521 mg;
Cholesterol 237 mg

| 20 minutes | 25 minutes |

1 Preheat the broiler and set the rack 4 inches from the heat. Heat 1 tablespoon of the oil in a 12-inch ovenproof skillet over moderate heat for 1 minute. Add the onion, green pepper, and potatoes, cover, and cook, stirring occasionally, for 5 minutes. Add the mushrooms, cover, and cook, stirring occasionally, for 4 minutes or until the potatoes are tender. Remove the cover, raise the heat to moderately high, and cook, stirring, 1 minute more or until all the liquid evaporates.

2 In a large bowl, whisk together the eggs, milk, all but 2 tablespoons of the cheese, and the salt and black pepper, then stir in the vegetable mixture.

3 Add the remaining 2 tablespoons of oil to the skillet and heat over moderately high heat for 1 minute. Add the egg and vegetable mixture, reduce the heat to moderately low, and cook, uncovered, for 8 to 10 minutes or until just set.

4 Sprinkle with the remaining cheese. Transfer the skillet to the broiler and broil for 1 to 2 minutes or until lightly golden. Top with the sour cream and sweet pepper. Serves 4.

201

Tomato and Spinach Tart

*Unlike prepared crusts, which are sold in pie tins, the refrigerated pie crust
called for in this recipe is sold folded and wrapped in plastic.*

1 refrigerated pie crust (from a
  15-ounce package)
½ cup orzo (rice-shaped pasta) or
  spaghetti broken into ½-inch
  lengths
2 tablespoons olive oil
1 large yellow onion, thinly sliced
2 cloves garlic, minced
1½ teaspoons dried basil,
  crumbled
1 cup low-fat cottage cheese
2 large eggs
1 package (10 ounces) frozen
  chopped spinach, thawed,
  drained, and squeezed dry
1 cup coarsely shredded low-fat
  Monterey Jack cheese (4
  ounces)
2 large tomatoes

Per serving:
Calories 593; Protein 25 g;
Carbohydrates 55 g;
Fat 31 g; Sodium 639 mg;
Cholesterol 129 mg

15 minutes | 1 hour

1 Preheat the oven to 450° F. Fit
the crust into a 9-inch pie pan
and make a fluted stand-up edge.
Place a square of foil on the crust and
weigh it down with dried beans, rice,
or pie weights. Bake, uncovered, until partially done—9 to 11 minutes—then take out of the oven and
remove the foil and beans. Meanwhile, cook the orzo according to
package directions and drain well.

2 Heat the oil in a 12-inch skillet
over moderately high heat for 1
minute. Add the onion and sauté
over moderate heat, stirring occasionally, until tender—5 minutes.
Add the garlic and basil and sauté,
stirring occasionally, for 2 minutes.
Remove the skillet from the heat
and stir in the orzo.

3 Purée the cottage cheese with
the eggs in a food processor or
an electric blender by whirling at
high speed for about 1 minute, then
add to the skillet. Mix in the spinach
and Monterey Jack cheese, mix well,
then spoon into the partially baked

pie crust. Smooth the top and
bake, uncovered, for 25 minutes.

4 Meanwhile, core and slice the
tomatoes, then let them drain on
paper toweling. When the tart has
baked for 25 minutes, remove it
from the oven and arrange the tomatoes in an overlapping circle on top.
Bake, uncovered, 20 minutes more
or until a knife inserted near the center comes out clean. Serves 4.

*What could be more festive for
a holiday brunch than
Tomato and Spinach Tart?*

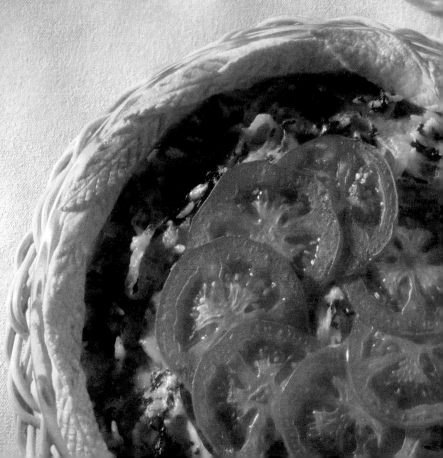

Asparagus Quiche

Our new version of this popular luncheon dish is lower in fat and cholesterol than the traditional recipe. Be sure to place the pie pan on a cookie sheet when it bakes so that the crust cooks through.

1 package (10 ounces) frozen asparagus tips, thawed and drained
1 frozen 9-inch pie crust
1 cup part-skim ricotta cheese or low-fat cottage cheese
1 cup plain low-fat yogurt or sour cream
2 large eggs
⅓ cup grated Parmesan cheese
⅓ cup finely chopped scallions, including tops
1 clove garlic, minced
⅓ cup unsifted all-purpose flour
2 teaspoons baking powder
2 teaspoons Dijon mustard
½ teaspoon salt
⅛ teaspoon ground red pepper (cayenne)

1 Preheat the oven to 350° F. Arrange the asparagus in a single layer in the pie crust.

2 Whirl the ricotta cheese, yogurt, eggs, half the Parmesan cheese, the scallions, garlic, flour, baking powder, mustard, salt, and red pepper in a food processor or an electic blender at high speed until smooth—about 10 seconds.

3 Pour over the asparagus, then sprinkle with the remaining Parmesan cheese. Cover with foil, place on a cookie sheet, and bake for 30 minutes, then remove the foil and bake 15 minutes more. Serves 4.

Per serving:
Calories 484; Protein 23 g;
Carbohydrates 40 g;
Fat 26 g; Sodium 1,052 mg;
Cholesterol 136 mg

10 minutes	45 minutes

Welsh Rarebit with Spinach

An all-time favorite with a zippy new twist.

1 package (1 pound) frozen leaf spinach, unthawed
½ cup unsifted all-purpose flour
2 cups low-fat milk
1½ teaspoons Worcestershire sauce
½ teaspoon dry mustard
¼ teaspoon salt
⅛ teaspoon ground red pepper (cayenne)
2 cups coarsely shredded sharp Cheddar cheese (8 ounces)
8 slices toast, halved diagonally
12 cherry tomatoes, quartered

Per serving:
Calories 522; Protein 28 g;
Carbohydrates 53 g;
Fat 23 g; Sodium 929 mg;
Cholesterol 65 mg

15 minutes	8 minutes

1 Cook the spinach according to package directions, then drain well, return to the saucepan, cover, and keep warm.

2 Meanwhile, place the flour and 1 cup of the milk in a jar with a tight-fitting lid, shake well to blend, then pour into a large saucepan. Stir in the remaining milk, the Worcestershire sauce, mustard, salt, and red pepper, and cook, stirring constantly, over moderate heat until thickened and smooth—about 5 minutes. Reduce the heat to low, add the cheese, then cook and stir for 2 to 3 minutes or until melted.

3 To serve, arrange the toast on 4 plates, spoon the spinach on top, and ladle the cheese mixture over all, dividing all amounts evenly. Garnish with the cherry tomatoes. Serves 4.

Stuffed Tomato Trio

Here are three versions of this attractive luncheon dish—tomatoes stuffed with rice, ham, and peas; with dilled shrimp and cucumber; and with a chutney, chicken, and rice mixture. Serve on a bed of lettuce.

1 cup long-grain white rice

1⅓ cups frozen green peas, thawed and drained

4 large ripe tomatoes

3 tablespoons olive or vegetable oil

1½ tablespoons red or white wine vinegar

½ teaspoon salt

8 ounces baked or boiled ham, cut into ½-inch cubes

1 medium-size carrot, peeled and coarsely shredded

Per serving:
Calories 440; Protein 17 g;
Carbohydrates 55 g;
Fat 17 g; Sodium 1,078 mg;
Cholesterol 32 mg

10 minutes   20 minutes

1 Cook the rice according to package directions, adding the peas during the last minute. Meanwhile, cut off the top third of each tomato, making a decorative zigzag edge if desired. Gently scoop out the seeds and pulp and discard. Dice the tops.

2 Stir the oil, vinegar, and salt into the rice and peas, then mix in the ham and diced tomato. Fill the tomato shells with the rice mixture, arrange on serving plates, then spoon any excess rice mixture around each tomato. Sprinkle the carrot on top. Serves 4.

Shrimp-Stuffed Variation

In Step 1, omit the peas; prepare the rice and tomatoes as directed. In Step 2, omit the vinegar and reduce the oil to 1 tablespoon. Whisk the oil and salt together in a small bowl with *¼ cup plain low-fat yogurt, 2 teaspoons sweet paprika, 2 chopped scallions, including tops, and 1 tablespoon snipped fresh dill or 1 teaspoon dill weed.* Mix the dressing into the rice as directed. Omit the ham and stir in *2 cups cooked shrimp, cut into bite-size pieces,* and *1 small diced cucumber.* Stuff and serve the tomatoes as directed. Garnish with *1 chopped scallion, including top,* if desired. Serves 4.

Per serving: Calories 316; Protein 19 g;
Carbohydrates 49 g; Fat 5 g;
Sodium 441 mg; Cholesterol 126 mg

Chicken-Stuffed Variation

In Step 1, prepare the rice as directed, omitting the peas and adding *2 teaspoons sweet paprika* during the last 5 minutes; prepare the tomatoes as directed. In Step 2, omit the oil and vinegar; instead, mix *2 tablespoons plain low-fat yogurt* into the rice along with *2 chopped scallions, including tops, 2 tablespoons mayonnaise, 2 tablespoons mango chutney, ½ teaspoon prepared mustard, ½ teaspoon salt,* and *⅛ teaspoon black pepper.* Omit the ham and stir in *1 pound cooked chicken, cut into ½-inch cubes.* Stuff the tomatoes as directed. Arrange *½ cup watercress, lettuce, or arugula leaves* on each plate, place 2 tomato halves on top. Garnish with *1 chopped scallion, including top,* if desired. Serves 4.

Per serving: Calories 475; Protein 42 g;
Carbohydrates 52 g; Fat 11 g;
Sodium 496 mg; Cholesterol 101 mg

*Serve Ham and Cheese Bread Bake
for either lunch or brunch.*

Ham and Cheese Bread Bake

A satisfying supper that you can put together in minutes.

1 tablespoon unsalted butter or margarine

1 medium-size yellow onion, finely chopped

1 package (10 ounces) frozen asparagus tips, chopped broccoli, or green peas, thawed and drained

1 pound baked or boiled ham, cut into 1-inch cubes

4 slices whole wheat bread, cut into 1-inch squares

3 large eggs

1 large egg white

2 cups milk

1 cup coarsely shredded Monterey Jack or Cheddar cheese (4 ounces)

½ teaspoon each salt and black pepper

1 tablespoon Dijon mustard

Per serving:
Calories 576; Protein 42 g;
Carbohydrates 28 g;
Fat 33 g; Sodium 2,264 mg;
Cholesterol 248 mg

| 20 minutes | 43 minutes |

1 Preheat the oven to 350° F. Melt the butter in a 12-inch nonstick skillet over moderate heat. Add the onion and sauté, stirring, for 2 to 3 minutes or until slightly softened. Add the asparagus tips and cook, stirring, for 2 minutes. Add the ham and bread and toss to mix. Set aside.

2 In a large bowl, beat the eggs and egg white with the milk, all but 2 tablespoons of the cheese, the salt, pepper, and mustard, just enough to combine. Stir in the skillet mixture.

3 Pour all into a greased flameproof 2-quart shallow baking dish and sprinkle with the remaining cheese. Cover with foil and bake for 30 to 35 minutes or until a knife inserted in the center comes out clean.

4 Transfer the dish to the broiler, and broil 4 inches from the heat for 2 minutes or until lightly golden. Serves 4.

Chicken Fajitas

To save time, marinate the chicken while you chop the vegetables.

- **2** tablespoons lime juice
- **1** tablespoon vegetable oil
- **1** large clove garlic, minced
- **¼** teaspoon salt
- **⅛** teaspoon black pepper
- **1** pound skinned and boned chicken breasts
- **8** flour tortillas, 8 inches in diameter
- **2** cups bottled salsa or Basic Salsa (page 339)
- **1** small avocado, peeled, pitted, and thinly sliced
- **2** cups coarsely shredded lettuce
- **½** cup plain low-fat yogurt or sour cream

1 Preheat the broiler and set the rack 5 inches from the heat. Combine the lime juice, oil, garlic, salt, and pepper in a medium-size bowl. Add the chicken, turn to coat, and marinate for 10 minutes.

2 Drain the chicken breasts and broil them until no longer pink on the inside—about 3 minutes on each side. Meanwhile, wrap the tortillas in foil, place them on the sides of the broiler pan, and heat for 5 minutes, turning once.

3 Cut the chicken into thin slices. Unwrap the tortillas and place some of the chicken in the center of each one. Top with the salsa, avocado slices, lettuce, and yogurt, then roll up each tortilla. Serves 4.

Per serving:
Calories 468; Protein 35 g;
Carbohydrates 49 g;
Fat 17 g; Sodium 678 mg;
Cholesterol 67 mg

15 minutes | 8 minutes

Smoked Turkey Sandwich with Cranberry Butter

A fabulous sandwich that combines the sweet, smooth flavor of Jarlsberg cheese with the tart taste of cranberries.

- **½** cup frozen cranberries, thawed and drained
- **3** tablespoons unsalted butter or margarine
- **1** teaspoon each honey and Dijon mustard
- **8** slices rye bread
- **12** ounces thinly sliced smoked turkey
- **12** ounces thinly sliced Jarlsberg cheese
- **8** romaine lettuce leaves
  Cherry tomatoes (optional garnish)

1 Purée the cranberries with the butter, honey, and mustard in a food processor or an electric blender by whirling at high speed for about 1 minute, then spread on one side of each slice of bread.

2 Stack the turkey, cheese, and lettuce on half of the bread slices, dividing the total amount evenly, and cover with the remaining slices. Halve diagonally, then garnish, if desired, with the cherry tomatoes. Serves 4.

Per serving:
Calories 698; Protein 44 g;
Carbohydrates 34 g;
Fat 43 g; Sodium 593 mg;
Cholesterol 102 mg

10 minutes | None

Tangy Egg Salad Sandwiches

An old standby tastes better than ever with a dash of mustard, vinegar, and anchovy paste.

- 2 tablespoons reduced-calorie mayonnaise
- 1 tablespoon Dijon mustard
- 1½ teaspoons balsamic or cider vinegar
- ½ teaspoon lemon juice
- ¼ teaspoon each salt and black pepper
- ⅛ teaspoon sugar
- ½ teaspoon anchovy paste (optional)
- 4 large hard-cooked eggs, peeled and coarsely chopped
- ¼ cup finely chopped celery
- ¼ cup finely chopped sweet red pepper
- 1 scallion, including top, finely chopped
- 1 clove garlic, minced
- 8 slices whole wheat bread, toasted
- 12 arugula leaves, watercress sprigs, or lettuce leaves

1 Combine the mayonnaise, mustard, vinegar, lemon juice, salt, black pepper, sugar, and anchovy paste, if desired, in a medium-size bowl. Add the eggs and mix well.

2 Stir in the celery, red pepper, scallion, and garlic. Spread the mixture on 4 slices of the toast and top with the arugula, dividing the total amount evenly. Place the remaining toast slices on top, then cut each sandwich in half. Serves 4.

Per serving:
Calories 295; Protein 16 g;
Carbohydrates 36 g;
Fat 11 g; Sodium 647 mg;
Cholesterol 277 mg

 15 minutes

 None

Tuna and Roasted Red Pepper Sandwich

Turn tuna fish into a four-star sandwich with this sensational recipe—from the Basque region of southern Europe.

- 1 loaf French or Italian bread
- 2 jars (7 ounces each) roasted red peppers, drained and cut into thin strips
- 2 cans (6½ ounces each) tuna in water, drained and flaked
- 2 tablespoons capers, drained and minced
- 2 large cloves garlic, minced
- 2 tablespoons minced parsley
- ¼ teaspoon each dried basil and oregano, crumbled
- ⅛ teaspoon black pepper
- 2 tablespoons olive or vegetable oil
- 1 tablespoon red wine vinegar or cider vinegar
- 1 tablespoon lemon juice
- 1 cup loosely packed watercress or torn red leaf lettuce leaves

1 Preheat the oven to 350° F. Cut the bread in half lengthwise and scoop out the soft center. Place the 2 halves, hollow sides up, on a baking sheet and bake, uncovered, for 10 minutes or until warm and crisp.

2 Meanwhile, mix the red peppers, tuna, capers, garlic, parsley, basil, oregano, black pepper, oil, vinegar, and lemon juice in a medium-size bowl. Place the watercress in one of the bread halves, spoon the tuna mixture on top, then cover with the other half. Cut the loaf crosswise into 4 equal portions. Serves 4.

Per serving:
Calories 605; Protein 42 g;
Carbohydrates 78 g;
Fat 13 g; Sodium 1,222 mg;
Cholesterol 33 mg

20 minutes | 10 minutes

A hero that hails from Spain: Tuna and Roasted Red Pepper Sandwich

Charleston Shrimp Pie

This dish is delicate, pretty, and deservedly popular.

2 cups skim or whole milk

3 large eggs, lightly beaten

3 tablespoons dry sherry (optional)

2 tablespoons Dijon mustard

½ teaspoon salt

¼ teaspoon ground mace or nutmeg

¼ teaspoon ground red pepper (cayenne)

4 slices firm-textured white bread, cut into 1-inch squares

2 tablespoons unsalted butter or margarine

1 medium-size yellow onion, finely chopped

1 pound large shrimp, shelled and deveined

1 package (10 ounces) frozen green peas, thawed and drained

2 tablespoons fine dry bread crumbs

Per serving:
Calories 409; Protein 37 g;
Carbohydrates 33 g;
Fat 13 g; Sodium 848 mg;
Cholesterol 334 mg

| 20 minutes | 1 hr. 9 min. |

---

1 Preheat the oven to 375° F. In a large bowl, combine the milk, eggs, sherry, if desired, mustard, salt, mace, and red pepper. Add the bread, toss well, and set aside.

2 Melt the butter in a 10-inch non-stick skillet over moderate heat. Add the onion and sauté, stirring, for 2 to 3 minutes or until slightly softened. Add the shrimp and peas and cook, stirring, for 2 to 3 minutes or until the shrimp turn opaque. Transfer to the bowl and mix well.

3 Spoon the mixture into a greased flameproof 2-quart soufflé dish and sprinkle the bread crumbs on top. Bake, uncovered, for 45 minutes to 1 hour or until a knife inserted in the center comes out clean.

4 Transfer the dish to the broiler and broil 4 inches from the heat for 1 to 2 minutes or until the top is golden brown. Serves 4.

All dressed up for a special occasion: Potatoes Stuffed with Crab and Spinach

Molded Shrimp Salad with Orzo

Prepare this salad at least 4 hours before serving so that it has time to set.

- ¼ cup cold water
- 1 tablespoon unflavored gelatin
- ¼ cup lemon juice (freshly squeezed preferred)
- ⅓ cup reduced-calorie mayonnaise
- 3 tablespoons plain low-fat yogurt
- ⅓ cup bottled chili sauce
- ¼ teaspoon salt
- ¼ teaspoon hot red pepper sauce
- 1 tablespoon grated yellow onion
- ⅓ cup coarsely chopped celery
- 1 pound cooked shrimp, cut into bite-size pieces
- ¾ cup frozen green peas, thawed and drained well
- 2 tablespoons coarsely chopped pimiento-stuffed olives

For the orzo:
- 1¼ cups orzo (rice-shaped pasta)
- ½ cup plain low-fat yogurt
- 2 tablespoons reduced-calorie mayonnaise
- 3 scallions, including tops, coarsely chopped
- ¼ teaspoon salt
- ⅛ teaspoon black pepper
- 8 lettuce leaves (any kind)

Per serving:
Calories 518; Protein 37 g;
Carbohydrates 68 g;
Fat 11 g; Sodium 961 mg;
Cholesterol 233 mg

10 minutes | 9 minutes

1 Place the water in a 1-cup heat-proof measuring cup, sprinkle in the gelatin, set in a small saucepan of simmering water, then warm over low heat until the gelatin dissolves completely—about 3 minutes. Remove from the heat and let cool slightly.

2 Meanwhile, mix the lemon juice, mayonnaise, yogurt, chili sauce, salt, red pepper sauce, onion, celery, shrimp, peas, and olives in a large bowl. Fold in the cooled gelatin. Spoon the mixture into a lightly greased 4-cup ring mold, patting it down so that no air spaces remain. Cover with plastic food wrap and refrigerate for at least 4 hours.

3 *For the orzo:* Cook the orzo according to package directions. Whisk together the yogurt, mayonnaise, scallions, salt, and pepper in a medium-size bowl. Drain the orzo well, add it to the yogurt mixture, and toss until well coated. Cover and refrigerate until ready to serve.

4 Arrange the lettuce on a medium-size round platter. Run a small spatula or knife around the edge and the central tube of the mold and invert on top of the lettuce. (If you have difficulty, dip the bottom of the mold into warm water for 10 seconds, then invert.) Mound the orzo in the center of the mold. Serves 4.

Potatoes Stuffed with Crab and Spinach

Once the potatoes are baked, you can put this beautiful dish together in just 5 minutes.

- 4 large baking potatoes
- 2 cans (6 ounces each) crabmeat, drained and picked over for bits of shell and cartilage
- 1 package (10 ounces) frozen chopped spinach, thawed, drained, and squeezed dry
- ½ cup plain low-fat yogurt
- ½ cup sour cream
- 2 teaspoons prepared mustard
- ¼ teaspoon dried tarragon, crumbled
- ⅛ teaspoon ground red pepper (cayenne)
- ¼ teaspoon paprika
  Snipped fresh dill or chopped scallion tops (optional garnish)

Per serving:
Calories 367; Protein 26 g;
Carbohydrates 49 g;
Fat 8 g; Sodium 422 mg;
Cholesterol 90 mg

10 minutes | 1 hour

1 Preheat the oven to 450° F. Prick the skin of each potato with a fork, cover with foil, and bake for 45 to 50 minutes or until tender. Remove the foil and let the potatoes sit until cool enough to handle.

2 Halve each potato lengthwise and scoop out the pulp, leaving a shell ¼ inch thick. Place the potato pulp in a large mixing bowl; set the shells aside.

3 Add the crab, spinach, yogurt, sour cream, mustard, tarragon, and red pepper to the potato pulp, and mix well. Stuff the potato shells with the mixture and sprinkle the paprika on top. Bake, uncovered, for 10 minutes. Sprinkle with dill if desired. Serves 4.

Main-Course Antipasto

Antipasto means "before the pasta," but with this superb platter, who needs a second course?

1 pound medium-size carrots, peeled and sliced diagonally ¼ inch thick

1 pound small new potatoes (about 8), sliced ¼ inch thick but not peeled

1 can (6½ ounces) tuna in water, drained and flaked

1 can (1 pound) cannellini (white kidney beans), drained and rinsed

1 can (14 ounces) artichoke hearts, drained and halved

8 ounces provolone or part-skim mozzarella cheese, cut into thin strips

1 jar (4 ounces) roasted sweet red peppers, drained

8 ounces salami, cut into thin strips (optional)

1 can (4 ounces) black olives (optional)

For the dressing:

3 tablespoons lemon juice

2 tablespoons balsamic or red wine vinegar

2 teaspoons Dijon mustard

½ teaspoon each salt and black pepper

1 to 2 cloves garlic, minced

¼ cup minced fresh basil or parsley

¼ cup each olive and vegetable oil

1 Place the carrots and potatoes in a large saucepan in enough boiling water to cover them by 1 inch. Cook, covered, for 9 to 10 minutes or until tender. Drain well, then rinse under cold running water and drain well again.

2 Arrange the carrots, potatoes, tuna, cannellini, artichoke hearts, cheese, red peppers, and, if desired, the salami and black olives on a large platter.

3 *For the dressing:* In a food processor or an electric blender at high speed, whirl the lemon juice, vinegar, mustard, salt, pepper, garlic, and basil for about 15 seconds or until smooth. With the motor running, add the olive and vegetable oils in a thin stream, then whirl about 60 seconds longer or until creamy. Pour into a bowl and serve with the antipasto. Serves 4.

You can add your own favorite ingredients to Main-Course Antipasto.

Per serving:
Calories 800; Protein 40 g;
Carbohydrates 65 g;
Fat 44 g; Sodium 1,437 mg;
Cholesterol 55 mg

| 30 minutes | 10 minutes |

Extra Quick 'n' Easy

When visitors drop by on short notice, when you're
looking for a way to lighten the load on a busy day, or when you
just don't feel like spending a lot of time in the kitchen, this is the place to turn.
All of these tempting dishes can be on your table in less than an hour,
thanks to frozen, canned, or packaged convenience foods. At the end of this chapter
you'll find several easy-to-use charts that show you how to turn a few
ordinary ingredients into a marvelous meal in short order.

Marinated Steak and Vegetables

A good start-ahead recipe that's ready to cook anytime. You can even begin it in the morning and let the meat and vegetables marinate until dinner. Use your favorite Italian dressing or ¾ cup Basic Vinaigrette (page 337) with ¼ teaspoon each dried basil and oregano crumbled into it.

- 8 ounces new potatoes, unpeeled and thinly sliced
- 1 large red onion, sliced ¼ inch thick
- 1 large sweet green pepper, cored, seeded, and quartered lengthwise
- 1 large sweet red pepper, cored, seeded, and quartered lengthwise
- 6 ounces large mushrooms
- 1¼ pounds flank steak
- ¾ cup bottled Italian dressing

Per serving:
Calories 501; Protein 46 g;
Carbohydrates 22 g;
Fat 25 g; Sodium 314 mg;
Cholesterol 129 mg

20 minutes   24 minutes

1 Place the potatoes, onion, green and red peppers, mushrooms, steak, and dressing in a large self-sealing plastic bag, seal, and shake well to distribute the dressing. Refrigerate for 2 to 24 hours.

2 Preheat the broiler and cover the broiler pan with foil if desired. Arrange the potatoes in a single layer in the pan and broil 6 inches from the heat for 7 minutes. Arrange the onion and peppers on top and broil for 5 minutes. Place the mushrooms and steak on top of the vegetables and broil 7 to 10 minutes for medium-rare or 10 to 12 minutes for medium, turning the steak once. Slice the steak and arrange it on a platter with the vegetables. Serves 4.

No-Time Chili

Few dishes are as popular as chili, and few chili recipes are as quick and easy as this one.

2	tablespoons vegetable oil
1	cup frozen chopped onion, unthawed
½	cup frozen chopped sweet green pepper, unthawed
1	pound lean ground beef
1	package (⅜ ounce) chili seasoning mix
¼	teaspoon black pepper
1	can (1 pound 12 ounces) crushed tomatoes in tomato purée
1	can (1 pound 3 ounces) kidney beans, drained and rinsed
1	package (9 ounces) frozen cut green beans, unthawed
¼	teaspoon red pepper flakes (optional)
1½	cups quick-cooking white rice

1 Heat the oil in a large saucepan over moderate heat for 1 minute. Add the onion and green pepper and sauté, stirring often, for 2 minutes or until slightly softened. Add the beef, breaking up large clumps, and cook, stirring, for 2 minutes or until no longer pink. Pour off the fat.

2 Add the seasoning mix and black pepper to the saucepan and cook, stirring, over moderate heat for 1 minute. Mix in the tomatoes and kidney beans and bring to a simmer, stirring often. Add the green beans and, if desired, the red pepper flakes. Cover and simmer for 5 minutes.

3 Meanwhile, cook the rice according to package directions. Divide the rice among 4 soup bowls and ladle the chili on top. Serves 4.

> Per serving:
> Calories 734; Protein 52 g;
> Carbohydrates 96 g;
> Fat 15 g; Sodium 1,077 mg;
> Cholesterol 103 mg

5 minutes | 13 minutes

Hurry-Up Hamburger Skillet

Tasty and hearty—terrific for lunch or supper.

2	tablespoons vegetable oil
8	ounces packaged shredded potatoes or frozen hash brown potatoes
1	pound lean ground beef
2	cans (14½ ounces each) no-salt-added stewed tomatoes with their juice
1⅓	cups frozen baby lima beans, thawed and drained
½	teaspoon dried marjoram, crumbled
½	teaspoon salt
¼	teaspoon black pepper
1⅓	cups frozen corn kernels, thawed and drained

1 Heat the oil in a 12-inch skillet over moderately high heat for 1 minute. Add the potatoes and sauté, stirring occasionally, for 5 minutes. Add the beef, breaking up any large clumps, and brown, stirring occasionally, for 4 minutes.

2 Add the tomatoes, lima beans, marjoram, salt, and pepper. Bring to a boil, uncovered, adjust the heat so that the mixture bubbles gently, cover, and simmer for 15 minutes. Stir in the corn, cover, and cook 5 minutes more. Serves 4.

> Per serving:
> Calories 546; Protein 45 g;
> Carbohydrates 48 g;
> Fat 21 g; Sodium 420 mg;
> Cholesterol 103 mg

5 minutes | 30 minutes

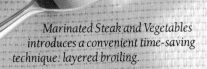

Marinated Steak and Vegetables introduces a convenient time-saving technique: layered broiling.

Burritos with Corn Salsa

If you transfer the burritos from the freezer to the refrigerator in the morning, they'll be defrosted in time for this fast Mexican supper.

- **1** jar (1 pound) mild or hot salsa or Basic Salsa (page 339)
- **1** package (10 ounces) frozen corn kernels, thawed and drained
- **1** cup frozen chopped sweet green pepper, thawed and drained
- **¼** cup minced fresh coriander (cilantro) or ¼ cup minced flat-leaf parsley plus ¼ teaspoon ground coriander

- **¾** teaspoon ground cumin
- **4** packages (5 ounces each) frozen beef and bean burritos, thawed
- **¾** cup coarsely shredded Monterey Jack cheese

Per serving:
Calories 555; Protein 21 g;
Carbohydrates 69 g;
Fat 29 g; Sodium 1,688 mg;
Cholesterol 20 mg

10 minutes	27 minutes

1 Preheat the oven to 375° F. Mix the salsa, corn, green pepper, coriander, and cumin in a large bowl.

2 Spoon about ⅓ of the salsa mixture over the bottom of an ungreased 13″ x 9″ x 2″ flameproof baking dish. Arrange the burritos on top, spacing evenly, and top with the remaining salsa mixture.

3 Bake, uncovered, for 25 minutes or until bubbling. Sprinkle with the cheese, transfer to the broiler, and broil 4 inches from the heat for 2 minutes or until tipped with brown. Serves 4.

For a delicious difference, try squeezing fresh lime juice over Burritos with Corn Salsa.

Corned Beef and Broccoli Hash

You don't need to add salt to this recipe—there's enough in the corned beef. For a moister, creamier hash, add the optional cream. If you have leftover roast beef or chicken, it can be used in place of the corned beef.

⅓ cup vegetable oil
1 large yellow onion, coarsely chopped
1 pound frozen hash brown potatoes
2 packages (10 ounces each) frozen chopped broccoli, unthawed
8 ounces corned beef, coarsely chopped (about 3 cups)
1 tablespoon Worcestershire sauce
¼ teaspoon black pepper
½ cup heavy cream or half-and-half (optional)

1 Heat the oil in a deep 12-inch skillet over moderate heat for 1 minute. Add the onion and sauté, stirring frequently, until tender— about 5 minutes.

2 Add the potatoes and sauté, stirring frequently, until they begin to brown—about 10 minutes. Meanwhile, cook the broccoli according to package directions; drain but do not season.

3 Stir the corned beef, broccoli, Worcestershire sauce, and pepper into the skillet. Cover and cook for 10 minutes, stirring occasionally.

4 Using a spatula, flatten the hash, then top with the cream if desired. Cook, uncovered, for 5 minutes or until the bottom is browned and crusty. Serves 4.

Per serving:
Calories 606; Protein 24 g;
Carbohydrates 43 g;
Fat 40 g; Sodium 681 mg;
Cholesterol 49 mg

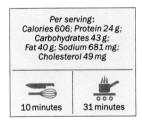

10 minutes | 31 minutes

Smoked Pork and Cabbage

A warming cold-weather dish that's particularly good topped with a little sour cream and a sprinkling of dill.

2 teaspoons vegetable oil
1 large yellow onion, halved and thinly sliced
1½ pounds cabbage, shredded, or 2 packages (10 ounces each) cole slaw mix
1 large Granny Smith apple, peeled, cored, and chopped
¼ cup water
8 ounces wide egg noodles
1 can (8 ounces) sliced beets, drained
1 pound boneless smoked pork butt or corned beef, cut into strips 2 inches wide
¾ cup sour cream or plain low-fat yogurt
2 tablespoons minced fresh dill or ½ teaspoon dill weed

1 Heat the oil in a large saucepan over moderate heat for 1 minute. Add the onion and sauté until limp—5 minutes. Add the cabbage, apple, and water, cover, and cook, stirring occasionally, for 10 minutes or until the cabbage has wilted.

2 Meanwhile, cook the noodles according to package directions, drain well, and set aside.

3 Add the beets and pork to the saucepan, cover, and cook for 4 minutes or until heated through. Smooth in the sour cream and bring just to serving temperature (but do not boil), then add the noodles, toss lightly, and sprinkle with the dill. Serves 4.

Per serving:
Calories 634; Protein 35 g;
Carbohydrates 64 g;
Fat 27 g; Sodium 1,062 mg;
Cholesterol 92 mg

20 minutes | 21 minutes

215

Pork-on-a-Bun

You can also serve this barbecued pork and vegetable combination over rice.

1 pound sliced boneless smoked pork butt, cut into thin strips
1 cup bottled barbecue sauce
1 small yellow onion, finely chopped
1 package (10 ounces) frozen cut green beans, thawed and drained
1 package (10 ounces) frozen corn kernels, thawed and drained
4 hamburger buns or large rolls, split and toasted

1 Brown the pork in a 12-inch non-stick skillet over moderate heat for 10 minutes, stirring frequently.

2 Stir in the barbecue sauce, onion, beans, and corn. Cover, reduce the heat to low, and simmer, stirring occasionally, until the beans are tender—about 15 minutes. Spoon over the buns. Serves 4.

Tangy and tasty on its own, Pork-on-a-Bun is even better with an informal "finger" salad and some fresh fruit for dessert.

Per serving:
Calories 457; Protein 33 g;
Carbohydrates 48 g;
Fat 15 g; Sodium 823 mg;
Cholesterol 80 mg

15 minutes | 25 minutes

216

Pepper Pork Chops

In this hassle-free recipe, the rice cooks right in the casserole.

- 1 tablespoon vegetable oil
- 6 loin pork chops, about ½ inch thick (1½ to 1¾ pounds)
- 1 can (1 pound 12 ounces) crushed tomatoes
- 1½ cups quick-cooking white rice
- ¾ cup water
- 1 teaspoon chili powder
- 1 teaspoon dried oregano, crumbled
- ¼ teaspoon salt
- ¼ teaspoon ground cumin
- ⅛ teaspoon black pepper
- 1 large yellow onion, thinly sliced
- 2 medium-size sweet green peppers, cored, seeded, and thinly sliced

1 Heat the oil in a deep 12-inch skillet over moderately high heat for 1 minute. Add the pork chops and brown on each side for 3 minutes. Drain on paper toweling.

2 Meanwhile, mix the tomatoes, rice, water, chili powder, oregano, salt, cumin, and black pepper in a medium-size bowl; set aside.

3 Return the chops to the skillet and layer the onion and green pepper slices on top. Pour the tomato mixture over all. Bring to a boil, reduce the heat to low, cover, and simmer for 30 minutes or until the pork chops and rice are tender and the liquid is absorbed. Serves 6.

Per serving:
Calories 401; Protein 24 g;
Carbohydrates 46 g;
Fat 13 g; Sodium 358 mg;
Cholesterol 63 mg

| 10 minutes | 39 minutes |

Stir-Fried Pork with Peanut Sauce

Peanut butter and soy sauce team up to give this dish a special flavor. Using a food processor to chop the vegetables cuts the preparation time in half.

- 2½ tablespoons cream-style peanut butter
- ½ cup water
- 1 tablespoon rice vinegar or cider vinegar
- 2 teaspoons reduced-sodium soy sauce
- ¾ teaspoon ground coriander
- ½ teaspoon ground ginger
- 1½ cups quick-cooking white rice
- 2 tablespoons vegetable oil
- 1 pound pork tenderloin, cut into ½-inch cubes
- 1 large sweet red pepper, cored, seeded, and cut into thin strips
- 2 medium-size carrots, peeled and thinly sliced
- 1 medium-size yellow onion, cut into eighths
- 2 scallions, including tops, thinly sliced

1 Combine the peanut butter, ¼ cup of the water, the vinegar, soy sauce, coriander, and ginger in a small bowl and set aside.

2 Cook the rice according to package directions. Meanwhile, heat the oil in a 12-inch skillet over moderately high heat for 1 minute. Add the pork and stir-fry for 5 minutes or until brown and cooked through. Remove with a slotted spoon and set aside.

3 Add the pepper, carrots, onion, and remaining ¼ cup water to the skillet and cook, uncovered, for 5 minutes.

4 Stir the peanut butter mixture into the skillet, add the pork, and cook, uncovered, for 1 minute. Stir in the scallions and serve over the rice. Serves 4.

Per serving:
Calories 551; Protein 34 g;
Carbohydrates 66 g;
Fat 17 g; Sodium 238 mg;
Cholesterol 79 mg

| 20 minutes | 12 minutes |

Rice-Meatballs and Summer Squash

Some folks call these porcupine meatballs because the rice gives them a grainy, or "porcupine," look.

8 ounces ground pork
8 ounces ground turkey
1 cup quick-cooking white or brown rice
1 large egg
3 tablespoons dry bread crumbs
3 tablespoons milk
½ teaspoon salt
½ teaspoon dried marjoram, crumbled

1 can (1 pound) sauerkraut, drained and rinsed
2 cans (14½ ounces each) no-salt-added stewed tomatoes with their juice
1 package (10 ounces) frozen sliced summer squash, thawed and drained
½ cup sour cream or plain low-fat yogurt (optional)

Per serving:
Calories 521; Protein 31 g;
Carbohydrates 58 g;
Fat 18 g; Sodium 974 mg;
Cholesterol 131 mg

5 minutes   15 minutes

1 Combine the pork, turkey, rice, egg, bread crumbs, milk, salt, and marjoram in a large bowl, then shape into 24 small balls—about 1 inch each—and set aside.

2 Mix the sauerkraut and tomatoes in a large saucepan and bring to a boil, uncovered, over moderate heat. Adjust the heat so that the mixture bubbles gently, then add the meatballs and squash.

3 Cover and simmer, stirring occasionally, for 10 minutes or until the meatballs and squash are both cooked through. Serve each portion with a dollop of sour cream if desired. Serves 4.

Rice-Meatballs and Summer Squash— a palate-pleasing combination of textures and flavors

Sausage, Pepper, and Potato Skillet

You can make this dish with hot sausage, sweet sausage, or a combination of both.

- **1** pound Italian-style sausage, sliced 1 inch thick
- **1** medium-size yellow onion, cut into 1-inch cubes
- **1** large sweet green pepper, cored, seeded, and cut into 1-inch squares
- **1** large sweet red pepper, cored, seeded, and cut into 1-inch squares
- **1¼** pounds small new potatoes, cut into ¾-inch cubes
- **¾** cup water
- **⅛** teaspoon black pepper

1 Brown the sausage on all sides in a deep 12-inch skillet over moderate heat—about 10 minutes. Drain off all but 2 tablespoons of the drippings.

2 Stir in the onion, green and red peppers, potatoes, water, and black pepper. Reduce the heat to low, cover, and cook for 15 to 20 minutes or until the potatoes are tender. Serves 4.

Per serving:
Calories 467; Protein 23 g;
Carbohydrates 35 g;
Fat 26 g; Sodium 924 mg;
Cholesterol 77 mg

15 minutes | 30 minutes

Ham and Yam Casserole

Try this winning combination for a quick put-together dinner.

- **1** pound boneless smoked ham, sliced ½ inch thick
- **2** tablespoons olive or vegetable oil
- **½** cup frozen chopped onion, unthawed
- **1** package (10 ounces) frozen chopped spinach, thawed and drained
- **¼** teaspoon black pepper
- **1** can (11 ounces) Cheddar cheese soup
- **½** cup low-fat or whole milk
- **1** can (1 pound 13 ounces) cut yams in light syrup, drained
- **¼** cup dry bread crumbs

1 Preheat the oven to 400° F. Sauté the ham in the oil in a 12-inch skillet over moderate heat for 1 minute on each side; transfer to a plate. Add the onion to the skillet and sauté, stirring, for 1 minute. Add the spinach and pepper and cook, stirring, for 1 minute. Transfer the spinach mixture to an ungreased shallow 2-quart casserole and arrange the ham on top.

2 Add the soup and milk to the skillet and cook, stirring, over moderate heat for 1 to 2 minutes or until smooth. Arrange the yams around the ham, then pour the soup mixture over all. Sprinkle with the bread crumbs.

3 Bake, uncovered, for 15 minutes or until bubbling. Transfer to the broiler and broil 4 inches from the heat for 2 minutes or until tipped with brown. Serves 4.

Per serving:
Calories 612; Protein 36 g;
Carbohydrates 75 g;
Fat 20 g; Sodium 2,039 mg;
Cholesterol 75 mg

10 minutes | 23 minutes

Chicken with Wild Rice and Walnuts

Fresh oranges and grated orange zest provide a rich citrus flavor while the walnuts add a flavorful crunch.

- 2 tablespoons vegetable oil
- 3 whole chicken breasts, skinned, boned, and halved (2 pounds)
- ¼ teaspoon each salt and black pepper
- 1¾ cups Basic Chicken Stock (page 333) or 1 can (13¾ ounces) low-sodium chicken broth
- 1 package (6 ounces) wild rice mix

- 1 tablespoon grated orange zest (colored part of the rind)
- 2 medium-size oranges, peeled, seeded, white pith removed, and coarsely chopped
- 1 package (10 ounces) frozen chopped kale or spinach, thawed and drained well
- 1 cup coarsely chopped walnuts

Per serving:
Calories 413; Protein 32 g;
Carbohydrates 21 g;
Fat 24 g; Sodium 248 mg;
Cholesterol 75 mg

25 minutes | 32 minutes

1 Heat the oil in a deep 12-inch skillet over moderately high heat for 1 minute. Sprinkle the chicken with the salt and pepper and brown in the oil for 2 minutes on each side. Drain on paper toweling.

2 Pour off the skillet drippings and add the stock, rice mix with seasoning packet, and orange zest. Return the chicken to the skillet and bring to a boil, then reduce the heat to low, cover, and simmer for 20 minutes or until most of the liquid is absorbed.

3 Transfer the chicken to a large platter and keep warm. Stir the oranges, kale, and walnuts into the skillet, cover, and simmer until the remaining liquid is absorbed— about 5 minutes. Spoon the rice mixture around the chicken on the platter and serve. Serves 6.

Welsh Rarebit Surprise

An attractive dish to serve when company suddenly appears on your doorstep.

- 2 whole chicken breasts, skinned, boned, and halved (1¼ pounds)
- ¼ teaspoon salt
- 2 tablespoons vegetable oil
- 2 cups quick-cooking white rice
- 1 package (10 ounces) frozen rarebit sauce, thawed
- ½ cup evaporated skim milk or whole milk
- 1 tablespoon Dijon mustard
- ¼ teaspoon each black pepper and dill weed
- 1 package (10 ounces) frozen asparagus tips, thawed and drained
- 2 tablespoons shredded Cheddar or grated Parmesan cheese

1 Preheat the oven to 400° F. Sprinkle the chicken with the salt. Heat the oil in a 12-inch non-stick skillet over moderate heat and sauté the chicken for 2 minutes on each side. Transfer to a plate.

2 Cook the rice according to package directions. Meanwhile, in a small bowl, whisk together the rarebit sauce, milk, mustard, pepper, and dill weed.

3 Spread the rice over the bottom of a greased 12" x 9½" x 2" baking dish, then layer in the asparagus and chicken. Top with the rarebit mixture and sprinkle with the cheese.

4 Bake, uncovered, for 20 to 25 minutes or until the sauce is bubbling and the chicken is no longer pink on the inside. Transfer to the broiler and broil 4 inches from the heat for 1 to 2 minutes or until lightly browned. Serves 4.

Per serving:
Calories 715; Protein 44 g;
Carbohydrates 86 g;
Fat 21 g; Sodium 698 mg;
Cholesterol 105 mg

5 minutes

36 minutes

Extra-Quick Chicken with Chick Peas

For a spicier meal, use the full ¼ teaspoon of ground red pepper. Serve any leftovers the next day at room temperature dressed with olive oil and lemon juice for a lovely luncheon salad.

- 2½ cups canned low-sodium chicken broth
- ¾ teaspoon ground cinnamon
- ½ teaspoon ground ginger
- ⅛ to ¼ teaspoon ground red pepper (cayenne)
- 1 package (10 ounces) frozen sliced carrots, thawed and drained
- 1¼ pounds chicken breasts or thighs, skinned, boned, and cut into 1-inch cubes
- 1 cup canned chick peas, drained and rinsed
- 1 cup couscous
- 2 tablespoons minced parsley

1 Bring the broth, cinnamon, ginger, and pepper to a simmer in a large uncovered saucepan over moderately low heat. Add the carrots and cook, uncovered, for 3 minutes.

2 Add the chicken and chick peas, cover, and cook for 5 minutes or until the chicken is cooked through.

3 Add the couscous and cook, uncovered, for 1 minute. Remove from the heat, cover, and let stand for 5 minutes. Fluff with a fork and sprinkle with the parsley. Serves 4.

Per serving:
Calories 434; Protein 37 g;
Carbohydrates 54 g;
Fat 8 g; Sodium 278 mg;
Cholesterol 70 mg

10 minutes

16 minutes

A triumphant trio: Chicken with Wild Rice and Walnuts

221

Almond-Crowned Chicken

For fish lovers, substitute canned tuna, shrimp, or crabmeat for the chicken.

- 1 package (10 ounces), frozen asparagus spears, unthawed
- 1 can (5 ounces) chow mein noodles
- 1 can (10½ ounces) cream of celery soup
- 1 cup evaporated skim milk or half-and-half
- 1 can (5 ounces) chicken, drained and coarsely diced
- ½ cup slivered blanched almonds
- 2 medium-size stalks celery, finely diced
- 1 small yellow onion, finely chopped
- 1 teaspoon Worcestershire sauce
- ¼ cup grated Parmesan cheese

Per serving:
Calories 480; Protein 26 g;
Carbohydrates 42 g;
Fat 25 g; Sodium 980 mg;
Cholesterol 40 mg

15 minutes | 35 minutes

1 Preheat the oven to 375° F. Cook the asparagus according to package directions and drain; set aside.

2 Meanwhile, scatter half the noodles over the bottom of a lightly greased 9¾" x 6" x 2½" baking dish. Lightly mix the soup, milk, chicken, ¼ cup of the almonds, the celery, onion, Worcestershire sauce, and cheese, then spoon half of it evenly over the noodles.

3 Arrange the asparagus on top in a single layer and cover with the remaining chicken mixture, then the remaining noodles. Bake, uncovered, for 20 minutes. Sprinkle the remaining almonds on top and bake 10 minutes more or until bubbling and lightly browned. Serves 4.

222

Last-Minute Chicken

The new preroasted chickens now carried in supermarket poultry sections make this an easy meal to prepare. This dish also tastes great made with cubed ham. Omit the pepperoni and sauté the onion in 2 tablespoons olive or vegetable oil.

- 1 package (3½ ounces) sliced pepperoni
- 1 cup frozen chopped onion, unthawed
- 1 clove garlic, minced
- 2 cups coarsely shredded cabbage
- 1 package (10 ounces) frozen sliced carrots, thawed and drained
- 1 can (10 ounces) black beans, drained and rinsed
- 1 can (10 ounces) chick peas, drained and rinsed
- 1 can (8 ounces) stewed tomatoes with their juice
- ¼ teaspoon black pepper
- 2½ pounds chicken nuggets or cooked chicken parts

1 Sauté the pepperoni in a 12-inch skillet over moderate heat, stirring occasionally, for 3 to 5 minutes. Drain on paper toweling.

2 Add the onion to the skillet and sauté, stirring occasionally, for 2 minutes or until softened. Add the garlic and sauté 3 minutes more. Add the cabbage, carrots, beans, chick peas, tomatoes, and pepper, and stir well to mix.

3 Place the chicken on top of the vegetable mixture. Cover, reduce the heat to low, and simmer for 15 minutes. Add the pepperoni and simmer 5 more minutes or until heated through. Serves 4 to 6.

Per serving:
Calories 1,149; Protein 69 g;
Carbohydrates 98 g;
Fat 55 g; Sodium 2,080 mg;
Cholesterol 163 mg

15 minutes | 30 minutes

Last-Minute Chicken presents nuggets with a special flair.

Tortilla Casserole

We used half sour cream and half yogurt for the topping to cut down on fat, but you can use all sour cream if you prefer.

- 2 cups coarsely chopped cooked or canned chicken
- 1 can (10½ ounces) black beans, drained and rinsed
- 1 can (4 ounces) chopped green chilies, drained
- 1 medium-size sweet green pepper, cored, seeded, and coarsely chopped
- 1 medium-size sweet red pepper, cored, seeded, and coarsely chopped
- 1 package (10 ounces) shredded Monterey Jack cheese
- 8 flour tortillas, 7 inches in diameter
- ½ cup sour cream
- ½ cup plain low-fat yogurt

Optional toppings:

- 1 medium-size avocado, peeled, pitted, and thinly sliced
- 1 large tomato, cored and thinly sliced

1 Preheat the oven to 375° F. Mix the chicken, beans, chilies, green and red peppers, and cheese in a medium-size bowl. Spoon a mound of the mixture in the center of each tortilla, dividing the total amount evenly, then roll up the tortillas.

2 Place the filled tortillas seam side down in a greased 11" x 7" x 2" baking dish. Combine the sour cream and yogurt in a small bowl and spoon over all. Bake, uncovered, for 10 minutes or until heated through. Top with the avocado and tomato slices if desired. Serves 4.

Per serving:
Calories 746; Protein 50 g;
Carbohydrates 60 g;
Fat 34 g; Sodium 463 mg;
Cholesterol 63 mg

15 minutes | 10 minutes

All-American turkey takes on an Italian accent in Turkey Cutlet Parmesan.

Turkey Cutlet Parmesan

Sprinkle a little Parmesan on top of the cheese in Step 4, then pass more at the table for those who want extra.

- **6 ounces spaghettini or thin spaghetti**
- **1 medium-size zucchini, quartered lengthwise and sliced 1 inch thick**
- **1 medium-size yellow squash, quartered lengthwise and sliced 1 inch thick**
- **¼ cup olive oil**
- **4 turkey cutlets, ¼ inch thick (1¼ pounds)**
- **1 large egg, lightly beaten**
- **⅔ cup plain or flavored dry bread crumbs**
- **¼ teaspoon black pepper**
- **1 jar (1 pound 12 ounces) marinara sauce**
- **2 cups shredded mozzarella cheese (8 ounces)**

Per serving:
Calories 820; Protein 44 g;
Carbohydrates 71 g;
Fat 41 g; Sodium 1,655 mg;
Cholesterol 153 mg

12 minutes	30 minutes

1 Preheat the oven to 400° F. Begin cooking the spaghettini according to package directions in a large kettle of boiling water over moderately high heat. After 6 minutes, add the zucchini and yellow squash and cook, uncovered, for 1 minute. Drain, run under cold water, and drain well again. Transfer the pasta and vegetables to a greased 13″ x 9″ x 2″ baking dish. Add 1 tablespoon of the oil and toss well.

2 Dip the cutlets into the egg, then dredge in the bread crumbs, shaking off any excess. Sprinkle with the pepper.

3 Heat the remaining 3 tablespoons oil for 1 minute in a 10-inch skillet over moderately high heat. Add the turkey cutlets and brown for 1 minute on each side.

4 Arrange the cutlets in a single layer on top of the pasta and vegetables, cover with the marinara sauce, and sprinkle with the cheese. Bake, uncovered, for about 20 minutes or until the sauce is bubbling and the cheese has melted. Serves 4.

Turkey Sausage Succotash

Serve this meal with crusty bread to soak up the sauce.

2 tablespoons olive oil

1 pound turkey sausage, sliced 1 inch thick

1 large yellow onion, coarsely chopped

2 cloves garlic, minced

1 can (1 pound) crushed tomatoes

1 package (10 ounces) frozen baby lima beans, unthawed

1 teaspoon dried marjoram, crumbled

⅛ teaspoon black pepper

1 package (10 ounces) frozen corn kernels, unthawed

Per serving:
Calories 409; Protein 27 g;
Carbohydrates 37 g;
Fat 20 g; Sodium 810 mg;
Cholesterol 69 mg

10 minutes

26 minutes

1 Heat the oil in a 12-inch skillet over moderately high heat for 1 minute. Add the sausage and sauté, stirring occasionally, for 5 minutes. Drain on paper toweling.

2 Reduce the heat to moderate, add the onion to the skillet, and sauté, stirring occasionally, for 3 minutes or until it begins to soften. Add the garlic and sauté, stirring occasionally, for 2 minutes or until the onion is soft.

3 Stir in the tomatoes, lima beans, marjoram, and pepper. Bring to a boil, then cover and cook for 10 minutes.

4 Stir in the corn and sausage, then return the mixture to a boil. Cover and cook for 5 minutes or until the lima beans are tender and the sausage is cooked through.
Serves 4.

A quick skilletful of family eating: Turkey Sausage Succotash

225

Fish and Potato Bake

A bread crumb topping keeps the fish crisp on the outside, moist on the inside. You can use cod, flounder, haddock, or halibut fillets. Frozen broccoli or artichoke hearts may be substituted for the spinach.

- 1 clove garlic, halved
- 2 medium-size all-purpose potatoes, peeled and thinly sliced, or 12 ounces frozen hash brown potatoes, thawed
- 3 tablespoons butter or margarine
- 1 package (10 ounces) frozen leaf spinach, thawed but not drained
- 4 fresh or frozen fish fillets (5 ounces each), thawed and drained if frozen
- 1 tablespoon lemon juice
- 2 tablespoons fine dry bread crumbs

1 Preheat the oven to 450° F. Rub an 11" x 7" x 2" baking pan with the garlic and discard. Arrange the potatoes in the pan, overlapping the slices slightly, and dot with 2 tablespoons of the butter. Cover with foil and bake for 15 minutes.

2 Spread the spinach over the potatoes and top with the fish. Sprinkle with the lemon juice and bread crumbs and dot with the remaining butter.

3 Cover with foil and bake for 10 minutes. Uncover and bake about 5 minutes more or until pale golden. Serves 4.

> **Per serving:**
> Calories 263; Protein 25 g;
> Carbohydrates 20 g;
> Fat 10 g; Sodium 254 mg;
> Cholesterol 94 mg

 10 minutes 30 minutes

Deviled Tuna Delight

In this recipe, the pasta cooks with the sauce. If you want to trim the baking time, cook the spaghettini according to package directions, drain, and add to the simmered sauce at the end of Step 2.

- 2 tablespoons vegetable oil
- ½ cup frozen chopped onion, unthawed
- 1 jar (7 ounces) sliced mushrooms, drained, with liquid reserved
- 1 package (10 ounces) frozen chopped broccoli, unthawed
- ¼ teaspoon black pepper
- 1 can (10¾ ounces) cream of mushroom soup
- 2 cups half-and-half or evaporated skim milk
- 3 tablespoons Dijon mustard
- 1 can (6½ ounces) tuna in water, drained
- 6 ounces spaghettini, or thin spaghetti, broken into 3-inch lengths
- ¼ cup dry bread crumbs

1 Preheat the oven to 375° F. Heat the oil in a medium-size saucepan over moderate heat for 1 minute. Add the onion and sauté, stirring often, until soft. Add the mushrooms, broccoli, and pepper, and cook, stirring, for 2 minutes.

2 Mix in the soup, half-and-half, and mushroom liquid, bring to a simmer, and cook, stirring, for 2 minutes. Mix in the mustard, tuna, and spaghettini, stirring gently to coat with the sauce, and bring to a simmer.

3 Transfer the mixture to a greased shallow 2-quart casserole. Top with the bread crumbs and bake, uncovered, for 35 minutes or until the pasta is tender. Serves 4.

> **Per serving:**
> Calories 590; Protein 27 g;
> Carbohydrates 56 g;
> Fat 30 g; Sodium 1,064 mg;
> Cholesterol 64 mg

5 minutes | 42 minutes

Tuna-Spinach Pie with Corn Bread Crust

Corn bread makes a quick crust for this creamy filling. For a decorative touch, garnish with sprigs of marjoram and thyme or with 2 tablespoons of chopped parsley.

1 large lemon, thinly sliced

2 large eggs

1 can (12½ ounces) tuna, drained and flaked, or 2 cups coarsely chopped cooked chicken, turkey, or ham

1 cup herbed stuffing mix or soft bread crumbs

1 small yellow onion, finely chopped

½ teaspoon each dried thyme and marjoram, crumbled

1 can (10¾ ounces) cream of chicken, mushroom, or celery soup

½ cup evaporated skim milk or half-and-half

2 packages (10 ounces each) frozen chopped spinach, thawed and drained

1 package (10 ounces) corn bread mix

Per serving:
Calories 422; Protein 29 g;
Carbohydrates 46 g;
Fat 14 g; Sodium 1,058 mg;
Cholesterol 100 mg

15 minutes

25 minutes

1 Preheat the oven to 400° F. Arrange the lemon slices on the bottom of a lightly greased ovenproof 10-inch skillet (not iron) or a 10-inch round cake pan.

2 In a large bowl, beat the eggs lightly. Add the tuna, stuffing mix, onion, thyme, marjoram, soup, and milk, and fold together. Spoon half of the mixture evenly over the lemon slices. Layer the spinach over it, then spread the remaining tuna mixture on top.

3 Prepare the corn bread mix according to package directions. Spread on top of the tuna mixture and bake, uncovered, for 20 to 25 minutes or until browned.

4 Place a large heatproof platter on top of the skillet, then carefully invert. Serves 6.

When Tuna-Spinach Pie is inverted onto a serving dish, the lemon slices baked on the bottom form a golden wreath on top.

Creamy Salmon and Fettuccine

A fast and fancy pink- and green-flecked white sauce that's perfect with long ribbons of pasta. A sprinkling of Parmesan cheese on top adds a tasty touch.

- 8 ounces fettuccine
- 2 tablespoons unsalted butter or margarine
- 2 scallions, including tops, thinly sliced
- 1 package (10 ounces) frozen cut asparagus, thawed and drained
- 1 can (15½ ounces) salmon, drained and flaked
- 1 tablespoon drained capers, finely chopped
- ⅛ teaspoon black pepper
- 1 cup heavy cream or half-and-half

1 Cook the fettuccine according to package directions. Meanwhile, melt the butter in a deep 12-inch skillet over moderate heat. Add the scallions and asparagus, cover, and cook for 5 minutes.

2 Stir the salmon, capers, pepper, and cream into the skillet and cook, uncovered, for 5 minutes, stirring occasionally.

3 Drain the fettuccine, add to the salmon mixture in the skillet, and toss just to coat. Serves 4.

Per serving:
Calories 636; Protein 32 g;
Carbohydrates 47 g;
Fat 35 g; Sodium 694 mg;
Cholesterol 97 mg

10 minutes | 10 minutes

Creamy Salmon and Fettuccine — an easy and elegant meal

Clam Hash

You can serve this crusty clam-and-potato hash topped with poached eggs or with English muffins on the side.

⅓ cup vegetable oil

1 large yellow onion, coarsely chopped

4 cups frozen hash brown potatoes, thawed

2 cans (10 ounces each) chopped clams, drained, with ½ cup juice reserved

1 package (10 ounces) frozen mixed vegetables, thawed and drained

1 teaspoon dried thyme, crumbled

Pinch ground red pepper (cayenne)

½ cup heavy cream, half-and-half, or evaporated skim milk

1 Heat the oil in a 12-inch skillet over moderate heat. Add the onion and sauté until tender—about 5 minutes. Add the potatoes and sauté, stirring occasionally, until they begin to brown—about 8 minutes.

2 Add the clams, clam juice, vegetables, thyme, and red pepper, and stir well. Cover and cook, stirring occasionally, for 10 minutes.

3 Stir in the cream and cook, uncovered, for 5 minutes or until the bottom is browned and crusty. Serves 4.

Per serving:
Calories 723; Protein 20 g;
Carbohydrates 60 g;
Fat 49 g; Sodium 164 mg;
Cholesterol 129 mg

5 minutes | 29 minutes

Sweet Shrimp and Angel Hair Pasta

The unlikely combination of ketchup, soy sauce, garlic, and coconut gives this dish a delightfully spicy-sweet flavor that pleases just about everyone. Try spiking it with the hot red pepper sauce for a sharper taste.

¼ cup ketchup

3 tablespoons reduced-sodium soy sauce

3 tablespoons water

4 to 6 dashes hot red pepper sauce or ⅛ teaspoon ground red pepper (cayenne), optional

1 tablespoon peanut or vegetable oil

1 large sweet red pepper, cored, seeded, and cut into ½-inch squares

2 medium-size carrots, peeled and coarsely shredded

2 cloves garlic, minced

8 ounces angel hair pasta (cappellini) or spaghettini

1 pound frozen shelled and deveined small shrimp, thawed and drained

3 scallions, including tops, thinly sliced,

⅓ cup unsalted dry-roasted peanuts

⅓ cup flaked coconut

1 Combine the ketchup, soy sauce, water, and red pepper sauce, if using, in a small bowl and set aside.

2 Heat the oil in a deep 12-inch skillet over moderately high heat for 1 minute. Add the sweet red pepper, carrots, and garlic, and sauté for 5 minutes or until softened.

3 Meanwhile, cook the pasta according to package directions until just tender—about 2 minutes—then drain and set aside.

4 Add the shrimp to the skillet and sauté until almost cooked through—about 2 minutes. Add the ketchup mixture, stir well, and cook 1 minute more. Stir in the scallions, peanuts, and coconut. Add the pasta and toss to mix. Serves 4.

Per serving:
Calories 492; Protein 33 g;
Carbohydrates 57 g;
Fat 14 g; Sodium 853 mg;
Cholesterol 157 mg

20 minutes | 9 minutes

Quick Lobster Newburg

A rich, elegant dish that is exceptionally easy to make, thanks to convenience foods. Use two baking dishes if you plan to double the recipe.

2 packages (8 ounces each) frozen sugar snap peas, thawed enough to break apart

2 packages (10 ounces each) frozen white and wild rice, thawed enough to loosen the rice grains

2 packages (6½ ounces each) frozen lobster Newburg, thawed

2 jars (4 ounces each) whole button mushrooms with their liquid

¼ cup fine dry bread crumbs

2 teaspoons melted butter or margarine

1 Preheat the oven to 350° F. Scatter the peas over the bottom of a lightly greased 13″ x 9″ x 2″ baking dish, then sprinkle the rice on top. Mix the lobster Newburg and mushrooms in a medium-size bowl and spoon evenly over the rice.

2 Bake, uncovered, for 15 minutes. Mix the bread crumbs with the butter, scatter on top of the lobster Newburg, and bake, uncovered, for 5 minutes or until bubbling. Serves 4.

Per serving:
Calories 482; Protein 20 g;
Carbohydrates 58 g;
Fat 20 g; Sodium 1,107 mg;
Cholesterol 79 mg

5 minutes   20 minutes

Jiffy Crab Bake

*Here's a dish you can make in a dash—a perfect choice
for lunch, dinner, or even brunch.*

*Jiffy Crab Bake
says "Welcome" to
a hungry group.*

6	ounces elbow macaroni
1	package (10 ounces) frozen mixed vegetables, unthawed
¼	teaspoon black pepper
1	can (6 ounces) crabmeat, drained, or 1 package (8 ounces) frozen crabmeat, thawed, drained, and picked over to remove bits of shell and cartilage
1	can (10¾ ounces) cream of shrimp soup
1	cup half-and-half or evaporated skim milk
2	tablespoons dry sherry (optional)
2	tablespoons shredded Gruyère or Swiss cheese
2	tablespoons grated Parmesan cheese

Per serving:
Calories 405; Protein 21 g;
Carbohydrates 49 g;
Fat 14 g; Sodium 928 mg;
Cholesterol 81 mg

12 minutes   32 minutes

1 Preheat the oven to 375°F. Cook the macaroni according to package directions. After 6 minutes, add the vegetables and cook, uncovered, for 2 minutes; drain well. Transfer to a well-greased shallow 2-quart casserole, sprinkle with the pepper, and top with the crabmeat.

2 In a medium-size saucepan over moderate heat, bring the soup and half-and-half to a simmer, stirring, and simmer for 1 minute. Stir in the sherry if desired, then pour over the casserole. Sprinkle both cheeses evenly on top.

3 Bake, uncovered, for 20 minutes or until bubbling. Transfer to the broiler and broil 4 inches from the heat for 2 minutes or until tipped with brown. Serves 4.

231

Tortellini Primavera with Pesto Sauce

A superb dish that's ideal for days when there's little time to cook.

- 1 **pound fresh or frozen cheese tortellini**
- 4 **medium-size carrots, peeled and sliced ¼ inch thick**
- 8 **ounces broccoli florets or 1 package (10 ounces) frozen broccoli florets, unthawed**
- 8 **ounces cherry tomatoes, halved**

For the sauce:

- 2 **cups loosely packed fresh basil leaves**
- 4 **ounces pine nuts or slivered blanched almonds**
- ½ **cup grated Parmesan cheese (2 ounces)**
- 1 **clove garlic, minced**
- ¼ **teaspoon black pepper**
- ⅓ **cup olive oil**

> Per serving:
> Calories 796; Protein 34 g;
> Carbohydrates 75 g;
> Fat 43 g; Sodium 830 mg;
> Cholesterol 73 mg

15 minutes   9 minutes

1 Cook the tortellini and carrots, uncovered, in a large saucepan of boiling water over moderately high heat for 4 minutes. Add the broccoli and cook, uncovered, 3 minutes more. Drain the tortellini and vegetables, run under cold water, drain well again, and transfer to a large bowl. Add the tomatoes.

2 *For the sauce:* Purée the basil, pine nuts, cheese, garlic, and pepper in a food processor or an electric blender at high speed for 15 to 20 seconds or until smooth. With the motor running, add the oil in a fine stream and continue to whirl until thick and smooth. Pour over the tortellini mixture and toss well. Serves 4.

Ricotta and Roasted Red Pepper Sauce Variation

Follow Step 1 as directed. In Step 2, substitute **1 container (15 ounces) ricotta cheese, 1 jar (7 ounces) drained roasted red peppers, ⅓ cup grated Parmesan or Romano cheese (or to taste), 2 tablespoons lemon juice, ¼ cup minced fresh basil or parsley, and ¼ teaspoon black pepper** for the sauce ingredients. Place in a food processor or an electric blender and whirl for 15 seconds or until smooth. Pour over the tortellini mixture and toss well. Serves 4.

Per serving: Calories 634; Protein 38 g; Carbohydrates 73 g; Fat 22 g; Sodium 796 mg; Cholesterol 122 mg

Macaroni and Cheese Deluxe

Here are three versions of an American standard.

- **1** package (1 pound 4 ounces) frozen macaroni and cheese, thawed
- **4** ounces baked or boiled ham, cut into ½- to ¾-inch cubes
- **1** package (10 ounces) frozen chopped broccoli, thawed and drained
- **1** large yellow onion, coarsely chopped, or 1 cup frozen chopped onion, thawed and drained
- **⅛** teaspoon ground red pepper (cayenne)

1 Preheat the oven to 350° F. Spoon the macaroni and cheese into an ungreased 11" x 7" x 2½" baking dish. Add the ham, broccoli, onion, and red pepper, then mix well. Bake, uncovered, until bubbling—about 30 minutes. Serves 4.

Mexican Variation

Omit the broccoli and ground red pepper. Substitute **2 cups chopped sweet green and red pepper (mixed), ¼ cup minced fresh coriander (cilantro)** or **parsley,** and **1 teaspoon ground cumin.** Proceed as directed. Serves 4.

Per serving: Calories 367; Protein 17 g; Carbohydrates 31 g; Fat 19 g; Sodium 1,145 mg; Cholesterol 46 mg

Three-Bean Variation

Omit the ham, broccoli, and ground red pepper. Substitute **1 thawed and drained package (9 ounces) frozen cut green beans, 1 cup each drained and rinsed black beans and kidney beans,** and **1 teaspoon dry mustard.** Proceed as directed. Serves 4.

Per serving: Calories 436; Protein 20 g; Carbohydrates 53 g; Fat 16 g; Sodium 986 mg; Cholesterol 30 mg

Per serving:
Calories 390; Protein 20 g;
Carbohydrates 36 g;
Fat 19 g; Sodium 1,160 mg;
Cholesterol 46 mg

10 minutes | 30 minutes

Tortellini Primavera with Pesto Sauce is served at room temperature.

Red Beans and Rice

A traditional duo is enhanced by peas and chorizo, a spicy sausage often used in Mexican and Spanish recipes.

- **1** tablespoon olive or vegetable oil
- **1** large yellow onion, finely chopped
- **1** can (1 pound) red kidney beans, drained and rinsed
- **1** can (8 ounces) tomato sauce
- **6** ounces chorizo, sliced ¼ inch thick, or boiled ham, cut into ½-inch cubes
- **1** cup water
- **¾** cup frozen green peas, thawed and drained
- **1½** cups quick-cooking white rice

1 Heat the oil in a large heavy saucepan over moderately low heat for 1 minute. Add the onion and sauté, stirring occasionally, for 5 minutes or until limp.

2 Add the beans, tomato sauce, chorizo, water, and peas, and bring to a boil over moderate heat. Adjust the heat so that the mixture bubbles gently, cover, and cook for 4 minutes.

3 Uncover, raise the heat to high, and bring to a full boil. Add the rice and cook, uncovered, for 1 minute. Remove from the heat, cover, and let stand for 5 minutes. Serves 4.

Per serving:
Calories 449; Protein 25 g;
Carbohydrates 87 g;
Fat 21 g; Sodium 420 mg;
Cholesterol 142 mg

10 minutes | 19 minutes

More Extra Quick 'n' Easy Meals

The recipes below and on the following six pages are arranged so that the dishes on a single chart all have the same simple directions. Make just *one* meal from a chart, and you've mastered *all* the recipes in that chart.

These recipes make the most of common ingredients and take into account a variety of individual tastes. Once you find a recipe that appeals to you, keep the ingredients on hand to save time in the future. Cooking-by-the-chart is handy in various situations. If time is limited, for example, try a simple stir-fry; to minimize cleanup, make a fast foil bake; when a trip to the market is out of the question, whip up a quick quiche or fluffy frittata; or if you have a pound of chicken or ground beef in the freezer, serve a family-pleasing casserole in next to no time.

And that's not all. Using these convenient charts as a guide, you can improvise recipes. Just tailor them to suit your taste, and create your very own extra quick 'n' easy one-dish meals.

Frittatas

Each Recipe Serves 4

RECIPE	PROTEIN	VEGETABLES	STARCH	OIL	SEASONINGS	TOPPING
Potatoes and Spinach	5 large eggs; ½ cup grated Parmesan cheese	10-oz pkg frozen chopped spinach, thawed & drained	2 cups frozen hash brown potatoes, thawed	2 tbs olive oil	1 tsp paprika; ⅛ tsp each dried thyme, garlic & onion powder	2 tbs grated Parmesan
Ham and Mozzarella	5 large eggs; 2 oz minced cooked ham; 1 cup shredded mozzarella cheese	10-oz pkg frozen green beans or cut asparagus, thawed & drained; ½ cup sliced mushrooms	1⅓ cups cooked orzo (rice-shaped pasta)	2 tbs olive oil	½ tsp dried basil; ¼ tsp dried oregano	¼ cup grated Parmesan + 2 tbs minced canned roasted red peppers
Frittata Niçoise	5 large eggs; ⅓ cup grated Parmesan cheese	10-oz pkg frozen green beans, thawed & drained; ⅓ cup chopped pitted black olives	2 cups cubed cooked potatoes	2 tbs olive oil	½ tsp dried basil; ¼ tsp dried thyme; 4-oz can caponata; ½ cup canned crushed tomatoes	¼ cup halved pitted black olives; 3 anchovy fillets, minced (optional)
Sausage and Broccoli	5 large eggs; 6 oz crumbled cooked sausage meat	10-oz pkg frozen chopped broccoli or cauliflower, thawed & drained; ½ cup chopped red onion	⅓ cup cornmeal soaked 5 minutes in ¾ cup hot milk	2 tbs olive oil	2 cloves garlic, minced; ½ tsp dried oregano; ¼ tsp red pepper flakes	2 tbs seasoned dry bread crumbs

Cooking Directions

1 Whisk the eggs from Protein in a bowl until frothy. Add the remaining Protein ingredients and all Vegetables, Starches, and Seasonings; mix well.
2 Heat the oil in a 10-inch skillet with a flameproof handle for 2 minutes over moderate heat.
3 Add the egg mixture to the skillet, reduce the heat to very low, and cook, uncovered, without stirring, for 12 minutes or until set around the edges and almost set on top. Meanwhile, preheat the broiler.
4 Sprinkle the Topping over the frittata, then broil 6 inches from the heat for 45 seconds or until the top is set. Run a thin-bladed spatula around the edge of the frittata, then invert on a serving plate.

Quiches

RECIPE	PROTEIN	VEGETABLES	STARCH	LIQUID	SEASONINGS	TOPPING
Ham and Broccoli	4 large eggs; 1 cup shredded Gruyère cheese; 6 oz cooked ham, diced	10-oz pkg frozen broccoli, asparagus, or green peas, thawed & drained	9" frozen pie shell, thawed	1¼ cups milk	1 tsp prepared mustard; ½ tsp dried thyme; ⅛ tsp black pepper	2 tbs slivered pimiento
Ricotta and Spinach	3 large eggs; 15 oz ricotta cheese; ¼ cup grated Parmesan cheese	10-oz pkg frozen chopped spinach or kale, thawed & drained	9" frozen pie shell, thawed	1 cup milk	1 clove garlic, minced; ¾ tsp dried rosemary or marjoram; ⅛ tsp ground nutmeg	¼ cup crisp bacon crumbles
Quiche Lorraine	3 large eggs; ½ cup crisp bacon crumbles; 1½ cups shredded Gruyère cheese	(see Topping)	9" frozen pie shell, thawed	1¼ cups milk	¼ tsp ground nutmeg	1 large ripe tomato, cored & thinly sliced but not peeled
Cheddar, Corn, and Chili	3 large eggs; 1¼ cups shredded low-fat Cheddar cheese	10-oz pkg frozen corn kernels, thawed & drained; 2 scallions, finely chopped; 4-oz can chopped green chilies, drained; 1 tbs minced pimiento	9" frozen pie shell, thawed	1 cup milk	2 tsp chili powder; ¼ tsp each ground cumin & coriander	½ cup finely diced avocado
Low-Cal Cottage Cheese	3 large eggs; 1 lb low-fat cottage cheese; 6 tbs sour cream or plain low-fat yogurt	10-oz pkg frozen chopped broccoli, thawed & drained	2 cups mashed potatoes (fresh or instant)	½ cup milk	2½ tsp paprika; ½ tsp ground coriander; ¼ tsp ground nutmeg; ⅛ tsp black pepper	½ tsp paprika; 2 scallions, finely chopped
Crab and Asparagus	3 large eggs; 6¼ oz can crab (fresh or frozen), drained and picked over	10-oz pkg frozen cut asparagus or broccoli florets, thawed and drained	9" frozen pie shell, thawed	1¼ cups milk	2 tbs dry port, Madeira, or sherry; 2 tbs prepared mustard	⅓ cup shredded Gruyère cheese + 2 tbs grated Parmesan cheese or toasted chopped pecans

Cooking Directions

1 Preheat the oven to 425°F. Place the pie shell from Starch on a baking sheet and bake, uncovered, for 5 minutes. Reduce oven temperature to 350°F. (For Low-Cal Cottage Cheese Quiche, preheat oven to 350°F, then pat the mashed potatoes over the bottom and up the sides of a greased 9" pie pan; set aside.)
2 Whisk the eggs from Protein in a large bowl until frothy. Mix in the remaining Protein ingredients, Vegetables, Liquid, and Seasonings. Pour into the pie shell. (For Low-Cal Cottage Cheese Quiche, use the mashed potato crust.)
3 Sprinkle with the Topping and bake, uncovered, for 35 to 40 minutes or until set and browned on top. (For Quiche Lorraine, bake without the Topping, then remove from the oven, add the Topping, and let stand for 5 minutes before serving.)

Chicken Casseroles

Each Recipe Serves 4

RECIPE	CHICKEN	VEGETABLES	STARCH	SAUCE	SEASONINGS	TOPPING
Chicken with Creamy Mushroom Sauce	1 broiler-fryer, 3–3½ lb, cut into 8 pieces	10-oz pkg frozen mixed peas & onions, thawed & drained	1-lb can new potatoes, drained, or 1 lb peeled new potatoes (about 1½" diam), halved and parboiled for 5 minutes	½ cup finely chopped yellow onion; 1¾ cups canned chicken broth; 8-oz can sliced mushrooms with liquid; ½ cup half-and-half; 3 tbs flour; 2 tsp Dijon mustard	½ tsp each salt, dried thyme & marjoram; ¼ tsp black pepper	⅓ cup seasoned dry bread crumbs
Oven Barbecued Chicken	1 broiler-fryer, 3–3½ lb, cut into 8 pieces	2 cups frozen mixed vegetables, thawed & drained; 2 cloves garlic, minced	2 pkg (10 oz each) frozen au gratin potatoes, thawed	½ cup finely chopped yellow onion; 1 cup each barbecue & tomato sauce	½ tsp each dried oregano & basil; ¼ tsp each salt & black pepper	2 tbs coarsely shredded Cheddar cheese mixed with 2 tbs dry bread crumbs
Mexicali Chicken	2 lb chicken parts	10-oz pkg each frozen corn kernels & green beans, thawed & drained; 8-oz can sliced mushrooms, drained	4 corn tortillas, warmed until pliable	½ cup finely chopped yellow onion; 2½ cups enchilada sauce; 4-oz can chopped green chilies, drained	½ tsp each salt, ground cumin & dried oregano; 2 tbs minced fresh coriander (cilantro)	1 cup coarsely shredded Monterey Jack cheese
Chicken Divan	1½ lb chicken cutlets	10-oz pkg frozen broccoli spears, thawed & drained	2 pkg (10 oz each) frozen mixed rice & wild rice, thawed	½ cup finely chopped yellow onion; 1 cup each canned chicken broth & milk; 1 cup coarsely shredded Cheddar cheese; 3 tbs flour	2 tbs dry sherry; add 2 tsp each Dijon mustard & Worcestershire sauce	½ cup coarsely shredded Cheddar cheese; ½ tsp paprika
Chicken, Italian Style	1½ lb chicken cutlets	1 cup 1" squares green pepper; 2 medium-size zucchini, cut into 1" cubes; 2 cloves garlic, minced	8 oz spaghetti, cooked & drained, then tossed with 1 tbs olive oil	½ cup finely chopped yellow onion; 2 jars (14 oz each) marinara sauce	½ tsp each dried basil & fennel seeds; ¼ tsp each salt & red pepper flakes	2 cups coarsely shredded mozzarella cheese + ¼ cup grated Parmesan

Cooking Directions

1 Preheat the oven to 350°F. Heat 2 tablespoons butter, margarine, or oil over moderate heat in a deep 12-inch skillet. Brown the Chicken, then transfer to a plate. Sauté the onion from Sauce ingredients for 3 minutes or until slightly softened.
2 Add the remaining Sauce ingredients and Seasonings to the skillet. Adjust the heat and simmer for 3 minutes. (For Chicken Divan, don't add the cheese until after the mixture has simmered.)
3 Arrange the Starch in a single layer on the bottom of a greased flameproof 11" x 9" x 2" baking dish or shallow 2½-quart casserole. (For Oven Barbecued Chicken, arrange the potatoes around the edge.) Layer the Vegetables on top, then the Chicken, then the skillet mixture. Sprinkle the Topping over all. Bake, uncovered, for 40 to 50 minutes or until bubbling and cooked through.

Ground Meat Casseroles

Each Recipe Serves 4

RECIPE	MEAT	VEGETABLES	STARCH	SAUCE	SEASONINGS	TOPPING
Beef 'n' Beans	1 lb lean ground beef	2 cups diced carrots; 1 cup diced green pepper; ½ cup diced yellow onion; 2 cloves garlic, minced	2 cans (1 lb each) baked beans, drained	1 cup tomato sauce; ⅓ cup chili sauce; 2 tbs molasses; 1 tbs Dijon mustard	½ tsp each celery seeds & dried savory; ¼ tsp each ground red pepper (cayenne) & salt	¼ cup seasoned dry bread crumbs
Italian Beef and Pasta	1 lb lean ground beef or 8 oz each lean ground beef & pork	½ cup finely chopped yellow onion; 10-oz pkg frozen chopped broccoli, thawed & drained; 2 cloves garlic, minced	8 oz ziti or penne, cooked & drained, then tossed with 1 tbs olive oil	1 cup tomato or marinara sauce; 7½-oz can caponata; 8-oz can sliced mushrooms with liquid	½ tsp each salt, dried oregano & fennel seeds; ¼ tsp red pepper flakes	2 cup coarsely shredded mozzarella cheese + ⅓ cup grated Parmesan
Tortilla Casserole	1 lb lean ground beef	½ cup finely chopped yellow onion, 1 large zucchini & 1 large yellow squash, cut into 1" cubes; 10-oz pkg frozen corn kernels, thawed & drained; 2 cloves garlic, minced	4 corn tortillas, cut into ¼" strips	2 cups taco or enchilada sauce; 4-oz can chopped green chilies, drained	2 tsp each ground cumin & chili powder; ½ tsp salt; ¼ tsp black pepper	1 cup coarsely shredded Monterey Jack or sharp Cheddar cheese
Beef in Mushroom Sauce	1 lb lean ground beef or 8 oz each lean ground beef & pork	½ cup finely chopped yellow onion; 2 cups frozen mixed vegetables, thawed & drained; 2 cloves garlic, minced	4 oz uncooked medium-wide egg noodles	10¾-oz can cream of mushroom soup; 1 cup milk; 8-oz can sliced mushrooms with liquid; 2 tsp Dijon mustard	½ tsp each dried thyme & marjoram; ¼ tsp each salt & black pepper	1 cup coarsely shredded Gruyère cheese or ½ cup each shredded Gruyère & grated Parmesan
Oriental Pork and Pineapple	1 lb lean ground pork or beef	½ cup finely chopped yellow onion; 1 cup 1" squares green pepper; 2 cloves garlic, minced	2 pkg (9⅞ oz each) frozen Oriental noodles & vegetables, thawed; 20-oz can pineapple chunks, drained (reserve juice for sauce)	⅓ cup each canned chicken broth & reserved pineapple juice; 2 tbs each soy sauce & cider vinegar; 1 tbs each brown sugar & cornstarch	¼ tsp each salt & black pepper	3-oz can chow mein noodles

Cooking Directions

1 Preheat the oven to 350° F. Sauté the Vegetables in 2 tablespoons oil, butter, or margarine in a deep 12-inch skillet over moderate heat until slightly softened—3 to 5 minutes. Add the Meat and Seasonings and cook, stirring, until the Meat is no longer pink—3 to 5 minutes.

2 Mix in the Sauce ingredients, bring to a simmer, then stir in the Starch. Spoon into a greased 11" x 9" x 2" baking dish or shallow 2½-quart casserole. Sprinkle with the Topping and bake, uncovered, for 35 to 45 minutes or until bubbling and lightly browned.

Fast Foil Bakes

RECIPE	PROTEIN	VEGETABLES	STARCH	SAUCE	SEASONINGS	TOPPING
Tex-Mex Burgers with Hash Browns	1 lb lean ground beef mixed with ½ tsp salt & ¼ tsp black pepper, then shaped into 4 patties	1 cup each frozen corn kernels & mixed chopped onion & sweet green pepper, thawed & drained; ¼ cup diced canned roasted red peppers or quartered cherry tomatoes	2 cups frozen hash brown potatoes, thawed	¾ cup canned beef broth mixed with 1 tsp flour or cornstarch	2 tbs chopped canned green chilies; 1 tbs chili powder; ¼ tsp each dried oregano, minced parsley, ground cumin & coriander	¼ cup diced pitted black olives
Red River Hash	1-lb can corned beef hash	8-oz can shredded beets, drained; 1 cup shredded red cabbage; ¼ cup finely chopped yellow onion	2 cups frozen hash brown potatoes, thawed	½ cup canned beef broth; ¼ cup orange juice blended with 1 tsp cornstarch or arrowroot	1 tbs minced parsley; ½ tsp each dill weed & caraway seeds. Optional: 1 tsp grated orange rind; ¼ tsp each ground cinnamon & allspice; ⅛ tsp ground nutmeg	1 tbs minced parsley mixed with 1 tsp grated orange rind
Hawaiian Ham Steaks	4 ham steaks (5 oz each)	½ cup each thinly sliced sweet red & green pepper; 1 cup chopped fresh pineapple, peaches, or papaya or 1 cup drained canned fruit cocktail or pineapple chunks	1-lb can sliced yams, drained & rinsed	½ cup canned chicken broth	2 tsp each soy sauce, grated lemon & orange rind & minced fresh ginger (or ½ tsp ground ginger); ¾ tsp curry powder	2 tbs slivered almonds
Chicken and Rice	4 skinned bone-in chicken thighs	½ cup each thinly sliced yellow onion & sweet red & green peppers, sautéed in 1 tbs olive oil for 3 minutes	1 cup uncooked quick-cooking brown rice	8-oz can stewed tomatoes with their juice or 7-oz can caponata; ¾ cup canned chicken broth	2 cloves garlic, minced; ¼ cup chopped pimiento-stuffed green olives; ¼ tsp each dried basil, oregano & fennel seeds	2 tsp finely slivered orange zest
Creamed Chicken and Potatoes	4 chicken cutlets (5 oz each)	10-oz pkg frozen chopped broccoli or cut asparagus, thawed & drained	1 cup thinly sliced unpeeled new potatoes, uncooked	1-oz pkg white sauce mix cooked with 1 cup milk (or ¾ cup milk & ¼ cup dry vermouth)	⅓ cup grated Parmesan cheese; ¼ tsp each dried thyme & nutmeg; ⅛ tsp ground red pepper (cayenne)	2 tbs sesame seeds or grated Parmesan cheese

Fast Foil Bakes

RECIPE	PROTEIN	VEGETABLES	STARCH	SAUCE	SEASONINGS	TOPPING
Turkey 'n' Dumplings	4 turkey cutlets (5 oz each)	10-oz pkg frozen mixed vegetables, thawed & drained; ¼ cup finely chopped yellow onion	10-oz can refrigerator biscuits	10-oz can cream of celery or mushroom soup or 1¼ cups canned chicken gravy	¼ tsp each dried sage, thyme & marjoram or ¾ tsp poultry seasoning	1 tsp lemon juice
Turkey with Stuffing	4 turkey cutlets (5 oz each) or 5 slices smoked turkey breast or leftover roast turkey	10-oz pkg frozen green peas in white sauce, thawed; 4-oz can sliced mushrooms, drained; ⅓ cup each diced celery & scallions	4 cups herb or corn bread stuffing mix	¾ cup canned chicken broth	None	2 tbs chopped pecans; 1 oz prosciutto or thinly sliced boiled or baked ham, finely slivered
Shrimp Madrid	1 lb small shrimp, shelled & deveined (fresh or thawed & drained frozen)	10-oz pkg frozen mixed peas & carrots, thawed & drained; 1 cup each frozen chopped onion & sweet green pepper	10-oz pkg Spanish rice mix; 1 cup drained canned chick peas	14½-oz can stewed tomatoes with their juice	2 cloves garlic, minced; 2 tsp grated orange rind; ½ tsp each dried basil & thyme; ¼ tsp dried oregano; ⅛ tsp ground cloves	2 tbs dry sherry or dry red wine
Dilled Fish Steaks	4 1"-thick salmon, scrod, or haddock steaks (1¼ lb in all)	10-oz pkg frozen cut asparagus or green beans + 1 cup frozen sliced carrots, thawed & drained	2 cups packaged scalloped or au gratin potatoes (omit cheese)	½ cup bottled clam juice or canned chicken broth; 4 tsp each dry white wine & lemon juice	2 tbs snipped fresh dill (or 1 tsp dill weed); 1 tsp grated lemon rind	2 tbs slivered pimiento; 4 fresh dill sprigs
Fillets of Fish with Snow Peas	4 flounder, haddock, or cod fillets (4 oz each) (fresh or thawed & drained frozen)	6-oz pkg frozen snow peas, thawed & drained; 1 cup each drained canned sliced carrots & mushrooms; ⅓ cup thinly sliced scallions	1⅓ cups cooked orzo (rice-shaped pasta) or 2 cups cooked medium-wide egg noodles	½ cup canned chicken broth; 2 tbs dry sherry; 1 tbs soy sauce	2 cloves garlic, minced; 2 tsp grated lemon or orange rind; 1 tsp minced fresh ginger (or ¼ tsp ground ginger)	¼ cup sliced water chestnuts or toasted slivered almonds

Cooking Directions

1 Preheat the oven to 400°F. Cut four 12-inch squares of heavy-duty foil. Lightly coat the middle of each with vegetable oil or nonstick cooking spray. Place the Starch on the coated area.

2 Mix the Vegetables, Sauce ingredients, and Seasonings together. Place on top of the Starch, then top with the Protein. Sprinkle with the Topping.

3 Lift 2 sides of the foil up, fold over twice to form a snug packet, then fold the ends over several times to seal. Place on baking sheet. Bake Tex-Mex Burgers with Hash Browns and Red River Hash for 20 minutes; Hawaiian Steaks, 12 minutes; Chicken and Rice, 35 minutes; Creamed Chicken and Potatoes, 25 minutes; Turkey 'n' Dumplings, 20 minutes (if crisper biscuits are desired, open foil and bake 5 minutes more); Turkey with Stuffing, 20 minutes; Shrimp Madrid, 12 minutes (check to see if shrimp are done; if not, reseal and bake 2 to 3 minutes more); Dilled Fish Steaks and Fillets of Fish with Snow Peas, 15 minutes.

Stir-Fry Meals

RECIPE	PROTEIN	VEGETABLES	STARCH	SAUCE	SEASONINGS	TOPPING
Oriental Steak in Orange Sauce	12 oz flank or minute steak, cut crosswise into strips ½" wide	10-oz pkg frozen Chinese vegetables, thawed & drained; 1 cup thinly sliced mushrooms	2 cups cooked orzo (rice-shaped pasta) or 1 cup uncooked quick-cooking white rice	¼ cup vegetable oil; ½ cup canned beef broth; 3 tbs orange juice	3 scallions, finely chopped; 1 tbs soy sauce; 2 tsp brown sugar; 1 tsp grated orange rind	½ cup each thinly sliced sweet red & green peppers
Hong Kong Pork with Baby Corn	12 oz pork cutlets, sliced crosswise into strips ½" wide	¾ cup frozen mixed chopped onion & sweet green pepper; ½ cup drained canned baby corn; 4-oz can sliced mushrooms, drained; 4-oz can sliced water chestnuts, drained	1 cup uncooked quick-cooking brown rice	¼ cup vegetable oil; ¾ cup canned beef broth; 1 tbs soy sauce blended with 1 tsp cornstarch	2 cloves garlic, minced; 2 tsp minced fresh ginger (or ¼ tsp ground ginger); 1 tsp Oriental sesame oil	2 tbs sesame seeds
Chinese Chicken and Vegetables	12 oz chicken cutlets, cut crosswise into strips ½" wide	4 oz snow peas; 1 cup each bean sprouts & thinly sliced mushrooms; ½ thinly sliced sweet red pepper	3 cups cooked fine egg noodles	¼ cup vegetable oil; ⅓ cup canned chicken broth	1 clove garlic, minced; 1 tbs minced fresh ginger (or ½ tsp ground ginger); 2 tbs soy sauce; 1 tbs dry sherry; ½ tsp sugar	½ cup slivered water chestnuts
Shrimp with Cashews and Broccoli	12 oz medium-size shrimp, shelled & deveined; ½ C roasted cashews	10-oz pkg frozen broccoli florets, thawed & drained; 1 cup finely sliced sweet red pepper	3 cups cooked medium-wide egg noodles	3 tbs vegetable oil; ½ cup canned chicken broth blended with 1 tbs dry sherry, 2 tsp soy sauce & 1½ tsp cornstarch	3 scallions, finely chopped; 1 clove garlic, minced; 2 tsp minced fresh ginger (or ¼ tsp ground ginger); 1 tsp grated lemon rind	2 tbs slivered canned roasted red peppers
Tofu and Snow Peas	1 lb firm tofu, cut into 2" cubes	6 oz snow peas; ½ cup thinly sliced carrot	2 cups cooked bulgur	3 tbs vegetable oil; ½ cup canned chicken broth blended with 2 tbs light soy sauce, 1 tbs chili sauce & 1½ tsp cornstarch	2 cloves garlic, minced; ½ cup diced yellow onion; 1 tsp each chili oil & Oriental sesame oil	2 tbs sesame seeds

Cooking Directions

1 Place the oil from Sauce in a deep 12-inch skillet or wok, then whisk the remaining Sauce ingredients together in a bowl; set aside. Heat the oil over high heat for 2 minutes.

2 Add any fresh garlic, ginger, onion, and/or scallions from Seasonings to the skillet and stir-fry for 1 minute. Add the Protein and stir-fry for 3 minutes. Add the Vegetables and stir-fry for 3 minutes.

3 Mix in the Sauce mixture and remaining Seasonings. If using uncooked rice, mix it in now, cover the skillet, adjust the heat, and simmer for 2 minutes. Turn off the heat and let stand, covered, for 3 minutes. Sprinkle with the Topping, toss to mix, and serve. If using cooked Starches, reduce the heat to moderate and cook the skillet mixture uncovered, stirring often, until it boils. Sprinkle with the Topping, toss to mix, and serve over Starch.

microwave meals

With these recipes created especially for microwaving,
you can easily bypass the hours it would take by traditional methods to
make delicious one-dish meals such as tangy Spanish Meatball Stew or smooth,
soothing Creamed Turkey and Spaghetti. A note of caution: be careful as you
uncover these dishes; although the pan may be barely warm, the
steam is scalding hot. To learn how oven power levels vary—and for other
important microwave tips—check the information on page 11.

Beef, Cabbage, and Potato Medley

Try this warming dish when the temperature plummets.

1 pound boneless top sirloin or round steak, cut into 4" x ¼" x ¼" strips
¼ cup olive oil
1 large yellow onion, halved and thinly sliced
1 large clove garlic, minced
1 tablespoon cornstarch blended with 2 tablespoons cold water
¾ cup boiling water
1 beef bouillon cube
1¼ teaspoons ground cumin
¾ teaspoon dried thyme, crumbled
½ teaspoon black pepper
1 pound cabbage, sliced ½ inch thick
3 cups refrigerated shredded potatoes or frozen hash brown potatoes, thawed and drained

> **Per serving:**
> *Calories 609; Protein 31 g;*
> *Carbohydrates 44 g;*
> *Fat 36 g; Sodium 339 mg;*
> *Cholesterol 75 mg*
>
> 20 minutes | 24 minutes

1 Toss the beef with 2 tablespoons of the oil in an ungreased 13" x 9" x 2" microwave-safe baking dish, then arrange around the edge of the dish. Microwave, uncovered, on *High* for 3½ to 4 minutes. At the midway point, push the beef to the center of the dish and continue to microwave on *High* until no longer pink. Transfer to a medium-size bowl and set aside.

2 Mix the onion, garlic, and remaining 2 tablespoons oil in the baking dish, cover with wax paper, and microwave on *High* for 4 minutes or until the onion is glassy.

3 In a small bowl, whisk the cornstarch mixture with the boiling water, then add the bouillon cube, cumin, thyme, and pepper. Stir until the cube dissolves, then mix in any juices that have accumulated in the bowl of meat.

4 Add the cabbage, potatoes, and cornstarch mixture to the baking dish and mix well. Cover with wax paper and microwave on *High* for 12 to 14 minutes or until the cabbage is tender, stirring midway.

5 Stir in the meat, cover with wax paper, and microwave on *High* until heated through—about 1½ minutes. Serves 4.

Mustcohola

A popular midwestern specialty made with three favorite ingredients— hamburger, macaroni, and tomatoes.

2 tablespoons vegetable oil
2 medium-size yellow onions, coarsely chopped
2 medium-size sweet green or red peppers (or 1 of each), cored, seeded, and coarsely chopped
1 pound lean ground beef
1 tablespoon chili powder
4 ounces mushrooms, thinly sliced
1 teaspoon salt
¼ teaspoon black pepper
1 can (14½ ounces) no-salt-added stewed tomatoes with their juice, coarsely chopped
6 ounces elbow macaroni

> **Per serving:**
> *Calories 495; Protein 44 g;*
> *Carbohydrates 45 g;*
> *Fat 15 g; Sodium 657 mg;*
> *Cholesterol 103 mg*
>
>
> 20 minutes | 31 minutes

1 Mix the oil, onions, and green peppers in an ungreased 2½-quart microwave-safe casserole. Cover with paper toweling and microwave on *High* for 4½ to 5 minutes or until the onions are glassy.

2 Crumble the beef into the casserole, cover with paper toweling, and microwave on *High* for 5 to 6 minutes or until the beef is no longer pink, stirring midway.

3 Break the beef up with a fork and stir in the chili powder, mushrooms, salt, black pepper, and tomatoes. Cover with the casserole lid and microwave on *High* for 15 minutes. Meanwhile, cook the macaroni according to package directions and drain well.

4 Stir the macaroni into the casserole, cover, and microwave on *Medium* for 5 minutes. Serves 4.

Spanish Meatball Stew

*In this adaptation of paella, the olives add an extra perk. If you like,
substitute ground veal or pork for the beef, pasta for the rice.*

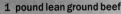

- 1 **pound lean ground beef**
- 1 **large egg, lightly beaten**
- ⅓ **cup dry bread crumbs**
- 4 **cloves garlic, minced**
- ½ **teaspoon each salt and black pepper**
- ½ **teaspoon each dried basil and thyme, crumbled**
- 2 **tablespoons olive oil**
- 1 **medium-size yellow onion, finely chopped**
- 1 **medium-size sweet red pepper, cored, seeded, and cut into 1-inch squares**
- 1 **cup canned tomatoes, drained and chopped**
- 1½ **cups Basic Beef Stock (page 332) or canned beef broth**
- 2 **tablespoons tomato paste**
- ⅓ **cup long-grain white rice**
- 1 **cup frozen green peas, unthawed**
- ½ **cup pimiento-stuffed green olives**

Optional garnishes:
- 1 **tablespoon minced fresh coriander (cilantro) or flat-leaf parsley**
- 1 **tablespoon drained small capers**

1 Combine the beef, egg, bread crumbs, 2 cloves of the garlic, and ¼ teaspoon each of the salt, black pepper, basil, and thyme in a large bowl. Shape into 16 balls about 1½ inches in diameter.

2 Arrange the meatballs around the edge of an ungreased 10- to 12-inch microwave-safe plate and cover with wax paper. Microwave on *High* for 5 minutes or until lightly browned; at the midway point, rearrange by moving the meatballs in the center to the outer edge and the meatballs from the outer edge to the center. Remove from the microwave oven and set aside.

3 Mix the oil, onion, red pepper, remaining 2 cloves garlic, and remaining ¼ teaspoon each salt, black pepper, basil, and thyme in an ungreased 3-quart microwave-safe casserole. Cover with the casserole lid and microwave on *High* for 4 minutes or until the onion is glassy, stirring once midway.

4 Mix in the tomatoes, stock, and tomato paste, add the meatballs, cover with the lid, and microwave on *High* for 5 minutes, stirring once midway. Mix in the rice, cover, and microwave on *High* for 3 minutes.

5 Reduce the power level to *Medium High* and microwave, covered, for 8 to 10 minutes or until the rice is just tender. Stir in the peas and olives, cover, and microwave on *High* until the peas are cooked—3 to 5 minutes.

6 Let the casserole stand, covered, in the turned-off microwave oven for 5 minutes. Just before serving, sprinkle with the coriander and capers if desired. Serves 4.

Spanish Meatball Stew, garnished with fragrant coriander

Per serving:
Calories 465; Protein 44 g;
Carbohydrates 33 g;
Fat 17 g; Sodium 928 mg;
Cholesterol 156 mg

20 minutes | 37 minutes

Lamb and Eggplant Gratin

Serve this casserole with a green salad and crusty bread.

1 eggplant (1 to 1¼ pounds), halved lengthwise

2 tablespoons vegetable oil

1 medium-size yellow onion, finely chopped

2 cloves garlic, minced

1½ pounds lean ground lamb or lean ground beef

½ teaspoon salt

½ teaspoon each dried oregano and basil, crumbled

¼ teaspoon each black pepper and ground cinnamon

1½ cups tomato sauce

2 packages (11½ ounces each) frozen potatoes au gratin, thawed

1 tablespoon minced fresh basil or parsley (optional)

Per serving:
Calories 593; Protein 59 g;
Carbohydrates 41 g;
Fat 21 g; Sodium 1,635 mg;
Cholesterol 176 mg

10 minutes

27 minutes

1 Prick the skin of the eggplant in several places with a fork. Arrange the eggplant halves, cut sides up, in an ungreased 11" x 9" x 2" microwave-safe baking dish. Cover with wax paper and microwave on *High* for 5 minutes; at the midway point, give the dish a half-turn. Slice the eggplant ¼ inch thick and arrange the slices, overlapping, in the baking dish; set aside.

2 Mix the oil, onion, and garlic in an ungreased 2-quart microwave-safe casserole. Cover with the casserole lid and microwave on *High* until the onion is glassy—3 to 4 minutes—stirring once midway.

3 Add the lamb to the casserole, arranging it in a circle around the edge, and cover with the lid. Microwave on *High* until the lamb is no longer pink—about 5 minutes; at the midway point, rearrange by moving the lamb nearest the center to the outer edge and the lamb from the outer edge closer to the center.

4 Pour all the drippings from the casserole, then mix in the salt, oregano, basil, pepper, cinnamon, and tomato sauce. Cover with the lid and microwave on *High* for 5 minutes, stirring once midway.

5 Spoon the casserole mixture over the eggplant slices, then cover with the potatoes, distributing them as evenly as possible. Cover with microwave-safe plastic food wrap and vent by turning back one corner. Microwave on *High* for 5 minutes; midway, give the baking dish a half-turn.

6 Remove the plastic wrap, reduce the power level to *Medium*, and microwave, uncovered, just until the mixture bubbles—about 3 minutes. Sprinkle, if you like, with the basil or parsley. Serves 4.

Sweet-and-Sour Pork

To save time, you can cook the rice on the top of your stove while the pork is in the microwave. In Step 1, be sure to rearrange the meat so that it cooks thoroughly.

1 pound boneless pork loin, cut into 4" x ¼" x ¼" strips
2 teaspoons Oriental sesame oil
1 medium-size yellow onion, cut into 1-inch cubes
1 small sweet green pepper, cored, seeded, and cut into ½-inch squares
2 cloves garlic, minced
1 tablespoon vegetable oil

1 package (1 pound) frozen mixed broccoli, baby carrots, and water chestnuts, unthawed
1 cup quick-cooking white rice
⅓ cup Basic Chicken Stock (page 333) or canned chicken broth
2 tablespoons each reduced-sodium soy sauce, honey, and cider vinegar
1 can (1 pound 4 ounces) pineapple chunks, drained, with ½ cup juice reserved
2 tablespoons cornstarch

Per serving:
Calories 676; Protein 36 g;
Carbohydrates 86 g;
Fat 22 g; Sodium 479 mg;
Cholesterol 95 mg

20 minutes | 19 minutes

1 Arrange the pork around the edge of an ungreased 9- or 10-inch microwave-safe plate. Sprinkle with the sesame oil, cover with wax paper, and microwave on *High* for 5 minutes. At the midway point, rearrange the pork by moving the inner strips to the outer edge of the plate and pushing the outer strips toward the center.

2 Mix the onion, pepper, garlic, and vegetable oil in an ungreased 3-quart microwave-safe casserole, cover with the lid, and microwave on *High* for 2 minutes. Add the frozen vegetables, cover, and microwave on *High* for 5 minutes, stirring midway. Remove from the microwave and set aside.

3 Cook the rice according to package directions. Meanwhile, combine the stock, soy sauce, honey, vinegar, and ⅓ cup of the pineapple juice in a microwave-safe 2-cup measure, and microwave, uncovered, on *High* for 2 minutes, stirring midway.

4 In a small bowl, blend the cornstarch with the remaining pineapple juice, then stir into the measuring cup. Microwave, uncovered, on *High* for 2 minutes or until slightly thickened, stirring midway.

5 Mix the pork, pineapple chunks, and soy sauce mixture into the casserole, cover, and microwave on *High* for 3 minutes or until the mixture is heated through, stirring midway. Serve over a bed of rice. Serves 4.

Good fortune will be yours when you cook Sweet-and-Sour Pork.

245

Smoked Pork, Cabbage, and Potato Casserole

If your family likes sauerkraut, use it in place of the fresh cabbage. You can also substitute boiled or baked ham, pork chops, or sausage for the smoked pork, and turnips or carrots for the potatoes.

1 medium-size yellow onion, finely chopped
1 tablespoon vegetable oil
1 pound cabbage, coarsely shredded
1 teaspoon caraway seeds
1 pound all-purpose potatoes, peeled and cut into 1-inch cubes
¼ cup Basic Chicken Stock (page 333), canned chicken broth, or water
1 pound boneless smoked pork butt, sliced ¾ inch thick
½ teaspoon salt
¼ teaspoon black pepper

> **Per serving:**
> Calories 322; Protein 29 g;
> Carbohydrates 31 g;
> Fat 9 g; Sodium 1,626 mg;
> Cholesterol 55 mg

| 20 minutes | 30 minutes |

1 Mix the onion and oil in an ungreased shallow 3-quart microwave-safe casserole. Cover with the lid, and microwave on *High* until glassy—about 3 minutes.

2 Mix in the cabbage and caraway seeds, then arrange the potatoes around the edge of the casserole. Pour in the stock, cover, and microwave on *High* for 12 minutes, stirring midway.

3 Scoop out half the cabbage. Arrange the pork in a single layer over the cabbage in the casserole, then spread the scooped-out cabbage on top.

4 Cover and microwave on *High* for 5 minutes. Give the casserole a half-turn, reduce the power to *Medium High,* and microwave for another 5 minutes. Remove from the oven and let stand, covered, for 5 minutes. Sprinkle with the salt and pepper. Serves 4.

Baked Beans with Ham and Maple Syrup

Dinner is ready in less than 30 minutes with this quick-and-easy recipe. Instead of maple syrup, try molasses, honey, or a combination of the two. To brown before serving, use a baking dish that is both microwave-safe and flameproof.

1 pound boneless precooked ham steak, cut into 1-inch cubes
2 medium-size carrots, peeled and sliced ¼ inch thick
⅓ cup maple syrup
1 tablespoon Dijon mustard
2 cans (1 pound each) baked beans, drained
2 tablespoons ketchup
½ teaspoon each dry mustard and chili powder
½ cup dry bread crumbs
1 tablespoon unsalted butter or margarine, melted

> **Per serving:**
> Calories 592; Protein 39 g;
> Carbohydrates 81 g;
> Fat 15 g; Sodium 2,882 mg;
> Cholesterol 75 mg

| 10 minutes | 18 minutes |

1 Place the ham in the center of an ungreased 11" x 9" x 2" microwave-safe baking dish. Arrange the carrots in a single layer around the edge of the dish. Combine the maple syrup and Dijon mustard in a small dish, then pour over the ham and carrots.

2 Cover with microwave-safe plastic food wrap, vent by turning back one corner, and microwave on *High* for 8 minutes, stirring the carrots once midway.

3 Mix the beans with the ketchup, dry mustard, and chili powder in a large bowl, then spoon on top of the ham and carrots. Microwave, uncovered, on *High* for 8 minutes, stirring midway.

4 Toss the bread crumbs with the butter in a small bowl, then sprinkle over the beans and microwave, uncovered, on *High* for another 2 minutes. Or, if you prefer, transfer to a preheated broiler and broil 4 inches from the heat for 1 minute or until tipped with brown. Serves 4.

Ham and Scalloped Potatoes

Made Grandmother's way, this homey dish must bake about 1½ hours, but with the microwave it takes only one-third the time. You may want to garnish the casserole with a few sweet red pepper rings or some chopped scallion tops.

1¼ pounds all-purpose potatoes, peeled and cut into ¾-inch cubes

¾ cup Basic Chicken Stock (page 333) or canned chicken broth

2 large scallions, including tops, thinly sliced

1 cup coarsely chopped sweet red pepper

1 tablespoon butter or margarine, cut into small pieces

4 teaspoons cornstarch

¼ teaspoon black pepper

¾ cup heavy cream

12 ounces boiled or baked ham, cut into ½-inch cubes

Per serving:
Calories 474; Protein 19 g;
Carbohydrates 36 g;
Fat 29 g; Sodium 1,218 mg;
Cholesterol 117 mg

 20 minutes   28 minutes

1 Mix the potatoes and ½ cup of the stock in an ungreased 2½-quart microwave-safe casserole. Cover with the lid and microwave on *High* until the potatoes are tender— 9 to 11 minutes. Drain, reserving the stock, then transfer the potatoes to a medium-size bowl and set aside.

2 Mix the scallions, red pepper, and butter in the same casserole, cover, and microwave on *High* for 3 minutes or until the pepper is slightly softened.

3 Blend the remaining ¼ cup stock with the cornstarch in a small bowl, then mix in the reserved stock, the black pepper, and cream.

4 Stir into the casserole, cover, and microwave on *High* just until the mixture boils—3 to 4 minutes. Stir in the potatoes and ham and microwave, uncovered, on *Medium* for 10 minutes, stirring occasionally. Serves 4.

Score a culinary touchdown with this after-the-game meal: Baked Beans with Ham and Maple Syrup.

247

Portuguese Bean Stew

Any canned beans will work in this recipe — you can try red kidney beans, chick peas, or black-eyed peas.

1½ ounces pepperoni, finely chopped

1 large yellow onion, coarsely chopped

1 medium-size sweet green pepper, cored, seeded, and coarsely chopped

1 clove garlic, minced

1 tablespoon olive oil

1 can (1 pound) stewed tomatoes with their juice

2 medium-size carrots, peeled and thinly sliced on the diagonal

1 large all-purpose potato, peeled and cut into ½-inch cubes

1 whole bay leaf

1 can (1 pound) cannellini (white kidney beans), drained and rinsed

1 package (10 ounces) frozen chopped kale or spinach, thawed and squeezed dry

⅔ cup finely diced boiled or baked ham

1 tablespoon cornstarch blended with 2 tablespoons canned chicken broth or water

⅛ teaspoon black pepper
Pinch ground red pepper (cayenne)

⅓ cup minced parsley

Per serving:
Calories 343; Protein 17 g;
Carbohydrates 45 g;
Fat 12 g; Sodium 1,195 mg;
Cholesterol 12 mg

30 minutes   30 minutes

1 Mix the pepperoni, onion, green pepper, garlic, and oil in an ungreased 2½-quart microwave-safe casserole. Cover with wax paper and microwave on *High* for 5 minutes or until the onion is glassy, stirring midway.

2 Mix in the tomatoes, carrots, potato, and bay leaf. Cover with the casserole lid and microwave on *High* until the vegetables are tender — 10 to 12 minutes.

3 Stir in the cannellini, kale, and ham, cover, and microwave on *Medium* for 10 minutes. Stir the cornstarch mixture into the casserole along with the black and red pepper. Cover and microwave on *High* just until the mixture boils — 2½ to 3 minutes. Remove the bay leaf and stir in the parsley. Serves 4.

Sausage and Ziti in Marinara Sauce

A fast midweek meal. If you prefer, use ground beef for the sausage, and tomato sauce, purée, or crushed tomatoes for the marinara sauce. Cook the pasta ahead of time if you like, toss with the oil, and chill until ready to use in Step 4.

8 ounces ziti or medium-size pasta shells
1 pound sweet Italian-style sausage
1 tablespoon olive oil
1 large yellow onion, finely chopped
1 large sweet green pepper, cored, seeded, and cut into 1-inch squares
3 cups prepared marinara sauce
½ teaspoon fennel seeds
½ teaspoon dried basil, crumbled
2 cups shredded mozzarella cheese (8 ounces)
½ cup grated Parmesan cheese (2 ounces)

Per serving:
Calories 927; Protein 47 g;
Carbohydrates 68 g;
Fat 52 g; Sodium 2,544 mg;
Cholesterol 131 mg

 15 minutes

 30 minutes

1 Cook the ziti according to package directions. Meanwhile, prick the skin of the sausage with a fork, then arrange the sausage around the sides of an ungreased 11" x 9" x 2" microwave-safe baking dish. Cover with wax paper and microwave on *High* for 5 minutes.

2 Pour off all the drippings, turn the sausage over, cover with wax paper, and microwave on *High* for another 3 minutes. Transfer the sausage to a cutting board and slice ½ inch thick. Again pour all the drippings from the baking dish. Drain the ziti well, toss with the oil, and set aside.

3 Add the onion, pepper, 1 cup of the marinara sauce, and the fennel seeds and basil to the baking dish, and stir well to mix. Cover with wax paper and microwave on *High* for 3 minutes, stirring once midway.

4 Mix in the ziti, sausage, remaining 2 cups marinara sauce, and half of the mozzarella and Parmesan cheeses. Cover with microwave-safe plastic food wrap and vent by turning back one corner. Microwave on *Medium High* for 12 minutes, giving the dish a half-turn every 4 minutes.

5 Uncover, sprinkle with the remaining mozzarella and Parmesan cheeses, and microwave on *Medium High* for 2 minutes. Remove from the microwave, cover with plastic wrap, and let stand for 5 minutes. Serves 4.

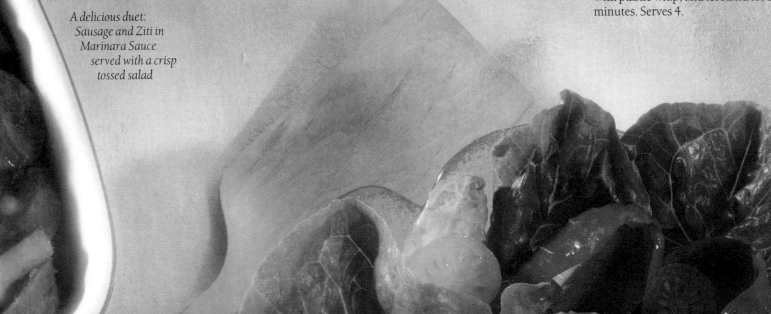

A delicious duet: Sausage and Ziti in Marinara Sauce served with a crisp tossed salad

Chicken Bundles with Rice

A great idea for hurry-up days. You can use any frozen rice mix instead of the pilaf, and turkey in place of the chicken.

- 1 package (10 ounces) frozen broccoli florets, unthawed
- 2 tablespoons water
- 1 medium-size carrot, peeled and coarsely shredded
- 2 teaspoons Dijon mustard
- ½ teaspoon salt
- ⅛ teaspoon black pepper
- 3 ounces Monterey Jack cheese, coarsely shredded
- 1 pound chicken cutlets, pounded thin as for scaloppine

- 1 tablespoon canned chicken broth or dry white wine
- ¼ teaspoon paprika
- 2 packages (10 ounces each) frozen rice pilaf with mushrooms, unthawed

Per serving:
Calories 382; Protein 37 g;
Carbohydrates 34 g;
Fat 10 g; Sodium 1,175 mg;
Cholesterol 66 mg

15 minutes   21 minutes

1 Place the broccoli and water in an ungreased shallow 10-inch-square microwave-safe casserole, cover with the casserole lid, and microwave on *High* for 7 minutes or until the broccoli is tender, stirring midway. Drain well, then chop fine.

2 Transfer the broccoli to a medium-size bowl and mix in the carrot, mustard, ¼ teaspoon of the salt, the pepper, and all but 1 tablespoon of the cheese.

3 Sprinkle both sides of the chicken with the remaining ¼ teaspoon salt, then spoon the broccoli mixture onto the center of each cutlet, dividing the total amount evenly. Fold over the ends of the chicken to enclose the broccoli mixture and secure with wooden toothpicks.

4 Sprinkle the broth into the casserole, then dust the chicken bundles with the paprika and arrange in the casserole, spoke fashion. Cover and microwave on *High* for 5 minutes or until the chicken is no longer pink on the inside.

5 Using a slotted spoon, transfer the bundles to a plate, cover, and keep warm. Remove the pilaf from the plastic pouches and place in the casserole. Cover and microwave on *High* for 7 minutes, stirring after 5 minutes.

6 Return the bundles to the casserole, arranging spoke fashion on top of the pilaf, and sprinkle with the remaining cheese. Cover and microwave on *High* until the cheese melts— 1½ to 2 minutes. Serves 4.

Tender cutlets enfold a broccoli stuffing in Chicken Bundles with Rice.

Stuffed Chicken Breasts with Fettuccine and Cheese Sauce

Here's a dish that's fast, easy — and satisfying.

4 chicken breasts, skinned and boned (1¼ pounds)

2 ounces part-skim mozzarella cheese, cut into ½-inch cubes

¼ cup dry bread crumbs mixed with ½ teaspoon paprika

2 packages (10⅝ ounces each) frozen fettuccine and vegetables in cheese sauce, thawed but not drained

½ cup frozen green peas, thawed and drained

1 Cut a pocket in the thicker side of each chicken breast. Tuck ¼ of the cheese cubes into each pocket. Spread the bread crumb mixture on a sheet of wax paper and coat each chicken breast with it. Set aside.

2 Mix the fettuccine mixture with the peas in an ungreased 8″ x 8″ x 2″ microwave-safe baking dish and spread evenly over the bottom of the dish. Arrange the chicken breasts, spoke fashion, on top, with the thicker edges toward the outside.

3 Cover the dish with wax paper and microwave on *High* for 10 minutes; after 6 minutes, give the dish a half-turn. Remove the paper and microwave on *High* 1 minute more. Remove the dish from the oven, cover with wax paper, and let stand for 3 minutes. Serves 4.

Per serving:
Calories 503; Protein 48 g;
Carbohydrates 36 g;
Fat 17 g; Sodium 1,456 mg;
Cholesterol 130 mg

8 minutes | 14 minutes

Chicken Gumbo

With the help of a microwave oven, you can make this traditionally slow-cooking Creole dish in less than an hour.

2 tablespoons unsalted butter or margarine

2 tablespoons all-purpose flour

1 medium-size yellow onion, finely chopped

1 medium-size stalk celery, finely chopped

1 medium-size sweet green pepper, cored, seeded, and finely chopped

2 cloves garlic, minced

2 cups canned crushed tomatoes

2 cups Basic Chicken Stock (page 333) or canned chicken broth

½ teaspoon each salt and black pepper

1 package (10 ounces) frozen sliced okra, unthawed

1 pound skinned and boned chicken breasts, cut into ½-inch cubes

1⅓ cups quick-cooking white rice

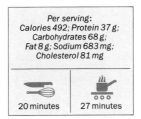

Per serving:
Calories 492; Protein 37 g;
Carbohydrates 68 g;
Fat 8 g; Sodium 683 mg;
Cholesterol 81 mg

20 minutes | 27 minutes

1 Place the butter in a microwave-safe 2-cup measure, cover with wax paper, and microwave on *High* for 35 to 40 seconds. Blend in the flour, cover with wax paper, and microwave on *High,* without stirring, until golden brown — 3 to 4 minutes.

2 Transfer to an ungreased microwave-safe 3-quart casserole and mix in the onion, celery, green pepper, and garlic. Cover with the lid and microwave on *High* until the onion, celery, and green pepper are limp — about 5 minutes — stirring once midway.

3 Mix in the tomatoes, stock, salt, and black pepper, cover, and microwave on *High* for 5 minutes, stirring once midway.

4 Add the okra and chicken. Cover and microwave on *High* until the okra is just cooked and the chicken is no longer pink on the inside — 10 to 12 minutes — stirring every 4 minutes to break up the okra.

5 Meanwhile, cook the rice according to package directions. To serve, spoon a mound of rice into 4 soup bowls and ladle the steaming gumbo on top. Serves 4.

251

Risotto with Chicken and Mushrooms

Be sure to use short-grain rice in this Italian-style dish so that it cooks to a deliciously creamy consistency.

1 medium-size yellow onion, finely chopped

1 small sweet red pepper, cored, seeded, and finely chopped

2 tablespoons unsalted butter or margarine, cut into small pieces

1 cup short-grain white rice, preferably arborio

1 can (14½ ounces) reduced-sodium chicken broth

¼ cup dry white wine or water

4 ounces mushrooms, thinly sliced

Pinch ground saffron (optional)

2 cups coarsely chopped cooked or canned chicken

¾ cup frozen green peas, thawed and drained

¼ cup grated Parmesan cheese

½ teaspoon salt

¼ teaspoon black pepper

1 Mix the onion, red pepper, and butter in an ungreased 2½-quart microwave-safe casserole, cover with wax paper, and microwave on *High* for 4 to 5 minutes or until the onion is glassy. Stir in the rice, cover, and microwave on *High* 2 minutes more.

2 Mix in the broth, wine, mushrooms, and saffron if desired. Cover with the casserole lid and microwave on *High* until the liquid boils—6 to 8 minutes. Stir well, cover, and microwave on *Medium* until the rice has absorbed almost all of the liquid—7 to 9 minutes.

3 Mix in the chicken and peas, cover, and microwave on *Medium* for 3 minutes. Let stand, covered, in the turned-off microwave oven for 5 minutes. Stir in the cheese, salt, and black pepper. Serves 4.

Per serving:
Calories 405; Protein 28 g;
Carbohydrates 47 g;
Fat 10 g; Sodium 571 mg;
Cholesterol 68 mg

15 minutes | 32 minutes

Creamed Turkey and Spaghetti

Whipped cream cheese melts into a satiny sauce in the microwave.

10 ounces thin spaghetti

1 large sweet red pepper, cored, seeded, and coarsely chopped

1 large clove garlic, minced

2½ tablespoons olive oil

1 pound turkey tenderloins, halved lengthwise, then sliced ½ inch thick

1¼ pounds yellow squash, cut into 2″ x ¼″ x ¼″ strips

1 container (4 ounces) whipped cream cheese

¼ cup Basic Chicken Stock (page 333) or canned chicken broth

¾ teaspoon salt

¼ teaspoon each dried thyme and marjoram, crumbled

¼ teaspoon black pepper

3 tablespoons grated Parmesan cheese

1 Cook the spaghetti according to package directions. Meanwhile, mix the red pepper, garlic, and 2 tablespoons of the oil in an ungreased 2½-quart microwave-safe casserole, cover with wax paper, and microwave on *High* for 3 minutes or until slightly softened.

2 Push the red pepper mixture to the center of the casserole and arrange the turkey around the edge. Cover with wax paper and microwave on *High* for 4 minutes. As soon as the spaghetti is tender, drain well, toss with the remaining ½ tablespoon oil, and set aside.

3 Stir the squash into the casserole, cover with the casserole lid, and microwave on *High* for 5 to 6 minutes or until the squash is tender, stirring midway.

4 In a small bowl, combine the cream cheese with the stock, salt, thyme, marjoram, and black pepper. Drain the casserole liquid into the cheese mixture and stir until smooth.

5 Add the cream cheese mixture, spaghetti, and Parmesan cheese to the casserole. Mix well, cover, and microwave on *High* until steaming hot—1 to 2 minutes. Serves 4.

Per serving:
Calories 602; Protein 30 g;
Carbohydrates 62 g;
Fat 26 g; Sodium 657 mg;
Cholesterol 79 mg

15 minutes | 15 minutes

Turkey Picadillo

This versatile Mexican dish is as easy to make as it is hearty. If you like, try ground beef, pork, veal, or chicken instead of turkey. Garnish with Monterey Jack or Cheddar cheese and with minced fresh coriander (cilantro) or flat-leaf parsley.

1 large yellow onion, finely chopped

1 large sweet green pepper, cored, seeded, and coarsely chopped

2 cloves garlic, minced

1 tablespoon vegetable oil

1¼ pounds ground turkey

1 teaspoon chili powder, or to taste

1 tablespoon red wine vinegar or cider vinegar

1 tablespoon capers, drained

½ teaspoon each ground cinnamon and dried oregano, crumbled

½ teaspoon each salt and black pepper

1 cup canned no-salt-added crushed tomatoes

1 can (1 pound) kidney beans, drained and rinsed

⅔ cup raisins

1⅓ cups quick-cooking white rice

1 Toss the onion, green pepper, and garlic in the oil in an ungreased 3-quart microwave-safe casserole. Cover with the lid and microwave on *High* for 3 minutes, stirring once midway.

2 Push the vegetables to the center of the casserole, arrange the turkey around the edge, cover, and microwave on *High* for 5 minutes, stirring the vegetables once midway.

3 Stir the turkey and vegetables together, then mix in the chili powder, wine, capers, cinnamon, oregano, salt, and black pepper, and microwave, uncovered, on *Medium High* for 1 minute.

4 Mix in the tomatoes, beans, and raisins, and microwave, uncovered, on *High* for 8 minutes, stirring

once midway. Meanwhile, cook the rice according to package directions.

5 Mix the rice into the casserole, cover, and microwave on *High* just until steaming hot—1 to 2 minutes. Serves 4.

Turkey Picadillo: Each cheese-topped serving in its own bowl.

Per serving:
Calories 635; Protein 44 g;
Carbohydrates 96 g;
Fat 9 g; Sodium 813 mg;
Cholesterol 92 mg

15 minutes | 19 minutes

Fish and Tomatoes with Couscous

To make a fish stock, place 2 quarts cold water, 1 pound fish bones, including heads and trimmings, and 1 tablespoon salt in a large saucepan, cover, and bring to a boil. Let the stock simmer for an hour, then strain it through a fine sieve. Make it ahead of time and store in the freezer.

- **1** medium-size yellow onion, finely chopped
- **2** large cloves garlic, minced
- **1** tablespoon olive oil
- **1** can (1 pound) tomatoes, drained and chopped
- **½** cup fish stock, bottled clam juice, or canned chicken broth
- **¼** teaspoon each dried thyme and basil, crumbled
- **¼** teaspoon black pepper
- **1** large zucchini, sliced ¼ inch thick
- **1** large yellow squash, sliced ¼ inch thick
- **4** flounder, haddock, or cod fillets (5 ounces each)
- **1** teaspoon lemon juice
- **¼** teaspoon salt
- **3** tablespoons snipped fresh dill or ½ teaspoon dill weed
- **1** cup couscous

Per serving:
Calories 371; Protein 30 g;
Carbohydrates 51 g;
Fat 5 g; Sodium 409 mg;
Cholesterol 71 mg

20 minutes | 19 minutes

---

1 Mix the onion, garlic, and oil in an ungreased 11″ x 9″ x 2″ microwave-safe baking dish, cover with wax paper, and microwave on *High* until the onion is glassy—3 to 4 minutes—stirring once midway.

2 Mix in the tomatoes, stock, thyme, basil, and half of the pepper, cover with wax paper, and microwave on *High* for 3 minutes, stirring once midway. Add the zucchini and yellow squash, toss to mix, cover with wax paper, and microwave on *High* for 2 minutes, stirring once midway.

3 Meanwhile, sprinkle both sides of the fish with the lemon juice, salt, remaining pepper, and 1 tablespoon of the dill (or ¼ teaspoon of the dill weed), then fold in half crosswise, with the skinned sides in.

4 Push the vegetables to the middle of the baking dish. Place the fish at both ends of the dish with the thickest portions toward the outside. Fold tapering ends toward the center of the fish.

5 Cover with microwave-safe plastic food wrap and vent by turning back one corner. Microwave on *High* until the fish just flakes—about 5 minutes; at the midway point, give the dish a half-turn.

6 Let the baking dish stand for 5 minutes, covered, in the turned-off microwave oven. Meanwhile, prepare the couscous according to package directions. To serve, spoon a mound of couscous onto each plate, top with the fish and vegetables, and sprinkle with the remaining dill. Serves 4.

Fish and Tomatoes with Couscous is at its summery best when seasoned with freshly snipped dill.

Stuffed Flounder Florentine

Here's a delicious dinner that puts convenience foods to imaginative use.

- 2 tablespoons unsalted butter or margarine
- ¼ cup finely chopped yellow onion
- ¼ cup finely chopped celery
- 2 tablespoons finely chopped sweet red pepper
- 2 cups packaged seasoned croutons
- ½ cup canned reduced-sodium chicken broth
- 2 flounder fillets (10 ounces each) or other firm-fleshed white fish
- 1 package (1 pound) frozen creamed spinach, thawed

Per serving:
Calories 374; Protein 28 g;
Carbohydrates 19 g;
Fat 20 g; Sodium 1,062 mg;
Cholesterol 86 mg

| 10 minutes | 15 minutes |

---

1 Place the butter in a 10-inch microwave-safe pie plate, cover with wax paper, and microwave on *High* until it melts—35 to 45 seconds. Stir in the onion, celery, and pepper, cover with wax paper, and microwave on *High* for 3 minutes or until limp.

2 Place the croutons in a large bowl, add the broth and the microwaved onion mixture, and stir to mix well.

3 Cut the flounder fillets in half lengthwise, bring the ends of each together to form 4 rings, and secure with wooden toothpicks.

4 Spread the spinach in the pie plate. Set the flounder rings on top of the spinach, spacing them evenly, then spoon the crouton mixture into the center of each.

5 Cover with wax paper and microwave on *High* for 7 to 9 minutes or until the fish flakes at the touch of a fork, giving the dish a half-turn midway. Let stand, covered, in the turned-off oven for 2 minutes before serving. Serves 4.

Salmon Cakes with White Sauce

For this creamy, dill-flavored dish, you can thaw the green peas quickly by putting them in a strainer and letting hot tap water run over them.

⅓ cup instant mashed potato granules (not flakes or buds)
¾ cup boiling water
1 large egg
1 scallion, including top, thinly sliced
1¼ teaspoons dill weed
3 teaspoons lemon juice (freshly squeezed preferred)
¼ teaspoon each salt and black pepper
1 can (15½ ounces) salmon, drained, skinned, and flaked
⅓ cup dry bread crumbs mixed with 1 teaspoon paprika

1 tablespoon butter or margarine
2¼ cups low-fat milk
1 envelope (1.8 ounces) white sauce mix
1 tablespoon Dijon mustard
1 package (10 ounces) frozen petite green peas, thawed and drained

Per serving:
Calories 440; Protein 35 g;
Carbohydrates 39 g;
Fat 16 g; Sodium 1,213 mg;
Cholesterol 73 mg

10 minutes   20 minutes

1 Place the potato granules in a medium-size heatproof bowl and add the water gradually, stirring until smooth. Mix in the egg, scallion, ½ teaspoon of the dill weed, 2 teaspoons of the lemon juice, and the salt and pepper. Gently fold in the salmon, then shape into 8 cakes about 2½ inches across. Coat evenly with the bread crumb mixture and set aside.

2 Place the butter in a 13″ x 9″ x 2″ microwave-safe baking dish, cover with wax paper, and microwave on *High* for 35 to 45 seconds. Stir to coat the bottom of the dish, then arrange the salmon cakes in the dish in a single layer, spacing them evenly. Cover with wax paper and microwave on *High* for 5 minutes, turning the cakes over after 3 minutes. Remove from the microwave and set aside.

3 Blend the milk and sauce mix in a 4-cup microwave-safe measure and microwave, uncovered, on *High* for 5 to 6 minutes or until the mixture boils, whisking every 2 minutes. Stir in the mustard, the remaining ¾ teaspoon dill weed and 1 teaspoon lemon juice, and the peas.

4 Carefully remove the salmon cakes from the baking dish. Pour the pea mixture into the dish, then arrange the cakes in the sauce, spacing them evenly. Cover with wax paper and microwave on *Medium High* for 6 minutes or until steaming hot. Let stand, covered, for 2 minutes before serving. Serves 4.

Decorative and delectable: Salmon Cakes with White Sauce

Shrimp and Fettuccine Mornay

A lovely, easy company dish in which you can substitute scallops for the shrimp and frozen cut green beans, broccoli florets, or asparagus tips for the green peas and onions.

9 ounces fettuccine

3 tablespoons unsalted butter or margarine, at room temperature

1 pound large shrimp, shelled and deveined

1 package (10 ounces) frozen green peas and onions, thawed and drained

1 package (10 ounces) frozen Welsh rarebit, thawed

½ cup milk

2 teaspoons Dijon mustard

⅛ teaspoon ground red pepper (cayenne)

⅓ cup seasoned dry bread crumbs

> *Per serving:*
> *Calories 632; Protein 39 g;*
> *Carbohydrates 65 g;*
> *Fat 22 g; Sodium 513 mg;*
> *Cholesterol 184 mg*

| 10 minutes | 16 minutes |

1 Cook the fettuccine according to package directions; drain well. Place in an ungreased 11" x 9" x 2" microwave-safe baking dish along with 2 tablespoons of the butter and toss well to mix. Set aside.

2 Arrange the shrimp on a 10-inch microwave-safe plate with their tails toward the center. Cover with microwave-safe plastic food wrap; vent by turning back one corner. Microwave on *High* for 2 minutes; at the midway point, rearrange by moving the shrimp in the center to the outer edge and the shrimp from the outer edge to the center, and give the plate a half-turn. Arrange the shrimp and the peas and onions in a single layer on top of the fettuccine; set aside.

3 Combine the rarebit, milk, mustard, and red pepper in a 2-cup microwave-safe measure and microwave, uncovered, on *High* for 1 minute. Pour evenly over the shrimp mixture, cover with vented plastic food wrap, and microwave on *High* for 4 minutes; midway, give the dish a half-turn.

4 In a small bowl, toss the bread crumbs with the remaining 1 tablespoon butter and sprinkle over the shrimp mixture. Microwave, uncovered, on *Medium High* for 1 minute. Serves 4.

Spicy Shrimp and Rice Stew

For a sharper flavor, increase the hot red pepper sauce to ¾ teaspoon.

1 large yellow onion, coarsely chopped

1 small sweet green pepper, cored, seeded, and coarsely chopped

2 cloves garlic, minced

2 tablespoons olive oil

1 can (14½ ounces) no-salt-added stewed tomatoes with their juice

1 cup Basic Chicken Stock (page 333) or canned chicken broth

1 package (10 ounces) frozen sliced okra, unthawed

½ teaspoon hot red pepper sauce

¼ teaspoon dried oregano, crumbled

1 pound medium-size shrimp, shelled and deveined

1 cup quick-cooking white rice

2 tablespoons minced parsley

1 teaspoon lemon juice

> *Per serving:*
> *Calories 407; Protein 29 g;*
> *Carbohydrates 52 g;*
> *Fat 9 g; Sodium 255 mg;*
> *Cholesterol 157 mg*

| 20 minutes | 25 minutes |

1 Mix the onion, pepper, garlic, and oil in an ungreased 2½-quart microwave-safe casserole. Cover with the lid and microwave on *High* for 4 to 5 minutes or until the onion is glassy, stirring midway.

2 Break up the tomatoes with a fork and stir into the casserole along with the stock, okra, red pepper sauce, and oregano. Cover with the lid and microwave on *High* for 12 minutes or until the okra is tender, stirring every 4 minutes. Add the shrimp, cover, and microwave on *High* until the shrimp are cooked through—2½ to 3 minutes.

3 Add the rice and stir until all of the grains are well moistened. Cover and microwave on *High* for 2 minutes.

4 Let the covered casserole stand in the turned-off microwave oven for 3 minutes, then stir in the parsley and lemon juice. Serves 4.

Seafood Creole

This Louisiana specialty has never been easier. If you prefer, the country-style rice can be replaced with any other type of frozen seasoned rice.

- 2 tablespoons vegetable oil
- 1 medium-size yellow onion, finely chopped
- 1 medium-size sweet green pepper, cored, seeded, and finely chopped
- 3 cloves garlic, minced
- ¼ teaspoon each dried basil and thyme, crumbled
- ¼ teaspoon each salt and black pepper
- ⅛ teaspoon ground red pepper (cayenne)
- 1½ cups canned crushed tomatoes
- 2 packages (10 ounces each) frozen country-style rice, thawed
- 1 package (10 ounces) frozen corn kernels, thawed and drained
- 1 pound medium-size shrimp, shelled and deveined, or scallops or crabmeat, picked over to remove bits of shell and cartilage

1 In an ungreased 2-quart microwave-safe casserole, mix the oil, onion, green pepper, and garlic. Cover with wax paper and microwave on *High* until the onion is glassy—4 to 5 minutes—stirring once midway.

2 Mix in the basil, thyme, salt, black pepper, red pepper, and tomatoes, cover with the casserole lid, and microwave on *High* for 5 minutes, stirring once midway.

3 Meanwhile, arrange the rice, corn, and shrimp in an ungreased 11″ x 9″ x 2″ microwave-safe baking dish. Spoon the casserole mixture evenly on top. Cover with microwave-safe plastic food wrap and vent by turning back one corner. Microwave on *High* for 5 minutes; at the midway point, give the dish a half-turn.

4 Let the baking dish stand, covered, in the turned-off microwave oven for 5 minutes. Serves 4.

Per serving:
Calories 418; Protein 28 g;
Carbohydrates 52 g;
Fat 12 g; Sodium 1,140 mg;
Cholesterol 157 mg

25 minutes | 20 minutes

New England Clam Chowder

With the added carrots, this American classic becomes a nutritionally balanced meal. For best results, cut the carrots and potatoes into ½-inch cubes. Serve with soup crackers.

- 2 tablespoons unsalted butter or margarine
- 1 medium-size yellow onion, finely chopped
- 4 large carrots, peeled and diced
- 2 tablespoons all-purpose flour
- 2 cans (6 ½ ounces each) minced clams, drained, with liquid reserved
- 1 to 1½ cups Basic Chicken Stock (page 333) or canned chicken broth
- 2 small all-purpose potatoes, peeled and diced
- 2 cups milk or half-and-half
- ¼ teaspoon each salt and white pepper
- Paprika (optional)

1 Place the butter in a 3½-quart microwave-safe casserole, cover with wax paper, and microwave on *High* for 1 minute. Add the onion and carrots, cover with the casserole lid, and microwave on *High* until the onion is glassy—about 5 minutes—stirring once midway. Blend in the flour, cover, and microwave on *High* for 1 minute. Set aside.

2 Place the clam liquid in a 2-cup measure and add enough chicken stock to total 2 cups. Add the stock mixture and the potatoes to the casserole, cover, and microwave on *High* until the potatoes are almost tender—about 8 minutes—stirring once midway.

3 Mix in the clams, milk, salt, and pepper. Cover and microwave on *High* until the chowder steams—4 to 5 minutes—stirring once midway. Reduce the power level to *Medium Low* and microwave, covered, for 3 minutes. Ladle into soup bowls and sprinkle with the paprika if desired. Serves 4.

Per serving:
Calories 282; Protein 16 g;
Carbohydrates 33 g;
Fat 11 g; Sodium 372 mg;
Cholesterol 89 mg

10 minutes | 23 minutes

Western-Style Egg Pie

Here's a vegetarian dish that's equally at home on the lunch or dinner table. You may even want to try it for a hearty breakfast.

1 small yellow onion, coarsely chopped

½ medium sweet red pepper, cored, seeded, and coarsely chopped

2 tablespoons olive oil

2 medium-size all-purpose potatoes, peeled and coarsely shredded

1 medium-size zucchini, coarsely shredded

½ cup frozen corn kernels, unthawed

4 large eggs

½ teaspoon salt

¼ teaspoon ground cumin

⅛ teaspoon each black pepper and chili powder

1 cup coarsely shredded Monterey Jack, Cheddar, or Muenster cheese (4 ounces)

Per serving:
Calories 335; Protein 16 g; Carbohydrates 22 g; Fat 21 g; Sodium 490 mg; Cholesterol 213 mg

 25 minutes | 23½ minutes

1 Mix the onion, red pepper, and oil in an ungreased 10-inch microwave-safe pie plate, cover with wax paper, and microwave on *High* for 3 to 4 minutes or until the onion is glassy.

2 Stir in the potatoes, zucchini, and corn, cover with wax paper, and microwave on *High* for 8 minutes, stirring midway.

3 Meanwhile, beat the eggs with the salt, cumin, black pepper, and chili powder until frothy. When the vegetable mixture has microwaved for 8 minutes, add the egg mixture and the cheese and mix well.

4 Cover with wax paper and microwave on *Medium* for 6 minutes; at the midway point, give the plate a half-turn. Remove the wax paper and microwave on *Medium* until the eggs look dry on top — 2½ to 3½ minutes more.

5 Remove the pie from the microwave, cover again with wax paper, and let stand for 2 minutes before serving. Serves 4.

Western-Style Egg Pie — whopping good and filling, too

Zucchini Pie

You may want to substitute yellow squash for the zucchini, and Swiss or Cheddar cheese for the Gruyère. No matter which you choose, the wreath of overlapping tomato slices creates a beautiful presentation.

- 2 tablespoons unsalted butter or margarine, cut into small pieces
- 1 medium-size yellow onion, coarsely chopped
- 2 cloves garlic, minced
- 1½ pounds small zucchini, halved lengthwise, then sliced ¼ inch thick (about 5 cups)
- 1½ cups soft whole wheat bread crumbs
- 3 large eggs, lightly beaten
- 1 cup coarsely shredded Gruyère cheese
- 2 tablespoons grated Parmesan cheese
- ¼ cup minced parsley
- ½ teaspoon salt
- ¼ teaspoon each black pepper and dried oregano, crumbled
- 2 medium-size tomatoes, cored and sliced ¼ inch thick
- 1 cup plain low-fat yogurt (optional topping)

Per serving:
Calories 316; Protein 19 g;
Carbohydrates 16 g;
Fat 21 g; Sodium 548 mg;
Cholesterol 209 mg

25 minutes | 32 minutes

1 Mix the butter, onion, and garlic in a 10-inch microwave-safe pie plate, cover with wax paper, and microwave on *High* for 3 minutes or until the onion is limp.

2 Mix in the zucchini, cover with wax paper, and microwave on *High* for 8 to 10 minutes or until the zucchini is crisp-tender, stirring once midway. Mix in the bread crumbs and set aside.

3 In a small bowl, combine the eggs, Gruyère cheese, Parmesan cheese, parsley, salt, pepper, and oregano, and pour over the zucchini. Mix well, then smooth evenly in the pie plate. Arrange the tomatoes around the edge of the pie, overlapping the slices slightly.

4 Microwave, uncovered, on *Medium* for 12 to 14 minutes or until a knife inserted in the center of the pie comes out clean. Let the pie stand for 5 minutes before serving. Cut into wedges and top, if you like, with the yogurt. Serves 4.

A slice of Zucchini Pie makes a perfect light lunch.

Outdoor Meals

Nothing boosts an appetite like the great outdoors.
Here are some one-dish meals that are ideally suited to backyard
barbecues, camping trips, or lazy afternoon picnics. With Grilled Chicken
Fajitas, Sunrise Skillet Scramble, Ham 'n' Yam Salad, and other
irresistible recipes, you can enjoy all the goodness of home-cooked food
while eating out. And remember the most important rule of outdoor
dining: if it's made with mayonnaise, keep it cool!

Steak Teriyaki Grill

*Once the steak has marinated for a couple of hours, it cooks
to melting tenderness in a matter of minutes.*

⅓ cup reduced-sodium soy sauce

¼ cup rice wine or dry sherry

2 cloves garlic, minced

1 sirloin or round steak, about
1½ inches thick (2 pounds)

2 packages (10 ounces each)
frozen white and wild rice, rice
pilaf, or other flavored rice

3 tablespoons hot water

6 ounces snow peas, trimmed

Per serving:
Calories 598; Protein 59 g;
Carbohydrates 39 g;
Fat 20 g; Sodium 1,457 mg;
Cholesterol 151 mg

10 minutes   18 minutes

1 Combine the soy sauce, wine, and garlic in a small bowl. Place the steak in a shallow baking dish, add the soy sauce mixture, cover with plastic food wrap, and refrigerate for at least 2 hours.

2 Meanwhile, thaw the rice, remove it from the bags, and place it in a wide-bottomed saucepan with the hot water. Lay the snow peas on top and cover.

3 On a grill set 6 inches above white-hot coals, cook the steak for 5 to 6 minutes on each side for rare, 6 to 7 minutes for medium-rare, or 7 to 8 minutes for medium. (Do not cook beyond medium or the steak will toughen.) Set the saucepan on the grill with the steak for 5 to 10 minutes or until the rice is heated through and the snow peas are crisp-tender.

4 Transfer the steak to a platter, cover, and let stand for 5 minutes. Cut the steak across the grain into thin slices, arrange on a platter, and surround with the rice and snow peas. Serves 4.

*Seaside seasoning: For an extra
dash of flavor, wrap Marinated Beef
Kebabs with sprigs of thyme
before grilling them.*

Marinated Beef Kebabs

The special marinating method used in this recipe is a neat and efficient way to distribute dry seasonings evenly over chunks of meat.

½ teaspoon salt

½ teaspoon dried thyme, crumbled

¼ teaspoon dried marjoram, crumbled

⅛ teaspoon black pepper

1 bay leaf

2 cloves garlic, minced

1 pound beef top round, cut into ¾-inch cubes

8 small new potatoes, unpeeled

1 large sweet red pepper, cored, seeded, quartered, then each quarter cut into thirds

1 medium-size zucchini, cut into 12 equal slices

Per serving:
Calories 299; Protein 24 g;
Carbohydrates 31 g;
Fat 9 g; Sodium 325 mg;
Cholesterol 62 mg

| 20 minutes | 22 minutes |

---

1 Combine ¼ teaspoon of the salt, the thyme, marjoram, black pepper, bay leaf, and garlic in a large self-sealing plastic food storage bag. Add the beef, seal, then massage lightly until the beef is well coated; refrigerate for 2 hours.

2 Meanwhile, cook the potatoes, uncovered, in a large saucepan of boiling water for 10 minutes or until almost tender. Drain, rinse under cold water, then drain well again. Place in a large bowl, add the red pepper and zucchini, sprinkle with the remaining ¼ teaspoon salt, and toss.

3 Thread the beef on four 10-inch metal skewers, alternating with the zucchini, potatoes, and red pepper; discard the bay leaf.

4 On a grill set 6 inches above white-hot coals, cook the kebabs for 10 minutes, turning after 5 minutes. Or, if you prefer, arrange the kebabs on a foil-lined broiler pan and broil 6 inches from the heat of a preheated broiler for 8 minutes, turning once. Serves 4.

Spicy Beef Kebabs Variation

In Step 1, marinate the beef in the plastic bag as directed but using the following mixture: *¼ teaspoon salt, ¾ teaspoon crumbled dried oregano, ½ teaspoon Worcestershire sauce, ¼ teaspoon each ground ginger and allspice, 2 tablespoons finely chopped scallion, ⅛ teaspoon black pepper*, and *2 minced cloves garlic*. Proceed as directed in Step 2, but substitute *2 medium-size peeled sweet potatoes or yams, quartered*, for the new potatoes and boil for 4 minutes only. Continue as directed. Serves 4.

Per serving: Calories 240; Protein 22 g; Carbohydrates 18 g; Fat 9 g; Sodium 198 mg; Cholesterol 62 mg

Oriental Baby Back Ribs

Here's an all-American favorite with a Far Eastern tang. This dish has great make-ahead possibilities, since the ribs must marinate for at least 4 hours (see Step 4).

- 3 large all-purpose potatoes, sliced ¾ inch thick but not peeled
- 4 large carrots, peeled and halved crosswise
- 3 pounds pork baby back ribs, divided into 4 equal portions
- ½ cup reduced-sodium soy sauce
- ¼ cup dry sherry or apple juice
- 3 tablespoons Oriental sesame oil
- ¼ to ½ teaspoon hot red pepper sauce

- 1 tablespoon minced fresh ginger or 1 teaspoon ground ginger
- 2 tablespoons dark brown sugar
- 6 whole cloves, crushed
- 3 cloves garlic, minced

Per serving:
Calories 862; Protein 54 g;
Carbohydrates 48 g;
Fat 52 g; Sodium 1,133 mg;
Cholesterol 167 mg

20 minutes | 58 minutes

1 Cook the potatoes and carrots in a large kettle of boiling water, uncovered, for 12 minutes or until you can pierce them easily with a knife. Using a slotted spoon, transfer the potatoes and carrots to a medium-size bowl, cover with plastic food wrap, and refrigerate.

2 Add the ribs to the kettle, adjust the heat so that the water bubbles gently, and simmer, uncovered, for 30 minutes.

3 Meanwhile, combine the soy sauce, sherry, oil, red pepper sauce, ginger, sugar, cloves, and garlic in a small bowl. Divide the mixture between 2 large self-sealing plastic food storage bags and set aside.

4 When the ribs have cooked for 30 minutes, drain them well, then put half into each plastic bag. Push out all the air from the bags and seal. Lay the bags flat in a large shallow pan, set in the refrigerator, and marinate for 4 to 48 hours, turning the bags occasionally.

5 Coat a barbecue rack with nonstick cooking spray, then set it 6 inches above white-hot coals. Remove the ribs from the plastic bags, reserving the marinade, and place them on the rack. Grill the ribs for 4 minutes, turn, and brush with the marinade.

6 Arrange the potatoes and carrots on either side of the ribs and brush with the marinade. Grill for 8 minutes, turning the ribs and vegetables once and brushing them with more of the marinade. Serves 4.

Oriental Baby Back Ribs: sweet, spicy, and sure to please

Barbecued Ribs 'n' Beans

The sauce used to baste the ribs is excellent for steaks, burgers, and chicken as well. If you're planning a party, just double the recipe.

3½ pounds pork spareribs

½ cup water

2 tablespoons unsalted butter or margarine

1 medium-size yellow onion, finely chopped

1 cup ketchup

1 cup orange juice (freshly squeezed preferred)

⅓ cup cider vinegar

⅓ cup sugar

1½ tablespoons Worcestershire sauce

1 large clove garlic, minced

1 can (1 pound) pork and beans

1 package (10 ounces) frozen cut green beans, thawed and drained

¼ cup molasses

3 tablespoons prepared yellow mustard

Per serving:
Calories 1,031; Protein 54 g;
Carbohydrates 84 g;
Fat 55 g; Sodium 1,437 mg;
Cholesterol 207 mg

| 10 minutes | 1 hr. 15 min. |

---

1 Set a grill 6 inches above white-hot coals. Divide the spareribs into 4 portions, place each on a square of heavy-duty foil large enough to enclose it, and sprinkle each with 2 tablespoons water. Wrap tightly in the foil, sealing the edges. Lay the packets on the grill and cook for 45 minutes, turning once and taking care not to pierce the foil.

2 Meanwhile, melt the butter in a small saucepan on the grill. Add the onion and sauté for 5 minutes or until limp. Stir in the ketchup, orange juice, vinegar, sugar, 1 tablespoon of the Worcestershire sauce, and the garlic. Bring to a simmer, then move the saucepan toward the edge of the grill. Simmer, uncovered, stirring occasionally, for about 25 minutes.

3 Remove the packets from the grill, open, transfer the ribs directly onto the grill, and brush with the ketchup mixture. Grill, turning and basting frequently, until tender and browned—about 30 minutes more.

4 Meanwhile, mix the pork and beans, green beans, molasses, mustard, and remaining ½ tablespoon Worcestershire sauce in a medium-size saucepan, place on the grill, and bring to a simmer. Cook, uncovered, stirring occasionally, for 10 minutes. Arrange the ribs on a platter and spoon the bean mixture on top. Serves 4.

Marinated Chicken Kebabs

A classic Chinese marinade not only gives the chicken a very special flavor but also tenderizes it.

2 tablespoons reduced-sodium soy sauce

1 tablespoon Oriental sesame oil

1 tablespoon dry sherry or apple juice

1 teaspoon ground ginger

1 clove garlic, minced

¼ teaspoon black pepper

1 pound skinned and boned chicken breasts, cut into ¾-inch cubes

12 ounces medium-size new potatoes, unpeeled

2 medium-size zucchini, cut into ¾-inch cubes

12 cherry tomatoes

Per serving:
Calories 188; Protein 21 g;
Carbohydrates 18 g;
Fat 4 g; Sodium 287 mg;
Cholesterol 44 mg

| 20 minutes | 30 minutes |

---

1 Combine the soy sauce, oil, sherry, ginger, garlic, and pepper in a medium-size bowl. Add the chicken, toss until well coated, then cover and refrigerate for 1 hour, stirring occasionally.

2 Meanwhile, cook the potatoes, uncovered, in a large saucepan of boiling water for 15 minutes. Drain well, cool, and halve.

3 Thread the potatoes onto six 14-inch metal skewers, alternating them with the chicken, zucchini, and tomatoes, and dividing all evenly.

4 On a grill set 6 inches above white-hot coals, cook the kebabs for 15 minutes, turning every 5 minutes, or until the chicken is no longer pink on the inside. Serves 6.

Barbecued Chicken with Corn and Sweet Peppers

For variety, you can substitute your favorite marinade for the barbecue sauce. Soaking the corn in water prevents it from catching fire on the grill; to cook corn in foil, see Swordfish Oreganata, page 270.

4 medium-size ears corn, unhusked

1 broiler-fryer (3½ pounds), quartered

2 cloves garlic, minced

½ teaspoon dried rosemary, crumbled

½ teaspoon each salt and black pepper

¼ cup olive oil

4 medium-size sweet red peppers

½ cup bottled barbecue sauce or Basic Barbecue Sauce (page 338)

1 loaf Italian bread, split lengthwise

1 Peel the corn husks back and remove the silks, then smooth the husks back in place and tie with a string. Soak in a large bowl of cold water for 30 minutes.

2 Meanwhile, using paper toweling, pat the chicken quarters dry, then rub the undersides with half the garlic, all of the rosemary, and ¼ teaspoon each of the salt and black pepper. Brush the chicken all over with 2 tablespoons of the oil.

3 On a grill set 6 inches above white-hot coals, place the chicken, skin side down, and surround with the corn and red peppers. Cover with the barbecue lid and grill—turning the chicken, corn, and peppers often—for 10 to 15 minutes or until the peppers are charred.

4 Remove the peppers, wrap or cover with foil, and set aside. Grill the chicken and corn 5 minutes more, then brush both sides of chicken with the barbecue sauce. Grill the chicken and corn 10 to 15 minutes more or until the chicken is no longer pink on the inside.

5 Meanwhile, unwrap the peppers, core, peel, and seed, then cut them lengthwise into 1-inch strips. Brush the cut sides of the bread with the remaining garlic, oil, salt, and black pepper. When the chicken and corn are done, place the bread, cut sides down, on the barbecue and grill until golden—1 to 2 minutes. Arrange the chicken, vegetables, and bread on a large platter. Serves 4.

Per serving:
Calories 1,081; Protein 71 g;
Carbohydrates 101 g;
Fat 43 g; Sodium 1,267 mg;
Cholesterol 176 mg

 20 minutes | 37 minutes

The perfect end to a lazy summer day: Barbecued Chicken with Corn and Sweet Peppers

Mediterranean Grilled Chicken and Vegetables

If your barbecue cannot accommodate everything at once, grill the vegetables first—they can be served at room temperature.

2 tablespoons fresh rosemary leaves or 2 teaspoons dried rosemary, crumbled

2 cloves garlic, minced

1 broiler-fryer (3½ pounds), cut into 8 pieces

4 small whole heads garlic

2 tablespoons plus 2 teaspoons olive oil

⅛ teaspoon black pepper

2 tablespoons minced parsley

2 medium-size tomatoes, peeled, cored, and halved crosswise

1 large eggplant, sliced ¾ inch thick

8 slices French bread, ½ inch thick

> Per serving:
> Calories 801 g; Protein 63 g;
> Carbohydrates 47 g;
> Fat 39 g; Sodium 560 mg;
> Cholesterol 176 mg

20 minutes	1 hour

1 Mix 1½ tablespoons of the fresh rosemary (or 1½ teaspoons of the dried rosemary) with the minced garlic and spread half of the mixture underneath the skin of the chicken. Rub the chicken with the remaining garlic mixture, cover, and refrigerate for at least 2 hours or overnight.

2 Remove and discard the papery outer skin from each head of garlic, leaving the heads intact. Place the garlic heads, remaining rosemary, and the 2 teaspoons oil on a 14-inch-long sheet of heavy-duty foil, and seal tight.

3 Set a grill 6 inches above white-hot coals. Sprinkle the chicken with half of the pepper and place on the grill along with the packet of garlic. Cook, turning often, for 40 minutes or until the chicken is no longer pink on the inside.

4 Meanwhile, mix the 2 tablespoons oil with the parsley and remaining pepper. Brush over the tomatoes and eggplant slices.

5 Move the chicken and packet of garlic to the edge of the grill, then place the tomatoes and eggplant slices in the middle. Grill, turning once, for 15 to 20 minutes or until the eggplant is tender. About 5 minutes before the eggplant is done, add the bread slices and grill, turning once, until lightly browned.

6 Arrange the chicken, tomatoes, eggplant, and bread on a large platter. Separate the heads of garlic into cloves, squeeze each clove to extract the pulp, and spread on the toast and vegetables. Serves 4.

Grilled Chicken Fajitas

A popular Tex-Mex combo that's equally good made with beef or salmon instead of chicken. Whatever you choose, allow time for marinating (Step 1).

- 2 tablespoons olive oil
- ¼ cup lime juice (freshly squeezed preferred)
- 2 cloves garlic, minced
- 1 teaspoon ground cumin
- 1 teaspoon dried oregano, crumbled
- ¼ teaspoon black pepper
- 1 pound skinned and boned chicken breasts
- 1 medium-size ripe avocado, peeled and pitted
- 1 medium-size ripe tomato, cored, seeded, and chopped
- 1 small yellow onion, finely chopped
- 2 tablespoons minced fresh coriander (cilantro) or flat-leaf parsley
- 2 tablespoons finely chopped canned green chili (wash your hands after handling the chili)
- 8 flour tortillas, 8 inches in diameter
- ½ cup prepared salsa or Basic Salsa (page 339)
- ½ cup sour cream

Toppings:
- ½ cup coarsely shredded Monterey Jack or Cheddar cheese (2 ounces)
- ½ cup shredded iceberg lettuce
- ½ cup coarsely chopped cored and seeded ripe tomato

1 Combine the oil, 2 tablespoons of the lime juice, the garlic, cumin, oregano, and pepper in a shallow nonmetallic bowl. Add the chicken, turn to coat, then cover and refrigerate for at least 2 hours or overnight.

2 Mash the avocado in a small bowl with a fork. Stir in the remaining 2 tablespoons lime juice, the tomato, onion, coriander, and chili. Smooth a piece of plastic food wrap flat on the surface of the mixture (to keep it from darkening), then refrigerate until ready to proceed.

3 On a grill set 6 inches above white-hot coals cook the chicken for 5 minutes. Meanwhile, wrap the tortillas in foil.

4 Turn the chicken over, lay the foil bundle on the grill with the chicken, and cook the chicken 5 minutes longer or until no longer pink on the inside.

5 To assemble the fajitas, cut the chicken breasts crosswise into thin slices, then layer on the tortillas along with the avocado mixture, salsa, and sour cream, dividing all equally. Add the toppings, then roll the tortillas to enclose the filling. Serves 4.

> *Per serving:*
> *Calories 602; Protein 38 g;*
> *Carbohydrates 47 g;*
> *Fat 31 g; Sodium 289 mg;*
> *Cholesterol 78 mg*
>
> 40 minutes | 10 minutes

Marinated Pork Kebabs

For the best possible flavor and make-ahead convenience, let the pork marinate in the refrigerator for 24 hours before cooking. Even the sweet potatoes can be boiled a day in advance.

- ¼ cup chili sauce or ketchup
- ¼ cup grape or red currant jelly
- ¼ teaspoon ground allspice
- ⅛ teaspoon ground red pepper (cayenne)
- 1 clove garlic, minced
- 1 pound boneless pork loin, cut into 1-inch cubes
- 2 medium-size sweet potatoes, quartered lengthwise but not peeled
- 1 medium-size red onion, cut into 1-inch cubes
- 2 medium-size zucchini, cut into 1-inch cubes

> *Per serving:*
> *Calories 516; Protein 35 g;*
> *Carbohydrates 63 g;*
> *Fat 14 g; Sodium 301 mg;*
> *Cholesterol 94 mg*
>
> 20 minutes | 30 minutes

1 Combine the chili sauce, jelly, allspice, red pepper, and garlic in a small bowl. Place the pork in a self-sealing plastic food storage bag, add half the chili sauce mixture, push out all the air, and seal. Marinate in the refrigerator for at least 30 minutes or overnight.

2 Meanwhile, cook the sweet potatoes, uncovered, in a medium-size saucepan of boiling water for 12 to 15 minutes or until firm-tender. Drain and set aside.

3 Thread the onion and zucchini cubes on eight 8-inch metal skewers, dividing the total amount evenly and alternating the vegetables. Thread the pork cubes on another four 8-inch metal skewers.

4 Lay the skewers in the center of a grill set 6 inches above white-hot coals, and arrange the potato quarters around the edge. Cook, turning every 5 minutes and brushing with the remaining chili sauce mixture. Allow 15 minutes for the potatoes and vegetable skewers, 10 to 12 minutes for the pork or until it is no longer pink on the inside. Serves 4.

Turkey Burger Bundles

Chutney and fresh coriander give these burgers a sweet, lemony flavor. To cook indoors, preheat the oven to 375° F, place the foil packet on the middle oven rack, and bake for 45 minutes.

- 1 **pound ground turkey**
- 4 **strips bacon, finely chopped**
- 1 **small sweet green pepper, cored, seeded, and finely chopped**
- 1 **small sweet red pepper, cored, seeded, and finely chopped**
- 1 **medium-size yellow onion, finely chopped**
- ¼ **cup minced fresh coriander (cilantro) or flat-leaf parsley**
- ¼ **cup finely chopped chutney**
- ½ **teaspoon each salt and pepper**
- 1 **package (10 ounces) frozen baby lima beans or cut green beans, thawed and drained**
- 1 **package (10 ounces) frozen corn kernels, thawed and drained**
- ½ **cup thin pimiento strips**

1 Mix the turkey with the bacon, green and red peppers, onion, coriander, chutney, and ¼ teaspoon each of the salt and black pepper in a large bowl. Shape into 4 patties and set aside.

2 On a 30-inch-long sheet of heavy-duty foil, toss the lima beans with the corn, pimientos, and remaining salt and pepper. Push the vegetables to the outer edges of the foil, place the burgers in the center, and seal all in a tight bundle.

3 Place the foil packet on a grill set 6 inches above white-hot coals and cook for 25 minutes. Open the packet, turn the burgers, reseal, and cook 20 minutes more. Serves 4.

Per serving:
Calories 326; Protein 34 g; Carbohydrates 34 g; Fat 7 g; Sodium 490 mg; Cholesterol 79 mg

20 minutes	45 minutes

Grilled Chicken Fajitas bring the great taste of the American Southwest into your own backyard.

269

Swordfish Oreganata

A grilled fish recipe that makes a patio-perfect meal. To cook corn in the husks, see Barbecued Chicken with Corn and Sweet Peppers, page 266.

2 tablespoons olive or vegetable oil

1 teaspoon finely grated lime rind

2 tablespoons lime juice (freshly squeezed preferred)

1 tablespoon honey

1 teaspoon reduced-sodium soy sauce

2 teaspoons dried oregano, crumbled

¼ teaspoon salt

¼ teaspoon hot red pepper sauce

4 thick swordfish steaks (1½ pounds)

4 medium-size ears corn, husked

2 tablespoons butter or margarine, melted

1¼ pounds small new potatoes, halved but not peeled

Per serving:
Calories 546; Protein 34 g;
Carbohydrates 64 g;
Fat 19 g; Sodium 416 mg;
Cholesterol 70 mg

| 20 minutes | 30 minutes |

1 Combine the oil, lime rind, lime juice, honey, soy sauce, oregano, salt, and red pepper sauce in a self-sealing plastic food storage bag. Add the swordfish, push out all the air, and seal. Let stand at room temperature for 20 minutes.

2 Meanwhile, place each ear of corn on a piece of heavy-duty foil, brush with the butter, and wrap tightly in the foil.

3 Cook the potatoes, uncovered, in a large saucepan of boiling water for 10 minutes or until tender. Drain well, then thread on four 8-inch metal skewers, dividing the total amount evenly.

4 Meanwhile, on a grill set 6 inches above white-hot coals, cook the corn for 20 minutes, turning one time.

5 Remove the swordfish steaks from the marinade, place on the grill alongside the corn, then place the potato skewers on the grill. Cook for 5 minutes, turn the swordfish, corn, and potato skewers, and grill another 5 minutes. Serves 4.

Fish Steak and Vegetable Packets

Delicious and healthful, this grilled fish dish will become one of your family's favorite meals and an ideal choice when guests are due. The sesame seeds add a distinctive crunch and flavor (directions for toasting them are on page 86).

4 thick halibut or cod steaks (1½ pounds)

4 medium-size carrots, peeled and thinly sliced

1 medium-size zucchini, thinly sliced

8 ounces medium-size mushrooms, thinly sliced

8 scallions, including tops, thinly sliced

3 tablespoons lemon juice (freshly squeezed preferred)

⅛ teaspoon black pepper

4 teaspoons olive oil

2 tablespoons toasted sesame seeds

1 loaf crusty Italian bread, thickly sliced

2 tablespoons butter or olive oil

Per serving:
Calories 763; Protein 53 g;
Carbohydrates 84 g;
Fat 27 g; Sodium 778 mg;
Cholesterol 100 mg

| 25 minutes | 15 minutes |

1 Tear off four 16-inch-long pieces of heavy-duty foil and place a fish steak in the middle of each one. Top each with ¼ of the carrots, zucchini, mushrooms, and scallions. Sprinkle with the lemon juice, pepper, oil, and sesame seeds, dividing all amounts evenly, and seal the foil into packets.

2 Place the packets on a grill set 6 inches above white-hot coals and cook for 15 minutes without turning, until the vegetables are tender and the fish flakes at the touch of a fork.

3 A few minutes before the fish is done, brush the bread slices with the butter, place on the grill, and toast lightly. Open the packets and accompany with the toast. Serves 4.

Marinated Shrimp Barbecue

If you substitute sea scallops, cut them into 1-inch cubes and grill them for about 2 minutes less. This recipe can easily be doubled if company's coming.

For the shrimp:

- ¼ cup water
- ¼ cup lemon juice (freshly squeezed preferred)
- 1 teaspoon finely grated lemon rind
- 2 tablespoons olive or vegetable oil
- ½ cup minced parsley
- 3 cloves garlic, minced
- ¼ teaspoon hot red pepper sauce
- ¼ teaspoon salt
- 1¼ pounds medium-size shrimp, shelled and deveined
- 1 loaf crusty Italian bread

For the vegetable packets:

- 2 medium-size zucchini, halved crosswise and cut lengthwise into strips ¼ inch wide
- 2 medium-size sweet red peppers, cored, seeded, and cut into 3″ x ¼″ x ¼″ strips
- 2 tablespoons olive or vegetable oil
- 2 tablespoons minced fresh mint or parsley
- ½ teaspoon salt
- 2 cloves garlic, minced

Per serving:
Calories 616; Protein 40 g;
Carbohydrates 73 g;
Fat 16 g; Sodium 1,192 mg;
Cholesterol 196 mg

30 minutes

18 minutes

1 *For the shrimp:* Combine the water, lemon juice, lemon rind, oil, parsley, garlic, red pepper sauce, and salt in a self-sealing plastic food storage bag. Add the shrimp, push out all the air, seal, and marinate at room temperature for 20 to 45 minutes.

2 *For the vegetable packets:* On four 18-inch-long sheets of heavy-duty foil, mound the zucchini and red peppers, dividing the total amount evenly. Sprinkle with the oil, mint, salt, and garlic, again dividing the total amount evenly. Seal the foil into packets.

3 On a grill set 6 inches above white-hot coals, cook the vegetable packets for 18 minutes. Meanwhile, thread the shrimp onto eight 8-inch metal skewers and set aside. Reserve the marinade.

4 Place the shrimp skewers on the grill after the vegetables have cooked for 10 minutes. Cook along with the vegetables for 4 minutes on one side, then turn, brush with the marinade, and grill 4 minutes more or until the shrimp are cooked through and the vegetables are tender.

5 Serve the shrimp and vegetable packets with chunks of crusty Italian bread and a small bowl of the remaining marinade in which to dunk the bread. Serves 4.

Marinated Shrimp Barbecue: The lime and garlic marinade makes a superb dipping sauce for the bread.

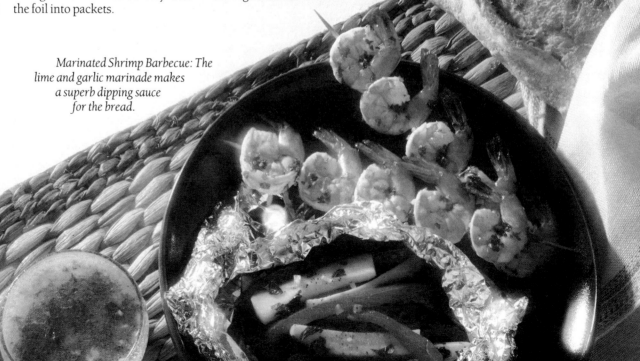

Sundown Stew

The aroma of beef simmering in gravy will summon hikers to dinner long before it's even time to add the dumplings.

2 tablespoons vegetable oil

1 pound lean boneless chuck steak (1 inch thick), cut crosswise into strips ¼ inch wide

1 envelope (¾ ounce) mushroom gravy mix

1 cup water

4 medium-size carrots, peeled and thickly sliced

2 cups fresh or 1 package (10 ounces) frozen green peas, unthawed

2 cups biscuit mix

⅔ cup low-fat milk

Per serving:
Calories 648; Protein 45 g;
Carbohydrates 62 g;
Fat 24 g; Sodium 1,227 mg;
Cholesterol 105 mg

10 minutes

1 hr. 34 min.

1 Heat the oil in a large saucepan over moderate heat for 1 minute. Add the steak and brown well on all sides—about 10 minutes.

2 Combine the gravy mix and water in a small bowl or by shaking in a self-sealing plastic food storage bag. Stir into the saucepan and bring to a simmer. Cook, stirring occasionally, for 2 minutes.

3 Add the carrots, adjust the heat so that the mixture bubbles gently, cover, and simmer for 1 hour or until the beef is almost tender. Stir in the peas.

4 Combine the biscuit mix and milk in a small bowl or plastic bag and drop by tablespoonfuls onto the simmering stew. Cover and cook for 10 minutes, then uncover and cook 10 minutes more. Serves 4.

Sundown Stew: Double the recipe for a crew of hungry campers.

Sausage 'n' Beans

A satisfying stew that's simple to prepare and perfect for campsite consumption.

1 tablespoon vegetable oil

1 medium-size yellow onion, thinly sliced

1 pound kielbasa, frankfurters, or knockwurst, sliced ¼ inch thick

2 cans (1 pound each) barbecued baked beans, drained

⅔ cup water

2 tablespoons tomato paste

2 tablespoons Dijon mustard or to taste

½ teaspoon dried thyme, crumbled

¼ teaspoon each salt and black pepper

2 medium-size yellow squash (or 1 zucchini and 1 yellow squash), halved lengthwise and sliced ½ inch thick

1 Heat the oil in a large saucepan over moderate heat for 1 minute. Add the onion and kielbasa, cover, and cook, stirring occasionally, for 5 minutes.

2 Add the beans, water, tomato paste, mustard, thyme, salt, and pepper. Bring the mixture to a boil, cover, adjust the heat so that the mixture bubbles gently, and simmer, stirring occasionally, for 8 minutes.

3 Add the squash, cover, and simmer 5 to 7 minutes more or until it is tender. Serves 4.

Per serving:
Calories 593; Protein 27 g;
Carbohydrates 57 g;
Fat 32 g; Sodium 2,273 mg;
Cholesterol 65 mg

15 minutes	22 minutes

Sunrise Skillet Scramble

A hearty outdoor beef and potato combo with few bulky packages to carry along. Dehydrated ingredients are often available at sporting goods stores that sell camping supplies.

3 tablespoons unsalted butter or margarine

1 package (5 ounces) dehydrated shredded potatoes, soaked in 3½ cups boiling water for 15 minutes and drained

1 package (5 ounces) dried chipped beef, rinsed in cold water, patted dry, and coarsely chopped

2 tablespoons freeze-dried chives

¼ teaspoon black pepper

4 firm ripe plum tomatoes

1 package (2 ounces) dehydrated scrambled egg mix

1 cup cold water

2 tablespoons parsley flakes

1 Melt 2 tablespoons of the butter in a 12-inch nonstick skillet over moderate heat. Add the potatoes, beef, chives, and pepper, and cook, uncovered, stirring occasionally, for 5 to 7 minutes or until heated through. Transfer to a large piece of wax paper or plastic food wrap and set aside.

2 Meanwhile, halve the tomatoes lengthwise, squeeze to remove juice and seeds, and cut into ¼-inch slices. Set aside.

3 Blend the egg mix with the water in a small bowl or by shaking in a self-sealing plastic food storage bag.

4 Melt the remaining 1 tablespoon butter in the skillet over moderate heat, add the potato mixture, then stir in the egg mixture to coat. Sprinkle with the parsley flakes, reduce the heat to moderately low, and cover. Cook for 3 to 4 minutes or until set, arranging the tomatoes in concentric circles on top for the last 1 to 2 minutes or until heated through. Cut into wedges. Serves 4.

Per serving:
Calories 310; Protein 22 g;
Carbohydrates 29 g;
Fat 12 g; Sodium 1,361 mg;
Cholesterol 137 mg

15 minutes	13 minutes

Pan-Fried Trout

Here's a meal to make fishermen proud and diners delighted. The recipe can easily be halved.

- 1 cup couscous
- 4 brook or rainbow trout (12 ounces each), cleaned and pan ready
- ½ teaspoon each salt and black pepper
- 4 rosemary or thyme sprigs (optional)
- 4 large, firm ripe tomatoes, cored
- ¼ cup vegetable or olive oil
- 2 tablespoons unsalted butter or margarine
- 2 tablespoons minced parsley (optional)
- 4 lemon wedges

> **Per serving:**
> Calories 819; Protein 60 g;
> Carbohydrates 45 g;
> Fat 46 g; Sodium 460 mg;
> Cholesterol 15 mg

 10 minutes   24 minutes

1 Prepare the couscous according to package directions, then cover to keep warm.

2 Meanwhile, using paper toweling, pat the fish dry. Sprinkle with half the salt and pepper, tuck a sprig of rosemary inside each fish if desired, and set aside. Halve the tomatoes and sprinkle the cut sides with the remaining salt and pepper.

3 Heat 2 tablespoons of the oil and 1 tablespoon of the butter in a 12-inch nonstick skillet over moderate heat for 2 minutes or until the butter is golden brown. Add 2 of the fish and 4 of the tomato halves, arranging the tomatoes cut sides down.

4 Fry the fish and tomatoes together, allowing 3 to 4 minutes per side for the tomatoes and 4 to 5 minutes per side for the fish. As the tomatoes and fish are done, transfer them to a platter, cover, and keep warm. Fry the remaining fish and tomatoes the same way in the remaining oil and butter.

5 Sprinkle the fish and tomatoes with the parsley if desired, then accompany with the lemon wedges and couscous. Serves 4.

A scooped-out cantaloupe is an attractive portable picnic dish for Chicken and Fruit Salad.

Picnic Salad

Enriched with chicken, this refreshing coleslaw can also be made with turkey, ham, or shellfish.

- 1 small head green or red cabbage, coarsely shredded (4 cups)
- 3 cups diced cooked chicken
- 2 cups cooked or drained canned cut green beans
- 2 medium-size carrots, peeled and coarsely shredded
- 1 medium-size red onion, finely chopped
- 1 medium-size sweet red pepper, cored, seeded, and finely chopped
- 2 tablespoons snipped fresh dill, chives, or minced parsley

For the dressing:
- 2 tablespoons white wine vinegar or cider vinegar
- 2 teaspoons Dijon mustard
- 1 teaspoon celery seeds
- ¼ teaspoon each salt, black pepper, and sugar
- ⅔ cup reduced-calorie mayonnaise

> **Per serving:**
> Calories 359; Protein 36 g;
> Carbohydrates 20 g;
> Fat 15 g; Sodium 277 mg;
> Cholesterol 103 mg

 25 minutes   None

1 Place the cabbage, chicken, beans, carrots, onion, red pepper, and dill in a large bowl and toss well.

2 *For the dressing:* Combine the vinegar, mustard, celery seeds, salt, black pepper, and sugar in a small bowl. Whisk in the mayonnaise, pour over the cabbage mixture, and toss gently. Cover and refrigerate until ready to serve. Serves 4.

Chicken and Fruit Salad

*A time-saving tip: Prepare the creamy dressing
for this refreshing dish ahead of time.*

2 small cantaloupes, halved and seeded

8 ounces snow peas, trimmed

1 cup quick-cooking brown rice, cooked according to package directions

3 cups diced cooked chicken

1 can (1 pound 4 ounces) pineapple chunks, drained

4 scallions, including tops, finely chopped

For the dressing:

½ cup plain low-fat yogurt

½ cup reduced-calorie mayonnaise

3 tablespoons lemon juice (freshly squeezed preferred)

2 teaspoons curry powder

½ teaspoon salt

¼ teaspoon black pepper

3 tablespoons minced fresh coriander (cilantro) or flat-leaf parsley

1 Using a melon baller, scoop out balls from the cantaloupes, placing them in a large bowl. Wrap the scooped-out melon halves in plastic food wrap.

2 Cook the snow peas, uncovered, in a large saucepan of boiling water for 1 minute or until crisp-tender. Drain, rinse under cool water, drain again, then slice crosswise into strips ¼ inch wide.

3 Add the snow peas, rice, chicken, pineapple, and scallions to the bowl with the cantaloupe balls; toss lightly. Transfer the mixture to a plastic container and snap the lid on tight.

4 *For the dressing:* In a large measuring cup, whisk together the yogurt, mayonnaise, lemon juice, curry powder, salt, pepper, and coriander until smooth. Pour the dressing into a plastic container and snap the lid on tight.

5 Refrigerate the melon halves, chicken mixture, and dressing until ready to transport. To serve, mound the mixture in the cantaloupe halves and pass the dressing. Serves 4.

> **Per serving:**
> *Calories 510; Protein 41 g;
> Carbohydrates 58 g;
> Fat 14 g; Sodium 382 mg;
> Cholesterol 101 mg*

 15 minutes   3 minutes

Red and Green Slaw with Ham

*To make short shrift of slicing the cabbage, use the food processor. For a change
of pace, substitute diced kielbasa or Cheddar cheese for the ham.*

1 small head red cabbage, thinly sliced (4 cups)

1 small head green cabbage, thinly sliced (4 cups)

1 package (10 ounces) frozen baby lima beans, unthawed

1 cup frozen corn kernels, unthawed (optional)

1 medium-size sweet green pepper, cored, seeded, and thinly sliced

1 medium-size red onion, thinly sliced

⅓ cup mayonnaise

⅓ cup sour cream or plain low-fat yogurt

3 tablespoons cider vinegar

1 tablespoon Dijon or spicy brown mustard

1 teaspoon sugar

¾ teaspoon salt

½ teaspoon caraway seeds

3 cups diced boiled or baked ham

1 Place the red and green cabbage in a large colander and set in the sink. Cook the lima beans, uncovered, in a large saucepan of boiling water for 10 minutes, adding the corn, if using, for the last 3 minutes. Add the pepper and onion to the saucepan, then pour all into the colander with the cabbage; drain well.

2 In a large serving bowl, whisk the mayonnaise with the sour cream, vinegar, mustard, sugar, salt, and caraway seeds until blended.

3 Add the cabbage mixture and toss well to mix. Sprinkle with the ham, chill for several hours and serve cold. Serves 6.

> **Per serving:**
> *Calories 335; Protein 18 g;
> Carbohydrates 22 g;
> Fat 21 g; Sodium 1,326 mg;
> Cholesterol 52 mg*

 20 minutes   10 minutes

Ham 'n' Yam Salad

*The dressing will be ready when you are if you make it a day in advance
and store it in the refrigerator in a tightly sealed container.*

8 ounces large new potatoes

8 ounces small yams or sweet potatoes

½ cup cottage cheese

⅓ cup plain low-fat yogurt

2 tablespoons reduced-calorie mayonnaise

4 teaspoons Dijon mustard

1 teaspoon balsamic or cider vinegar

1 teaspoon dried rosemary, crumbled

½ teaspoon lemon juice (freshly squeezed preferred)

½ teaspoon salt

¼ teaspoon black pepper

1 pound boiled or baked ham, cut into ½-inch cubes

1 large sweet green pepper, cored, seeded, and coarsely chopped

2 medium-size stalks celery, thinly sliced

1 cup thinly sliced radishes

Per serving:
Calories 390; Protein 27 g;
Carbohydrates 34 g;
Fat 16 g; Sodium 1,972 mg;
Cholesterol 71 mg

20 minutes   20 minutes

1 Cook the potatoes and yams together, uncovered, in a large saucepan of boiling water until firm-tender—about 20 minutes. Drain, let cool until easy to handle, peel, and cut into 1-inch cubes. Transfer to a large bowl and set aside.

2 Purée the cottage cheese in a food processor or an electric blender at high speed for about 1 minute or until smooth. Add the yogurt, mayonnaise, mustard, vinegar, rosemary, lemon juice, salt, and black pepper, and whirl for 10 to 15 seconds to blend well.

3 Pour over the potatoes, then add the ham, green pepper, celery, and radishes; toss well. Serves 4.

*The irresistible combination
in Ham 'n' Yam Salad makes
it a picnic-perfect choice.*

Rigatoni with Tuna, Tomatoes, and Broccoli

A picnic dish that traces its roots to Sicily.

1 pound rigatoni, ziti, or medium-size pasta shells

1 large bunch broccoli, cut into florets, stems peeled and thickly sliced

¼ cup olive oil

2 tablespoons balsamic or red wine vinegar

1 tablespoon Dijon mustard

¼ teaspoon black pepper

1 can (2 ounces) flat anchovy fillets, drained and finely chopped (optional)

3 scallions, including tops, coarsely chopped

2 medium-size ripe tomatoes, cored and cut into eighths

1 can (6½ ounces) Italian-style tuna or tuna in water, drained and flaked

¼ cup minced parsley

1 Cook the rigatoni according to package directions, adding the broccoli after 5 minutes.

2 Meanwhile, whisk the oil in a small bowl with the vinegar, mustard, and pepper until smooth. Stir in the anchovies if desired.

3 When the broccoli and rigatoni are tender, drain well, reserving ¼ cup of the cooking water. Place the broccoli and rigatoni in a large bowl.

4 Pour the the oil mixture and cooking water over the broccoli and rigatoni and toss well. Add the scallions, tomatoes, tuna, and parsley, and toss again. Serve at room temperature or slightly chilled. Serves 4.

Per serving:
Calories 638; Protein 29 g;
Carbohydrates 91 g;
Fat 16 g; Sodium 259 mg;
Cholesterol 19 mg

| 20 minutes | 12 minutes |

Tortellini Salad

You can vary this salad by using Italian green beans instead of peas and ravioli instead of tortellini.

3 tablespoons olive oil

2 large sweet red peppers, cored and seeded, 1 thinly sliced, 1 diced

2 medium-size yellow onions, thinly sliced

3 cloves garlic, minced

1 pound cheese or meat tortellini

1 cup frozen green peas, thawed and drained

1½ tablespoons red wine vinegar

½ cup Basic Chicken Stock (page 333) or canned chicken broth

¼ cup unblanched whole almonds

½ teaspoon salt

1 Heat 1 tablespoon of the oil in a 10-inch skillet over moderate heat for 1 minute. Add the sliced pepper, onions, and garlic, cover, and cook for 15 minutes, stirring occasionally, or until mushy.

2 Meanwhile, cook the tortellini according to package directions. About 1 minute before the tortellini is done, add the peas and diced pepper to the pot and cook, uncovered, for the final minute. Drain, rinse well, and place in a large bowl.

3 Transfer the skillet mixture to a food processor or an electric blender, add the vinegar, stock, almonds, salt, and remaining 2 tablespoons oil, and purée for 1 minute or until smooth. Add to the bowl and toss well to mix. Serves 4 to 6.

Per serving:
Calories 543; Protein 24 g;
Carbohydrates 69 g;
Fat 20 g; Sodium 843 mg;
Cholesterol 62 mg

| 10 minutes | 16 minutes |

Country Meat Loaf Sandwiches

If you're planning a picnic for four, you can use just one loaf of bread and only half of the meat loaf; freeze the other half for a quick supper.

- 1 tablespoon olive oil
- 1 medium-size yellow onion, finely chopped
- 1 small sweet green pepper, cored, seeded, and finely chopped
- 1 small sweet red pepper, cored, seeded, and finely chopped
- 1 clove garlic, minced
- ½ teaspoon each dried basil and thyme, crumbled
- 1 large egg

- 1 pound lean ground beef
- 4 ounces lean ground veal or pork
- 1 cup frozen corn kernels, unthawed
- ½ cup old-fashioned rolled oats
- 2 ounces part-skim mozzarella cheese, cut into ¼-inch cubes
- ¼ cup grated Parmesan cheese
- ½ teaspoon salt
- ⅛ teaspoon black pepper
- ¼ cup ketchup
- 2 loaves crusty Italian bread, split lengthwise

> Per serving:
> Calories 579; Protein 37 g;
> Carbohydrates 76 g;
> Fat 12 g; Sodium 939 mg;
> Cholesterol 95 mg

20 minutes	59 minutes

1 Preheat the oven to 375° F. Heat the oil in a 10-inch skillet over moderate heat for 1 minute. Add the onion and sauté for 3 minutes. Add the green and red peppers, garlic, basil, and thyme, and sauté, stirring occasionally, for 5 minutes or until the vegetables are limp; set aside.

2 Beat the egg in a large bowl until frothy. Add the beef, veal, corn, oats, mozzarella cheese, Parmesan, salt, black pepper, and skillet mixture. Mix well with your hands, then pat into a lightly greased 9" x 5" x 3" loaf pan.

3 Bake, uncovered, for 25 minutes. Remove the pan from the oven and brush the top of the meat loaf with the ketchup. Return to the oven and bake, uncovered, 25 minutes more or until the loaf is no longer pink on the inside. Let stand for 10 minutes, then cut into ¼-inch slices, arrange along the bottom half of each loaf of bread, and cover with the tops. Cut each loaf into 4 pieces. Serves 8.

Picnic rained out? Serve these Country Meat Loaf Sandwiches warm at home.

278

Magic with Leftovers

Just because food is making its second appearance on your table doesn't
mean it can't be first-rate. With a pinch of patience and a dash of ingenuity, we've
taken yesterday's extras and transformed them into today's extra-special treats.
From Monday Hash to Post-Thanksgiving Turkey Soup, these dishes are so sensational
that you may find yourself cooking more than you need just so you'll be able
to enjoy an encore. And remember: even if you don't have leftovers,
any of these nifty, thrifty meals can be made from scratch.

Spaghetti with Creamy Chicken-Mushroom Sauce

*Here's a smooth and soothing meal that's destined
to be a winner any night of the week.*

- 2 **tablespoons unsalted butter or margarine**
- 2 **shallots or scallions, including tops, or 1 medium-size yellow onion, finely chopped**
- 8 **ounces mushrooms, thinly sliced**
- 1½ **cups Basic Chicken Stock (page 333) or canned low-sodium chicken broth**
- 12 **ounces spaghetti or other long, thin pasta**
- ½ **cup half-and-half, whole milk, or evaporated skim milk**
- 4 **teaspoons cornstarch**
- 2 **cups diced leftover cooked chicken**
- 1 **package (10 ounces) frozen green peas, thawed and drained**
- 2 **teaspoons Dijon mustard**
- ¼ **teaspoon each salt and black pepper**
- 2 **tablespoons snipped fresh dill or ½ teaspoon dill weed**
- ¼ **cup grated Parmesan cheese (optional)**

1 Melt the butter in a 10-inch non-stick skillet over moderate heat. Add the shallots and sauté, stirring, for 1 minute. Add the mushrooms and sauté, stirring occasionally, for 3 minutes or until limp.

2 Pour in the stock, bring to a boil, then adjust the heat so that the mixture bubbles gently. Simmer, uncovered, stirring occasionally, for 5 minutes.

3 Meanwhile, cook the spaghetti according to package directions. Also blend the half-and-half with the cornstarch in a small bowl.

4 Whisk the cornstarch mixture into the skillet and cook, stirring constantly, for 2 to 3 minutes or until thickened. Mix in the chicken, peas, mustard, salt, and pepper. Simmer, uncovered, stirring occasionally, for 5 minutes, then stir in the dill.

5 Drain the spaghetti well, transfer to a large serving bowl, add the skillet mixture, and toss well. Accompany with the cheese if desired. Serves 4.

Per serving:
Calories 633; Protein 41 g;
Carbohydrates 85 g;
Fat 13 g; Sodium 395 mg;
Cholesterol 86 mg

15 minutes | 20 minutes

Creamed Chicken and Biscuits

*Chicken drowned in velvety white sauce has always been a basic
comfort food; here biscuits add a southern touch.*

- 3 **tablespoons unsalted butter or margarine**
- 1 **medium-size yellow onion, finely chopped**
- 1 **small sweet green pepper, cored, seeded, and finely chopped**
- 3 **tablespoons all-purpose flour**
- 1 **cup Basic Chicken Stock (page 333) or canned low-sodium chicken broth**
- 1 **cup milk**
- 2 **cups diced leftover cooked chicken**
- 2 **cups mixed leftover cooked vegetables (any combination) or 2 cups frozen mixed vegetables, partially thawed and drained**
- 2 **tablespoons minced parsley**
- 2 **tablespoons snipped fresh dill or ½ teaspoon dill weed**
- ¼ **teaspoon each salt and black pepper**
- 8 **leftover biscuits or dinner rolls, heated and split, or 4 slices white or whole wheat toast or 4 English muffins, split and toasted**

1 Melt the butter in a large saucepan over moderately low heat. Add the onion and green pepper and sauté, stirring occasionally, for 10 minutes or until very soft.

2 Blend in the flour and cook, stirring constantly, for 2 minutes. Gradually whisk in the stock and milk, adjust the heat so that the mixture bubbles gently, then cook, stirring constantly, until thickened—3 to 5 minutes.

3 Mix in the chicken, vegetables, parsley, dill, salt, and black pepper. Bring to a simmer, adjust the heat so that the mixture bubbles gently, then simmer, uncovered, for 5 minutes. Ladle over the biscuits. Serves 4.

*Pinwheel Chicken Pot Pie:
pot pie never looked—or
tasted—so good.*

Per serving:
Calories 533; Protein 33 g;
Carbohydrates 48 g;
Fat 23 g; Sodium 663 mg;
Cholesterol 91 mg

20 minutes | 25 minutes

Pinwheel Chicken Pot Pie

To save time, you can make the scallion and pimiento mixtures ahead. Refrigerate them in small bowls covered with plastic food wrap until ready to use.

2 tablespoons vegetable oil

2 tablespoons butter or margarine

1 large yellow onion, finely chopped

6 tablespoons all-purpose flour

1 teaspoon dried rosemary, crumbled

½ teaspoon salt

¼ teaspoon black pepper

1¾ cups Basic Chicken Stock (page 333) or canned low-sodium chicken broth

1 cup low-fat milk

2½ cups diced leftover cooked chicken

1 package (10 ounces) frozen cut green beans, thawed and drained

1 package (10 ounces) frozen sliced carrots, thawed and drained

1 package (10 ounces) frozen corn kernels, thawed and drained

For the topping:

1 scallion, including top, finely chopped

2 tablespoons minced fresh coriander (cilantro) or flat-leaf parsley

2 tablespoons chopped pimiento

2 tablespoons grated Parmesan cheese

1 package (8 ounces) refrigerated crescent roll dough

1 Preheat the oven to 400° F. Heat the oil and butter in a large saucepan over moderate heat for 1 minute. Add the onion and sauté, stirring occasionally, for 3 to 5 minutes or until soft.

2 Blend in the flour, rosemary, salt, and pepper, and cook, stirring, for 2 minutes. Gradually stir in the stock and milk, then cook, stirring constantly, for 3 minutes or until thickened. Mix in the chicken, beans, carrots, and corn. Reduce the heat to its lowest point, cover, and simmer for 5 to 8 minutes while you prepare the topping.

3 *For the topping:* Combine the scallion and coriander in one bowl, and the pimiento and cheese in another. Unroll the crescent roll dough and divide into 4 rectangles by keeping each 2 triangles attached. Spread 2 rectangles with the scallion mixture and 2 with the pimiento mixture. Starting at the narrow end, roll up each rectangle, jelly-roll style, and cut into 4 slices.

4 Transfer the chicken mixture to a 2-quart round casserole and arrange the dough pinwheels on top, alternating the colors.

5 Set the casserole on a baking sheet and bake, uncovered, for 20 to 25 minutes or until the pinwheels are lightly browned and the chicken mixture is bubbling. (If the pinwheels brown too fast, cover the casserole loosely with foil.) Let stand for 10 minutes before serving. Serves 4.

Per serving:
Calories 669; Protein 42 g;
Carbohydrates 64 g;
Fat 29 g; Sodium 1,108 mg;
Cholesterol 95 mg

45 minutes | 44 minutes

Hot Chicken Salad

Here's a beautiful biscuit-topped salad that's not only a fine family dinner but also a perfect buffet centerpiece. When company's expected, simply double the recipe.

- 2 tablespoons vegetable oil
- 2 medium-size stalks celery, finely diced
- 1 small sweet red pepper, cored, seeded, and finely diced
- 3 scallions, including tops, or 1 small yellow onion, finely chopped
- 2 tablespoons all-purpose flour
- 1 cup skim or low-fat milk
- ½ cup reduced-calorie mayonnaise
- ⅓ cup grated Parmesan cheese
- 2 cups diced leftover cooked chicken or turkey
- 1 medium-size zucchini, finely diced, or 1 package (10 ounces) frozen chopped broccoli or cut green beans, thawed and drained
- ¼ teaspoon black pepper
- 1 package (8 ounces) refrigerator biscuits

1 Preheat the oven to 400° F. Heat the oil in a 12-inch nonstick skillet over moderate heat for 1 minute. Add the celery, red pepper, and scallions, and sauté, stirring, for 1 minute or until slightly softened.

2 Blend in the flour and cook and stir for 1 minute. Add the milk and cook, stirring constantly, until thickened—about 3 minutes.

3 Remove from the heat and mix in the mayonnaise, ¼ cup of the cheese, the chicken, zucchini, and black pepper. Transfer all to a lightly greased shallow 2-quart casserole, sprinkle with the remaining cheese, then arrange the biscuits on top.

4 Bake, uncovered, for 15 to 20 minutes or until the chicken mixture is bubbling and the biscuits are nicely browned. Serves 4.

Per serving:
Calories 528; Protein 33 g;
Carbohydrates 39 g;
Fat 27 g; Sodium 956 mg;
Cholesterol 77 mg

15 minutes | 26 minutes

Chicken Chow Mein

An ideal way to use up leftover chicken.

- 2 tablespoons vegetable or peanut oil
- 1 medium-size yellow onion, finely chopped
- 2 cups diced leftover cooked chicken
- 2 cloves garlic, minced
- 2 cans (1 pound each) Chinese vegetables, drained and rinsed
- 1 cup Basic Chicken Stock (page 333) or canned low-sodium chicken broth
- 2 tablespoons reduced-sodium soy sauce
- 2 teaspons Oriental sesame oil
- 2 teaspoons cornstarch
- 2 cans (3 ounces each) chow mein noodles

1 Heat the vegetable oil in a wok or deep 12-inch skillet over moderately high heat for 1 minute. Add the onion and sauté, stirring, for 1 minute.

2 Add the chicken and garlic and sauté, stirring, for 2 minutes. Add the vegetables and cook, stirring, 3 minutes more or until the vegetables are heated through.

3 Meanwhile, combine the stock, soy sauce, sesame oil, and cornstarch in a small bowl, then stir into the chicken mixture. Cook, stirring constantly, for 2 to 3 minutes or until the sauce is slightly thickened.

4 Arrange the chow mein noodles on 4 dinner plates and ladle the skillet mixture on top. Serves 4.

Per serving:
Calories 539; Protein 36 g;
Carbohydrates 50 g;
Fat 23 g; Sodium 796 mg;
Cholesterol 64 mg

10 minutes | 10 minutes

Oriental Fried Rice

If you prefer, substitute pork or shrimp for the chicken.

- **1** cup long-grain white or brown rice
- **3** tablespoons vegetable oil
- **2** medium-size stalks celery, thinly sliced
- **2** cups diced leftover cooked chicken
- **1** to 2 cups leftover cooked green peas or 1 package (10 ounces) frozen green peas, thawed and drained
- **1** can (8 ounces) sliced water chestnuts, drained
- **1** carrot, shredded (optional)
- **1½** tablespoons reduced-sodium soy sauce
- **2** large eggs, lightly beaten
- **2** scallions, including tops, finely chopped

1 Cook the rice according to package directions and set aside. Heat the oil in a wok or deep 12-inch skillet over moderate heat for 1 minute. Add the celery and stir-fry for 2 minutes.

2 Mix in the rice, chicken, peas, water chestnuts, carrot if desired, and soy sauce. Cook, uncovered, stirring frequently, for 5 to 7 minutes or until heated through.

3 Stir in the eggs and cook, stirring constantly, just until the eggs are set—about 1 minute. Sprinkle with the scallions. Serves 4.

Per serving:
Calories 562; Protein 33 g;
Carbohydrates 70 g;
Fat 16 g; Sodium 398 mg;
Cholesterol 166 mg

15 minutes | 31 minutes

When leftover chicken, rice, or peas go into Oriental Fried Rice, the result is pure magic.

Family-Style Chicken

For variety, try this dish over noodles or boiled potatoes instead of rice.

1 cup long-grain white rice

2 tablespoons olive or vegetable oil

4 large cloves garlic, minced

4 large scallions, including tops, finely chopped (½ cup)

3 tablespoons all-purpose flour

2 cups Basic Chicken Stock (page 333) or canned low-sodium chicken broth

½ cup minced parsley

1 cup frozen green peas, thawed and drained

2 medium-size zucchini, cut into ½-inch cubes

½ teaspoon salt

¼ teaspoon black pepper

2 cups diced leftover cooked chicken

Per serving:
Calories 434; Protein 32 g;
Carbohydrates 54 g;
Fat 10 g; Sodium 489 mg;
Cholesterol 59 mg

 20 minutes 20 minutes

1 Cook the rice according to package directions. Meanwhile, heat the oil in a large saucepan over moderate heat for 1 minute. Add the garlic and scallions and sauté, stirring constantly, for 2 minutes or until slightly softened.

2 Blend in the flour and cook, stirring constantly, for 1 minute. Gradually whisk in the stock, adjust the heat so that the mixture bubbles gently, then cook, stirring constantly, until thickened—3 to 5 minutes.

3 Add the parsley, peas, zucchini, salt, and pepper. Cook, uncovered, stirring occasionally, for 5 minutes. Mix in the chicken and cook, uncovered, stirring occasionally, just until heated through—about 2 minutes longer.

4 Mound the rice on a small platter and ladle the chicken mixture on top. Serves 4.

Spring color and sprightly flavor make Family-Style Chicken a merry dish for family and friends.

284

Chicken Patties

*Crisp and golden-brown, these patties are also good
smothered with white sauce or leftover gravy.*

- 2 cups leftover mashed potatoes
- 2 cups finely chopped leftover cooked chicken
- 1½ cups frozen peas and carrots, thawed and drained
- 2 scallions, including tops, finely chopped
- 1 large egg
- ½ teaspoon salt
- ½ teaspoon dried rosemary, crumbled
- ½ cup plain dry bread crumbs
- 2 tablespoons vegetable or olive oil
- 1 lemon, cut into thin wedges

Per serving:
Calories 389; Protein 29 g;
Carbohydrates 36 g;
Fat 16 g; Sodium 777 mg;
Cholesterol 115 mg

15 minutes | 12 minutes

1 Preheat the oven to 400° F. Mix the potatoes, chicken, peas and carrots, scallions, egg, salt, and rosemary in a large bowl. Shape into 8 patties, each about 5 inches in diameter, then dredge on both sides in the bread crumbs.

2 Heat 1 tablespoon of the oil in a 12-inch skillet over moderately high heat for 1 minute. Add the patties and brown in batches, allowing about 2 minutes per side and adding the remaining tablespoon of oil as needed.

3 As the patties brown, transfer them to a lightly greased baking sheet. When all of the patties are browned, transfer to the oven and bake, uncovered, for 3 minutes. Garnish with the lemon wedges. Serves 4.

Chicken Nachos

*Everybody likes nachos, so serve this irresistible finger
food at an impromptu lunch or supper.*

- 6 ounces large round tortilla chips (8 cups)
- 1½ cups coarsely chopped leftover cooked chicken or turkey
- 3 tablespoons prepared salsa or Basic Salsa (page 339)
- 1 can (4 ounces) chopped mild green chilies, drained
- 1½ cups coarsely shredded low-fat Cheddar cheese (6 ounces)

For the toppings:
- 3 cups thinly sliced iceberg lettuce
- 8 ounces plum tomatoes, cored and finely diced
- 1 sweet red pepper, cored, seeded, and chopped
- ½ cup thinly sliced pitted black olives
- ½ cup prepared salsa or Basic Salsa (page 339)
- ½ cup sour cream or plain low-fat yogurt (optional)

Per serving:
Calories 446; Protein 30 g;
Carbohydrates 42 g;
Fat 20 g; Sodium 1,124 mg;
Cholesterol 62 mg

20 minutes | 10 minutes

1 Preheat the oven to 375° F. Lightly coat a 15" x 10" x 1" baking pan with nonstick cooking spray and spread the chips in an even layer in the bottom of the pan.

2 Toss the chicken with 3 tablespoons salsa in a small bowl and scatter over the chips, then sprinkle the chilies and cheese evenly on top. Bake, uncovered, for 10 minutes or until the cheese is melted.

3 *For the toppings:* Arrange the lettuce, tomatoes, pepper, olives, ½ cup salsa, and, if desired, the sour cream in separate serving bowls. Serve the nachos immediately and pass the toppings. Serves 4.

Post-Thanksgiving Turkey Soup

A wonderful way to make the most of the big bird. Start this soup a day ahead to allow time for chilling and skimming the fat (see Step 3).

Carcass of a 12- to 20-pound turkey

- ¼ cup cider vinegar
- 2 teaspoons salt, or to taste
- 5 quarts cold water
- 2 tablespoons unsalted butter or margarine
- ¼ cup whole wheat or all-purpose flour
- 1 teaspoon ground sage, or to taste
- ½ teaspoon black pepper
- 2 cups leftover or canned turkey gravy
- 2 medium-size yellow onions, coarsely chopped, or 1 cup coarsely chopped scallions, including tops
- ½ cup coarsely chopped celery
- ¼ cup minced parsley
- 8 ounces green beans, trimmed and snapped, or 2 cups leftover cooked green beans (optional)
- 2 medium-size carrots, peeled and diced
- 1 medium-size baking potato, peeled and diced, and/or 2 cups cooked long-grain white rice
- 2 cups diced leftover cooked turkey
- 1 cup pecan halves
- 1 cup light cream or half-and-half (optional)

1 Place the turkey carcass in a 6- to 7-quart Dutch oven, pulling some of the bones apart if necessary. Add the vinegar and salt, then pour in the water.

2 Set over moderate heat, cover, and bring to a boil—about 15 minutes. Adjust the heat so that the liquid bubbles gently, partially cover, and simmer for 3 hours or until the stock has a rich turkey flavor.

3 Remove the carcass and discard. Strain the turkey stock, pour into a large heatproof bowl, and cover with plastic food wrap. Refrigerate for 6 hours or overnight or until the fat has risen to the top and solidified (the stock underneath will have gelled).

4 Melt the butter in the Dutch oven over moderate heat. Blend in the flour, sage, and pepper, and cook, stirring, for 2 minutes.

5 Gradually whisk in 2 quarts of the turkey stock. When it liquefies, stir in the gravy, onions, celery, parsley, beans if desired, carrots, and potato and/or rice. Simmer, uncovered, for 15 to 20 minutes or until the vegetables are tender.

6 Add the turkey and pecans and adjust the heat so that the soup just simmers; stir in the cream if desired.

7 Taste for salt, pepper, and sage, and adjust if necessary. Heat, uncovered, for 10 minutes or just until the soup is steaming hot; if using cream, do not boil or the soup may curdle. Serves 8.

Per serving:
Calories 278; Protein 20 g;
Carbohydrates 20 g;
Fat 14 g; Sodium 822 mg;
Cholesterol 38 mg

 25 minutes | 3 hr. 56 min.

Turkey Turnovers

What a great way to recycle the Thanksgiving turkey! And there's no need to make the pastry—simply open a package of refrigerated crescent roll dough.

- **1** package (8 ounces) refrigerated crescent rolls
- **3** cups diced leftover cooked turkey
- **1⅓** cups coarsely chopped cooked or canned sweet potatoes
- **1** medium-size yellow onion, coarsely chopped
- **1** package (10 ounces) frozen chopped spinach, thawed and well drained
- **½** cup cranberry sauce
- **2** tablespoons Basic Chicken Stock (page 333), canned low-sodium chicken broth, or water

1 Preheat the oven to 375° F. Separate the rolls into 4 rectangles. On a lightly floured surface, roll each rectangle of dough until it measures about 8 by 7 inches.

2 Mix the turkey, sweet potatoes, onion, spinach, cranberry sauce, and stock in a medium-size bowl. Spoon ¼ of the mixture diagonally onto half of each piece of dough, leaving a ¼-inch border all around. Lightly brush the edges of the dough with water, then fold the dough over, forming triangles. Press the edges together to seal.

3 Place the turnovers on a lightly greased baking sheet and bake, uncovered, for 15 minutes or until golden. Serves 4.

Per serving:
Calories 464; Protein 39 g;
Carbohydrates 51 g;
Fat 12 g; Sodium 601 mg;
Cholesterol 88 mg

15 minutes

15 minutes

For a seasonal sensation, fill your tureen with robust Post-Thanksgiving Turkey Soup.

Curried Turkey with Apples

A light, simple, fruity dish with a decidedly Indian flavor. For accompaniments, serve any combination of coconut, raisins, chutney, or chopped hard-cooked eggs.

1½ cups quick-cooking white rice

3 tablespoons vegetable oil

2 large yellow onions, thinly sliced

1 package (9 ounces) frozen snow peas, thawed and drained

1 large red cooking apple (such as Rome Beauty), cored and coarsely chopped but not peeled

2 tablespoons curry powder

5 teaspoons all-purpose flour

¼ teaspoon salt, or to taste

1 cup Basic Chicken Stock (page 333) or canned low-sodium chicken broth

1 cup milk

1 tablespoon lemon juice (freshly squeezed preferred)

¼ teaspoon black pepper

2 cups diced leftover cooked turkey or chicken

½ cup unsalted dry-roasted peanuts

1 Cook the rice according to package directions. Transfer to a large bowl, cover with foil, and keep warm.

2 Heat 1 tablespoon of the oil in a 12-inch skillet over moderately high heat for 1 minute. Add the onions and sauté, stirring occasionally, for 5 minutes or until soft. Add the snow peas and apple and cook, uncovered, stirring now and then, for 2 to 3 minutes or until the apple is golden brown. Add to the rice.

3 Heat the remaining 2 tablespoons oil in the skillet for 1 minute. Blend in the curry powder, flour, and salt, and cook, stirring, for 2 minutes. Gradually whisk in the stock and milk and cook, stirring constantly, for 3 to 5 minutes or until thickened.

4 Mix in the lemon juice, pepper, turkey, and rice mixture. Cook, uncovered, stirring occasionally, 2 to 3 minutes more—just until steaming hot. Sprinkle some of the peanuts over each portion. Serves 4.

> **Per serving:**
> *Calories 707; Protein 40 g;*
> *Carbohydrates 87 g;*
> *Fat 23 g; Sodium 275 mg;*
> *Cholesterol 67 mg*
>
>
> 15 minutes — 25 minutes

Turkey Rice Bake

The buttery toasted topping on this creamy dish is so good you'll want to double the amount.

1 can (10¾ ounces) condensed cream of mushroom soup

½ cup low-fat milk

1½ teaspoons dried thyme, crumbled

½ teaspoon lemon juice

¼ teaspoon black pepper

2 cups diced leftover cooked turkey

2 cups leftover cooked long-grain brown or white rice

1 package (10 ounces) frozen broccoli spears, thawed and drained

2 teaspoons unsalted butter or margarine

¼ cup seasoned dry bread crumbs

1 tablespoon grated Parmesan cheese

1 Preheat the oven to 350° F. Combine the soup, low-fat milk, thyme, lemon juice, and pepper in a large mixing bowl. Set aside ½ cup of the mixture. Add the turkey and rice to the bowl and toss well to mix.

2 Lightly coat an 8" x 8" x 2" baking dish with nonstick cooking spray. Spoon the turkey mixture into the dish, arrange the broccoli on top, then pour the reserved ½ cup soup mixture evenly over all.

3 Melt the butter in a small saucepan, then stir in the bread crumbs and cheese. Scatter evenly over the casserole. Bake, uncovered, for 30 minutes or until the topping is lightly browned and the mixture underneath is bubbling. Serves 4.

> **Per serving:**
> *Calories 297; Protein 29 g;*
> *Carbohydrates 41 g;*
> *Fat 10 g; Sodium 755 mg;*
> *Cholesterol 67 mg*
>
>
> 10 minutes — 32 minutes

Enchiladas with Turkey

If you prefer, substitute leftover hamburgers, coarsely crumbled.

- 2 tablespoons vegetable oil
- 1 small yellow onion, coarsely chopped
- 2 cans (15 ounces each) tomato sauce
- 1 can (4 ounces) chopped green chilies, drained
- 2 tablespoons chili powder
- ½ teaspoon dried oregano, crumbled
- ½ teaspoon ground cumin
- 2 cups coarsely chopped leftover cooked turkey
- 1 can (1 pound) red kidney beans, drained and rinsed
- 12 corn tortillas
- 1 cup coarsely shredded Monterey Jack cheese (4 ounces)
- 8 large scallions, including tops, finely chopped (1 cup)

1 Preheat the oven to 350° F. Heat the oil in a medium-size saucepan over moderate heat for 1 minute. Add the onion and sauté, stirring occasionally, for 5 minutes or until limp. Add the tomato sauce, chilies, chili powder, oregano, and cumin, cover, and simmer for 30 minutes.

2 Spread a thin layer of the tomato mixture in the bottom of an ungreased 13" x 9" x 2" baking pan. Mix 1½ cups of the remaining tomato mixture with the turkey and beans. Spoon the mixture over half of each tortilla. Fold the tortillas over and arrange, slightly overlapping, in the tomato mixture in the baking pan.

3 Spoon the remaining tomato mixture evenly over the tortillas, then sprinkle with the cheese and scallions. Bake, uncovered, for 20 minutes or until bubbling. Serves 4 to 6.

Per serving: Calories 658; Protein 45 g; Carbohydrates 78 g; Fat 21 g; Sodium 2,046 mg; Cholesterol 58 mg	
15 minutes	56 minutes

Turkey Rice Bake — quick, easy, and a boon to budget-watchers

Fiesta Frittata

*Dark green spinach and bright red peppers make a
colorful feast of this nicely seasoned omelet.*

- 2 tablespoons unsalted butter or margarine
- 1 large yellow onion, coarsely chopped
- 1 large sweet red pepper, cored, seeded, and finely diced
- 1 teaspoon each dried basil and oregano, crumbled
- 1 package (10 ounces) frozen chopped spinach, thawed, drained, and squeezed dry
- 2 cups finely diced leftover cooked turkey or pork, or boiled or baked ham
- ⅓ cup plus 2 tablespoons grated Parmesan cheese
- 4 large eggs
- 3 large egg whites
- ½ cup milk
- ½ teaspoon salt
- ⅛ teaspoon ground red pepper (cayenne)
- 2 cups leftover cooked long-grain white or brown rice

> Per serving:
> Calories 304; Protein 27 g;
> Carbohydrates 24 g;
> Fat 11 g; Sodium 468 mg;
> Cholesterol 200 mg

| 15 minutes | 37 minutes |

1 Preheat the oven to 400° F. Coat a 10-inch ovenproof skillet with nonstick cooking spray, add the butter, and melt over moderate heat. Add the onion and sweet red pepper and sauté, stirring occasionally, until very soft — about 8 minutes.

2 Mix in the basil and oregano and cook and stir for 1 minute. Mix in the spinach and turkey and cook, uncovered, for 2 minutes or until heated through.

3 Meanwhile, whisk the ⅓ cup cheese with the eggs, egg whites, milk, salt, and ground red pepper in a large bowl until frothy.

4 Mix into the skillet along with the rice, reduce the heat to moderately low, and cook, uncovered, without stirring, for 5 minutes. Sprinkle the remaining 2 tablespoons cheese on top.

5 Transfer to the oven and bake, uncovered, for 15 to 20 minutes or until golden brown and set in the center. Remove from the oven and let stand for 10 minutes before cutting into wedges. Serves 6.

Hearty Beef Pot Pie

*An English classic guaranteed to make good beef
even better the second time around.*

- 1½ tablespoons vegetable oil
- 1½ tablespoons unsalted butter or margarine
- 1 package (10 ounces) frozen sliced carrots, thawed and drained
- 1 cup frozen small white onions, thawed and drained
- 1 package (8 ounces) frozen mushrooms, thawed and drained
- 3 tablespoons all-purpose flour
- ½ teaspoon dried marjoram, crumbled
- ⅛ teaspoon black pepper
- 1½ cups Basic Beef Stock (page 332) or canned low-sodium beef broth
- 2 cups diced leftover roast beef or steak
- 1 refrigerated pie crust (from a 15-ounce package)

> Per serving:
> Calories 804; Protein 27 g;
> Carbohydrates 63 g;
> Fat 49 g; Sodium 615 mg;
> Cholesterol 68 mg

| 15 minutes | 51 minutes |

1 Preheat the oven to 400° F. Heat the oil and butter in a large saucepan over moderate heat for 1 minute. Add the carrots and onions and sauté, stirring occasionally, for 5 minutes. Add the mushrooms and sauté, stirring now and then, 3 minutes longer. Using a slotted spoon, transfer the vegetables to a bowl.

2 Blend the flour, marjoram, and pepper into the pan drippings and cook and stir for 5 minutes. Gradually whisk in the stock and cook, stirring constantly, for 3 to 5 minutes or until thickened.

3 Mix in the beef and sautéed vegetables, bring to a boil, then adjust the heat so that the mixture bubbles gently and cook, uncovered, for 5 minutes. Transfer to a lightly greased 1½-quart casserole that measures about 8 inches across.

4 Center the pie crust on top of the casserole. Trim the overhang so that it is 1 inch larger than the casserole, then roll under until it is even with the rim. Crimp the edge, then cut 3 to 4 decorative steam vents in the pastry.

5 Bake the pot pie, uncovered, for 20 to 25 minutes or until the crust is golden and the filling bubbling. If the crust begins to brown too much, cover loosely with foil. Let the pie stand for 10 minutes before serving. Serves 4.

Shepherd's Pie

*In this version of an old favorite, cornstarch is used instead
of flour to make the sauce smooth and silky.*

1 cup frozen cut green beans, thawed but not drained

1 cup frozen green peas and pearl onions, thawed but not drained

1 carrot, peeled and thinly sliced

1⅓ cups Basic Chicken or Beef Stock (page 333 or 332) or canned low-sodium chicken or beef broth

¼ teaspoon salt

¼ teaspoon each dried thyme and savory, crumbled

2 teaspoons cornstarch

2 tablespoons cold water

3 cups coarsely chopped leftover roast beef, pot roast, or steak

4 cups leftover mashed potatoes

¼ teaspoon paprika

6 sprigs parsley or summer savory for garnish

Per serving:
Calories 536; Protein 37 g;
Carbohydrates 47 g;
Fat 24 g; Sodium 957 mg;
Cholesterol 89 mg

10 minutes   27 minutes

1 Preheat the oven to 400° F. Mix the beans, peas and onions, carrot, stock, salt, thyme, and savory in a 10-inch skillet over moderate heat, and bring to a boil. Adjust the heat so that the mixture bubbles gently, cover, and simmer for 7 minutes or until the vegetables are tender.

2 Blend the cornstarch and water in a small cup and stir into the skillet mixture. Raise the heat to moderate and cook, stirring constantly, until slightly thickened—about 3 minutes. Stir in the beef and remove from the heat.

3 Transfer all to an ungreased 10-inch pie pan or quiche dish. "Frost" with the potatoes and sprinkle with the paprika.

4 Slide the pie onto a baking sheet and bake, uncovered, for 15 minutes or until bubbling and lightly browned. Garnish with the parsley. Serves 4.

*In this Shepherd's Pie, sprigs
of savory are the jewels on a
crown of mashed potatoes.*

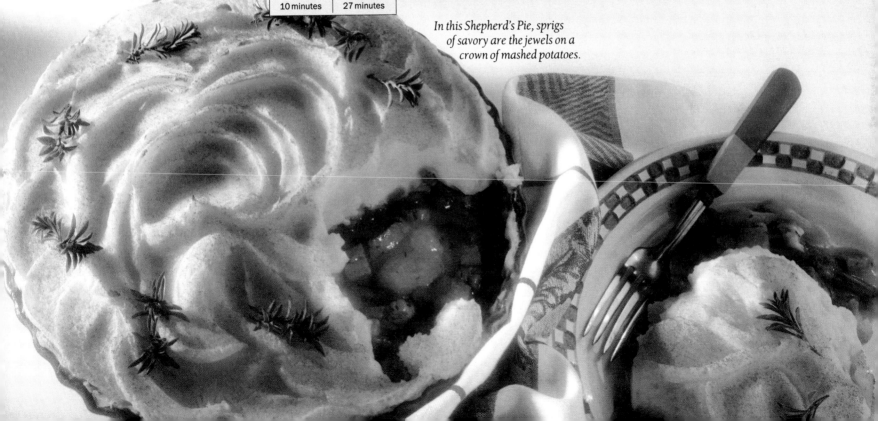

Bubble and Squeak

This English classic is made from leftover mashed potatoes, meat, and whatever green vegetable is on hand.

- 2 tablespoons vegetable oil
- 1 large yellow onion, coarsely chopped
- 1 small cabbage, coarsely chopped (4 cups)
- ¼ teaspoon salt
- ¼ teaspoon dried marjoram, crumbled
- 3 cups coarsely chopped leftover roast beef, pork, or lamb
- 2 cups leftover mashed potatoes

1 Preheat the oven to 425° F. Heat 1 tablespoon of the oil in a 12-inch ovenproof skillet over moderate heat for 1 minute. Add the onion and sauté, stirring frequently, until golden—about 7 minutes.

2 Mix in the cabbage, remaining oil, salt, and marjoram, then toss lightly. Reduce the heat to low, cover, and cook for 7 minutes or until the cabbage is wilted.

3 Stir in the beef and potatoes, transfer the skillet to the oven, and bake, uncovered, for 20 minutes or until heated through. Brown under the broiler, if desired. Serves 4.

Per serving:
Calories 458; Protein 32 g;
Carbohydrates 25 g;
Fat 26 g; Sodium 538 mg;
Cholesterol 87 mg

15 minutes | 35 minutes

Bubble and Squeak is named for the sizzling sounds the potatoes make when they hit the hot pan.

Spaghetti with Meat and Onions

Here's a recipe you can repeat often without boredom, for each kind of meat suggested lends a unique flavor to the sauce.

2 tablespoons unsalted butter or margarine or vegetable oil

3 large yellow onions, halved and thinly sliced

2 medium-size carrots, peeled, halved lengthwise, and thinly sliced

10 ounces spaghetti or other long, thin pasta

3 cups diced leftover roast beef, veal, pork, lamb, or boiled or baked ham

1 tablespoon all-purpose flour

2 cups Basic Chicken Stock (page 333) or canned low-sodium chicken broth

½ cup water

1 tablespoon red wine vinegar or cider vinegar

½ teaspoon salt

½ teaspoon dried savory, crumbled

⅛ teaspoon black pepper

¼ cup grated Parmesan cheese

1 Melt the butter in a 12-inch skillet over low heat. Add the onions, cover, and cook, stirring occasionally, until very soft—about 10 minutes.

2 Add the carrots, cover, and cook, stirring occasionally, for 15 minutes or until the carrots are crisp-tender. Meanwhile, start cooking the spaghetti.

3 Add the beef to the skillet, stirring until well mixed. Blend in the flour and cook, stirring constantly, for 2 minutes. Add the stock, water, vinegar, salt, savory, and pepper, raise the heat to high, and cook, uncovered, stirring often, for 3 to 5 minutes or until the sauce is slightly thickened.

4 Drain the spaghetti well, and transfer to a large serving bowl. Add the skillet mixture and toss to mix. Top each portion with 1 tablespoon of the cheese. Serves 4.

Per serving:
Calories 667; Protein 44 g;
Carbohydrates 67 g;
Fat 23 g; Sodium 605 mg;
Cholesterol 105 mg

20 minutes	32 minutes

Monday Hash

Start the week with a clear refrigerator by combining all those leftover bits of this and that in an undemanding crusty hash.

2 tablespoons vegetable oil

1 large yellow onion, coarsely chopped

¾ teaspoon dried rosemary, crumbled

¼ teaspoon caraway seeds (optional)

½ teaspoon salt

¼ cup minced parsley

3 cups coarsely chopped leftover cooked vegetables (cabbage, carrots, cauliflower, broccoli, etc.)

2 cups coarsely chopped leftover roast beef, pork, veal, lamb, or boiled or baked ham

2 cups finely diced boiled or baked potatoes

1 tablespoon milk

1 Heat the oil in a 10-inch nonstick skillet over moderate heat for 1 minute. Add the onion, rosemary, and caraway seeds if desired, and sauté, stirring occasionally, for 5 minutes or until the onion is soft.

2 Mix in the salt, parsley, vegetables, beef, potatoes, and milk, then press flat with a pancake turner. Reduce the heat to moderately low and cook, uncovered, for 15 minutes or until crusty on the bottom.

3 Loosen the hash around the edges and invert on a large platter. Serves 4.

Per serving:
Calories 334; Protein 22 g;
Carbohydrates 24 g;
Fat 17 g; Sodium 360 mg;
Cholesterol 57 mg

20 minutes	21 minutes

Pizza Roll

Use a serrated bread knife to cut this loaf into neat, colorful slices.

2 tablespoons olive oil
1 large yellow onion, thinly sliced
1 large sweet green pepper, cored, seeded, and cut into matchstick strips
¼ teaspoon each salt and black pepper
2 packages (10 ounces each) refrigerated pizza dough

1½ cups leftover thick tomato and meat sauce
1 cup coarsely shredded part-skim mozzarella cheese (4 ounces)
¼ cup grated Parmesan cheese

Per serving:
Calories 643; Protein 24 g;
Carbohydrates 84 g;
Fat 22 g; Sodium 1,529 mg;
Cholesterol 22 mg

20 minutes   31 minutes

1 Heat the oil in a 10-inch skillet over moderate heat for 1 minute. Add the onion and green pepper and sauté, stirring until soft. Mix in the salt and black pepper and set aside.

2 Preheat the oven to 400° F. Flour a 17- by 14-inch baking sheet. Unroll both doughs on the sheet, overlapping them 1 inch. Brush the overlapping dough with water, pinching it slightly. Gently roll the dough into a 16- by 10-inch rectangle.

3 Spread the tomato sauce on top, leaving a 1-inch border. Top with the skillet mixture, then sprinkle with the mozzarella and Parmesan cheeses.

4 Starting from the 16-inch side, carefully roll up the dough. Keeping the seam side down, gently adjust the roll to fit on the baking sheet. (Pinch the overlapping edges together if necessary.) Tuck the ends of the roll underneath.

5 With another baking sheet set on the lower oven rack, bake the pizza roll, uncovered, for 25 minutes or until golden brown. Let cool for 10 minutes. Using 2 wide metal spatulas, ease the roll onto a cutting board. Cut into 1-inch-thick slices. Serves 4.

Look what happens when a familiar favorite is rolled up—Pizza Roll!

Pork with Barbecue Sauce

A rich red sauce enlivens this lip-smacking open-face sandwich.

- 2 tablespoons vegetable oil
- 1 medium-size yellow onion, coarsely chopped
- 1 medium-size sweet green pepper, cored, seeded, and coarsely chopped
- 2 cloves garlic, minced
- 1½ cups canned crushed tomatoes
- ½ cup bottled barbecue sauce or Basic Barbecue Sauce (page 338)
- ¼ teaspoon each dried thyme and basil, crumbled
- ¼ teaspoon each salt and black pepper
- 1 pound leftover roast pork or turkey, cut into 2″ x ¼″ x ¼″ strips
- 1 package (10 ounces) frozen corn kernels, thawed and drained
- 4 large hard rolls, about 4 inches in diameter, split horizontally

1 Heat the oil in a medium-size saucepan over moderate heat for 1 minute. Add the onion and green pepper and sauté, stirring occasionally, for 3 minutes or until slightly softened. Add the garlic and sauté 1 minute more.

2 Mix in the tomatoes, barbecue sauce, thyme, basil, salt, and black pepper, and bring to a boil. Adjust the heat so that the mixture bubbles gently, cover, and cook for 5 minutes.

3 Add the pork and corn, cover, and simmer 10 minutes more. Meanwhile, toast the rolls lightly and arrange, cut sides up, on 4 heated plates. Ladle the pork mixture on top, dividing the total amount evenly. Serves 4.

Per serving:
Calories 614; Protein 43 g;
Carbohydrates 56 g;
Fat 25 g; Sodium 933 mg;
Cholesterol 107 mg

15 minutes | 22 minutes

Lamb, Barley, and Vegetable Soup

Turnips, sometimes harsh when cooked in other ways, acquire a sweet, nutty flavor in this hearty broth of Scottish origin.

- 2 tablespoons vegetable oil
- 2 large yellow onions, coarsely chopped
- 3 cups diced leftover roast lamb or beef
- 4 cups Basic Beef Stock (page 332) or canned low-sodium beef broth
- 3 cups water
- 1 pound rutabaga or turnips, peeled and cut into ½-inch cubes
- 2 medium-size carrots, peeled and thickly sliced
- 1 large all-purpose potato, peeled and cut into ½-inch cubes
- 2 medium-size stalks celery, coarsely chopped
- ½ cup medium pearl barley
- ½ teaspoon dried thyme, crumbled
- ½ teaspoon salt
- ¼ teaspoon black pepper

1 Heat the oil in a 6-quart Dutch oven over moderate heat for 1 minute. Add the onions and sauté, stirring frequently, for 10 minutes or until very soft.

2 Add the lamb, stock, and water, and bring to a simmer. Adjust the heat so that the liquid bubbles gently, then cook, uncovered, for 10 minutes. Skim all foam from the surface and discard.

3 Add the rutabaga, carrots, potato, celery, barley, thyme, salt, and pepper. Simmer, uncovered, for 45 minutes to 1 hour or until the barley is tender. Serves 6.

Per serving:
Calories 317; Protein 25 g;
Carbohydrates 32 g;
Fat 10 g; Sodium 432 mg;
Cholesterol 66 mg

25 minutes | 1 hr. 26 min.

295

Ham and Macaroni with Ricotta Cheese Sauce

A first-rate last-minute meal whether you make it with ham, chicken, or turkey.

- 8 ounces elbow macaroni, rotelle, or small pasta shells
- 1 package (10 ounces) frozen sugar snap peas or snow peas, unthawed
- ½ cup part-skim ricotta cheese
- 2 tablespoons Dijon mustard
- 2 teaspoons balsamic or cider vinegar
- ¼ teaspoon each sugar and black pepper
- 2 cups diced leftover boiled or baked ham, cooked chicken, or cooked turkey

1 Cook the macaroni according to package directions, adding the peas during the last 3 minutes.

2 Meanwhile, whirl the cheese, mustard, vinegar, sugar, and pepper in a food processor or an electric blender at high speed until smooth—about 30 seconds. Transfer to a large bowl.

3 Drain the macaroni and peas, then add to the bowl along with the ham. Toss well to mix. Serve at once or cover and chill for several hours. Serves 4.

Per serving:
Calories 448; Protein 28 g;
Carbohydrates 57 g;
Fat 11 g; Sodium 1,062 mg;
Cholesterol 49 mg

10 minutes | 8 minutes

Cheddar, Ham, and Rice Pudding

An old standby, rice pudding, takes on delectable main-dish dimensions.

- 1 cup long-grain white or brown rice
- 1½ cups diced leftover baked or boiled ham
- 1 cup coarsely shredded low-fat Cheddar cheese (4 ounces)
- 1 package (10 ounces) frozen peas, carrots, or corn kernels, thawed and drained
- 2 scallions, including tops, or 1 medium-size yellow onion, finely chopped
- ⅛ teaspoon ground red pepper (cayenne)
- 1 cup whole or low-fat milk
- 2 large eggs, lightly beaten

1 Preheat the oven to 375° F. Cook the rice according to package directions. Mix the rice, ham, ¾ cup of the cheese, the peas, scallions, red pepper, milk, and eggs in a large bowl.

2 Transfer the mixture to a greased 11" x 9" x 2" flameproof baking dish, sprinkle the remaining ¼ cup cheese evenly over all, cover with foil, and bake for 30 to 35 minutes or until bubbling.

3 Remove the foil, transfer to the broiler, and broil 4 inches from the heat for 1 to 2 minutes or until lightly browned. Serves 4.

Per serving:
Calories 552; Protein 29 g;
Carbohydrates 74 g;
Fat 15 g; Sodium 1,224 mg;
Cholesterol 157 mg

15 minutes | 57 minutes

Ham and Sweet Potato Salad

Shredded cabbage gives this salad the crunch of coleslaw; for more bite, add a pinch of dried mustard or a teaspoon of horseradish to the dressing.

- ½ cup low-fat cottage cheese
- 1 tablespoon reduced-calorie mayonnaise
- 1 tablespoon Dijon mustard
- ¼ teaspoon black pepper
- ⅛ teaspoon sugar
- 2 cups leftover boiled or baked ham, cut into matchstick strips
- 2 cups finely shredded cabbage
- 2 cups diced leftover boiled or baked sweet potatoes

1 Whirl the cottage cheese, mayonnaise, mustard, pepper, and sugar in a food processor or an electric blender at high speed for about 30 seconds or until smooth. Transfer to a large bowl.

2 Add the ham and cabbage and toss well to mix. Add the sweet potatoes and stir gently. Serve at once or cover and chill for several hours before serving. Serves 4.

Per serving:
Calories 239; Protein 18 g;
Carbohydrates 19 g;
Fat 6 g; Sodium 1,100 mg;
Cholesterol 44 mg

20 minutes | None

Stuffed Acorn Squash — a tasty stuffing made like meatloaf bakes inside a sweet squash.

Stuffed Acorn Squash

If you're making this recipe in advance, don't apply the glaze in Step 4. Instead, glaze the mounds of stuffing when you reheat the squash.

- 3 medium-size acorn squash, halved crosswise and seeded
- 1 small yellow onion, finely chopped
- 1 large egg
- 3 tablespoons ketchup
- 1 tablespoon Dijon mustard
- ¾ teaspoon dried basil, crumbled
- ¼ teaspoon dried thyme, crumbled
- 1 pound ground turkey
- 1 cup finely chopped leftover boiled or baked ham
- ½ cup dry bread crumbs
- 1½ cups frozen green peas, unthawed

For the glaze:
- ⅓ cup ketchup
- 1 tablespoon dark brown sugar
- 1 teaspoon Dijon mustard

1 Preheat the oven to 350° F. Trim the bottom of the squash halves so that they will stand without wobbling; set aside.

2 Combine the onion, egg, ketchup, mustard, basil, and thyme in a large bowl. Using your hands, mix in the turkey, ham, bread crumbs, and peas. Stuff the squash halves with the mixture, mounding it up in the middle.

3 Arrange the squash halves in an ungreased 13" x 9" x 2" baking pan, cover snugly with foil, and bake for 1 hour or until the squash is almost tender.

4 *For the glaze:* Combine the ketchup, sugar, and mustard in a small bowl. Using a pastry brush, spread the glaze over each mound of stuffing. Return the squash to the oven and bake, uncovered, 10 minutes more or until the squash is tender when pierced with a knife. Serves 6.

Per serving:
Calories 405; Protein 28 g;
Carbohydrates 63 g;
Fat 7 g; Sodium 742 mg;
Cholesterol 98 mg

25 minutes | 1 hr. 10 min.

297

Ham and Lima Bean Soup

*Be sure that the ham bone you use still has plenty of meat
left on it so this soup will be hearty and flavorful.*

1 pound dried large lima beans,
    sorted and rinsed

3 quarts plus 2 cups cold water

1 large leftover meaty ham bone
    or 1½ pounds leftover boiled or
    baked ham cut into ½-inch
    cubes

2 medium-size all-purpose
    potatoes, peeled and cut into
    ½-inch cubes

2 large carrots, peeled and
    sliced ¼ inch thick

1 large stalk celery, diced

1 cup minced fresh chives or
    scallions, including tops

1 cup coarsely chopped fresh
    sorrel or 1 cup coarsely
    chopped fresh spinach plus 2
    tablespoons lemon juice

¼ cup minced parsley

½ teaspoon black pepper

Per serving:
Calories 272; Protein 21 g;
Carbohydrates 26 g;
Fat 9 g; Sodium 1,139 mg;
Cholesterol 48 mg

1 hour | 1 hr. 16 min.

1 Place the beans and 4 cups of the water in a 5-quart Dutch oven, cover, and bring to a boil over moderate heat. Boil, covered, for 2 minutes. Remove from the heat and let stand, covered, for 1 hour.

2 Drain the beans, rinse, drain again, and return to the Dutch oven. Add the ham bone and the remaining 10 cups water. (Or, if you still have the pan in which the ham was cooked, skim off all of the fat and discard, leaving the pan juices and browned bits. Pour 2 cups of the water into the pan, scrape up the browned bits and juices, then add enough water to the pan to total 10 cups liquid; add the mixture to the Dutch oven.) Simmer, covered, for 45 minutes, stirring occasionally, until the beans are just tender.

3 Transfer the ham bone to a cutting board and let cool until easy to handle. Remove the meat from the bone, cut it into ½-inch cubes, and set aside. Discard the bone.

4 Add the potatoes, carrots, and celery to the soup and simmer, uncovered, over moderate heat for 15 minutes. Add the chives, sorrel, parsley, pepper, and ham. Simmer, uncovered, 10 minutes more. Serves 8.

*With Ham and Lima Bean Soup,
Sunday's ham makes a spectacular
encore, accompanied by lima
beans, carrots, and potatoes.*

Empanadas

If you have several kinds of leftover meat, you can make a variety of empanadas. Instead of adding the meat to the sauce, spread one kind of meat over the sauce on each uncooked empanada just before you roll it up. Be sure to allow an extra 20 minutes for the dough to rise.

1 tablespoon vegetable oil
2 cloves garlic, minced
4 scallions, including tops, finely chopped
¾ teaspoon dried oregano, crumbled
¾ teaspoon ground cumin
¼ teaspoon ground cloves
2 tablespoons tomato paste
2 teaspoons sugar
½ teaspoon salt
2 cups coarsely chopped leftover roast pork, beef, or chicken
1 cup frozen (or leftover) green peas or corn kernels, thawed and drained
1 cup coarsely chopped leftover baked or boiled potato
¼ cup thinly sliced pimiento-stuffed green olives
1 pound frozen bread dough, thawed and divided into 4 equal parts
1 cup plain low-fat yogurt (optional)

Per serving:
Calories 526; Protein 32 g;
Carbohydrates 64 g;
Fat 16 g; Sodium 1,100 mg;
Cholesterol 66 mg

25 minutes | 31 minutes

1 Heat the oil in a 10-inch skillet over moderate heat for 1 minute. Add the garlic, scallions, oregano, cumin, and cloves, and sauté, stirring now and then, for 5 minutes or until the scallions are soft. Blend in the tomato paste, sugar, and salt, then mix in the pork, peas, potato, and olives and set aside.

2 Roll each piece of dough into an 8- by 6-inch oval on a lightly floured surface and let rest for 10 minutes. Spoon 1 cup of the skillet mixture down the center of each oval, leaving a 1-inch border all around. Fold the dough over, enclosing the filling, then press the edges together firmly to seal.

3 Arrange the empanadas on a baking sheet that has been lightly coated with nonstick cooking spray, cover with a dry clean cloth, and allow to rise for 20 minutes in a warm, dry place. Meanwhile, preheat the oven to 375° F.

4 Brush the empanadas lightly with water and bake, uncovered, for 20 to 25 minutes or until golden brown. Top, if desired, with dollops of yogurt. Serves 4.

Twice-Baked Potatoes with Ham and Cheese

The next time you bake potatoes, make an extra four just so you'll have leftovers for this version of everybody's favorite comfort food.

4 large leftover baked potatoes
1 cup finely diced boiled or baked ham
1 package (10 ounces) frozen corn kernels, thawed and drained
2 scallions, including tops, or 1 medium-size yellow onion, finely chopped
½ cup plain low-fat yogurt
1 cup coarsely shredded Monterey Jack cheese (4 ounces)
½ teaspoon ground cumin
⅛ to ¼ teaspoon ground red pepper (cayenne)

Per serving:
Calories 429; Protein 21 g;
Carbohydrates 60 g;
Fat 13 g; Sodium 647 mg;
Cholesterol 21 mg

20 minutes | 32 minutes

1 Preheat the oven to 400° F. Halve the potatoes lengthwise and, leaving shells ¼ inch thick, scoop the pulp into a medium-size bowl. Mash well, then mix in the ham, corn, scallions, yogurt, ½ cup of the cheese, the cumin, and red pepper.

2 Stuff the potato shells with the mixture, mounding it in the center. Sprinkle with the remaining ½ cup cheese, dividing the total amount evenly, then arrange the potatoes in an ungreased 13″ x 9″ x 2″ baking pan.

3 Bake, uncovered, for 25 to 30 minutes or until the potatoes are heated through. Transfer to the broiler and broil 4 inches from the heat for 1 to 2 minutes or until lightly browned. Serves 4.

Baked Ham and Cheese with Mushrooms

A cozy one-dish meal made with everyday ingredients.

2 tablespoons unsalted butter or margarine or vegetable oil

1 medium-size yellow onion, finely chopped

8 ounces mushrooms, thinly sliced, or 1 can (8 ounces) sliced mushrooms, drained

1 package (10 ounces) frozen chopped spinach, thawed, drained, and squeezed dry

2 cloves garlic, minced

¼ teaspoon black pepper

1½ cups milk

3 large eggs

2 teaspoons Dijon mustard

1 cup part-skim ricotta cheese

½ cup grated Parmesan cheese

1 cup diced leftover boiled or baked ham

6 slices firm-textured whole wheat or white bread, cut into ½-inch cubes (4 cups)

Per serving:
Calories 510; Protein 34 g;
Carbohydrates 36 g;
Fat 27 g; Sodium 1,199 mg;
Cholesterol 236 mg

20 minutes	41 minutes

---

1 Preheat the oven to 375° F. Melt the butter in a 10-inch nonstick skillet over moderate heat. Add the onion and sauté, stirring occasionally, for 3 minutes or until slightly softened.

2 Add the mushrooms and sauté, stirring now and then, for 3 minutes or until limp. Mix in the spinach, garlic, and pepper, and cook, stirring, 1 to 2 minutes more or until almost all of the liquid has evaporated.

3 Meanwhile, combine the milk, eggs, mustard, ricotta cheese, and ⅓ cup of the Parmesan in a medium-size bowl. Fold in the ham, bread cubes, and skillet mixture.

4 Transfer all to a lightly greased 9″ x 9″ x 2″ flameproof baking dish and sprinkle with the remaining Parmesan. Cover with foil and bake for 30 minutes or until bubbling.

5 Uncover the dish, transfer to the broiler, and broil 4 inches from the heat for 1 to 2 minutes or until lightly browned. Serves 4.

Baked Ham and Cheese with Mushrooms—an out-of-this-world bread pudding, delicately seasoned with a touch of mustard

Appetizers and Desserts

Every musical masterpiece has a prelude and a finale, and so
do great meals. While each entrée in this book is a complete meal in itself,
there are certain occasions that call for a before- or after-dinner treat. These tantalizing
appetizers and desserts add an exquisite grace note to any meal. Try one the
next time you celebrate a holiday, host a dinner party, or simply want to reward
yourself or your family with a little something special.

South-of-the-Border Appetizer

This colorfully served dip is not only a treat to the eye—just wait till you taste it.

- 2 large ripe avocados, peeled and pitted
- ¼ cup minced fresh coriander (cilantro) or flat-leaf parsley or ½ teaspoon ground coriander
- 2 tablespoons lime juice (freshly squeezed preferred)
- ½ teaspoon hot red pepper sauce
- ¼ teaspoon each salt and black pepper
- 1 cup plain low-fat yogurt
- ⅓ cup reduced-calorie mayonnaise
- 1 teaspoon ground cumin
- ¾ teaspoon chili powder
- ½ teaspoon garlic powder
- 2 cans (10½ ounces each) bean dip
- 3 medium-size ripe tomatoes, cored, seeded, and coarsely chopped but not peeled
- 4 scallions, including tops, coarsely chopped
- 1 cup coarsely shredded iceberg or romaine lettuce
- 3 packages (8 ounces each) tortilla chips (for dipping)

1 Place the avocados, coriander, lime juice, red pepper sauce, salt, and black pepper in a large bowl and mash well; set aside.

2 Combine the yogurt, mayonnaise, cumin, chili powder, and garlic powder in a small bowl, then set aside.

3 Spread the bean dip over the bottom of a large round or oval platter. Spoon the avocado mixture on top, leaving a ½-inch margin of bean dip all around.

4 Smooth the yogurt mixture on top of the avocado mixture, leaving a 1-inch border of green all around. Sprinkle with the tomatoes, then the scallions. Surround with a border of lettuce. Accompany with tortilla chips. Serves 12.

Per serving:
Calories 442; Protein 9 g;
Carbohydrates 49 g;
Fat 24 g; Sodium 720 mg;
Cholesterol 5 mg

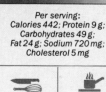

35 minutes	None

Tangy Cheddar Cheese Spread

This creamy spread is equally delicious with crackers or French bread.

- 1 large shallot or scallion, including top, cut into 1-inch pieces
- 1 tablespoon unsalted butter, at room temperature
- 1 tablespoon Dijon mustard
- 1 teaspoon dried sage
- 2 cups shredded sharp Cheddar cheese (8 ounces)
- ¼ cup dry white wine or apple juice
- ¼ teaspoon ground red pepper (cayenne)
- 1 package (8 ounces) cream cheese, cut into 1-inch cubes

1 Place the shallot, butter, mustard, and sage in a food processor and whirl for 15 seconds.

2 Add the Cheddar cheese, wine, and red pepper, and whirl for 10 seconds. Add the cream cheese, then whirl for 40 seconds longer or until creamy.

3 Transfer the mixture to a serving bowl, cover with plastic food wrap, and refrigerate for several hours. Before serving, let stand at room temperature for 30 minutes. Makes 2 cups.

Per cup:
Calories 945; Protein 38 g;
Carbohydrates 8 g;
Fat 84 g; Sodium 1,164 mg;
Cholesterol 260 mg

10 minutes	None

Spicy Sour Cream Dip

This dip, which can be prepared a day ahead, is ideal to serve with crisp chunks of celery, cucumber, scallions, raw zucchini or carrots, broccoli or cauliflower florets, or any other seasonal vegetable.

- ⅔ cup reduced-fat sour cream
- ⅓ cup reduced-calorie mayonnaise
- 4 scallions, including tops, finely chopped
- 1 tablespoon white wine vinegar or cider vinegar
- 1 teaspoon Dijon mustard
- 1 clove garlic, minced
- ¼ teaspoon salt
- ⅛ teaspoon ground red pepper (cayenne)
- 2 tablespoons minced fresh basil or parsley

Per cup:
Calories 508; Protein 6 g;
Carbohydrates 17 g;
Fat 48 g; Sodium 767 mg;
Cholesterol 27 mg

15 minutes | None

1 Combine the sour cream, mayonnaise, scallions, vinegar, mustard, garlic, salt, red pepper, and basil in a small bowl. Cover with plastic food wrap and chill until ready to serve. Makes about 1 cup.

Horseradish Variation

Prepare as directed, but add **3 tablespoons well-drained prepared horseradish** and substitute **2 tablespoons snipped fresh dill** or **½ teaspoon dill weed** for the basil. Makes about 1 cup.

Per cup: Calories 526; Protein 7 g;
Carbohydrates 21 g; Fat 48 g;
Sodium 1,262mg; Cholesterol 27 mg

Curry Variation

Prepare as directed, but add **1 to 2 teaspoons curry powder** and substitute **1 tablespoon lemon juice** for the vinegar and **2 tablespoons minced fresh coriander (cilantro)** or **flat-leaf parsley** for the basil. Makes about 1 cup.

Per cup: Calories 515; Protein 7 g;
Carbohydrates 18 g; Fat 48 g;
Sodium 765 mg; Cholesterol 27 mg

Yogurt Variation

Prepare as directed, but substitute **⅔ cup low-fat cottage cheese** or **part-skim ricotta** for the sour cream and **⅓ cup plain low-fat yogurt** for the mayonnaise. Reduce the vinegar to 2 teaspoons and add, if desired, **3 tablespoons finely grated cucumber** that has been squeezed dry. Makes about 1 cup.

Per cup: Calories 206; Protein 26 g;
Carbohydrates 16 g; Fat 5 g;
Sodium 1,272 mg; Cholesterol 17 mg

South-of-the-Border Appetizer will make you an instant Tex-Mex fan.

303

Deviled Ham Dip

Dust this easy-to-make dip with paprika and serve with a selection of crackers.

1 small yellow onion, quartered

8 ounces boiled or baked ham, cut into 1-inch cubes

2 tablespoons Dijon mustard

3 tablespoons mayonnaise

2 tablespoons light cream or milk

¼ teaspoon ground red pepper (cayenne)

1 Place the onion, ham, mustard, mayonnaise, cream, and red pepper in a food processor or an electric blender and whirl for 15 seconds. Scrape the sides of the container, then whirl until smooth and creamy.

2 Transfer the mixture to a serving bowl, cover with plastic food wrap, and refrigerate until ready to use. Makes 2 cups.

Per cup:
Calories 394; Protein 22 g;
Carbohydrates 9 g;
Fat 30 g; Sodium 1,820 mg;
Cholesterol 78 mg

10 minutes | None

Hummus

The traditional accompaniment for this Middle Eastern dip is pita bread cut into triangles, but you can also use your favorite raw vegetables.

4 cloves garlic

1 can (1 pound 14 ounces) chick peas, drained well

1 cup tahini (sesame seed paste) or creamy peanut butter

¼ cup lemon juice (freshly squeezed preferred)

⅓ cup water

¾ teaspoon salt, or to taste

¼ teaspoon black pepper, or to taste

1 Place the garlic, chick peas, tahini, lemon juice, water, salt, and pepper in a food processor or an electric blender and purée for 1 to 2 minutes or until smooth and creamy.

2 Transfer to a serving bowl. Cover with plastic food wrap and refrigerate for several hours. Before serving, let stand at room temperature for 30 minutes. Taste and add more salt or pepper if desired. Makes 2 cups.

Per cup:
Calories 1,537; Protein 80 g;
Carbohydrates 154 g;
Fat 75 g; Sodium 1,457 mg;
Cholesterol 0 mg

5 minutes | None

Deviled Ham Dip, Eggplant Pâté, and Hummus make a terrific trio for parties, and singly, any one of them will deliver a superb solo performance with a one-dish meal.

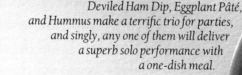

Eggplant Pâté

Serve this pâté as a dip for crisp crackers, triangles of pita bread, or chunks of crisp raw vegetables.

- 1 large eggplant (1¼ pounds)
- 4 scallions, including tops, finely chopped
- 1 medium-size tomato, peeled, cored, seeded, and coarsely chopped, or 1 cup chopped drained canned tomatoes
- 1 clove garlic, minced
- 2 tablespoons olive or vegetable oil
- 1 tablespoon red wine vinegar or cider vinegar
- ½ teaspoon salt
- ⅛ teaspoon ground red pepper (cayenne)
- ¼ cup minced parsley

1 Preheat the oven to 400° F. Using a sharp fork, pierce the eggplant in 3 or 4 different spots. Place the eggplant on an ungreased baking sheet and bake, uncovered, for 40 to 45 minutes or until tender. Let cool until easy to handle.

2 Peel the eggplant, finely chop the pulp, then place in a medium-size bowl. Add the scallions, tomato, garlic, oil, vinegar, salt, and red pepper; mix well.

3 Sprinkle with the parsley, cover with plastic food wrap, and chill for at least 1 hour. Serves 6 to 8.

Per serving:
Calories 72; Protein 1 g;
Carbohydrates 8 g;
Fat 5 g; Sodium 183 mg;
Cholesterol 0 mg

 20 minutes   45 minutes

Tortellini and Pesto Pickups

You can prepare this recipe through Step 1 as much as 2 hours in advance. Simply cover the tortellini and refrigerate until ready to serve.

- 1 package (9 ounces) meat or cheese tortellini
- 1 tablespoon olive or vegetable oil
- ½ cup pesto sauce (page 232)
- 2 tablespoons reduced-fat sour cream

1 Cook the tortellini according to package directions; drain well. Place in a large bowl, add the oil, and toss well.

2 Combine the pesto sauce and sour cream in a small bowl. Set the bowl in the middle of a large platter, surround with the tortellini, and place a small container of toothpicks nearby. Serves 6 to 8.

Per serving:
Calories 236; Protein 10 g;
Carbohydrates 22 g;
Fat 13 g; Sodium 246 mg;
Cholesterol 25 mg

 15 minutes   8 minutes

Bread Round Stuffed with Baked Cheese

*For a lower-calorie appetizer, omit the bread cubes and
use chunks of crisp raw vegetables for dunking.*

1 round loaf (1 pound) firm-
   textured white bread, about 6
   inches in diameter
1 cup coarsely shredded part-
   skim mozzarella cheese
¾ cup part-skim ricotta cheese
1 small sweet green pepper,
   cored, seeded, and finely
   chopped
1 small sweet red pepper, cored,
   seeded, and finely chopped
¼ cup grated Parmesan cheese
1 teaspoon ground cumin
½ teaspoon garlic powder
¼ teaspoon each salt and white
   pepper

Per serving:
Calories 316; Protein 16 g;
Carbohydrates 40 g;
Fat 10 g; Sodium 682 mg;
Cholesterol 24 mg

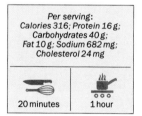

20 minutes | 1 hour

1 Place an oven rack in the middle of the oven and a second rack underneath it, then preheat the oven to 400° F. Slice 1 inch off the top of the bread and set it aside. Scoop out the center of the bread, leaving a ½ inch shell; set aside. Cut the scooped-out bread into 1½-inch cubes and set aside.

2 Combine the mozzarella and ricotta cheeses, green and red peppers, Parmesan, cumin, garlic powder, salt, and white pepper in a medium-size bowl. Spoon the mixture into the bread shell and replace the top. Wrap the loaf snugly in foil, then place on an ungreased baking sheet and bake on the middle oven rack for 1 hour.

3 Meanwhile, spread the bread cubes on an ungreased baking sheet, place on the lower rack, and bake, uncovered, until crisp and golden—about 10 minutes.

4 Carefully remove the foil, lift off the top, and stir the cheese filling until creamy. Replace the top, slightly askew, and center the stuffed bread on a large round serving platter. Surround with the bread cubes. Serves 6 to 8.

*When a dinner party calls for a festive touch, serve this
Bread Round Stuffed with Baked Cheese.*

Stuffed Mushroom Caps

We've used wheat germ in this recipe because it's so healthful, but if you prefer you can substitute fine dry bread crumbs.

1 pound large mushrooms, wiped clean
1 tablespoon olive or vegetable oil
3 cloves garlic, minced
2 scallions, including tops, finely chopped
3 tablespoons toasted or plain wheat germ
1 tablespoon minced parsley
1 tablespoon lemon juice
¼ teaspoon salt
¼ cup water

Per mushroom:
Calories 24; Protein 1 g;
Carbohydrates 3 g;
Fat 1 g; Sodium 39 mg;
Cholesterol 0 mg

15 minutes   22 minutes

1 Preheat the oven to 375° F. Remove the mushroom stems and set the caps aside. Trim off the tough ends of the stems and discard. Chop enough of the remaining stems to make 1 cup.

2 Heat the oil in a 10-inch skillet over moderate heat for 1 minute. Add the garlic and scallions and sauté for 2 minutes. Add the chopped mushroom stems and sauté for 2 to 3 minutes or until they are soft and have released their juices. Stir in the wheat germ and sauté 30 seconds longer.

3 Remove from the heat, then mix in the parsley, lemon juice, and salt. Spoon about 2 teaspoons of the mixture into each mushroom cap. Arrange the caps in a single layer in an ungreased 9" x 9" x 2" baking pan.

4 Pour the water into the pan around the mushroom caps and bake, uncovered, for 12 to 15 minutes or until the mushrooms are tender. Makes about 14 mushrooms.

Savory Stuffed Celery

Any time is a good time for these bite-size bundles of contradictions—creamy but crunchy, sweet but snappy, light but very satisfying.

1 package (8 ounces) cream cheese or light cream cheese, at room temperature
2 tablespoons milk
3½ tablespoons finely chopped mango chutney or apricot preserves
1 teaspoon Dijon mustard
4 ounces boiled or baked ham, finely chopped
2 tablespoons minced parsley
9 medium-size stalks celery, trimmed to 8-inch lengths
36 celery leaves (optional garnish)

Per piece:
Calories 36; Protein 1 g;
Carbohydrates 2 g;
Fat 3 g; Sodium 72 mg;
Cholesterol 9 mg

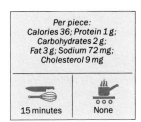

15 minutes   None

1 Beat the cheese with the milk in a small electric mixer bowl at high speed until creamy—about 2 minutes. Add the chutney and mustard, beat just enough to combine, then fold in the ham and parsley with a wooden spoon.

2 Stuff the hollow of each celery stalk with 3 tablespoons of the cheese mixture. Cut each stalk into four 2-inch lengths and garnish each piece, if desired, with a celery leaf. Makes 3 dozen.

Roasted Red Pepper and Mozzarella Toasts

This recipe also works well with Monterey Jack or goat cheese in place of the mozzarella and reconstituted sun-dried tomatoes in place of the roasted peppers.

1 loaf Italian or French bread (about 15 inches long), cut into ½-inch slices

3 tablespoons olive or vegetable oil

1 clove garlic, minced

2 jars (7 ounces each) roasted red peppers, drained and coarsely chopped

1 to 2 teaspoons balsamic or cider vinegar, or to taste

¼ teaspoon each salt and black pepper

2 tablespoons minced fresh basil or parsley

2 cups shredded part-skim mozzarella cheese (8 ounces)

1 Preheat the oven to 400° F. Arrange the bread slices in a single layer on an ungreased baking sheet.

2 Combine the oil and garlic in a small bowl. Using a pastry brush, lightly brush each slice with the mixture, using about half of the total amount. Bake, uncovered, for 5 minutes.

3 Meanwhile, add the red peppers, vinegar, salt, black pepper, and basil to the remaining oil mixture and mix well.

4 When the bread has baked for 5 minutes, remove from the oven and spread each slice with a thin layer of the red pepper mixture. Sprinkle with the cheese.

5 With the rack set 4 inches from the heat, broil for 30 seconds to 1 minute or until the cheese melts. Makes 2½ dozen.

Per piece:
Calories 78; Protein 4 g;
Carbohydrates 10 g;
Fat 3 g; Sodium 130 mg;
Cholesterol 4 mg

15 minutes | 6 minutes

Marvelous to munch on:
Baked Pita Chips, Roasted
Red Pepper and Mozzarella
Toasts, Potato Skin Nachos, and
Orange Spiced Walnuts

Potato Skin Nachos

Save the scooped-out potatoes from these nippy hors d'oeuvres to make mashed potatoes for another day.

4 large baking potatoes, scrubbed

¼ teaspoon each chili powder and salt

1 jar (8 ounces) taco sauce

1½ cups shredded Monterey Jack or Cheddar cheese (6 ounces)

2 canned jalapeño peppers, seeded and finely chopped (wash your hands after handling the peppers)

1 clove garlic, minced

2 tablespoons minced fresh coriander (cilantro) or flat-leaf parsley

1 Preheat the oven to 400° F. Bake the potatoes in the oven for 1 hour. Remove, leaving the oven on, and let cool until easy to handle.

2 Halve the potatoes lengthwise and scoop out the pulp, leaving shells ⅛ inch thick. Halve each potato shell lengthwise, then halve each piece crosswise.

3 Arrange the potato skins, flesh side up, on an ungreased baking sheet. Sprinkle with the chili powder and salt. Bake, uncovered, for 10 minutes or until heated through.

4 Meanwhile, combine the taco sauce, cheese, peppers, garlic, and coriander in a small bowl. Spoon the mixture onto the hot potato skins.

5 With the oven rack set 4 inches from the heat, broil the potato skins for 1 to 2 minutes or until the cheese melts. Makes 32 nachos.

Per piece:
Calories 30; Protein 2 g;
Carbohydrates 2 g;
Fat 2 g; Sodium 118 mg;
Cholesterol 0 mg

15 minutes | 1 hr. 12 min.

Baked Pita Chips

If you don't have pita bread on hand, you can use thinly sliced bagels or day-old rye bread. If the pitas around the edge of the baking sheet brown too fast, move them toward the center and the paler ones toward the edges.

- 2 tablespoons olive or vegetable oil
- 1 clove garlic, minced
- 1 teaspoon Dijon mustard
- 1 teaspoon lemon juice
- ½ teaspoon dried basil, crumbled
- 1 package (6 ounces) small pita breads
- ⅛ teaspoon each salt and black pepper

1 Preheat the oven to 375° F. Combine the oil, garlic, mustard, lemon juice, and basil in a small bowl. Split the pitas in half horizontally. Using a pastry brush dampened with water, brush the cut sides of each piece of pita with the oil mixture.

2 Stack the pitas into 2 piles. Using a sharp knife, cut each stack into quarters.

3 Arrange the pitas in a single layer on 2 ungreased baking sheets, sprinkle with the salt and pepper, and bake, uncovered, for 15 to 20 minutes or until golden brown. Makes 10 dozen.

Per dozen: Calories 72; Protein 2 g; Carbohydrates 9 g; Fat 3 g; Sodium 130 mg; Cholesterol 0 mg	
15 minutes	20 minutes

Orange Spiced Walnuts

These crispy nuts are wonderful to nibble on. If they should soften during storage, crisp them by spreading in a single layer on an ungreased baking sheet and warming, uncovered, in a 325° F oven for 5 to 10 minutes.

- 1 medium-size orange
- ¼ cup sugar
- 1 tablespoon vegetable oil
- ¼ teaspoon hot red pepper sauce
- 8 ounces shelled walnuts
- 2 teaspoons ground cinnamon
- ½ teaspoon ground cloves
- ¼ teaspoon salt

1 Preheat the oven to 350° F. Finely grate the orange zest (colored part of the rind) and set aside. Squeeze the orange and pour 2 tablespoons of the juice into a 13″ x 9″ x 2″ baking pan. Stir in the sugar, oil, and red pepper sauce, and mix well. Add the nuts and toss to coat.

2 Bake, uncovered, for 15 to 20 minutes or until golden, stirring halfway. Remove from the oven, stir in the reserved orange zest, cinnamon, and cloves, and toss to coat. Spoon onto a sheet of wax paper, separating the walnuts, and sprinkle with the salt, then let cool to room temperature. Keeps in an airtight container stored in a cool, dry place for 3 weeks. Makes 2 cups.

Per cup: Calories 909; Protein 17 g; Carbohydrates 53 g; Fat 77 g; Sodium 281 mg; Cholesterol 0 mg	
10 minutes	20 minutes

Celebration Cake

Here is a cake for every occasion, from birthdays to holidays, and a version—from rich chocolate to fresh lemon—
for every taste. For more servings, make a single-layer cake in a 13″ x 9″ x 2″ baking pan.

2½ cups sifted cake flour
1½ teaspoons baking powder
½ teaspoon baking soda
¾ cup (1½ sticks) unsalted butter, at room temperature
1½ cups granulated sugar
3 large eggs, lightly beaten
1 teaspoon vanilla extract
1 cup buttermilk

For the frosting:
6 tablespoons unsalted butter or margarine, at room temperature
6 squares (1 ounce each) unsweetened chocolate, melted
1 box (1 pound) confectioners sugar, sifted
6 to 8 tablespoons heavy cream, half-and-half, or evaporated skim milk

> *Per serving:*
> *Calories 881; Protein 8 g;*
> *Carbohydrates 125 g;*
> *Fat 44 g; Sodium 180 mg;*
> *Cholesterol 166 mg*

35 minutes   35 minutes

1 Preheat the oven to 350° F. Line the bottom of 2 well-greased 9-inch round cake pans with wax paper. Grease the wax paper, then dust lightly with flour. Tap out the excess flour and set aside. Sift the flour, baking powder, and soda together on a piece of wax paper; set aside.

2 Place the butter in a large electric mixer bowl and beat at high speed for about 2 minutes. Add the granulated sugar gradually and continue beating until fluffy—4 to 5 minutes.

3 Reduce the mixer speed to medium. Add the eggs, one at a time, beating only enough to combine after each addition. Add the vanilla and beat until light and fluffy—3 to 4 minutes.

4 Reduce the mixer speed to low. Add the sifted dry ingredients alternately with the buttermilk, beginning and ending with the dry ingredients and adding about ¼ of the total amount at a time. Beat the batter just until smooth.

5 Spoon the batter into the prepared pans, dividing the amount evenly, and bake, uncovered, for 30 to 35 minutes or until a toothpick inserted in the center of each cake comes out clean.

6 Transfer the pans to a wire rack and let cool, upright, for 5 minutes. Invert the pans on the rack, lift off the pans, and let the cakes cool to room temperature.

7 *For the frosting:* Place the butter in a small electric mixer bowl and beat at high speed for about 2 minutes. Add the chocolate and beat just until combined. Reduce the mixer speed to low, then add the confectioners sugar a little at a time, alternating with the cream. Continue beating until fluffy. (If the frosting is too thick to spread easily, beat in a little more cream.)

8 Place 1 cake layer on a round plate and spread with a thin layer of frosting. Top with the second layer, then frost the top and sides of the cake. Serves 8 to 10.

Chocolate Cake Variation

Follow Steps 1 and 2 as directed. In Step 3, add **3 melted squares (1 ounce each) unsweetened chocolate** to the batter after beating in the eggs. Proceed as directed. Serves 8 to 10.

Per serving: Calories 936; Protein 9 g;
Carbohydrates 128 g; Fat 49 g;
Sodium 181 mg; Cholesterol 166 mg

Lemon Cake Variation

Follow Steps 1 and 2 as directed. In Step 3, add **1 tablespoon finely grated lemon rind** along with the vanilla. Follow Steps 4 through 6 as directed. In Step 7, substitute Lemon Frosting (below) for the chocolate frosting and proceed as directed. Serves 8 to 10.

Per serving: Calories 735; Protein 6 g;
Carbohydrates 119 g; Fat 28 g;
Sodium 175 mg; Cholesterol 150 mg

Lemon Frosting Variation

In Step 7, omit the chocolate, add **1 tablespoon finely grated lemon rind**, and substitute **¼ cup lemon juice** for the cream. Proceed as directed.

Per serving: Calories 296; Protein 0 g;
Carbohydrates 58 g; Fat 9 g;
Sodium 2 mg; Cholesterol 23 mg

Vanilla Frosting Variation

In Step 7, omit the chocolate, add **2 teaspoons vanilla extract**, and proceed as directed.

Per serving: Calories 269; Protein 0 g;
Carbohydrates 57 g; Fat 13 g;
Sodium 6 mg; Cholesterol 38 mg

Celebration Cake—plain vanilla dressed up in confetti candy

No-Bake Cheesecake

Much lighter than the baked version and just as smooth and creamy. You can even make it with low-fat cottage cheese. Be sure to allow at least 4 hours for the cheesecake to chill before serving.

2 envelopes unflavored gelatin
¾ cup sugar
¼ teaspoon salt
2 large egg yolks
1 cup milk
1 tablespoon grated lemon rind
2 tablespoons lemon juice
3 cups whole-milk or part-skim ricotta cheese or creamed small curd or low-fat cottage cheese
1 cup heavy cream
Whole strawberries or raspberries (optional garnish)

For the crust:
1½ cups graham cracker crumbs (about 18 cracker squares)
¼ cup sugar
⅓ cup unsalted butter or margarine, melted

Per serving:
Calories 523; Protein 15 g;
Carbohydrates 41 g;
Fat 34 g; Sodium 250 mg;
Cholesterol 165 mg

35 minutes	10 minutes

1 Mix the gelatin, sugar, and salt in a medium-size saucepan. Add the egg yolks and half the milk, then beat until smooth. Stir in the remaining milk and cook over moderate heat, stirring constantly, until the mixture thickens slightly—7 to 10 minutes. (Do not let the mixture boil or it will curdle.) Remove from the heat and stir in the lemon rind and juice. Let cool for about 10 minutes.

2 *For the crust:* Mix the graham cracker crumbs, sugar, and butter in a small bowl. Lightly press the mixture over the bottom and about halfway up the sides of a 9-inch springform pan. Place in the freezer while preparing the filling.

3 Press the ricotta cheese through a large fine-meshed sieve set over a large mixing bowl. Blend in the cooled milk mixture. Beat the heavy cream in a medium-size bowl until stiff peaks form, then fold it into the milk and cheese.

4 Pour the filling into the prepared crust, cover with plastic food wrap, and chill for 4 hours or overnight. Garnish with strawberries or raspberries if desired. Serves 8 to 10.

Black Forest Roll

This impressive dessert requires a little patience and a jelly roll pan (a rectangular baking pan with 1-inch-deep sides). But the combination of chocolate sponge cake, raspberry jam, and whipped cream is so good, you'll want to make it time and again.

- **6** large eggs, separated
- **¾** cup granulated sugar
- **1** teaspoon vanilla extract
- **⅓** cup unsweetened cocoa powder
- **½** cup seedless raspberry jam
- **1** cup heavy cream, whipped
- **2** tablespoons confectioners sugar

Per serving:
Calories 239; Protein 5 g;
Carbohydrates 30 g;
Fat 12 g; Sodium 48 mg;
Cholesterol 160 mg

40 minutes | 30 minutes

1 Preheat the oven to 350° F. Grease a 15″ x 10″ x 1″ jelly roll pan, line the bottom with wax paper, then grease the paper and dust lightly with flour. Tap out any excess flour and set the pan aside.

2 Beat the egg yolks in a small electric mixer bowl at high speed until pale and thick—about 5 minutes. Add ½ cup of the granulated sugar and the vanilla and beat 5 minutes more. Reduce the mixer speed to low, add the cocoa, and beat just until blended. Set aside.

3 Quickly wash and dry the beaters, then beat the egg whites in a large mixer bowl at high speed until foamy—about 1 minute. Beating at high speed, gradually add the remaining ¼ cup granulated sugar and continue beating until the whites form stiff peaks.

4 Fold ⅓ of the beaten whites into the yolk mixture, then gently fold the yolk mixture into the remaining whites until no streaks of white or brown show. Pour the batter into the prepared pan and spread evenly with a spatula. Bake, uncovered, for 30 minutes or until the cake springs back when pressed lightly in the center.

5 Dampen a clean dish towel by sprinkling it with water. As soon as the cake comes from the oven, invert it onto the towel. Remove the pan and peel off the wax paper. Starting at one of the long sides, roll up the cake and towel together (jelly roll fashion) to prevent the cake from sticking to itself. Place on a wire rack and let cool to room temperature.

6 Unroll the cake, leaving the towel underneath, and spread with the jam, leaving a 1-inch margin all around. Spread the whipped cream on top of the jam, then roll up the cake. Using the towel to lift the cake, transfer it to a platter or cutting board, setting it seam side down. Remove the towel. Trim a diagonal slice off each end, then dust the top with the confectioners sugar. Serves 10 to 12.

When you want something grand, serve this beautiful Black Forest Roll, garnished with fresh raspberries.

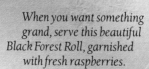

One-Bowl Chocolate Cake

For an elegant touch, arrange a few mint leaves or pretty cutouts on the cake, dust the surface with confectioners sugar, then remove the leaves or cutouts.

- 6 tablespoons hot water
- ½ cup unsweetened cocoa powder
- 1¼ cups sifted all-purpose flour
- ½ teaspoon baking powder
- ¼ teaspoon ground cinnamon
- ⅛ teaspoon salt
- ½ cup (1 stick) plus 2 tablespoons unsalted butter or margarine, at room temperature
- ¾ cup firmly packed light brown sugar

- 2 tablespoons honey
- 3 large eggs
- ½ teaspoon vanilla extract
- 2 tablespoons confectioners sugar

Per serving:
Calories 334; Protein 5 g;
Carbohydrates 43 g;
Fat 17 g; Sodium 87 mg;
Cholesterol 118 mg

15 minutes   30 minutes

1 Place an oven rack in the lower third of the oven, then preheat the oven to 350° F. Place the water in a large electric mixer bowl, add the cocoa, and whisk until smooth; let cool to room temperature.

2 Sift the flour with the baking powder, cinnamon, and salt onto a sheet of wax paper and set aside. Grease the bottom and sides of an 8-inch round cake pan, line the bottom with a circle of wax paper, and grease the paper; set aside.

3 Add the butter and brown sugar to the chocolate mixture and beat at medium speed until light and creamy—about 3 minutes. Beat in the honey, then add the eggs, one at a time, beating after each addition. Beat in the vanilla. Using a spoon, gently fold in the sifted dry ingredients.

4 Pour the batter into the prepared pan. Bake, uncovered, for 25 to 30 minutes or until a toothpick inserted in the center of the cake comes out clean. (Do not overbake or the cake will be dry.)

5 Transfer the pan to a wire rack and let cool, upright, for 10 minutes. Remove the cake from the pan and let cool to room temperature. Dust with the confectioners sugar. Serves 8.

Summer Peach Cake

Lovely to look at, easy to make, this cake will please everyone. For variety,
use your favorite seasonal fruit or a combination.

3 large ripe peaches, peeled and sliced, or 2½ cups frozen unsweetened sliced peaches, partially thawed

¾ cup plus 2 tablespoons granulated sugar

½ teaspoon ground cinnamon

1 cup sifted all-purpose flour

1 teaspoon baking powder

½ cup unsalted butter or margarine, at room temperature

2 large eggs

Confectioners sugar

Per serving:
Calories 244; Protein 3 g;
Carbohydrates 34 g;
Fat 11 g; Sodium 53 mg;
Cholesterol 75 mg

20 minutes | 50 minutes

---

1 Preheat the oven to 350° F. Place the peaches, 2 tablespoons of the granulated sugar, and the cinnamon in a large bowl and toss.

2 On a piece of wax paper, sift together the flour and baking powder. Cream the butter and remaining granulated sugar in the large bowl of an electric mixer at high speed until very light and fluffy—about 5 minutes. Beat in the eggs, one at a time, until well blended. On low speed, mix in the flour just until blended.

3 Pour the batter into a greased 8″ x 8″ x 2″ pan and arrange the peaches attractively on top. Bake for 50 minutes or until lightly browned and a toothpick inserted in the center comes out clean. Let cool in the pan on a wire rack. Dust with the confectioners sugar and serve warm or at room temperature. Serves 9.

Pineapple-Carrot Loaf

This lovely tea cake will keep for 5 days covered with plastic food wrap and stored in a cool, dry place.

- 1½ cups sifted all-purpose flour
- 1½ teaspoons baking powder
- ¾ teaspoon baking soda
- 1 teaspoon ground cinnamon
- 1 cup granulated sugar
- ½ cup finely chopped walnuts or pecans
- 2 large eggs
- ½ cup vegetable oil
- 1½ cups finely grated carrots
- ¾ cup canned crushed pineapple with its juice
- 2 teaspoons finely grated orange rind
- 2 tablespoons confectioners sugar

1 Preheat the oven to 350° F. Sift the flour, baking powder, soda, cinnamon, and granulated sugar together into a large bowl. Add the walnuts, toss well to mix, then make a well in the center.

2 Mix the eggs, oil, carrots, pineapple, and orange rind in a medium-size bowl, pour into the well, and stir just enough to combine. The batter should be lumpy.

3 Pour the batter into a well-greased 9″ x 5″ x 3″ loaf pan, spreading smoothly to the corners, and bake, uncovered, for 1 to 1¼ hours or until the cake begins to pull away from the sides of the pan and a toothpick inserted in the center comes out clean.

4 Let cool upright in the pan on a wire rack for 10 minutes, then turn out onto the rack and let cool completely. Sift the confectioners sugar over the top. Serves 12.

Per serving:
Calories 256; Protein 3 g;
Carbohydrates 33 g;
Fat 13 g; Sodium 110 mg;
Cholesterol 36 mg

 25 minutes 1 hr. 15 min.

Black Cherry Trifle

Trifles — tender concoctions of cake, fruit, and custard — are of British origin. This quick version substitutes yogurt for custard for a lighter dessert. Allow 1 hour for the trifle to chill before serving.

- 1 package (10 ounces) frozen pound cake, thawed
- ⅓ cup black cherry or other all-fruit spread
- 3 containers (8 ounces each) black cherry low-fat yogurt
- 1 cup frozen light whipped dessert topping, thawed
- ⅓ cup coarsely chopped walnuts or pecans

1 Cut the cake into 14 slices ½ inch thick. Spread 1 side of each slice with 1 level teaspoon of the fruit spread. Line the sides of a 1-quart glass bowl or soufflé dish with 8 slices of the cake, with the spread sides in. Lay 2 slices, spread sides up, in the bottom of the dish.

2 Spoon 1 container of yogurt evenly on top of the cake in the bottom of the dish. Top with ⅓ cup of the whipped topping, then sprinkle with 2 tablespoons of the walnuts.

3 Repeat each of the layers twice, ending with a dollop of whipped topping and a sprinkling of walnuts. Chill for 1 hour. Serves 4 to 6.

Per serving:
Calories 704; Protein 14 g;
Carbohydrates 89 g;
Fat 34 g; Sodium 230 mg;
Cholesterol 154 mg

 15 minutes None

The pick of the crop makes Summer Peach Cake the cream of the crop.

315

Chocolate Decadence

This sinfully rich dessert needs 4 hours to chill, but it can be made up to 4 days in advance. If you prefer, you can omit the pound cake. Simply prepare the chocolate mixture as directed, then pour it into eight 5- to 6-ounce custard cups.

3 squares (1 ounce each) unsweetened chocolate, coarsely chopped

¾ cup unsweetened cocoa powder

1½ cups sugar

1 teaspoon unflavored gelatin

½ cup strong coffee

¾ cup (1½ sticks) unsalted butter or margarine, at room temperature

1 teaspoon vanilla extract

1 cup heavy cream, whipped, or 2 cups frozen whipped dessert topping, thawed

6 ounces prepared pound cake, cut into ¾-inch cubes

1 Line an 8" x 4" x 2" loaf pan with plastic food wrap and coat with nonstick cooking spray; set aside.

2 Place the chocolate and cocoa in a food processor or an electric blender and whirl for 2 minutes or until powdery.

3 Combine the sugar, gelatin, and coffee in a small saucepan. Bring to a boil over moderate heat, then cook, stirring constantly, for 1 minute or until the gelatin dissolves completely.

4 With the processor on, add the boiling coffee mixture to the chocolate and process for 1 minute, scraping down the sides of the container midway. Add the butter and vanilla and process for 30 seconds or until smooth, again scraping down the sides midway.

5 Spoon the whipped cream around the edge of the container and pulse 3 times. Scrape down the sides and pulse until well mixed.

Spoon about ⅓ of the chocolate mixture into the prepared pan, sprinkle the cake cubes on top, then cover with the remaining chocolate mixture.

6 Rap the pan sharply on the counter several times, cover with plastic food wrap, and chill for at least 4 hours or until firm. To serve, invert the loaf on a platter, lift off the pan, and remove the plastic wrap. Using a knife dipped in hot water, cut into ½-inch slices. Serves 16.

Per serving:
Calories 286; Protein 2 g;
Carbohydrates 27 g;
Fat 21 g; Sodium 26 mg;
Cholesterol 65 mg

15 minutes 3 minutes

Lemon Pudding Cake

This down-home recipe gives you two desserts in one: a creamy custard topped with a cloud-light sponge cake. It's easy to make, too— the batter separates all by itself while the cake bakes.

3 tablespoons unsalted butter or margarine, at room temperature

½ cup granulated sugar

2 large eggs, separated

¼ cup lemon juice (freshly squeezed preferred)

⅓ cup sifted all-purpose flour

1 cup milk

2 teaspoons finely grated lemon rind

1 teaspoon vanilla extract

2 tablespoons confectioners sugar

Per serving:
Calories 295; Protein 6 g;
Carbohydrates 39 g;
Fat 13 g; Sodium 63 mg;
Cholesterol 138 mg

 25 minutes   45 minutes

1 Preheat the oven to 350° F. Beat the butter in a large electric mixer bowl at high speed until creamy— about 2 minutes. Add ⅓ cup of the granulated sugar, a little at a time, beating after each addition. Continue beating at high speed until fluffy—about 2 minutes.

2 Add the egg yolks, one at a time, beating at medium speed after each addition only enough to incorporate. Beat in the lemon juice, then the flour, and continue beating at medium speed for 2 minutes. Add the milk, lemon rind, and vanilla, and beat just enough to combine.

3 Quickly wash and dry the beaters. Place the egg whites in a small electric mixer bowl and beat at high speed until frothy. While beating, add the remaining granulated sugar gradually, then continue beating until stiff peaks form. Fold ¼ of the whites into the batter, then fold in the remaining whites.

4 Spoon the mixture into a buttered 1-quart soufflé dish or straight-sided baking dish and set in a large shallow baking pan. Pour enough hot water into the pan to come halfway up the sides of the soufflé dish. Bake, uncovered, in the hot water bath for 40 to 45 minutes or until puffed and golden. Sift the confectioners sugar over the top and serve warm or, if you prefer, chilled. Serves 4.

The proof, as they say, is in the pudding—or in this case the Lemon Pudding Cake.

317

Chocolate Bread Pudding

This chocolate lover's delight can also be made with other kinds of bread, such as white, granola, or cinnamon-raisin.

- 3 tablespoons golden raisins
- ½ cup warm water
- ½ cup firmly packed light brown sugar
- ¼ cup unsweetened cocoa powder
- 3 large eggs
- 2½ cups low-fat milk
- 1 tablespoon unsalted butter or margarine
- ½ teaspoon vanilla extract
- ⅛ teaspoon each ground nutmeg and salt
- 8 slices whole wheat bread, cut into ½-inch cubes (4 cups)

1 Preheat the oven to 375° F. Place the raisins and water in a small bowl and let stand for 10 to 15 minutes or until the raisins are soft. Drain the raisins, discarding the water, and set aside.

2 Whisk the sugar with the cocoa and eggs in a medium-size bowl until smooth; set aside. Heat the milk and butter, uncovered, in a medium-size saucepan over low heat until the butter melts—about 3 minutes. Whisk the milk mixture into the cocoa mixture along with the vanilla, nutmeg, and salt.

3 Place the bread cubes in a lightly greased 8″ x 8″ x 2″ baking pan. Sprinkle with the raisins, then pour in the cocoa mixture. Let stand for 10 minutes.

4 Set the pan in a larger baking pan, then pour enough hot water into the larger pan to come halfway up the sides of the pudding pan.

5 Bake the pudding, uncovered, in the hot water bath for 25 minutes or until a toothpick inserted in the center comes out clean. Serve warm or at room temperature. Serves 4.

Per serving:
Calories 421; Protein 16 g;
Carbohydrates 68 g;
Fat 12 g; Sodium 556 mg;
Cholesterol 174 mg

 25 minutes 28 minutes

Quick Brown Rice Pudding

This simple rice pudding makes a nutritious snack for kids. Keep the cooked grain and raisin mixture in the refrigerator, stirring in ¼ cup whipped topping per person just before serving.

- 1¼ cups water
- ¼ cup sugar
- ¼ teaspoon salt
- 1 cup quick-cooking brown rice
- ½ cup golden raisins
- 1 teaspoon vanilla extract
- 1 cup frozen whipped dessert topping, thawed

1 Place the water, sugar, and salt in a medium-size saucepan and bring to a boil over high heat. Add the rice, reduce the heat to low, cover, and simmer for 5 minutes.

2 Stir in the raisins, cover, and cook 5 minutes longer or until all the liquid has been absorbed. Stir in the vanilla.

3 Transfer the rice mixture to a medium-size bowl. Cover with plastic food wrap and refrigerate for several hours or until well chilled.

4 Just before serving, gently but thoroughly fold in the whipped topping. Serves 4.

Per serving:
Calories 218; Protein 2 g;
Carbohydrates 43 g;
Fat 5 g; Sodium 141 mg;
Cholesterol 0 mg

 10 minutes 12 minutes

The perfect pick-me-up for any afternoon—soft and chewy Chocolate Bread Pudding with a steaming cup of tea

Maple-Nut Chocolate Pudding

Who could possibly resist chocolate chips and other goodies blended to the consistency of an extra-thick shake and topped with nuts? Allow several hours for the pudding to chill.

1 cup evaporated skim milk

1 package (6 ounces) chocolate chips

4 teaspoons maple extract or 1 teaspoon other extract

¼ cup coarsely chopped walnuts or pecans

> Per serving:
> Calories 317; Protein 8 g;
> Carbohydrates 33 g;
> Fat 20 g; Sodium 75 mg;
> Cholesterol 3 mg

8 minutes | 5 minutes

1 Heat the milk in a small saucepan over low heat until small bubbles form around the edge of the pan—about 5 minutes.

2 Place the chocolate chips and maple extract in an electric blender, pour in the hot milk, and whirl at high speed for about 3 minutes or until the chocolate chips melt and the mixture is smooth.

3 Pour into a medium-size bowl, cover with plastic food wrap, and refrigerate for several hours or until slightly thickened. Stir in the walnuts before serving. Serves 4.

Coffee Parfait

This cool, refreshing dessert is easy on the cook and the waistline. For a festive look, top it with a dollop of whipped cream, chocolate curls, and fresh coffee beans. Allow several hours for the parfait to chill before serving.

2 cups low-fat milk

2 envelopes unflavored gelatin

½ cup sugar

2 tablespoons instant coffee granules

1 cup half-and-half

1 teaspoon vanilla extract

1 cup ice cubes (6 to 8)

> Per serving:
> Calories 161; Protein 6 g;
> Carbohydrates 23 g;
> Fat 6 g; Sodium 61 mg;
> Cholesterol 18 mg

10 minutes | 5 minutes

1 Heat 1 cup of the milk, uncovered, in a small saucepan over low heat until tiny bubbles form around the edge of the pan—about 5 minutes. Meanwhile, pour the remaining 1 cup milk into an electric blender, sprinkle in the gelatin, and let stand for 5 minutes.

2 Pour the hot milk over the gelatin mixture and whirl at low speed for 2 minutes or until the gelatin is completely dissolved. Add the sugar and coffee granules and whirl at high speed for about 1 minute or until the coffee dissolves and the mixture is well blended.

3 With the motor running at high speed, add the half-and-half, then the vanilla, then the ice cubes, one at a time, and continue whirling until all of the ice cubes have melted. Pour into six 8-ounce parfait glasses or wine goblets and refrigerate for several hours or until set. Serves 6.

Mocha Parfait Variation

Prepare as directed, but in Step 2, add *1 tablespoon unsweetened cocoa powder* along with the sugar and coffee granules. Serves 6.

Per serving: Calories 164; Protein 6 g;
Carbohydrates 24 g; Fat 6 g;
Sodium 61 mg; Cholesterol 18 mg

319

Raspberry Chocolate Pie

A lovely summer dessert. If you're pressed for time, use a packaged 9-inch graham cracker crust in place of the chocolate wafers. Allow 4 hours before serving for the filling to chill.

For the crust:

- 1½ cups chocolate wafer crumbs (25 to 30 thin chocolate wafers)
- 3 tablespoons unsalted butter or margarine, at room temperature
- 2 tablespoons sugar

For the filling:

- ¼ cup cold water
- 1 envelope unflavored gelatin
- 12 ounces fresh or frozen raspberries with their juice, thawed
- 1 cup plain low-fat yogurt
- ½ cup sugar
- ½ teaspoon finely grated lemon rind
- 1 cup frozen light whipped topping, thawed

Per serving:
Calories 495; Protein 8 g;
Carbohydrates 75 g;
Fat 20 g; Sodium 298 mg;
Cholesterol 27 mg

 20 minutes   13 minutes

1 *For the crust:* Preheat the oven to 350° F. Combine the crumbs, butter, and sugar in a medium-size bowl. Pat the mixture over the bottom and up the sides of a greased 9-inch pie pan. Bake, uncovered, for 10 minutes. Let cool to room temperature.

2 *For the filling:* Place the water in a small heatproof bowl, sprinkle with the gelatin, and let soften for 10 minutes. Set the bowl of gelatin in a saucepan of simmering water. Cook, stirring, over moderate heat for 2 to 3 minutes or until the gelatin dissolves completely.

3 Purée the raspberries in a food processor or an electric blender—about 30 seconds. Press the purée through a fine sieve set over a medium-size bowl. Discard the seeds.

4 Mix the yogurt into the raspberry purée along with the gelatin, sugar, and lemon rind. Fold in the whipped topping. Pour the raspberry mixture into the pie shell and chill, uncovered, for 3 to 4 hours or until set. Serves 4 to 6.

Blueberry Yogurt Pie

You can make this gorgeous dessert in just 15 minutes, but you must allow 1 hour for the filling to chill.

- 2 cups plain nonfat yogurt
- 1 package (3½ ounces) instant vanilla pudding and pie filling mix
- ½ teaspoon finely grated lemon rind
- 1 9-inch graham cracker pie shell
- 1 pint fresh blueberries or 1 package (12 ounces) frozen unsweetened blueberries, unthawed
- ¼ cup red currant jelly

Per serving:
Calories 244; Protein 4 g;
Carbohydrates 36 g;
Fat 10 g; Sodium 163 mg;
Cholesterol 24 mg

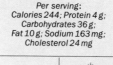 13 minutes 2 minutes

1 Combine the yogurt, pudding mix, and lemon rind in a small bowl. Chill, uncovered, in the refrigerator for 5 minutes.

2 Spoon the mixture into the pie shell, then arrange the blueberries on top. Warm the jelly in a small heavy saucepan over low heat, stirring often, until melted—2 minutes. Brush over the blueberries.

3 Chill the pie, uncovered, in the refrigerator for 1 hour or until firm. Serves 8.

Lime Angel Pie

This pie is best started the day before you plan to serve it because the meringue shell needs 5 hours to dry and the filling must be chilled another 5 hours. Surely a taste of heaven is worth the wait.

For the meringue crust:
- 4 large egg whites
- ¼ teaspoon cream of tartar
- ¼ teaspoon salt
- ¾ cup sugar
- ¼ teaspoon almond extract

For the filling:
- ½ cup sugar
- ⅛ teaspoon salt
- 4 large egg yolks
- 3 tablespoons fresh lime juice
- ½ teaspoon finely grated lime rind

For the topping:
- 1 cup heavy cream or 2 cups frozen whipped dessert topping, thawed

Per serving:
Calories 340; Protein 5 g;
Carbohydrates 42 g;
Fat 18 g; Sodium 190 mg;
Cholesterol 196 mg

35 minutes   1 hr. 7 min.

1 *For the meringue crust:* Place an oven rack in the lower third of the oven and preheat the oven to 250° F. Place the egg whites, cream of tartar, and salt in the largest electric mixer bowl and beat at medium speed until soft peaks form. Raise the mixer speed to high and add the sugar, 1 tablespoon at a time, beating continuously, until stiff peaks form. Beat in the almond extract.

2 Spread the meringue over the bottom and up the sides of a lightly greased 9-inch pie pan (preferably ovenproof glass) to form a pie shell. Bake for 1 hour. Turn off the heat but leave the meringue in the oven without opening the door for at least 5 hours or overnight so that it crisps and dries.

3 *For the filling:* Combine the sugar, salt, egg yolks, lime juice, and rind in the top of a double boiler. Set over simmering water and cook, stirring constantly, for 6 to 7 minutes or until the mixture

thickens. Remove from the heat, set the double boiler top in a pan of cold water, and let cool to room temperature, stirring occasionally. Pour the cooled filling into the meringue shell.

4 *For the topping:* Whip the cream until stiff and spread over the filling, swirling into peaks and valleys. Tent the pie loosely with foil and chill for at least 5 hours or overnight. Serves 6 to 8.

Chocolate Angel Variation

Follow Steps 1 and 2 as directed. Omit Step 3. Instead, melt **4 squares (1 ounce each) semisweet chocolate** in the top of a double boiler over simmering water; let cool to room temperature. Whip **1 cup heavy cream** until stiff, then fold into the melted chocolate along with **1 teaspoon vanilla extract**. Pour into the shell and chill as directed in Step 4. Serves 6 to 8.

Per serving: Calories 473; Protein 5 g;
Carbohydrates 37 g; Fat 36 g;
Sodium 156 mg; Cholesterol 109 mg

Jelly glaze adds professional gloss to Blueberry Yogurt Pie.

321

Fruit Crisp

The sugar and flour crisp up as they bake, giving this dish its name and making a wonderfully crunchy topping for the soft, warm fruit.

1¼ pounds pears, peaches, apples, or nectarines, peeled, cored, and thinly sliced

1 tablespoon lemon juice (freshly squeezed preferred)

¼ teaspoon each ground cinnamon and cloves

½ cup firmly packed light brown sugar

½ cup unsifted whole wheat or all-purpose flour

¼ cup (½ stick) unsalted butter or margarine

½ cup heavy cream, whipped, or 1 cup frozen whipped dessert topping, thawed, or 4 scoops vanilla ice cream (optional topping)

1 Preheat the oven to 375° F. Coat an 8" x 8" x 2" baking dish with nonstick cooking spray. Place the fruit, lemon juice, cinnamon, cloves, 2 tablespoons of the sugar, and 1 tablespoon of the flour in the baking dish and mix well.

2 Combine the remaining sugar and flour in a small bowl, add the butter, then, using a pastry blender or 2 knives, cut the butter in until the texture of coarse meal. Sprinkle evenly over the fruit mixture.

3 Bake, uncovered, for 30 to 40 minutes or until the topping is golden brown. Serve hot or at room temperature. Top, if you like, with whipped cream. Serves 4 to 6.

Per serving:
Calories 338; Protein 3 g;
Carbohydrates 59 g;
Fat 12 g; Sodium 11 mg;
Cholesterol 31 mg

 20 minutes | 40 minutes

Ginger Pear Crisp Variation

Follow Step 1 as directed, but add **1 tablespoon coarsely chopped crystallized ginger** to the pear mixture. In Step 2, omit the flour. Place **1½ cups gingersnap crumbs** in a large bowl. Reduce the brown sugar to ¼ cup, add it to the gingersnap crumbs, and mix well with your fingers. Reduce the butter to 3 tablespoons and, using a pastry blender, cut it in until the texture of coarse meal. Sprinkle evenly over the pear mixture. Follow Step 3 as directed. Serves 4 to 6.

Per serving: Calories 344; Protein 2 g;
Carbohydrates 51 g; Fat 16 g;
Sodium 97 mg; Cholesterol 23 mg

Cranberry Tarts

For variety, you can fill the tart shells with 1½ cups of your favorite prepared pie filling or pudding. Garnish with sour cream or whipped cream and a sprinkling of coarsely chopped nuts.

1½ cups whole cranberry sauce

1 tablespoon honey

½ teaspoon finely grated orange rind

½ cup toasted chopped walnuts (see page 86)

1 package (10 ounces) refrigerator biscuits

¼ cup reduced-fat sour cream

1 Preheat the oven to 400° F. Mix the cranberry sauce, honey, and orange rind in a small bowl. Stir in the walnuts and set aside.

2 Using a rolling pin, gently flatten each biscuit into a 3½-inch round. Put each round in a muffin pan cup so that it covers the bottom and comes halfway up the sides. Using a tablespoon, flatten the dough against the bottom and sides of the cup to form tart shells.

3 Bake the shells, uncovered, for 4 to 7 minutes or until golden brown. Transfer to a serving platter.

4 Fill the shells with the cranberry mixture. Top each one with a small dollop of the sour cream. Makes 10 tarts.

Per tart:
Calories 209; Protein 3 g;
Carbohydrates 33 g;
Fat 8 g; Sodium 368 mg;
Cholesterol 0 mg

 20 minutes | 7 minutes

Blueberry-Raspberry Cobbler

If you're in a rush, top the cobbler with packaged biscuits. To make a peach-raspberry cobbler, substitute peaches for the blueberries. To separate the frozen fruit, place the package under cold running water just long enough to loosen.

- **4 cups** fresh or **1 package (12 ounces)** frozen unsweetened blueberries, unthawed
- **1 cup** fresh or frozen unsweetened raspberries, unthawed
- **¼ cup** sugar
- **4 teaspoons** cornstarch
- **1 tablespoon** lemon juice or kirsch

For the topping:
- **2 cups** unsifted all-purpose flour
- **2½ tablespoons** sugar
- **1 tablespoon** baking powder
- **¼ teaspoon** salt
- **6 tablespoons** unsalted butter or margarine, cut into pats
- **⅔ cup** milk
- **1 cup** heavy cream, whipped, or **½ pint** vanilla ice milk (optional)

Per serving:
Calories 589; Protein 9 g;
Carbohydrates 96 g;
Fat 20 g; Sodium 420 mg;
Cholesterol 52 mg

20 minutes | 40 minutes

1 Preheat the oven to 425° F. Mix the blueberries and raspberries in an ungreased 9" x 9" x 2" baking pan. Combine the sugar and cornstarch in a small bowl, then sprinkle over the berries. Drizzle the lemon juice evenly over all and set aside.

2 *For the topping:* Sift the flour, 2 tablespoons of the sugar, the baking powder, and salt together in a large bowl. Using a pastry blender or 2 knives, cut the butter in until the texture of coarse meal. Add the milk and mix with a fork just until the dough holds together.

3 On a floured surface, pat the dough out to a thickness of ½ inch, then cut into ten 2½-inch rounds. Arrange the rounds, slightly overlapping, on top of the berry mixture. Sprinkle with the remaining ½ tablespoon sugar.

4 Bake, uncovered, for 30 to 40 minutes or until the fruit is bubbling and the topping lightly browned. If the topping seems to be browning too fast, tent with foil. Serve hot or warm, topped, if desired, with whipped cream or vanilla ice milk. Serves 4 to 6.

A dandy dessert for the day after Thanksgiving — Cranberry Tarts topped with a dollop of sour cream

Easy Apple Strudel

We used applesauce and frozen phyllo pastry to take most of the work out of this traditional Hungarian dessert.

1 jar (1 pound 7 ounces) chunky applesauce

½ cup raisins

2 tablespoons granulated sugar

2 tablespoons fine dry bread crumbs, gingersnap crumbs, or vanilla wafer crumbs

½ teaspoon ground cinnamon

¼ teaspoon each ground cloves and nutmeg

8 sheets phyllo dough, thawed if frozen

¼ cup unsalted butter or margarine, melted

2 tablespoons confectioners sugar

Per serving:
Calories 287; Protein 2 g;
Carbohydrates 38 g;
Fat 15 g; Sodium 140 mg;
Cholesterol 15 mg

20 minutes 35 minutes

1 Preheat the oven to 350° F. Mix the applesauce, raisins, granulated sugar, bread crumbs, cinnamon, cloves, and nutmeg in a medium-size bowl and set aside.

2 Spread 1 sheet of the phyllo dough on a piece of wax paper. Cover the remaining dough with a damp cloth to keep it from drying out. Brush the dough with a little of the melted butter. Place a second sheet of dough on top and brush with a little more butter. Repeat until you have used up all of the phyllo dough and butter.

3 Spoon the applesauce mixture along one long side of the phyllo dough, leaving a 1-inch margin at each end. Fold the ends of the dough over the applesauce mixture, then roll up, tucking in the ends as you go. Using the wax paper to lift the strudel, ease it onto a lightly greased baking sheet, seam side down.

4 Bake, uncovered, for 30 to 35 minutes or until golden. Transfer to a wire rack and let cool to room temperature. Place the confectioners sugar in a small fine sieve and dust over the top. Serves 8.

Cherry Clafouti

This classic French dessert is usually made with fresh cherries, but you can also use frozen cherries or, if you prefer, sliced peaches or apricots.

⅔ cup milk

⅓ cup sifted all-purpose flour

⅓ cup granulated sugar

2 large eggs

2 teaspoons vanilla extract

⅛ teaspoon salt

1½ cups pitted fresh dark sweet cherries or 1 package (12 ounces) frozen pitted dark sweet cherries, unthawed but patted dry

2 tablespoons confectioners sugar

Per serving:
Calories 222; Protein 6 g;
Carbohydrates 40 g;
Fat 5 g; Sodium 119 mg;
Cholesterol 112 mg

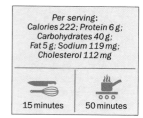

15 minutes 50 minutes

1 Preheat the oven to 350° F. Place the milk, flour, granulated sugar, eggs, vanilla, and salt in a food processor or an electric blender and whirl until smooth—5 to 10 seconds.

2 Arrange the cherries in the bottom of a buttered 9-inch glass pie plate. Pour the batter evenly over the cherries.

3 Bake, uncovered, for 45 to 50 minutes or until puffed, lightly browned, and set. Let cool for 15 minutes, then dust with the confectioners sugar. Serves 4.

Strawberry Fool—rich, creamy, and elegant

Strawberry Fool

This luscious old-fashioned dessert can also be made with blueberries or raspberries. Allow at least 1 hour (or as long as overnight) for the cooked fruit to chill before adding the whipped cream.

1 pint fresh strawberries, blueberries, or raspberries, rinsed and hulled
¼ cup honey
1 tablespoon strawberry or red raspberry jam
2 teaspoons lemon juice (freshly squeezed preferred)
¾ cup heavy cream
¼ cup plain low-fat yogurt
4 large strawberries, thinly sliced (optional garnish)

Per serving:
Calories 265; Protein 2 g;
Carbohydrates 28 g;
Fat 17 g; Sodium 29 mg;
Cholesterol 62 mg

15 minutes	5 minutes

1 Place the whole strawberries and 3 tablespoons of the honey in a food processor or an electric blender and purée—about 30 seconds.

2 Transfer the mixture to a medium-size nonmetallic saucepan, add the jam, and boil over moderate heat, uncovered, for 3 minutes. Remove from the heat and stir in the lemon juice. Transfer to a small bowl, cover with plastic food wrap, and chill—about 1 hour.

3 Less than an hour before serving, combine the cream and yogurt in a medium-size bowl and whip until frothy. Drizzle in the remaining 1 tablespoon honey and beat until soft peaks form.

4 Gently fold the whipped mixture into the strawberry mixture and spoon into 4 parfait glasses or wine goblets. Serve at once or refrigerate and serve within 1 hour. Garnish, if desired, with the sliced strawberries. Serves 4.

325

Baked Apples with Cranberry-Nut Stuffing

What could beat a baked apple with cream on a cold day—only this new version made with chopped nuts and cranberry-orange relish.

4 medium-size baking apples such as Rome Beauties

3 tablespoons prepared cranberry-orange relish

2 tablespoons coarsely chopped blanched pistachios (see page 145) or walnuts

½ teaspoon pumpkin pie spice

1 tablespoon unsalted butter or margarine

½ cup boiling water

2 tablespoons honey

½ cup heavy cream, whipped, or 1 cup frozen whipped dessert topping, thawed (optional topping)

Per serving:
Calories 204; Protein 1 g;
Carbohydrates 41 g;
Fat 5 g; Sodium 4 mg;
Cholesterol 8 mg

20 minutes | 40 minutes

1 Preheat the oven to 375° F. Core the apples to within ½ inch of the bottom (a melon baller or paring knife makes this easy) and set aside. Mix the cranberry-orange relish, pistachios, and pumpkin pie spice in a small bowl, then spoon into the hollows of the apples and dot with the butter.

2 Stand the apples in an ungreased 9-inch round cake pan. Combine the water and honey in a 1-cup measure and pour into the pan around the apples. Bake, uncovered, for 30 to 40 minutes or until the apples are tender when pierced with a toothpick. Spoon the pan juices over the apples and serve hot or warm, topped, if desired, with dollops of whipped cream. Serves 4.

Good things in small packages: Pastry-crowned variations of Baked Apples with Cranberry-nut Stuffing.

Pastry-Crowned Apples Variation

Thaw the 2 sheets of *frozen puff pastry* (from a 17¼-ounce package) according to package directions. Follow Step 1 as directed. In Step 2, place the apples in individual custard cups. Omit the water; drizzle the honey over the apples. Roll out the pastry sheets on a floured surface to a thickness of ⅛ inch; cut two 5½-inch rounds out of each sheet. Place a pastry round on top of each apple and crimp to the edges of the custard cup. Bake as directed; serve at once. Serves 4.

Per serving: Calories 391; Protein 3 g;
Carbohydrates 55 g; Fat 8 g;
Sodium 187 mg; Cholesterol 8 mg

Stuffed Apple Dumplings Variation

Thaw the 2 sheets of *frozen puff pastry* according to package directions. Follow Step 1 as directed. In Step 2, roll out the pastry as directed in variation above. Cut each sheet into two 7-inch squares; place a stuffed apple in the center of each one. Omit the water; drizzle the apples with the honey. Gather the 4 corners of each square, bring up, then pinch all edges to seal. Place the apples, not touching, on an ungreased foil-lined baking sheet; bake as directed. Serves 4.

Per serving: Calories 453; Protein 4 g;
Carbohydrates 59 g; Fat 24 g;
Sodium 249 mg; Cholesterol 8 mg

Pumpkin Mousse

A feather-light dessert that can be served as a mousse or spooned into a baked 9-inch pie shell to make the world's best pumpkin pie. Allow 4 hours for the mousse to chill before serving.

- 1 envelope unflavored gelatin
- ½ cup sugar
- 2 large eggs
- ⅛ teaspoon salt
- ¼ cup cold water
- 1 cup fresh or canned pumpkin purée or 1 cup frozen winter squash, thawed
- ¾ teaspoon ground cinnamon
- ½ teaspoon ground ginger
- ¼ teaspoon each ground nutmeg and allspice
- 3 cups frozen whipped dessert topping, thawed, or 1½ cups heavy cream, whipped

Optional garnishes:

- 1 cup frozen whipped dessert topping, thawed or ½ cup heavy cream, whipped
- 2 tablespoons slivered crystallized ginger

1 Place the gelatin, sugar, eggs, salt, and water in a small saucepan, and beat until smooth. Cook, stirring constantly, over moderately low heat until the sugar and gelatin dissolve and the mixture thickens slightly—about 5 minutes. (Do not boil or the mixture may curdle.)

2 Remove from the heat and set in a large pan of cold water. Let the gelatin mixture cool to lukewarm, stirring occasionally. Beat in the pumpkin, then the cinnamon, ginger, nutmeg, and allspice.

3 Refrigerate, uncovered, for 15 minutes, then fold in the dessert topping. Spoon into a large serving bowl or into 6 to 8 individual dessert dishes. Cover with plastic food wrap and refrigerate for 4 hours or overnight.

4 Just before serving, decorate, if desired, with swirls of whipped topping and slivers of crystallized ginger. Serves 6 to 8.

Per serving:
Calories 223; Protein 4 g;
Carbohydrates 28 g;
Fat 11 g; Sodium 78 mg;
Cholesterol 71 mg

30 minutes   5 minutes

Low-Cal Orange Mousse

Garnish this refreshing dessert with slices of fresh orange or a sprig of mint. Allow 3 hours for the mousse to chill.

- ½ cup water
- 1 envelope unflavored gelatin
- ⅓ cup sugar
- ¼ cup frozen orange juice concentrate, thawed
- 1 cup plain low-fat yogurt
- 1 envelope (1.3 ounces) nondairy whipped topping mix
- ½ cup cold milk

Per serving:
Calories 200; Protein 7 g;
Carbohydrates 32 g;
Fat 5 g; Sodium 58 mg;
Cholesterol 8 mg

5 minutes   18 minutes

1 Place the water in a small saucepan over low heat, sprinkle with the gelatin, and bring to a simmer, stirring. Continue stirring until the gelatin dissolves—about 1 minute.

2 Stir in the sugar, orange juice concentrate, and yogurt, then place the pan in a large bowl of ice water. Stir until the mixture begins to mound—about 15 minutes.

3 Whip the topping and milk to soft peaks. Fold into the yogurt mixture. Spoon into a medium-size bowl, cover with plastic wrap, and chill 3 hours or until softly set. Serves 4.

Lemon Mousse Variation

Follow Step 1 as directed. In Step 2, increase the sugar to ⅔ cup and substitute **6 tablespoons freshly squeezed lemon juice** for the orange juice. Proceed as directed. Serves 4.

Per Serving: Calories 244; Protein 6 g; Carbohydrates 45 g; Fat 5 g; Sodium 58 mg; Cholesterol 8 mg

Grapefruit Mousse Variation

Follow Step 1 as directed. In Step 2, substitute **¼ cup thawed frozen pink grapefruit juice concentrate** for the orange juice. Add **½ teaspoon grenadine** to the gelatin mixture if desired. Proceed as directed. Serves 4.

Per Serving: Calories 201; Protein 6 g; Carbohydrates 32 g; Fat 6 g; Sodium 58 mg; Cholesterol 8 mg

Bananas with Double Chocolate Sauce

If you're in a hurry, you can make this dessert with your favorite store-bought chocolate sauce. But if you have a little time, try our Double Chocolate recipe. Absolutely scrumptious, it makes 2 cups, so there will be enough left over to serve another day over cake or ice cream.

For the sauce:
- 2 cups water
- 1⅓ cups sugar
- ¼ cup unsweetened cocoa powder
- 4 ounces chocolate chips
- 2 tablespoons unsalted butter or margarine
- ¼ teaspoon salt
- 1 teaspoon vanilla extract

For the bananas:
- 4 medium-size ripe bananas, peeled and sliced diagonally ½ inch thick
- 4 teaspoons hulled pumpkin seeds
- 1 tablespoon golden raisins
- 2 teaspoons toasted wheat germ

1 *For the sauce:* Combine the water and sugar in a medium-size saucepan and bring to a boil, uncovered, over moderate heat, stirring until the sugar dissolves. Then boil, uncovered, without stirring, for 4 minutes or until slightly thickened.

2 Remove from the heat and mix in the cocoa, chocolate chips, butter, and salt, stirring until the chocolate melts. Mix in the vanilla. Use as directed in Step 3. Pour the remaining sauce into a ½ pint preserving jar, and store in the refrigerator for up to 2 weeks. Warm over low heat before serving.

3 *For the bananas:* Divide the bananas among 4 dessert dishes. Top each with 2 tablespoons of the chocolate sauce, 1 teaspoon pumpkin seeds, ¾ teaspoon raisins, and ½ teaspoon wheat germ. Serves 4.

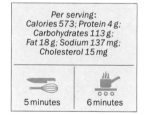

Per serving:
Calories 573; Protein 4 g;
Carbohydrates 113 g;
Fat 18 g; Sodium 137 mg;
Cholesterol 15 mg

5 minutes   6 minutes

Almond Cream with Strawberry Sauce

This is the easiest strawberry sauce ever—just purée frozen berries in the blender. Allow 3 hours for the almond cream to chill.

- ⅔ cup sugar
- 6 tablespoons cornstarch
- ⅛ teaspoon salt
- 2 cups milk
- 2 cups half-and-half
- ½ teaspoon almond extract
- 1 package (10 ounces) frozen strawberries in syrup, partially thawed and undrained

1 Combine the sugar, cornstarch, and salt in a medium-size heavy saucepan. Gradually stir in the milk, then the half-and-half. Cook over moderate heat, stirring constantly, until the mixture boils—about 10 minutes—then boil, uncovered, for 1 minute. Remove from the heat, let cool for 5 minutes, then stir in the almond extract.

2 Pour into 6 to 8 individual serving dishes, let cool for 15 minutes, then cover with plastic food wrap and refrigerate for at least 3 hours. Meanwhile, purée the strawberries in a food processor or an electric blender—about 30 seconds. Pour into a small sauceboat, cover with plastic food wrap, and refrigerate until ready to serve. Serves 6 to 8.

Per serving:
Calories 310; Protein 5 g;
Carbohydrates 48 g;
Fat 12 g; Sodium 119 mg;
Cholesterol 41 mg

20 minutes   11 minutes

Frozen Fruit Yogurt

During the hottest days of summer, make several batches of this icy treat, and store after Step 1. Then you can whip up the finished dessert whenever you need it. If fresh fruit is not available, you can substitute 2 cups of frozen unsweetened fruit, not thawed.

1 pint fresh strawberries or blueberries, hulled, or one pound peaches or nectarines, peeled and pitted

1½ cups plain low-fat yogurt

⅔ cup confectioners sugar

1 tablespoon lemon juice

½ teaspoon finely grated lemon rind

Per serving:
Calories 142; Protein 5 g;
Carbohydrates 28 g;
Fat 2 g; Sodium 61 mg;
Cholesterol 5 mg

 10 minutes | None

1 Place the strawberries, yogurt, sugar, lemon juice, and lemon rind in a food processor and whirl for about 20 seconds or until smooth. Pour into a 9" x 5" x 3" loaf pan and freeze, covered, until firm—3 hours or overnight.

2 Break the frozen yogurt into chunks and transfer to a food processor or an electric blender and whirl at high speed for about 1 minute or until fluffy.

3 Return to the loaf pan and freeze just until mushy—about 1 hour. Serves 4.

Strawberry Buttermilk Sherbet

If you prefer pineapple sherbet, in Step 1 substitute 1 can (1 pound 4 ounces) undrained crushed pineapple for the strawberries, then proceed as directed. For blueberry sherbet, use 1 pint fresh blueberries or 2 cups frozen unsweetened blueberries.

1 pint fresh strawberries, hulled, or 2 cups frozen unsweetened strawberries, partially thawed

½ cup sugar

1½ cups buttermilk

2 tablespoons lime juice (freshly squeezed preferred)

Per cup:
Calories 152; Protein 4 g;
Carbohydrates 34 g;
Fat 1 g; Sodium 98 mg;
Cholesterol 3 mg

 15 minutes | None

1 Mix the strawberries and sugar in a medium-size bowl and let stand for 10 minutes. Transfer to a food processor or an electric blender and purée—about 30 seconds. Add the buttermilk and lime juice and whirl briefly to combine.

2 Pour the mixture into an ungreased 9" x 9" x 2" baking pan, cover with plastic food wrap, and freeze until firm—about 3 hours.

3 Break the sherbet into large chunks and place in the processor or blender. Whirl until light and fluffy—about 1 minute. Serve immediately or freeze. Makes about 1 quart.

When the temperature rises, refresh yourself with Strawberry Buttermilk Sherbet, shown here with its frosty companions, pineapple and blueberry.

Do-It-Yourself Ice Cream Pie

You can make this pie as rich and gooey as you like. Substitute your favorite flavor of ice cream for the vanilla, then add some banana slices, raisins, peanut brittle, or toffee bars. Top it off with the Double Chocolate Sauce on page 328 or your favorite ice cream sauce. Allow 2 hours for the pie to freeze.

1 quart vanilla ice cream or frozen yogurt, softened until mushy

9 whole graham crackers or wheatmeal biscuits, coarsely broken (4 ounces)

14 bite-size (¼ ounce) chocolate bars (plain, crunchy, or nut), coarsely broken

½ cup coarsely chopped unblanched almonds or walnuts

1 prepared 9-inch chocolate or graham cracker crumb crust

Optional garnishes:

2 graham crackers or wheatmeal biscuits, coarsely broken

3 bite-size chocolate bars, coarsely broken

2 tablespoons coarsely chopped unblanched almonds

Per serving:
Calories 429; Protein 7 g;
Carbohydrates 47 g;
Fat 25 g; Sodium 184 mg;
Cholesterol 50 mg

10 minutes | None

1 Spoon the ice cream into a large bowl and gently fold in the graham crackers, chocolate bars, and almonds.

2 Spoon the mixture into the crumb crust and smooth the top. Garnish, if desired, with additional crackers, chocolate bars, and almonds. Freeze until firm—about 2 hours. Serves 8 to 10.

Have fun with Do-It-Yourself Ice Cream Pie and let your imagination run free.

Make-Ahead Basics

These convenient recipes can be made in advance, then retrieved
from the refrigerator, freezer, or pantry whenever they're needed—everything
from Basic Biscuit Mix to Basic Vinaigrette, from Meat Sauce to
Refrigerator Cookies. Perhaps the most useful recipes you'll find here are
the ones for Basic Beef Stock and Basic Chicken Stock, which are
called for in dozens of recipes throughout this book.

Basic Beef Stock

With this one recipe you can make a large repertoire of soups, sauces, and gravies.

3½ pounds meaty beef shanks
2 pounds short beef ribs
14 cups (3½ quarts) cold water
2 large yellow onions, quartered
4 medium-size carrots, peeled and thinly sliced
1 large ripe tomato, cored and coarsely chopped, or 1 cup drained canned tomatoes, coarsely chopped
6 whole cloves garlic
2 whole bay leaves
8 sprigs parsley
4 sprigs fresh thyme or 1 teaspoon dried thyme, crumbled
¼ teaspoon salt

Per cup:
Calories 15; Protein 3 g; Carbohydrates 0 g; Fat 0 g; Sodium 254 mg; Cholesterol 0 mg

15 minutes	5 hours

Slow simmering gives Basic Chicken Stock its rich flavor and home-sweet-home aroma.

1 Preheat the oven to 375° F. Arrange the beef shanks and short ribs in a single layer in an ungreased large shallow roasting pan. Roast, uncovered, for 45 minutes or until richly browned.

2 Transfer the shanks and ribs to a stockpot. Pour off all the fat from the roasting pan; add 2 cups of the water to the pan and swirl it around, scraping up any browned bits. Add to the stockpot along with the remaining water.

3 Bring the water to a boil, uncovered, over high heat, skimming off any scum. Add all the remaining ingredients, partially cover, and simmer for 3 hours, occasionally skimming off the scum.

4 Remove the short ribs and save to use on another day. Continue simmering the stock, partially covered, 1 hour longer.

5 Pour all through a large sieve set over a very large heatproof bowl. Save the shank meat for another use but discard the other solids. Let the stock cool, cover it with plastic food wrap, and refrigerate overnight. Discard the fat that has solidified on top, then ladle the stock into ice cube trays and freeze.

6 Transfer the frozen cubes to a plastic freezer bag, label, date, and return to the freezer. This stock keeps in the freezer for about 6 months. Makes 11 cups. (*Note: 1 standard ice cube equals about 3 tablespoons; 5 to 6 cubes equal 1 cup.*)

Basic Chicken Stock

Use this basic stock whenever a recipe calls for chicken stock or broth, or turn it into a quick soup when unexpected company shows up.

- 1 **roasting chicken (about 6 pounds), cut into 8 pieces and giblets reserved**
- 12 **cups (3 quarts) cold water**
- 2 **medium-size yellow onions, quartered**
- 3 **medium-size carrots, peeled and thinly sliced**
- 4 **whole cloves garlic**
- 2 **whole bay leaves**
- 6 **sprigs parsley**
- 2 **sprigs fresh rosemary or 1 teaspoon dried rosemary, crumbled**
- 4 **black peppercorns**
- ¼ **teaspoon salt**

> **Per cup:**
> *Calories 24; Protein 5 g;*
> *Carbohydrates 1 g;*
> *Fat 0 g; Sodium 254 mg;*
> *Cholesterol 0 mg*

| 15 minutes | 3¼ hours |

1 Place the chicken and giblets (except the liver, which can be used another day) in a large stockpot. Add the water and bring to a boil, uncovered, over high heat, skimming off any scum.

2 Adjust the heat so that the water bubbles gently, then add the remaining ingredients. Simmer, uncovered, for 3 hours, occasionally skimming off the scum.

3 Pour all through a large sieve set over a very large heatproof bowl. Save the chicken to use in soups, salads, or sandwiches, and discard the other solids. Let the stock cool, cover it with plastic food wrap, and refrigerate overnight. Discard the fat that has solidified on top, then ladle the stock into ice cube trays and freeze.

4 Transfer the frozen cubes to a plastic freezer bag, label, date, and return to the freezer. This stock will keep in the freezer for about 6 months. Makes 11 cups. (*Note: 1 standard ice cube equals about 3 tablespoons; 5 to 6 cubes equal 1 cup.*)

Speedy Soup Broth

An enriched stock substitute that's suitable for any recipe calling for beef or chicken stock or broth.

- 1 **can (46 ounces) beef or chicken broth or low-sodium beef or chicken broth**
- 1 **pound chicken backs or wings**
- 1 **medium-size yellow onion, quartered but not peeled**
- 2 **medium-size carrots, halved lengthwise but not peeled**
- 1 **medium-size stalk celery, quartered**
- 6 **sprigs parsley**
- 6 **black peppercorns**
- 1 **whole bay leaf**
- 1 **clove garlic, crushed lightly but not peeled**

> **Per cup:**
> *Calories 16; Protein 3 g;*
> *Carbohydrates 0 g;*
> *Fat 1 g; Sodium 773 mg;*
> *Cholesterol 1 mg*

| 15 minutes | 35 minutes |

1 Place the broth, chicken backs, onion, carrots, celery, parsley, peppercorns, bay leaf, and garlic in a large saucepan. Bring to a boil, uncovered, over moderate heat. Adjust the heat so that the mixture bubbles gently and simmer, uncovered, for 30 minutes.

2 Set a large fine sieve over a large heatproof bowl, pour in the broth mixture, then press the solids to extract all the liquid.

3 Discard the solids and let the broth cool. Pour it into 3 sterilized 1-pint preserving jars, and chill for 2 to 3 hours or until the fat solidifies; remove the fat and discard. Keeps in the refrigerator for 5 days; in the freezer for 6 months. Makes 5½ cups.

Basic Corn Bread Mix

Corn bread makes an excellent topping for some dishes and a perfect accompaniment for others. If you like, double or triple the ingredients so that you'll have extra mix on hand for the recipes below.

2 cups yellow or white cornmeal
2 cups unsifted all-purpose flour
6 tablespoons sugar
5 teaspoons baking powder
1 teaspoon salt

> Per 2¼ cups:
> Calories 1,103; Protein 24 g;
> Carbohydrates 242 g;
> Fat 3 g; Sodium 1,917 mg;
> Cholesterol 0 mg

5 minutes	None

1 Place the cornmeal, flour, sugar, baking powder, and salt in a large bowl and stir together. Transfer to a 1½-quart preserving jar. Keeps in a cool, dry place for 2 months. Makes 4½ cups (enough for two 8" x 8" x 2" or 9" x 9" x 2" pans of corn bread).

Corn Bread

Preheat the oven to 400° F. Place 2¼ cups of the Corn Bread Mix in a large bowl and make a well in the center. Whisk **1 cup whole or low-fat milk, ¼ cup vegetable oil or melted butter or margarine,** and **2 lightly beaten eggs** together in a small bowl until combined. Pour into the well of the Corn Bread Mix and stir just enough to mix (the batter should be lumpy).

Pour the batter into a greased 8" x 8" x 2" baking pan and smooth the top. Bake, uncovered, for 20 to 25 minutes or until the corn bread is lightly browned and a toothpick inserted in the center comes out clean. Cut into squares. Serves 8.

Per serving: Calories 236; Protein 6 g; Carbohydrates 32 g; Fat 9 g; Sodium 270 mg; Cholesterol 57 mg

Tex-Mex Corn Bread Variation

Preheat the oven to 400° F. Place 2¼ cups of the Corn Bread Mix in a large bowl. Add **1 teaspoon chili powder, 1 teaspoon unsweetened cocoa powder,** and **⅛ teaspoon each ground cinnamon, cloves,** and **ground red pepper (cayenne),** and stir to combine. Make a well in the center. Put **1 cup whole or low-fat milk, ¼ cup vegetable oil, 1 lightly beaten egg, 1 can (4 ounces) chopped drained green chilies,** and **½ cup shredded Monterey Jack or Cheddar cheese** in the well. Stir just enough to mix.

Pour the batter into a greased 9" x 9" x 2" baking pan and smooth the top. Bake, uncovered, for 20 minutes. Sprinkle another **½ cup Monterey Jack or Cheddar cheese** on top and bake 5 to 10 minutes longer or until the corn bread begins to pull from the sides of the pan. Serves 8.

Per serving: Calories 284; Protein 8 g; Carbohydrates 33 g; Fat 13 g; Sodium 339 mg; Cholesterol 31 mg

Basic Biscuit Mix

Keep this Basic Biscuit Mix on hand to use when biscuits are called for in various recipes. Or enjoy them all by themselves!

6 cups unsifted all-purpose flour
½ cup plus 1 tablespoon nonfat dry milk
2½ tablespoons baking powder
1½ teaspoons salt
¾ cup (1½ sticks) cold unsalted butter, margarine, or vegetable shortening, cut into bits

---

Per 2⅔ cups:
Calories 1,371; Protein 30 g;
Carbohydrates 199 g;
Fat 48 g; Sodium 1,994 mg;
Cholesterol 125 mg

| 12 minutes | None |

1 Sift the flour, dry milk, baking powder, and salt into a large bowl. Add the butter and, using a pastry blender or 2 knives, cut it in until the texture of coarse meal. Transfer the mixture to a 2-quart preserving jar. Keeps in the refrigerator for 2 weeks. Makes about 8 cups (enough for 30 biscuits).

Biscuits

Preheat the oven to 425° F. Place ⅓ of the Biscuit Mix (2 cups plus a scant ⅔ cup) in a large bowl, then drizzle in ⅔ to ¾ cup ice water. Mix with a fork just until the dough holds together. Knead the dough 4 to 6 times on a lightly floured surface, then pat out into a round ½ inch thick.

Using a floured 2½-inch round cutter, cut out the biscuits and space 1 inch apart on a lightly greased baking sheet. Brush the tops of the biscuits with a little cream or milk and bake, uncovered, for 10 to 12 minutes or until lightly browned. Makes 10 biscuits.

*Per biscuit: Calories 137; Protein 3 g;
Carbohydrates 20 g; Fat 5 g;
Sodium 199 mg; Cholesterol 13 mg*

Scone Variation

Place ⅓ of the Biscuit Mix (2 cups plus a scant ⅔ cup) in a large bowl. Follow the directions for Biscuits, adding **½ cup dried currants** and **1 tablespoon sugar**; mix well. Proceed as directed. Makes 10 scones.

*Per scone: Calories 163; Protein 3 g;
Carbohydrates 27 g; Fat 5 g;
Sodium 200 mg; Cholesterol 13 mg*

Whether it's time for breakfast, lunch, or dinner, what could be more welcome than a basket of oven-fresh biscuits made from Basic Biscuit Mix?

Cheese Biscuits Variation

Place ⅓ of the Biscuit Mix (2 cups plus a scant ⅔ cup) in a large bowl. Add **½ cup coarsely shredded sharp Cheddar cheese** and **⅛ teaspoon ground red pepper (cayenne)** and mix well. Proceed as directed. Makes 10 biscuits.

*Per biscuit: Calories 160; Protein 4 g;
Carbohydrates 20 g; Fat 7 g;
Sodium 234 mg; Cholesterol 19 mg*

Herbed Biscuits Variation

Place ⅓ of the Biscuit Mix (2 cups plus a scant ⅔ cup) in a large bowl. Add **¼ cup minced fresh herbs**, such as **parsley, dill, or basil,** to the mix. Proceed as directed. Makes 10 biscuits.

*Per biscuit: Calories 138; Protein 3 g;
Carbohydrates 20 g; Fat 5 g;
Sodium 200 mg; Cholesterol 13 mg*

Corn Muffin Variation

Follow the directions for Biscuits but substitute **½ cup cornmeal** for ½ cup of the Biscuit Mix. Add **2 tablespoons sugar**, increase the **ice water** to **1 cup**, and add **1 lightly beaten egg**. Stir just until combined. Spoon into a greased muffin tin, filling ⅔ of each muffin cup. Bake, uncovered, for 10 to 12 minutes or until lightly browned. Makes 10 muffins.

*Per muffin: Calories 153; Protein 4 g;
Carbohydrates 24 g; Fat 5 g;
Sodium 169 mg; Cholesterol 38 mg*

335

Basic White Sauce Mix

Here are several kinds of sauces, as well as some suggestions for the foods they enhance.

1⅓ cups nonfat dry milk
1 cup unsifted all-purpose flour
2 teaspoons salt
1 teaspoon white pepper

Per ½ cup:
Calories 197; Protein 11 g;
Carbohydrates 36 g;
Fat 0 g; Sodium 1,191 mg;
Cholesterol 4 mg

| 5 minutes | None |

---

1 Combine the dry milk, flour, salt, and pepper in a medium-size bowl, then transfer to a 1-pint preserving jar. Keeps in a cool, dark, dry place for 3 months. Makes 2⅓ cups (enough for 8 cups of white sauce).

White Sauce

Place ½ cup plus 1½ tablespoons of the mix in a medium-size saucepan. Blend in **2 cups water, chicken broth, or fish broth.** Bring to a boil, uncovered, over moderate heat, whisking or stirring constantly. Adjust the heat so that the mixture bubbles gently, then cook, uncovered, whisking occasionally, until thickened and smooth—3 to 5 minutes. Serve over chicken, fish, or green or yellow vegetables. Makes 2 cups.

Per cup: Calories 98; Protein 6 g;
Carbohydrates 18 g; Fat 0 g;
Sodium 595 mg; Cholesterol 2 mg

Parsley or Herb Sauce Variation

Prepare the White Sauce as directed, then mix in *¼ cup minced fresh parsley, dill, basil, or other fresh herb* or *1 tablespoon parsley flakes, 2 teaspoons crumbled dried basil, or 1 teaspoon dill weed, thyme, tarragon, or marjoram.* Serve over fish, chicken, or vegetables. Makes 2 cups.

Per cup: Calories 101; Protein 6 g;
Carbohydrates 19 g; Fat 0 g;
Sodium 599 mg; Cholesterol 2 mg

Cheese Sauce Variation

Prepare the White Sauce as directed, then mix in *2 teaspoons Dijon mustard, ⅛ teaspoon ground red pepper (cayenne),* and *1 cup shredded Cheddar or Swiss cheese* or *1 cup grated Parmesan cheese.* Whisk or stir over low heat just until the cheese melts—about 2 minutes. Serve over potatoes, cauliflower, cabbage, Brussels sprouts, or broccoli. Makes 2 cups.

Per cup: Calories 331; Protein 20 g;
Carbohydrates 19 g; Fat 19 g;
Sodium 1,014 mg; Cholesterol 61 mg

Mustard Sauce Variation

Prepare the White Sauce as directed, then smooth in *2 tablespoons Dijon mustard.* Serve over fish, green beans, asparagus, or any vegetable in the cabbage family. Makes 2 cups.

Per cup: Calories 113; Protein 7 g;
Carbohydrates 19 g; Fat 1 g;
Sodium 800 mg; Cholesterol 2 mg

Curry Sauce Variation

Combine *2 to 3 teaspoons curry powder* with the mix, then prepare the White Sauce as directed. Just before serving, stir in *1 tablespoon lemon juice* and *¼ teaspoon ground red pepper (cayenne).* Use when making curried chicken, fish, lamb, or vegetables. Or serve over grilled chicken, fish, or any green or yellow vegetable. Makes 2 cups.

Per cup: Calories 107; Protein 6 g;
Carbohydrates 20 g; Fat 1 g;
Sodium 597 mg; Cholesterol 2 mg

Thanks to a choice of four ingredients, this creamy variation of Basic Vinaigrette can be light, luscious, or anything in between.

Basic Vinaigrette

These two dressings can be used on any type of salad, but they are especially good on a tossed green salad.

- 1½ cups olive or vegetable oil
- ¾ cup red wine vinegar or cider vinegar
- 3 tablespoons Dijon mustard
- 1 tablespoon honey
- 2 tablespoons parsley flakes
- ¼ teaspoon garlic powder
- 1½ teaspoons each salt and black pepper

1 Place the oil, vinegar, mustard, honey, parsley flakes, garlic powder, salt, and pepper in a sterilized 1-quart preserving jar and shake well to blend. Keeps in the refrigerator for 3 weeks. Shake well before using. Makes 3 cups.

Creamy Vinaigrette Variation

Prepare as directed, adding ⅓ *cup buttermilk, plain low-fat yogurt, reduced-fat sour cream,* or *heavy cream.* Keeps in the refrigerator for 10 days. Shake well before using. Makes 3⅓ cups.

Per tablespoon: Calories 57; Protein 0 g; Carbohydrates 1 g; Fat 6 g; Sodium 74 mg; Cholesterol 0 mg

Per tablespoon: Calories 62; Protein 0 g; Carbohydrates 1 g; Fat 7 g; Sodium 80 mg; Cholesterol 0 mg	
5 minutes	None

Creamy Low-Cal Dressing

This mustard-flavored dressing is so rich and tasty you'd never guess that it's low in fat, cholesterol, and calories. Use it to dress almost any kind of green salad.

- 2 cups buttermilk
- ¼ cup grated Parmesan cheese
- 2 tablespoons Dijon mustard
- 2 tablespoons olive oil
- 1 tablespoon dried basil, crumbled
- 2 teaspoons sugar
- 1½ teaspoons garlic powder
- 1 teaspoon each paprika, freeze-dried chives, and dried marjoram, crumbled
- ½ teaspoon black pepper

1 Place all of the ingredients in a 1-quart preserving jar and shake well to mix. Keeps in the refrigerator for 10 days. Shake well before using. Makes 2½ cups.

Per tablespoon: Calories 15; Protein 1 g; Carbohydrates 1 g; Fat 1 g; Sodium 35 mg; Cholesterol 1 mg	
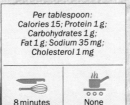 8 minutes	 None

337

Rice Seasoning Mix

*For each cup of long-grain white or brown rice,
add ⅓ cup Rice Seasoning Mix and 1 teaspoon salt, then cook
the rice according to package directions.*

- 6 tablespoons onion flakes
- 6 tablespoons parsley flakes
- 3 tablespoon celery flakes
- 4½ teaspoons garlic flakes
- ¾ teaspoon ground turmeric, coriander, or cumin
- ¾ teaspoon black pepper

1 Place the onion flakes, parsley flakes, celery flakes, garlic flakes, turmeric, and pepper in a 1-pint preserving jar. Store the mix in a cool, dark, dry place. Keeps for up to 3 months. Shake well before using. Makes 1½ cups.

Per ⅓ cup:
Calories 37; Protein 2 g;
Carbohydrates 7 g;
Fat 1 g; Sodium 11 mg;
Cholesterol 0 mg

5 minutes	None

Basic Barbecue Sauce

Brush over chicken, fish, or chops as they bake, broil, or grill.

- 1 can (8 ounces) tomato sauce
- ¼ cup cider vinegar or white vinegar
- ¼ cup ketchup
- ¼ cup water
- 2 tablespoons molasses or brown sugar
- 2 tablespoons Dijon mustard
- 1 tablespoon Worcestershire sauce
- ¼ teaspoon salt
- ⅛ teaspoon black pepper

1 Combine the tomato sauce, vinegar, ketchup, water, molasses, mustard, Worcestershire sauce, salt, and pepper in a small nonmetallic saucepan. Bring to a boil, uncovered, over moderate heat.

2 Reduce the heat to low and simmer, uncovered, for 15 minutes or until the flavors mellow and the sauce thickens slightly. Spoon into a sterilized 1-pint preserving jar. Keeps in the refrigerator for up to 2 weeks. Makes 1⅔ cups.

Spicy Sauce Variation

In Step 1, add ¾ *teaspoon chili powder* and ¼ *teaspoon hot red pepper sauce*, then proceed as directed. Makes 1⅔ cups.

Per cup: Calories 165; Protein 3 g;
Carbohydrates 41 g; Fat 2 g;
Sodium 1,865 mg; Cholesterol 0 mg

Per cup:
Calories 162; Protein 3 g;
Carbohydrates 40 g;
Fat 1 g; Sodium 1,850 mg;
Cholesterol 0 mg

8 minutes	17 minutes

The beauty of Basic Salsa and its Red Hot Variation is that you can make your meal as mild or spicy as you wish.

338

Basic Salsa

*Keep this savory sauce—or its zesty variation—
on hand as a dip for taco chips, a topping for scrambled
eggs, or an accompaniment for Tex-Mex dishes.*

1　whole clove garlic
1　pound ripe plum tomatoes,
　　cored and finely diced but not
　　peeled
½　small red onion, finely chopped
¼　cup minced fresh coriander
　　(cilantro) or ¼ cup minced flat-
　　leaf parsley plus ½ teaspoon
　　ground coriander
1　tablespoon lime juice (freshly
　　squeezed preferred)
¼　teaspoon salt

1 Drop the garlic into a small sauce-pan of boiling water. Let boil, uncovered, over moderate heat for 2 minutes. Drain well, then mince.

2 Place the minced garlic in a medium-size bowl and mix in the tomatoes, onion, coriander, lime juice, and salt. Cover with plastic food wrap and let stand at room temperature for 1 hour.

3 Transfer the mixture to a 1-quart preserving jar. Keeps in the refrigerator for 10 days. Makes 2⅓ cups.

Per cup:
Calories 55; Protein 2 g;
Carbohydrates 12 g;
Fat 1 g; Sodium 249 mg;
Cholesterol 0 mg

15 minutes　　2 minutes

Red Hot Salsa Variation

Follow Step 1 as directed, but *increase the garlic* to 2 cloves. In Step 2, *increase the lime juice* to 1½ tablespoons and add *1 tablespoon chopped jalapeño pepper* (wash hands after handling the pepper) and *¼ teaspoon red pepper sauce.* Proceed as directed. Makes 2⅓ cups.

Per cup: Calories 58; Protein 3 g;
Carbohydrates 13 g; Fat 1 g;
Sodium 305 mg; Cholesterol 0 mg

Meat Sauce

If the sauce is ready, can the pasta be far behind?

2　tablespoons olive oil
1　large yellow onion, chopped
2　large cloves garlic, minced
1　pound lean ground beef
2　cans (1 pound 12 ounces each)
　　crushed tomatoes
2　tablespoons minced fresh basil
　　or 2 teaspoons dried basil,
　　crumbled
¼　teaspoon each salt and black
　　pepper

1 Heat the oil in a 4-quart Dutch oven over moderate heat for 1 minute. Add the onion and sauté, uncovered, stirring occasionally, for 10 minutes or until very soft. Stir in the garlic and sauté 1 minute more.

2 Add the beef and cook, stirring occasionally, for 10 minutes or until the meat is browned. Add the tomatoes, basil, salt, and pepper, then bring to a simmer. Reduce the heat and cook, uncovered, until the sauce is thick—about 1 hour.

3 Let cool. Refrigerate for up to 5 days or freeze for up to 3 months. Makes 2 quarts.

Per cup:
Calories 184; Protein 20 g;
Carbohydrates 10 g;
Fat 7 g; Sodium 434 mg;
Cholesterol 52 mg

10 minutes　　1 hr. 22 min.

Vegetable Sauce Variation

In Step 1, sauté *1 cored, seeded, chopped sweet green pepper* with the onion and garlic in *¼ cup olive oil.* In Step 2, omit the beef. Substitute *2 peeled and chopped carrots* and *2 chopped stalks celery;* sauté, stirring often, for 5 minutes. Add *2 cups chopped mushrooms;* sauté, stirring occasionally, 5 minutes more, then add the tomatoes, basil, salt and pepper. Add *2 teaspoons sugar* and *½ teaspoon crumbled dried oregano,* then simmer, uncovered, over moderately low heat for about 1 hour or until thick. Follow Step 3 as directed. Makes 2 quarts.

Per cup: Calories 127; Protein 3 g;
Carbohydrates 15 g; Fat 7 g;
Sodium 406 mg; Cholesterol 0 mg

Refrigerator Cookies

Here are four recipes in one, since you can make these cookies plain, with chocolate chips or nuts, or with both. Each kind of dough will keep for up to 3 days in the refrigerator or 1 month in the freezer.

2 cups sifted all-purpose flour
½ teaspoon each salt and baking soda
¼ cup unsalted butter or vegetable shortening
½ cup granulated sugar
½ cup firmly packed light brown sugar
1 large egg, lightly beaten
1 teaspoon vanilla extract
1 cup chocolate chips (optional)
1 cup coarsely chopped pecans or walnuts (optional)

Per cookie:
Calories 58; Protein 1 g;
Carbohydrates 11 g;
Fat 1 g; Sodium 44 mg;
Cholesterol 9 mg

15 minutes | 10 minutes

---

1 Sift the flour, salt, and baking soda together onto a piece of wax paper and set aside.

2 Cream the butter in the large electric mixer bowl at medium speed until light—about 3 minutes. Add the granulated sugar gradually, beating continuously, then the brown sugar. Reduce the mixer speed to low. Beat in the egg, the sifted flour mixture, and the vanilla. Stir in the chocolate chips and/or nuts with a wooden spoon if desired.

3 Shape the dough into a roll about 2 inches in diameter, wrap in foil or plastic food wrap, and refrigerate overnight or freeze if desired.

4 *To bake:* Preheat the oven to 400° F. Slice the roll of dough into slices ¼ inch thick, then arrange the cookies ½ inch apart on lightly greased baking sheets. Bake, uncovered, for 8 to 10 minutes or until cookies are golden brown at the edges. Transfer to wire racks and let cool. Store in airtight containers. Makes about 3 dozen cookies.

With Refrigerator Cookies, all you have to do is slice and bake.

Melba Sauce

Ladle this scarlet sauce over ice cream, pudding, or fruit. It's also delicious over your favorite pound cake or angel food cake.

1 package (10 ounces) frozen raspberries in syrup, unthawed
¼ cup seedless raspberry jam
4 teaspoons cornstarch
1 tablespoon water
1 teaspoon lemon juice (freshly squeezed preferred)

Per cup:
Calories 414; Protein 2 g;
Carbohydrates 105 g;
Fat 0 g; Sodium 7 mg;
Cholesterol 0 mg

8 minutes | 23 minutes

---

1 Place the raspberries and jam in a small saucepan and bring to a boil, uncovered, over moderate heat. Adjust the heat so that the mixture bubbles gently and simmer, uncovered, stirring occasionally, for 15 to 20 minutes.

2 Blend the cornstarch and water in a small cup to make a smooth paste, then gradually whisk into the raspberry mixture. Cook, stirring constantly, until the mixture thickens and clears—about 3 minutes.

3 Remove from the heat and stir in the lemon juice. Press through a fine sieve, if desired, to remove the seeds.

4 Pour the sauce into a sterilized 1-pint preserving jar. Keeps in the refrigerator for about 1 week. Makes 1⅓ cups.

Credits and Acknowledgments

The editors are grateful to these organizations for their courtesy in providing the following items for the photography in this book.

26–27 Soup bowl and dinner plate: Villeroy & Boch Tableware Ltd. **30** Soup bowl: Wedgwood. **35** Napkins: Le Jacquard Français. **36** Soup cup and saucer: Eigen Arts Inc. **39** Napkin: Le Jacquard Français; tray: The Museum of Modern Art Design Store. **41** Soup bowl and dinner plate: Hutschenreuther. **44–45** Spoon: The Pottery Barn; bowl and underliner: Eigen Arts Inc. **46–47** Napkin: Le Jacquard Français; soup bowl and dinner plate: Villeroy & Boch Tableware Ltd. **48** Bowls and tray: The Museum of Modern Art Design Store. **51** Platter, salt and pepper shakers, and wineglasses: Royal Copenhagen/Georg Jensen Silversmiths. **58–59** Napkin: Le Jacquard Français; plate: Eigen Arts Inc. **60–61** Trivet: Dansk International Designs Ltd.; small bowl: Eigen Arts Inc. **64–65** Oval plate: Hutschenreuther; napkins: Dansk International Designs Ltd. **66–67** Tablecloth surface and dinner plate: Spode; fork and flatware: Jean Couzon Inc.; tablecloth: Le Jacquard Français. **69** Tablecloth and napkin: Le Jacquard Français. **71** Plate: Eigen Arts Inc. **73** Square plate: Eigen Arts Inc. **75** Platter: Hutschenreuther. **76–77** Platter: Hutschenreuther; carving fork and gravy ladle: Jean Couzon Inc.; gravy boat: Royal Copenhagen/Georg Jensen Silversmiths. **78** Serving fork and spoon: Jean Couzon Inc.; salad bowl and platter: Royal Copenhagen/Georg Jensen Silversmiths; platter: Spode. **82–83** Platter: Dansk International Designs Ltd. **84–85** Carving set: Jean Couzon Inc.; casserole: Wedgwood. **88–89** Platter: Hutschenreuther. **95** Platter and glasses: Dansk International Designs Ltd.; tablecloth: The Bebe Winkler Collection. **99** Plate: Dansk International Designs Ltd. **100** Condiment bowls: Eigen Arts Inc.; platter: Wedgwood. **104–105** Plate: Wedgwood; linen surface: Le Jacquard Français. **106–107** Serving fork and spoon: Jean Couzon Inc.; platter, salt and pepper shakers, bowl, gravy boat, and saucer: Dansk International Designs Ltd. **108–109** Plate and bowl: Dansk International Designs Ltd. **110–111** Platter and plate: Wedgwood; serving fork: Jean Couzon Inc. **112** Plate: Dansk International Designs Ltd. **115** Platter: Williams-Sonoma Inc. **116–117** Glass fish plate: Williams-Sonoma Inc. **120** Flatware: The Pottery Barn. **122–123** Napkin: Le Jacquard Français. **128** Au gratin: Williams-Sonoma Inc. **131** Skillet: All-Clad Metalcrafters Inc. **139** Baking dish: Williams-Sonoma Inc.; napkin: The Pottery Barn. **144–145** Casserole: All-Clad Metalcrafters Inc.; stack of plates: Spode. **159** Salad plate: Wedgwood (Johnson Brothers). **160** Flatware: Royal Copenhagen/Georg Jensen Silversmiths. **165** Casserole and dinner plate: Blanc de Blanc Porcelain. **166–167** Pan: All-Clad Metalcrafters Inc. **175** Platter: Annieglass Studio. **176–177** Tablecloth: Le Jacquard Français. **182–183** Small glass plate: The Museum of Modern Art Design Store; flatware: Jean Couzon Inc. **184** Tablecloth: Le Jacquard Français. **191** Tablecloth: Le Jacquard Français; plates, serving bowl, and silver salad utensils: Royal Copenhagen/Georg Jensen Silversmiths. **193** Dinner plate: Eigen Arts Inc. **199** Salt and pepper shakers: The Pottery Barn. **212–213** Carving set: Jean Couzon Inc; salad bowl: Wedgwood. **214** Flatware: The Pottery Barn. **222–223** Plate: Eigen Arts Inc.; salad plate: Annieglass Studio. **224** Dinner plate: Wedgwood; flatware, stemware, and decanter: The Museum of Modern Art Design Store. **226–227** Platter and plate: Villeroy & Boch Tableware Ltd. **228** Salt and pepper shakers: The Pottery Barn. **232–233** Kitchen linen and mortar and pestle: Williams-Sonoma Inc. **267** Napkin: Le Jacquard Français. **274–275** Tablecloth: Le Jacquard Français. **276** Plate and fork: The Pottery Barn. **286–287** Pumpkin tureen and bowl: Eigen Arts Inc. **291** Towel: Le Jacquard Français. **294–295** Cutting board: The Museum of Modern Art Design Store. **296–297** Square plate: Eigen Arts Inc. **298** Soup bowl: Eigen Arts Inc. **300** Tablecloth and napkin: Le Jacquard Français; casserole: The Museum of Modern Art Design Store. **304–305** Small bowls: Eigen Arts Inc. **311** Champagne glasses, white pitcher, and dessert plate: Waterford Wedgwood USA Inc.; tablecloth: Le Jacquard Français. **312–313** Tablecloth: Le Jacquard Français; dessert plate and dessert tray: Wedgwood. **325** Teapot, cups, saucers, and crystal tray: Waterford Wedgwood USA Inc. **329** Crystal glassware: Waterford.

Grateful acknowledgment is made to the following sources for permission to use or adapt their recipes. Note: When our recipe title differs from that of the original, our title appears in parentheses.

Doubleday Publishing Co. *The Doubleday Cookbook* by Jean Anderson and Elaine Hanna: "Rice and Black-Eyed Pea Salad" ("Tomatoes Stuffed with Rice and Black-Eyed Peas"), copyright © 1975 by Doubleday & Company Inc. *Micro Ways* by Jean Anderson and Elaine Hanna: "Maple Ham and Bean Casserole" ("Baked Beans with Ham and Maple Syrup"), "Mustcohola," copyright © 1990 by Doubleday, a division of Bantam Doubleday Dell Publishing Group. Reprinted by permission. **Gallery Books.** *The New Family Cookbook* by Carol Edwards: "Fish and Pasta Creole" ("Fish and Pasta Pronto"), copyright © 1985 by Bison Books Corp. Reprinted by permission. **The Junior Service League.** *Chapel Hill Cook Book*: "Molded Shrimp Salad" ("Molded Shrimp Salad with Orzo"), copyright © 1964 by The Junior Service League. **William Morrow and Company, Inc.** *Jean Anderson Cooks* by Jean Anderson: "Creamed White Meat of Chicken, Broccoli and Red Peppers with Fettuccine" ("Chicken Fettucine with Broccoli"), copyright © 1982 by Jean Anderson. Reprinted by permission of William Morrow and Company, Inc., and McIntosh and Otis, Inc. *Jean Anderson's New Processor Cooking* by Jean Anderson: "Deviled Ham Spread" ("Deviled Ham Dip"), "Fresh Sage and Cheddar Spread" ("Tangy Cheddar Cheese Spread"), "Hummus," copyright © 1979, 1983 by Jean Anderson. Reprinted by permission. **Ortho Books.** *Elegant Meals with Inexpensive Meats*: "Turkey Drumsticks and Barley Soup" ("Turkey, Tomato, and Barley Soup"), "Greek Meatball and Zucchini Soup" ("Meatball and Zucchini Soup"), copyright © 1978 by Chevron Chemical Company. Reprinted by permission. **Francis W. Parker School.** *Parker Cooks*: "Shellfish and Avocado Salad" ("Shrimp, Corn, and Avocado Salad"), copyright © 1983 by Francis W. Parker School. Reprinted by permission. **Simon & Schuster, Inc.** *Mastering Microwave Cookery* by Marcia Cone and Thelma Snyder: "Summer Squash Pie" ("Zucchini Pie"), copyright © 1986 by Marcia Cone and Thelma Snyder. Reprinted by permission. **The Viking Press.** *American Home Cooking* by Nika Hazelton: "Potato-Shrimp Salad" ("Shrimp Salad with Sugar Snap Peas"), copyright © 1980 by Nika Hazelton. Reprinted by permission of Viking Penguin, a division of Penguin Books USA Inc.

Index

Page numbers in *italic* type refer to illustrations.

Page numbers in *italic* type refer to illustrations.

Page numbers in *italic* type refer to illustrations.

348

Page numbers in *italic* type refer to illustrations.

Reader's Digest Fund for the Blind is publisher of the Large-Type Edition of *Reader's Digest.* For subscription information about this magazine, please contact Reader's Digest Fund for the Blind, Inc., Dept. 250, Pleasantville, N.Y. 10570.

Page numbers in *italic* type refer to illustrations.

EQUIVALENTS AND YIELDS OF INGREDIENTS

FOOD	AMOUNT	APPROXIMATE MEASURE
Almonds,		
in shell	1 lb	1–1¼ cups nutmeats
shelled, blanched	5⅓ oz	1 cup
Apples	1 lb	3 medium, 3 cups peeled, sliced
Bananas	1 lb	3 medium, 1¾ cups mashed
Beans, green, fresh	1 lb	3 cups uncooked, 2½ cups cooked
Beans, kidney, dried	1 lb	2½ cups uncooked, 6 cups cooked
Beans, navy, dried	1 lb	2 cups uncooked, 6 cups cooked
Berries	1 dry pt	1¾ cups
Bread crumbs, dry	1 slice bread	¼ cup
Bread crumbs, soft	1 slice bread	½ cup
Broccoli	1 lb	2 cups cooked
Butter or margarine	4 oz	1 stick, or ½ cup
Butter, whipped	1 lb	3 cups
Cabbage	1 lb	1 small, 4 cups shredded
Carrots	1 lb	3 cups shredded, 2½ cups diced
Celery	1 bunch	4½ cups chopped
Cheese, blue	4 oz	1 cup crumbled
Cheese, Cheddar	4 oz	1 cup shredded
Cheese, cottage	1 lb	2 cups
Cheese, cream	3-oz pkg	6 tbs
	8-oz pkg	1 cup (16 tbs)

FOOD	AMOUNT	APPROXIMATE MEASURE
Chicken, broiler-fryer	3½ lb	2 cups diced cooked
Chocolate	1 oz	1 square, ¼ cup grated
Coconut,		
flaked	3½ oz	1⅓ cups
shredded	4 oz	1⅓ cups
Cream, heavy	1 cup	2 cups whipped
Flour, all-purpose	1 lb	3½ cups unsifted, 4 cups sifted
Flour, cake	1 lb	4½ cups sifted
Lemon	1 medium	3 tbs juice, 1 tbs grated rind
Lime	1 medium	1½–2 tbs juice, 1 tsp grated rind
Macaroni	8 oz	4 cups cooked
Mushrooms,		
canned	4 oz	⅔ cup
fresh	1 lb	6 cups sliced uncooked, 2 cups cooked
Noodles	8 oz	3½ cups cooked
Oatmeal	1 cup	1¾ cups cooked
Onion	1 medium	½ cup chopped
	1 large	1 cup chopped
Orange	1 medium	⅓ cup juice, 2 tbs grated rind
Peach	4 oz	1 medium, ½ cup sliced
Peanuts,		
in shell	1 lb	2–2½ cups nutmeats
shelled	1 lb	3 cups
Pecans,		
in shell	1 lb	2¼ cups chopped nutmeats
shelled, chopped	4¼ oz	1 cup